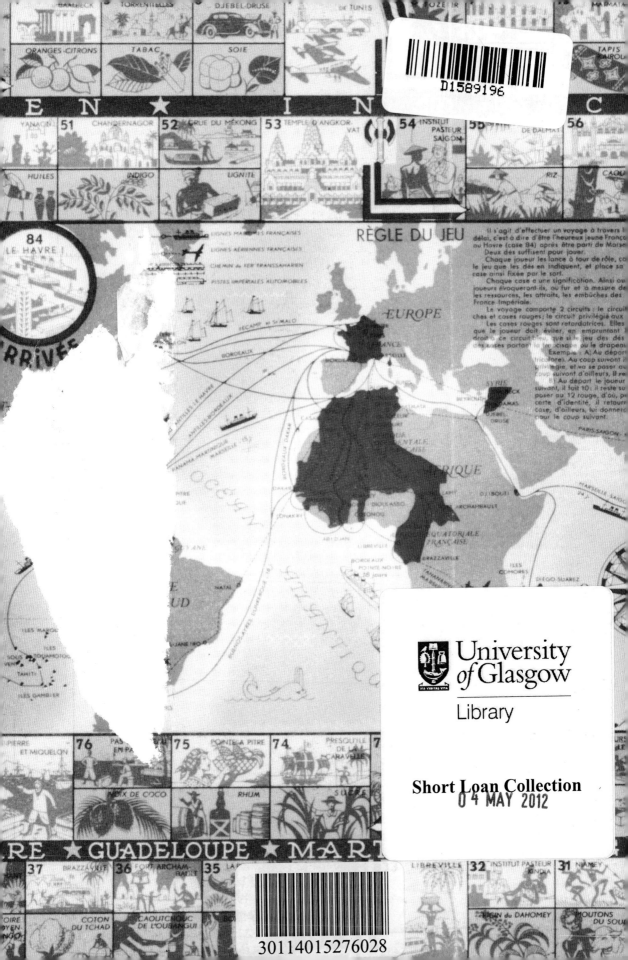

The Ar

Coloni

chaeology of

alism

The Ar

Coloni

Published by the Getty Research Institute

chaeology of

alism

Edited by Claire L. Lyons and John K. Papadopoulos

Issues & Debates

The Getty Research Institute Publications Program

Issues & Debates
Thomas Crow, *Director, Getty Research Institute*
Julia Bloomfield, Michael Roth, and Salvatore Settis, *Publications Committee*

The Archaeology of Colonialism
Edited by Claire L. Lyons and John K. Papadopoulos
Michelle Ghaffari, *Manuscript Editor*

This volume, the ninth in the series Issues & Debates, evolved from "Archaeology of Colonialism: Comparative Perspectives," a symposium sponsored by the Getty Research Institute and held at the Fourth World Archaeological Congress in Cape Town, South Africa, 10–14 January 1999

Published by the Getty Research Institute
Getty Publications
1200 Getty Center Drive, Suite 500
Los Angeles, CA 90049-1682
www.getty.edu
© 2002 The J. Paul Getty Trust
Printed in the United States of America

06 05 04 03 02   5 4 3 2 1

Cover: Allan Hughan, *Case canaque—Uarail* (mirror image), ca. 1874–81. See page 4
Frontispiece: Raoul Auger, *Jeu de l'Empire français* (detail), 1941. See page 10

Library of Congress Cataloging-in-Publication Data
The archaeology of colonialism / edited by Claire L. Lyons and John K. Papadopoulos.
    p. cm. — (Issues & debates)
  Includes bibliographical references and index.
  ISBN 0-89236-635-4 (pbk.)
  1. Archaeology and history. 2. Social archaeology. 3. Ethnoarchaeology.
4. Colonies—History. 5. Colonization—Social aspects—History. I. Lyons, Claire L., 1955–
II. Papadopoulos, John K., 1958– III. Series.
CC77.H5 A717 2001
930.1—dc21

2001007051

Contents

1 Archaeology and Colonialism
Claire L. Lyons and John K. Papadopoulos

Part I. Objects

27 Colonies without Colonialism: A Trade Diaspora Model of Fourth Millennium B.C. Mesopotamian Enclaves in Anatolia
Gil Stein

65 Greeks in Iberia: Colonialism without Colonization
Adolfo J. Domínguez

96 Indigenous Responses to Colonial Encounters on the West African Coast: Hueda and Dahomey from the Seventeenth through Nineteenth Century
Kenneth Kelly

121 Ambiguous Matters: Colonialism and Local Identities in Punic Sardinia
Peter van Dommelen

Part II. Ideologies

151 A Colonial Middle Ground: Greek, Etruscan, and Local Elites in the Bay of Naples
Irad Malkin

182 Colonizing Cloth: Interpreting the Material Culture of Nineteenth-Century Oceania
Nicholas Thomas

199 Forms of Andean Colonial Towns, Free Will, and Marriage
Tom Cummins

241 Material Culture and the Roots of Colonial Society at the South African Cape of Good Hope
Stacey Jordan and Carmel Schrire

273 Biographical Notes on the Contributors

275 Illustration Credits

277 Index

Archaeology and Colonialism

Claire L. Lyons and John K. Papadopoulos

Few human communities have remained untouched by outsiders, in antiquity as in the present. The subject of much archaeological research concerns contact among different peoples, transformations brought about by the exchange of goods and ideas, and episodes of encounter that were colonial by intent or outcome. As a worldwide phenomenon that traces its roots back to the earliest complex societies, colonization offers cultural historians a bounty of situations to analyze across time and place. Under this rubric fall vast territories that came under the sway of implanted settlements as well as the homelands from which entrepreneurs and colonists first set forth.

A variety of colonial systems operate simultaneously at different scales. The move to found new towns on distant shores may be motivated by large-scale factors of economic opportunity, territorial expansion, imperial ambition, or migration. Colonial relationships are embedded in the organization of social life through such shared community activities as trade, resource exploitation, labor, record keeping, land division, and political alliances. The policies of the dominant may govern individual interchanges between colonists and natives, with uneasy or even devastating consequences. Often, however, they are maintained at the small scale by shifts in social practices through which new ways of being are forged. The signs of change are evident in artistic expression, architecture and town planning, clothing, foodways, gender and caste identities, marriage, naming, storytelling, and religious ritual. In order to understand the transformations that colonial movements set in motion, one must approach the evidence on each of these levels. While written histories furnish information at the broader end of the scale, archaeology is particularly effective at its opposite end, where the details of domestic and social life structure the conduct of communal activities, activities that in turn constitute the larger patterns of the cultural landscape.

As a crucible of change in which differences between colonizer and colonized seem to stand in sharp outline, colonization opens a window onto the conditions that induced people to refashion their worlds. Archaeology, as Kent Lightfoot has pointed out, provides a common baseline for comparing the near past with remote antiquity. Any study that attempts to understand the long-term implications of intercultural contacts must consider the evidence of precontact societies and their responses to change. Long before writing recorded the confrontation between Europeans and native peoples, the long-distance spread of foreign merchandise, unfamiliar crops and livestock, and deadly diseases was already having a strong impact on indigenous socie-ties.[1] Without a prehistoric perspective, one cannot undertake comparative analyses of cultural transformations that took place before and after migrants, merchants, and militias embarked on ventures abroad.[2] The ramifications of colonization quickly become all-encompassing and unwieldy if one considers its numerous motivations and effects. The many ways in which a colonial dia-logue is carried on, in fact, challenge attempts to use the term *colonialism* as a category of analysis. Yet, by looking at both the subtle and the more blatant signs of change over time, we gain insights into the dynamics of past behav-iors, choices, and understandings.

Archaeology is enmeshed with colonialism, not only in the subject of its investigations and methods of practice but also in the visual, cultural, and national representations that it engenders. It is now generally recognized that colonialist mentalities have been among the most significant structuring fac-tors in the intellectual history of anthropology and archaeology.[3] Our imagina-tion of the past has been colored by recent colonial enterprises and studies of native peoples that may, in fact, have little bearing on the realities of societies preceding the advent of Europe as a world power. Archaeological investigation has unavoidably directed its gaze toward colonies, especially in regions like the ancient Mediterranean where a substantial portion of preserved sites came into being in the orbit of Near Eastern kingdoms, Greek city-states, or the Roman imperium. In other areas of the globe, the past has only been excavated more recently and colonial era remains often do not receive the scrutiny accorded to ruins and monuments of "original" cultures. This is due in part to the interests of classically trained archaeologists and travelers who set out to discover exotic civilizations in the Americas, Southeast Asia, and the Indian subcontinent. A mixture of Orientalist attitudes and adventure impelled the primitivist search for "pure" cultures and was not balanced by any reflexive inclination to consider the material consequences of colonialism itself. Nationalist archaeology, furthermore, valued the indigenous heritage of pre-colonial eras as a cornerstone of the nation's authenticity and legitimacy.[4]

The recovery of the non-European past was a project enthusiastically endorsed by Continental powers and implemented through various overseas institutes and scientific missions (figs. 1, 2). Nineteenth-century field archae-ology advanced a step forward from artifact description when topographical surveys were underwritten by government administrators keen to comprehend the pasts of their colonial subjects. The mapping and inventory of ancient ruins, sculptures, and inscriptions carried out by pioneer British archaeolo-gists in India, for example, fulfilled a number of unwritten aims. Their projects extended the terrain of Western knowledge over its possessions and situated India's past accomplishments within the developmental frame of European art, law, language, and literature. The task they performed, in short, was the creation of the colonial subject. "Indian" as an identity (or Algerian, Mexican, Cambodian, and so forth) was superimposed on certain privileged relics,

Fig. 1. Urbain Basset (French, 1842–1924)
French colonial mission to cast sculptures and photograph
ruins, Angkor Wat, Cambodia, ca. 1890–99
Los Angeles, Getty Research Institute

Fig. 2. W. L. Walton (British, active 1834–55)
Lowering the Great Winged Bull
From Austin Henry Layard, *Nineveh and Its Remains . . .*
(London: J. Murray, 1849), vol. 1, frontispiece

Fig. 3. Allan Hughan (British, 1834–83)
Case canaque — Uarail [French colonial officer and
Melanesians in front of native hut, Uarail, New Caledonia]
From E. de Lorine, "Souvenirs de voyages," album of
photographs, ca. 1874–81
Los Angeles, Getty Research Institute

which embodied the essence of local culture.[5] The examples of Khmer, Mayan, and Buddhist sculpture that explorers found occupied the lowest rungs of an aesthetic hierarchy whose peak was the art of Classical Greece. This aesthetic ordering served the twin purposes of establishing a "golden age" for non-Western art and demonstrating, by implication, just how far contemporary colonial subjects fell short of the ideal.

As the universal standing of Classical antiquity was unquestioned, early scholarship in the Mediterranean was more at liberty to focus instead on the fraught issues of interaction with barbarian races, domination and submission, progress and decline. Roman civilization was the model against which contemporary political situations might be evaluated. Projecting experiences from modern colonial regimes onto the distant past reinforced the perception of colonization as a unilateral initiative in which the advantages of power led to the assimilation (civilizing) of the native.[6] Both approaches to Classical and nonclassical antiquities reflected the unresolved tensions and insecurities of maintaining empires in the nineteenth and early twentieth centuries.

In the volumes of scientific reports and in the halls of national museums ornamented with the treasures of continents, it is not difficult to see how the methodology of archaeology and anthropology created products—knowledge and visual representations—that are based on colonialist perspectives. Ethnographic photography and artifact collecting assemble visual information that is far from an objective record, but that communicates a particular cultural rhetoric (fig. 3).[7] When one is confronted with museum galleries that isolate art objects from ethnographic artifacts, filtering material culture through the lens of ethnicity and inequality, certain presumptions about primitive and advanced societies become inevitable.[8] Our appreciation of the tasks that objects perform within a culture is hampered by their relocation in displays and catalogues that highlight Western conventions of style over meaning. The selection of objects frequently overemphasizes certain materials (for example, imported fine pottery), while other meaningful artifacts (such as coarseware and handicrafts) may be overlooked. Even the basic correlation of people and things to classify cultures pushes the viewer to equate a change in artifact types with a fundamental change in the people who made and used them. The reality of how objects work is actually more complex, and much more revealing.

Critical studies of colonialism have tended to keep step with evolving attitudes toward native peoples—the colonized as opposed to the colonizers. Scholars and administrators educated in the classics applied the lessons of ancient Rome's encounters with barbarian tribes and drew analogies to current preoccupations (fig. 4). In many early archaeological or anthropological studies, if and when native communities were considered outside the boundaries of their prehistoric "core-identity," they were often represented as passive recipients of new habits, progressively abandoning ancestral lifeways as they were subsumed into the dominant colonial culture. Foreign goods such as textiles or weaponry were usually presumed to be accepted by natives who

Fig. 4. Pietro Santi Bartoli (Italian, 1635–1700)
Presentation of Dacian heads to the Emperor Trajan,
Trajan's Column, Rome, ca. A.D. 113
From Pietro Santi Bartoli, *Colonna Traiana eretta dal Senato,
e popolo romano all'imperatore Traiano Augusto nel suo foro
in Roma* (Rome: Gio. Giacomo de Rossi, 1673), pl. 51

became acculturated by emulating the superior achievements of outsiders. Looking superficially at objects of everyday life, assimilation appears to be an inevitability, varying only in the depth of its success. Critics of this theory of acculturation observe that it presents a one-sided view and considers neither reciprocal influences nor the responses of colonists to the demands of life among alien others. It divides settler culture (European, Western, Classical) and indigenous culture (native, non-Western) into separate, impermeable spheres, and positions technologically advanced societies over primitive ones. Later attempts to redress the imbalance were concerned with *l'image de l'autre*. The formulation of "Self versus Other" challenged this one-sided perspective and examined how colonial situations and actors were represented, but still maintained sharp dichotomies between essentialized, polarized groups.

With the dissolution of colonial empires, an interest in native resistance to colonial power soon emerged. More emphasis has been given to the indigenous role in manipulating externally imposed systems and in reinterpreting novel products to suit needs and ambitions. Assimilation was seen not as the endpoint of interaction but as a creative strategy by which native peoples incorporated selected ideas and objects into existing categories of meaning, while maintaining their traditional beliefs and customs. As the mechanisms of colonialism were recognized to operate deeply on internal grounds, the idea of individual agency was adopted in order to move away from colonialism as a mechanical, externally imposed system, and to recognize its internal logic.[9] Cases of indigenous autonomy and collaboration have thus been foregrounded, and the results can counter our stereotypes. While this approach rightly recognizes that groups frequently act with assured self-interest (particularly in the interests of their political elite), it often fails to acknowledge other possibilities. Such actions may be *reactions* to a menu of limited options made available under circumstances not freely chosen, or by the same token they can be broadly innovative and not merely last-ditch attempts to preserve the status quo.

As colonists are also constrained by the unpredictabilities of a strange environment and unfamiliar customs, it is important to consider how the ideologies of the "center" are enacted and to query monolithic formulations of colonial power. The mixed character of colonial populations, in which elements of settler and local culture combined to shape a distinct cultural entity, has suggested that hybridity and ambiguity more accurately characterize colonial relations.[10] In keeping with the directions of critical studies throughout the humanities, scholars turned from examining centers to peripheries, the marginal spaces where difference is negotiated and where actions and expectations take on new senses. The periphery, of course, is not an external geographical point but represents those borderland settings in which meanings are displaced and reinvented. Postcolonial thought has focused on situations for which metaphors of "between-ness" — "the Middle Ground" — are very apt. From this vantage point, the objects, images, and texts that are mobilized in new cultural contexts do not simply gauge the rate of change or "influence" imposed on fixed, predetermined relationships, but in significant ways they activate and constitute anew those relationships.

There has been an ongoing reevaluation of the role of objects, which, just like people, present themselves flexibly. The impetus for the centrality of objects draws on the premise that things lead social lives and can be described through quasi-biographical narratives, in much the same way that individuals are described. The career of an object is traced from its creation through successive stages of use and reuse by different audiences. The usefulness of biographical accounts lies both in showing how objects are variously experienced and in providing a glimpse into "the social system and collective understandings on which it rests."[11] In *Lives of Indian Images,* Richard Davis extends this idea to ritually enlivened religious images—alive in more than a metaphorical sense.[12] Interpreting these animated objects from within the cultural epistemologies of those who created them provides one way to enter into the Others' modes of thought and bridges the gap between scientific and vernacular ways of seeing. Even in the case of material culture that is not animated per se, certain objects are invested with symbolic attributes during the performance of ceremonies or, as gifts, confer the potency of prior owners on the recipient.[13] Refracted through ethnographic comparison, familiar objects that we assume are self-evident can be deflected into very different categories.

Our perspective in this volume takes as its central notion the idea that objects— the material world of creativity and commerce—are not simply residues of social interaction but are active agents in shaping identities and communities. From the most mundane artifacts to the most exalted forms of artistic expression, the multiple messages inherent in the objects grant certain opportunities for explanation not forthcoming from texts alone. If such commonplace items as wine cups and tobacco pipes can sway the direction and quality of human lifestyles, imagine the power of images, icons, and built spaces. Looked at as instruments of change having their own social existence, art, architecture, and other less tangible although equally powerful cultural productions, such as literature and ritual, can be seen to exert an overwhelming influence on the shape and substance of people's lives. Considered from such a perspective, it is not necessary to separate the aesthetic or stylistic qualities of an artifact from the social conditions of its making, although this false dichotomy has engendered much debate within the fields of art history and archaeology.[14] We need only consider very closely and integrally things, the social settings in which they are mobilized, and the relations they epitomize.

In the introduction to their chapter paper on the roots of colonial society in South Africa (see pp. 241–42), Stacey Jordan and Carmel Schrire pose a question often asked of archaeology: How can we infer identity from residues? If artifacts are understood as symbolic surrogates that operate beyond their everyday uses to mediate social relationships, then the experiences in which they function can be analyzed to reveal how communities are structured. The various roles that even modest artifacts play, and the ambiguities that enter as they pass from hand to hand and place to place, offer the possibility of interpretation and reinterpretation. Consider, for example, glass trade beads that were manufactured in Europe by the millions. A string of varied shapes and colors adorns a girl's neckline, ornamenting her body and cueing others to her availability and status. Different colors are valued according to their rarity or symbolic associations. Nearly worthless in the hands of settlers, beads functioned as one-way currency in unequal exchanges—trinkets offered in return for livestock and land, or pawned for alcohol and tobacco. Beauty, desire, commerce, exploitation...each new use and response introduces other commodities, acts, and consequences.[15] Commonplace artifacts—an elegant vase painted with a favorite story, a sculptured monument honoring the dead, or the geometric designs worked on ceremonial cloth—embody actions and intentions that determine the way individuals think of themselves and their place in the world.

Archaeologists, art historians, anthropologists, and historians approach the question of how material culture works in a variety of ways. Although a comparative archaeology of colonial settlements was one of the foci of the symposium that inspired these essays, the pervasiveness of colonialism past and present demands conversation not only among regional specialists but also among disciplines. Precisely because colonialism is a central concern of the humanities and the social sciences, our adoption of a comparative approach advocates a wider exchange of information and methods.[16] Colonialism represents an ideal subject for cross-cultural comparison because it is, at the same time, a culturally specific local phenomenon as well as a system that transcends specific regions and time periods. Its actions leave an imprint, however subtle or distinct, on the physical and mental landscape. Despite a worldwide trend toward decolonization over the past century, the ramifications of colonialist practices and thinking are so enduring that they merit ongoing reinterpretation. This has been continuously demonstrated in the decades since the publications of Edward Said, Gayatri Spivak, and Homi Bhabha first formulated nonhistoricist ways of writing history as part of a larger postcolonial project to decolonize history and deconstruct the West.[17] A skeptical view holds that colonial experiences are incommensurable and defy comparison, particularly across the divide between ancient and early modern history. An essential difference exists in the mechanisms of industrialization, global capital, and the means to deploy international force to secure economic or political interests. Long-term transformation, however, can take root only by individual actions. The small-scale workings of objects and ideologies may be a place where cross-cultural analogies can, in fact, illuminate underlying patterns and spark fresh hypotheses.

Our aim here is not, however, to promote a consensus model of colonization. Any such model is bound to carry the cultural baggage of its own time. As it soon becomes clear, no single theoretical position can encompass the

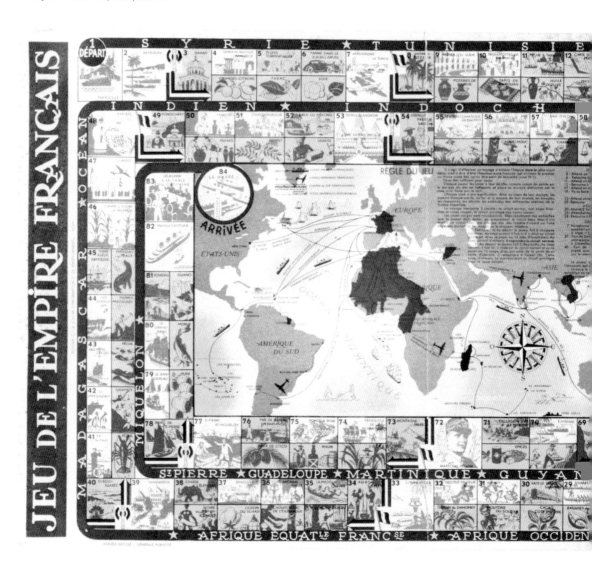

Fig. 5. Raoul Auger
Jeu de l'Empire français
Éditions Centre d'informations et de renseignements, Vichy; Imp. Delattre, Paris
France, 1941, board game: cardboard, lithographs, 32 × 50 cm (12⅝ × 19⅝ in.)
Los Angeles, Getty Research Institute

multiple instances of historical colonization and the practices that shaped them. The founding of colonies is a world phenomenon that is carried out locally. It is grounded on attitudes and accidents as much as institutional policies. Nicholas Thomas, for instance, has argued against general analyses of colonialism, proposing instead that a contextualized, ethnographic investigation would best lead to a fruitful discussion of its continued effects.[18] Any of the theoretical approaches taken in recent cultural criticism may offer relevant and informative insights into a given situation. It is in acts both deliberate and unconscious that we can observe the complex choices and responses to intercultural contact that are otherwise subsumed in the *longue durée* (long duration) of colonial history.

Texts have loomed large in the study of colonization and colonialism, often to the neglect of the physical evidence. Although some archaeologists have embraced the notion of "archaeology as text" to question their own methodology, many who work in historical periods are still reluctant to challenge the validity of the literary sources.[19] This is exactly the place where integrating history and prehistory proves beneficial. Explaining the effects of history as textuality, Robert Young provides a cogent perspective on current work around questions of writing and difference.[20] The fact remains that history is written by the winners. Archaeology, we recognize, provides the only means to study cultures and peoples who did not inscribe their own narratives in writing. More than this, archaeology gives voice to people marginally represented or excluded even in literate cultures. At a given time and place, human lives were dissimilar, often worlds apart. To cite Christopher Chippindale's classic example: "to be a slave girl at the wrong end of town in Classical Athens was not to experience Plato's world."[21] Classical literature describing the foundations of *apoikiai* (literally, homes away from home; colonies) has been regarded as journalism, when its underlying message was at least in part propaganda. Later tales of discovery and travelogues relay similarly motivated messages, but at the same time are essential guides to the social context in which they were read. Invaluable are primary sources (archives, legal instruments, and inventories) and popular culture (postcards, games, and cookbooks) that record the texture of day-to-day transactions and attitudes (fig. 5).

The case studies in this volume point to different ways in which a comparative approach can be productive. They also highlight a number of problems that are central to colonial relationships. An immediate issue is that of definition. In general, colonization refers to the processes of establishing and maintaining settlements in foreign territory, whether an isolated trading post perched on a protected headland or a network of fortified cities that act as proxies for distant military powers. A number of scholars have found it useful to apply the term loosely in order to embrace a range of situations and the social mechanisms through which they operate. The success of colonial movements often depends on subtle shifts in habits and state of mind. Colonialism, by this token, encompasses those ideologies that govern the relationships engendered by the interplay of settler and native communities. Founding a colony may be contingent on the effort to revise existing social orders through coercion, but this is not always the case.

Through a detailed analysis of the physical remains of an Uruk ethnic enclave established at the fourth-millennium B.C. village of Hacınebi in Turkey, Gil Stein concludes that colonization need not imply economic or cultural hegemony over the host community. Access to raw materials motivated the Uruk expansion into Anatolia, an exchange network that is explained on the analogy of West African trade diasporas. In this model, merchant groups that are culturally cohesive and distinct from their hosts operate as intermediaries and brokers. They are particularly useful where transportation routes or centralized state institutions cannot guarantee exchanges. The organization of trade diasporas depends very much on that of their local partners. They can assume the status of marginal pariah, useful client/ally, or dominant empire. The question of how to recognize the existence of an ethnic enclave and the nature of its presence must rely on a close reading of a complete assemblage of material culture and not just a single diagnostic type of object. As we have noted, pottery too often fulfills this purpose,[22] but Stein's analysis of architectural and artifactual discontinuities demonstrates how, for example, lithics, faunal remains, and household goods can be used to expose identity in culinary habits, writing systems, and social rituals.

Using explicitly defined ethnographic models as a basis for a holistic interpretation of archaeological contexts can facilitate cross-cultural analysis of, for instance, Uruk trading networks, the Greek emporia scattered throughout the Mediterranean, and other forms of trading that foreshadow more direct colonial intervention and exploitation. A similar diaspora of traders seeking to develop overseas natural resources is posited in ancient Iberia. Adolfo Domínguez describes a reversal of the situation investigated by Stein. Assessing the strong Greek influence on Iberian sculpture and language from the sixth to the fourth century B.C., Domínguez suggests that colonialist agendas were asserted without the presence of substantial settlements of resident colonists. Similar processes have been expressed in very different terms in Serge Gruzinski's work on the westernization of the New World, particularly in Mexico.[23] Large parts of the southeastern Iberian Peninsula were invested with a tangible Greek "spirit": the toponymy was hellenized and the landscape itself became a locale for the exploits of Greek mythological heroes. Indigenous elites leveraged their own prestige and political standing internally through commerce with Phoenician and Greek middlemen, exchanging valuables like silver ore for foreign commodities. Their power was made visible in impressive sculptural funerary monuments imitating Greek prototypes, the accoutrements of wine drinking and hospitality, and in the use of Greek alphabetic script through which economic transactions were regulated.

Iberian aristocrats employed visual art to broadcast messages of personal status and affiliations in their endeavor to achieve regional dominance, a desire hastily taken advantage of by savvy foreigners. Cooperation with native elites has long been a hallmark of colonialism, precisely because it promotes certain natives to the rank of translators and role models who are emulated by other community members. The quid pro quo in Spain appears to have struck a certain equilibrium, at least until a widespread rejection of alien elements and substitution of local ones in the third century B.C. and after, when Iberian national identity was resurgent and other groups came to the fore. Michel Foucault's notion of hegemony clarifies the nuances of cultural transformation, as it essentially involves securing social cohesion, not by overt pressure but by methods that infiltrate human minds and bodies.[24] Such techniques cultivate behavior and beliefs and mold the tastes, desires, and needs of individuals and society. The Iberian scenario represents a colonial exchange system that was not enforced by duress, servitude, and death. It is one in which indigenous agency is reflected in the selection and reconfiguration of prestige commodities to further mutual goals of social advancement and political profit.

The accommodations that the Hueda and Dahomey states of seventeenth-century Benin reached with European trade partners and with one another were similar in many ways to the Iberian arrangement. Economic relationships observed by Kenneth Kelly are unique on the African coast and offer a useful cautionary tale against extrapolating back from nineteenth- and twentieth-century historical records. Several European nations contended for niches in the market for consumables and natural resources that competing African states angled to control. When the demand for human cargo — slaves — to work plantations in the New World escalated, a European trade post was established at coastal Savi and elevated the Hueda to a key position of political autonomy. Dahomey later overthrew Hueda and removed European traders to Ouidah, an act of strategic surveillance over their movements and access. Excavation of trade posts at Savi and Ouidah shows that lodges were isolated from the sea within elite precincts to incorporate them within the symbolic structures of local power. The distribution patterns of imported artifacts signal the native elite's management of foreign influence and contrast with the patterns evident at Elmina (Ghana), another European entrepôt defended from a fortified promontory and exerting much greater authority over the surrounding territory. The European-African encounter involved exploitation and force to guarantee mercantile interests on both sides, calling into question the dominant role of the colonizer in this case. The distribution of imported products (pipes, ceramics, and beads) within the settlements at Elmina and Savi indicates when and how European material culture supplanted facets of local life and how such goods might have been used by residents living near trade precincts to set themselves apart from hinterland communities. Artifact and architectural patterning furnish key evidence for understanding how creole identities and colonial relationships are constructed on the household and local level.[25]

Kelly's essay indirectly raises two further issues that are central to colonial-ism. The first is the slave trade, a recurrent feature of colonization that is over-whelmingly attested in the written records of ships' manifests and plantation chattel, but sometimes harder to discern by archaeological means. Its impact in the homelands must be teased out of settlement shifts and depopulation, the plotting of trade routes, and increasing social complexity. The displace-ment of West African slaves as "involuntary colonists"[26] to the fields of Brazil and Virginia sets the West African plight quite apart from that of Greek immi-grants to south Italy or the English pilgrimage to North America. Involuntary colonization creates a nebulous situation in which the populations deported for forced labor are, in a sense, both colonizers and colonized. Forced to change their own identities and lifestyles radically, they in turn alter the culture of their new surroundings in visible ways. Freed Afro-Brazilian slaves returning to West Africa registered a stronger impact than early European slave-traders when they brought back new foodways, religious practices, and architecturally distinctive commercial buildings.

A second issue central to colonization is that it is driven by resource exploitation as opposed to territorial expansion, which leaves a notably dif-ferent imprint on the landscape and on the material record. The effect of the latter is on a large scale, while that of the former is more elusive, particularly when the item driving colonization frequently does not survive in the archae-ological record. In addition to human bodies, such trade commodities include some of the most crucial resources: textiles, livestock and pelts, metal ores, timber — "soft things," as Robin Osborne calls them[27] — grain, oil, sugar, tobacco, and alcohol. Here the archaeologist faces a potential dilemma: if we are to focus on the physical residues, intractable obstacles exist in the plain fact that what we know took place in specific contexts leaves barely a trace. Prehistoric archaeology, after all, is the only social science that has no *direct* access to human behavior.

The challenge of exploiting archaeological residues to the fullest is con-fronted by Peter van Dommelen in his study of the Mediterranean island of Sardinia under Carthaginian and Roman rule. Drawing on the results of field surveys of classical and Hellenistic settlements, he observes discontinuities in the ways coastal, inland, rural, and urban sites reacted to the Carthaginian presence. Situated within a limited geographic zone, these sites inhabit multiple cultural landscapes by manufacturing and distributing different commodities, practicing different burial rituals, and displaying different attitudes to the indigenous "nuraghic" heritage. Given the ambiguities, van Dommelen is con-cerned about the application of the term *colony* in antiquity, too easily trans-posed for the Latin *colonia*. The obvious disparity between Punic and local culture (the "colonial divide") makes the label convenient, but ignores the intermediate and hybrid identities that evolved. Difference is grounded in liter-ary and cultural representation as much as military and economic superiority, as Edward Said's seminal study *Orientalism* has made apparent.[28] Contrasting them with southern Punic Sardinians, Roman writers saw a threat in the wild "skin-clad" Sardinians of the northern mountains, although the most dangerous revolts took place in the south.

By rejecting binary oppositions, van Dommelen stresses that the blending of subordinate and dominant cultures is characterized by a thorough reworking of various elements, rather than merely combining two or more complete cultures. An analogy is offered in the example of Annaba in Algeria, where many different ethnic groups resided and where the "natives" were neither fully French nor fully Algerian. It is easy to imagine that in the fluid world of ancient Mediterranean commerce, guest friendship, and population movements, multicultural communities sprang up and thrived without the heavy modern apparatus of racial and religious subdivisions. The resulting reformulations or subversions of the dominant culture, as well as colonial reproductions of indigenous features, can be framed in terms of Homi Bhabha's notions of ambivalence, ambiguity, and hybridization.[29]

The roles that myth, ritual, and religion play in the ideological formation of colonial identities is the focus of the second section of this volume. Unlike the case studies of the first section, which deal with comparative interpretations of field excavation data, the following essays pursue the relationship between colonial artifacts and texts, traversing disciplines from classical philology, ethnography, and architecture, to art history. Theoretical currents in these and other relevant fields can inform archaeological practice in provocative ways.

In the eighth century B.C., the islands and inlets of the Bay of Naples were the grounds where Italic and Etruscan civilizations first undertook regular exchanges with Greeks, Phoenicians, northern Syrians, Cypriots, and others bringing luxury goods—transport amphorae filled with wine, and perfume in small ornamental containers. Perhaps most important, Greek traders also brought a vivid mythological tradition. The interplay of myth and identity is at the center of Irad Malkin's analysis of Greek-Etruscan interaction at the sites of Pithekoussai and Kymē. Malkin adopts the theory of the "Middle Ground" developed by Richard White in his study of Great Lakes frontier cultures of North America, to theorize the geographical and cognitive space in which Greeks and Italians articulated their historical origins. Rejecting "Self versus Other" as a binary model of alterity, Malkin looks at how these two groups built a mutually comprehensible world. Through tales of ancestor-founders, they conceptualized their ethnicity within the frame of Greek scientific myth-history. Whether this anticipates or derives from the growing social and political cohesion of Etruscan elites in the sixth and fifth centuries B.C. is moot. We can observe the process unfolding already at the dawn of Magna Graecian colonization, in the material remains of the earliest settlements.[30]

As a transcultural arbiter and icon, the hero Odysseus (like Aeneas in Rome) represented a progenitor who was congenial to the aristocratic ethos of the Etruscans. His travels following the Trojan War are a "colonial narrative" par excellence. Among the earliest iconographic representations found in Western Greek contexts is Odysseus's blinding of Polyphemos, the monstrous

Fig. 6. Allan Hughan (British, 1834–83)
Sortie de la messe à Vau
From E. de Lorine, "Souvenirs de voyages," album of
photographs, ca. 1874–81
Los Angeles, Getty Research Institute

Sicilian shepherd untutored in the Hellenic social etiquette of wine and hospitality. These myths entered into local cultures as stories painted on the paraphernalia of the *symposion* (wine-drinking party) and written in the Euboean Greek alphabet, imported commodities that registered strongly on the local culture. Homeric epics of return and exploration were likewise commodities that mediated early colonial encounters. The epics were superimposed on peripheral non-Greek cultures, which appropriated and internalized them to consolidate their own conception of descent and unity as a people.

Irad Malkin's essay is linked to a number of others in this volume by the question of how this new sense of self-identity evolved on the deepest levels of ideology and social practice. A number of recent and penetrating archaeological studies of ethnic identity in antiquity have demonstrated that ethnicity is not ultimately based on race, language, or religion but rather on social groupings whose origins are just as often imagined as they were real.[31] Ethnicity, like gender, is a social rather than a biological phenomenon, one defined by discursively constructed criteria. It can, therefore, be effectively manipulated by both dominant and subordinate groups within the colonial nexus. Colonization is a normative process that co-opts "mother cities," settlers, and natives alike. This perspective is echoed in recent work on the "poetics of colonization," particularly the manner in which colonial narratives constituted a way for the Greeks as a culture to authorize their common past.[32] Much is drawn on the seminal work of Stephen Greenblatt, including the term "cultural poetics," coined in an attempt to break down the barriers between literary text and its cultural and historical context.[33] This approach encourages us to read "texts as context and history itself as text, both informed by multiple competing symbolic strategies and symbolic economies."[34]

Dress constitutes a fundamental marker of social and ethnic identity and was one of the ways in which Christian missionaries in Oceania sought to alter native self-representation. Nicholas Thomas analyzes colonially introduced styles of clothing among Samoan and Tahitian communities that had a rich and complex tradition of wearing decorated tapa. Departing from the premise that colonialism is not domination but the "efforts to produce relations of dominance," he views material culture and technology as central to the transformative work of colonialism. Textiles were a key vector for the Christianization of the Pacific. Sewing kept young women usefully occupied, and the plain cloth stitched into Mother Hubbard-style dresses conformed to French missionaries' expectations of appropriate modesty. Beyond this, clothing facilitated a new moral and religious consciousness, as well as changes in work, calendar, and gender relationships (fig. 6). Rather than seeing objects as passive, however — as things that carry properties or certain efficacies that follow from their physical qualities and histories — Thomas considers how objects actively "text" their context. European-style clothing was not accepted because it mirrored prior native understandings of the body as empowered by wrapping. Rather, new clothes were an extension and twisting of that practice, and offered an opportunity for personal display in the spatial and temporal setting of Sunday church. This case demonstrates how potentially powerful material culture can be in a multilayered reading of past cultures, not as a corollary of history but as an independent entity.

Clothing was only one of the means by which Spanish missionaries in the New World undertook what would prove to be a radical refashioning of native lives. Conversion to Christianity involved more than systematic instruction in church doctrine using texts and images; it also entailed a process by which "imperial imagination . . . become colonial habitus in . . . space, action, and subjectivity."[35] Through an analysis of sixteenth-century Andean urban planning and kinship relations, Tom Cummins examines the re-creation of Inka subjects within a universalizing Christian domain. In Spanish, the operative term *reducir* — a bringing to better order — was objectified in the newly founded *reducciones,* towns built on a grid plan. Indians relocated to *reducciones* inhabited a physical space that was an assembly point of goods and labor to work the Potosí silver mines. The layout of plaza, church, and residential blocks further reinforced divine and secular authority. Just as the Quechua tongue was "reduced" along the precepts of Latin grammar in order to achieve linguistic unity, the physical organization of the geometric grid brought discipline and civilizing harmony to Andean social life. The redesign of house plans to accommodate nuclear families and to discourage sexual relations between family members effectively transformed the way indigenous marriage and kinship were conceived.

Although little archaeology has been undertaken in Andean colonial towns, a study of domestic contexts could reveal how Indians accommodated the strictures of Spanish civic and religious reformation that are so amply documented in official archives. This essay offers a number of propositions that could be tested by archaeological excavation in order to assess the missionizing project. "Resistance" is implied in the repeated edicts that the Spanish government issued in an effort to control and contain indigenous customs. Cummins, however, is more interested in the implementation of Christian rituals that intruded into the most intimate aspects of conduct. Recognition of the strength of native kinship structures is apparent in the diagrams of degrees of consanguinity, used by priests as visual didactic aids to inculcate the requirements of the marriage sacrament among the congregants. Very relevant to the operation of the *reducciones* are Pierre Bourdieu's observations on the household as a principal locus of generative schemes, and on symbolic violence as a penetrating condition that permeates day-to-day social encounters.[36]

Stacey Jordan and Carmel Schrire's contribution to this volume is a model for integrating all the kinds of evidence other authors rely on — artifacts, urban landscapes, visual imagery, archives, popular culture, and ethnographic analogy. Their focus is the Dutch East India Company (Dutch Verenigde Oostindische Compagnie, known as the VOC) settlement at the Cape of Good Hope. Initially established as a wayfaring station to trade with native pastoralists for the provisioning of ships, the settlement was positioned as an

Fig. 7. F. Riedel
Vue du Promontoire du Bonne Espérance
Germany (Augsburg), ca. 1750–80, pricked and handcolored
etching, 26.7 × 39.4 cm (10½ × 15½ in.)
Los Angeles, Getty Research Institute, Werner Nekes Collection

early toehold in the eventual colonial takeover of a continent (fig. 7). The social composition of the Cape was incorporated into the subsequent British colony, continuing until modern times, when its deeply enmeshed components were disarticulated under the infamous rulings of apartheid. Exploring the antecedents of institutional racism through the material signature of colonization, Jordan and Schrire investigate how social and ethnic identities are expressed in the simple crockery of lower-class colonial tables.

Traditional approaches to Cape history devise a basic tripartite division among "white," "Khoikhoi," and "slave" communities. Europeans, however, were sharply segregated by class. As historical documents illustrate, colonial authority had to exert control not only over the indigenous population but also over its own subordinates. Circumscribing access to commodities that signaled one's status accomplished this end. The lower echelons of colonial society occupied a liminal position, at once inferior to the ruling elite and yet active agents of its culture. Dutch-style earthenwares sustained an imagined European community in a world of blurred boundaries, creating a new sense of nationalism out of mercantile trade. Whereas imported Asian ceramics conferred a mark of distinction, earthenware integrated lower-class users into the colonizing community while simultaneously excluding them from the prerogatives of elite colonial identity. The dialectical nature of objects becomes all the more evident when gender and ethnicity are brought into the picture. Intermarriage introduced Malay women into colonial households, a necessity at a time when European women were unavailable. The authors consider inventories of cooking implements and the appearance of exotic condiments as signs of the progressive creolization of households. Despite the fact that vessel forms were intended to be icons of Dutch domestic morality, they contributed to the growth of a specifically colonial Eurasian culture in Africa.

Archaeology reveals the complexities of the polycultural Cape context and the consequences that colonialism has had for contemporary South African society. Even the modest furnishings of domestic life embody a dynamic that continues to shape the destiny of large parts of the world today. At issue in the chapters presented in this volume is the question of how objects and individuals interact to produce communities. Schrire and Jordan's case study offers both an apt summation and a point of departure for future comparative research. Identity (and particularly colonial identities) is enacted "where the 'unspeakable' stories of subjectivity meet the narratives of a history, of a culture."[37] The ideals of the homeland encounter colonial realities, creating instabilities and contradictions that material culture—artifacts, art, and architecture—work to manage.

Notes

A number of the contributions published in this volume were first presented as papers in the symposium "Archaeology of Colonialism: Comparative Perspectives," which was held at the Fourth World Archaeological Congress, University of Cape Town, South

Africa, 10–14 January 1999. This symposium was sponsored by the Getty Research Institute and benefited from the support and advice of Michael Roth, Marion True, and successive directors Salvatore Settis and Thomas Crow. We are especially grateful to Richard Lindstrom for the essential role he played in organizing the symposium's logistics and helping to shape its interdisciplinary themes. Our thanks are also due to the many colleagues in different fields who offered their expertise and insights on aspects of colonialism ancient and modern, particularly Sabine MacCormack, Patricia Samford, and Sarah Morris. We gratefully express our appreciation to our colleagues in the Research Institute's departments of Special Collections, Visual Media Services, and Publications; to Getty Publications and to Michelle Ghaffari for their careful attention to the production of this volume.

1. See Kent Lightfoot, "Culture Contact Studies: Redefining the Relationship between Prehistoric and Historical Archaeology," *American Antiquity* 60 (1995): 199–217.

2. James Deetz, "Archaeological Evidence of Sixteenth- and Seventeenth-Century Encounters," in Lisa Falk, ed., *Historical Archaeology in Global Perspective* (Washington, D.C.: Smithsonian Institution Press, 1991), 1–10, esp. 5–6; and Samuel M. Wilson and J. Daniel Rogers, "Historical Dynamics in the Contact Era," in J. Daniel Rogers and Samuel M. Wilson, eds., *Ethnohistory and Archaeology: Approaches to Postcontact Change in the Americas* (New York: Plenum, 1993), 3–15.

3. Peter Pels, "The Anthropology of Colonialism: Culture, History, and the Emergence of Western Governmentality," *Annual Review of Anthropology* 26 (1997): 163–93.

4. Bruce Trigger, "Alternative Archaeologies: Nationalist, Colonialist, Imperialist," *Man*, n.s., 19 (1984): 355–70; and Claire L. Lyons, "Objects and Identities: Claiming and Reclaiming the Past," in Elazar Barkan and Ronald Bush, eds., *Claiming the Stones/Naming the Bones: Cultural Property and the Negotiation of National and Ethnic Identity* (Los Angeles: Getty Research Institute, 2002).

5. Tapati Guha-Thakurta, "Monuments and Lost Histories: The Archaeological Imagination in Colonial India," in Suzanne Marchand and Elizabeth Lunbeck, eds., *Proof and Persuasion: Essays in Authority, Objectivity, and Evidence* (Turnhout, Belgium: Brepols, 1996), 144–70; and Javed Majeed, "Comparativism and References to Rome in British Imperial Attitudes to India," in Catherine Edwards, ed., *Roman Presences: Receptions of Rome in European Culture, 1789–1945* (Cambridge: Cambridge Univ. Press, 1999), 88–109.

6. Franco de Angelis, "Ancient Past, Imperial Present: The British Empire in T. J. Dunbabin's *The Western Greeks*," *Antiquity* 72 (1998): 539–49.

7. Elizabeth Edwards, *Anthropology and Photography, 1860–1920* (London: Yale Univ. Press, 1997); and Brian L. Molyneaux, ed., *The Cultural Life of Images: Visual Representation in Archaeology* (London: Routledge, 1997).

8. Tim Barringer and Tom Flynn, eds., *Colonialism and the Object: Empire, Material Culture, and the Museum* (London: Routledge, 1998), 1–8. Nicholas Thomas, *Possessions: Indigenous Art, Colonial Culture* (London: Thames & Hudson, 1999), 16, describes contemporary reactions against the "purist aesthetic."

9. Marcia Anne Dobres and John Ernest Robb, eds., *Agency in Archaeology* (London: Routledge, 2000).

10. J. Jorge Klor de Alva, "The Postcolonization of the (Latin) American Experience: A Reconsideration of 'Colonialism,' 'Postcolonialism,' and 'Mestizaje,'" in Gyan Prakash, ed., *After Colonialism: Imperial Histories and Postcolonial Displacements* (Princeton: Princeton Univ. Press, 1995), 241–75.

11. Igor Kopytoff, "The Cultural Biography of Things: Commoditization as Process," in Arjun Appadurai, ed., *The Social Life of Things: Commodities in Cultural Perspective* (Cambridge: Cambridge Univ. Press, 1986), 64–91, esp. 89.

12. Richard H. Davis, *Lives of Indian Images* (Princeton: Princeton Univ. Press, 1997).

13. For a review of the recent literature, see Chris Gosden and Yvonne Marshall, "The Cultural Biography of Objects," *World Archaeology* 31 (1999): 169–78.

14. Alfred Gell, *Art and Agency* (Oxford: Clarendon, 1998), 1–11.

15. Carmel Schrire, *Digging through Darkness: Chronicles of an Archaeologist* (Charlottesville: Univ. Press of Virginia, 1996), 111–12.

16. The editorial by Sylvia Thrupp that prefaced the first volume of *Comparative Studies in Society and History* 1 (1958): 1–4, still provides a useful introduction on the idea of comparative study.

17. Robert Young, *White Mythologies: Writing History and the West* (London: Routledge, 1990).

18. Nicholas Thomas, *Colonialism's Culture: Anthropology, Travel, and Government* (Princeton: Princeton Univ. Press, 1994).

19. See Ian Hodder, *Reading the Past: Current Approaches to Interpretation in Archaeology,* 2d ed. (Cambridge: Cambridge Univ. Press, 1986), esp. 80–106, 153–55, 160; Ian Hodder, "This Is Not an Article about Material Culture as Text," *Journal of Anthropological Archaeology* 8 (1989): 250–69; Christopher Tilley, *Material Culture and Text: The Art of Ambiguity* (London: Routledge, 1991); and John K. Papadopoulos, "Archaeology, Myth-History and the Tyranny of the Text: Chalkidike, Torone and Thucydides," *Oxford Journal of Archaeology* 18 (1999): 377–94.

20. Young, *White Mythologies* (note 17).

21. Christopher Chippindale, "Theory in Archaeology: A World Perspective," *TLS: Times Literary Supplement*, 20 October 1995, 11–12.

22. John K. Papadopoulos, "Phantom Euboians," *Journal of Mediterranean Archaeology* 10 (1997): 191–219.

23. Serge Gruzinski, "Colonization and the War of Images in Colonial and Modern Mexico," *International Social Science Journal* 44, no. 4 (1992): 503–18.

24. For Foucault's notion of hegemony, see Barry Smart, "The Politics of Truth and the Problem of Hegemony," in David C. Hoy, ed., *Foucault: A Critical Reader* (Oxford: Basil Blackwell, 1986), esp. 160.

25. A model study is Kathleen A. Deagan, "Spanish-Indian Interaction in Sixteenth-Century Florida and Hispaniola," in William W. Fitzhugh, ed., *Cultures in Contact: The Impact of European Contacts on Native American Cultural Institutions, A.D. 1000–1800* (Washington, D.C.: Smithsonian Institution Press, 1985), 281–318.

26. The term *involuntary colonists* is used in Felipe Fernandez-Armesto, *Millennium: A History of the Last Thousand Years* (New York: Simon & Schuster, 1995), 269.

27. Robin Osborne, "Early Greek Colonization? The Nature of Greek Settlement in

the West," in Nick Fisher and Hans van Wees, eds., *Archaic Greece: New Approaches and New Evidence* (London: Duckworth, 1998), 251–69.

28. Edward Said, *Orientalism* (Harmondsworth, England: Penguin, 1995).

29. See the papers assembled in Homi Bhabha, *The Location of Culture* (London: Routledge, 1994), for discussion of these terms. Note also the term *creolization,* for which see Ulf Hannerz, "The World in Creolisation," *Africa* 57 (1987): 546–59.

30. On luxury trade goods as emblems of aristocratic lifestyle in ancient Italy, see Michael Shanks, *Art and the Greek City-State: An Interpretive Archaeology* (Cambridge: Cambridge Univ. Press, 1999).

31. See, most recently, Jonathan M. Hall, *Ethnic Identity in Greek Antiquity* (Cambridge: Cambridge Univ. Press, 1997); and Siân Jones, *The Archaeology of Ethnicity: Constructing Identities in the Past and Present* (London: Routledge, 1997).

32. Carol Dougherty, *The Poetics of Colonization: From City to Text in Ancient Greece* (Oxford: Oxford Univ. Press, 1993).

33. See Stephen Greenblatt, *Marvelous Possessions: The Wonder of the New World* (Chicago: Univ. of Chicago Press, 1991).

34. Leslie Kurke, "The Economy of Kudos," in Carol Dougherty and Leslie Kurke, eds., *Cultural Poetics in Archaic Greece: Cult, Performance, Politics* (Cambridge: Cambridge Univ. Press, 1993), 131.

35. See Tom Cummins, in this volume, pp. 199–200.

36. Pierre Bourdieu, *Outline of a Theory of Practice* (Cambridge: Cambridge Univ. Press, 1977), 89.

37. See Stacey C. Jordan and Carmel Schrire, in this volume, p. 265, quoting Stuart Hall, "Minimal Selves," in Houston A. Baker Jr., Manthia Diawara, and Ruth H. Lindeborg, eds., *Black British Cultural Studies: A Reader* (Chicago: Univ. of Chicago Press, 1996).

Part I

Objects

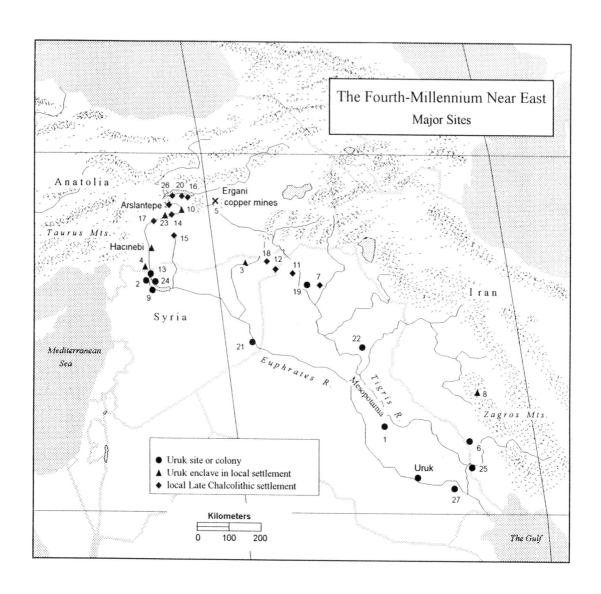

Fig. 1. Near East, 4000–3000 B.C.

1. Abu Salabikh
2. Aruda
3. Brak
4. Carchemish
5. Ergani Copper Mines
6. Farrukhabad
7. Gawra

8. Godin
9. Habuba Kabira
10. Hassek
11. Hawa
12. Hamoukar
13. Jerablus Tahtani
14. Karatut Mevkii

15. Kazane
16. Korucutepe
17. Kurban
18. Leilan
19. Nineveh
20. Norsuntepe
21. Qrayya

22. Rubeidheh
23. Samsat
24. Sheikh Hassan
25. Susa
26. Tepecik
27. Ur

Colonies without Colonialism: A Trade Diaspora Model of Fourth Millennium B.C. Mesopotamian Enclaves in Anatolia

Gil Stein

It has become clear over the last two decades that many, if not most, early state societies in the Old and New World established colonies as one aspect of their overall expansionary dynamics, such as trade, alliance formation, or conquest.[1] Although colonies existed in a wide variety of ancient, non-Western, and precapitalist cultural contexts, archaeological interpretations of these systems have been heavily influenced by the structure of European colonialism in the sixteenth through twentieth century. The uncritical extension of the European colonialism model's assumptions of dominance and asymmetric relations to non-Western and precapitalist cases is especially evident in current interpretations of ancient Mesopotamian colonies. As early as 3700 B.C., the newly emergent Mesopotamian city-states of the Uruk period expanded into neighboring areas of Syria and southeast Anatolia. They established a series of settlements apparently intended to gain access to vital raw materials such as copper or lumber, in the world's earliest known network of colonies.[2] The Mesopotamian trade colonies are generally viewed as controlling, either formally or informally, the exchange system and, through that, the indigenous populations with whom they interacted.[3] It is important to note that the arguments for Mesopotamian colonial dominance have been based on a heavily biased archaeological record. Although Uruk colonies in Syria and Anatolia have been excavated, until recently we knew almost nothing about either the dynamics of Mesopotamian and local interaction or the impact of this interregional trade system on the development of indigenous cultures in southeast Anatolia.

Excavations at the site of Hacınebi in the Euphrates River valley of southeast Anatolia investigate the organization of interaction between Mesopotamians and local peoples of Anatolia as a way to test the applicability of the colonial dominance model to prehistoric networks of interregional interaction. In 3700 B.C. a small Uruk trading enclave was established in the northeast corner of Hacınebi, more than 1,200 kilometers upstream from the Uruk homeland in southern Mesopotamia (fig. 1). The complex of material culture and available evidence for behavioral patterning strongly support the idea that an enclave of ethnically distinct Mesopotamians was present at the site. Comparative analyses of material culture from the enclave and surrounding indigenous contexts suggest that the foreigners did not dominate their local Anatolian host community as might be expected under the assumptions of the European model of colonialist domination. Instead, the Uruk enclave was a socially and economically autonomous diaspora whose members raised their own food, produced their own crafts, and administered their own separate exchange system. Although they were in close contact (and may even have intermarried) with their Anatolian host community, the foreigners seem to have maintained a distinct social identity over an extended period of time. The encapsulated organization of the Mesopotamian enclave and the essential parity in its social relations with the Anatolian host community at Hacınebi are best explained in terms of the "trade diaspora" model developed by Abner Cohen in his analyses of commercial enclaves in modern West Africa.[4] The Hacınebi data thus indicate that considerable variation exists in the organization of power relations and colonial-local economic interaction in ancient, non-Western colonial systems.

Colonialism and Colonies

To develop realistic models of organizational variation in ancient colonial systems and in their relations with indigenous societies, we need to emphasize the distinction between "colonialism" and "colonies." Colonialism is "the establishment and maintenance, for an extended time, of rule over an alien people that is separate from and subordinate to the ruling power."[5] It is a form of unequal social relations between polities, and entails the idea of political, military, or economic dominance by intrusive foreign groups over local populations.[6] Colonialism is not just an abstract concept, however; it is embedded in a culturally specific historical experience. In Western thought, the central defining case of colonialism is the expansion of early capitalist Europe by extending its control over the Americas, Africa, south Asia, and Southeast Asia from the sixteenth through the mid-twentieth century. The connection between colonialism and the last four centuries of Western history is so deeply rooted that a number of scholars in different disciplines have argued that the European colonial encounter continues to structure not only Western intellectual conceptions of other cultures, including the discipline of anthropology and the culture concept,[7] but even the West's very definition of itself as a distinct entity.[8] Colonialism is inextricably bound up with notions drawn from the European experience such as "domination of an alien minority, asserting racial and cultural superiority over a materially inferior native majority; contact between a machine oriented civilization with Christian origins, a powerful economy, and a rapid rhythm of life and a non-Christian civilization that lacks machines and is marked by a backward economy and a slow rhythm of life; and the imposition of the first civilization upon the second."[9] This close connection of colonialism with the experience of the last four centuries of capitalist expansion makes it virtually impossible to apply this concept to the interregional interaction systems of ancient, non-Western, or precapitalist societies without incorporating a whole set of a priori assumptions about inherently unequal power relationships derived from European domination over Asia, Africa, and the Americas.

In historians' usage, the traditional view of colonies is almost completely structured by the European experience. In one of the few attempts to develop a typology of colonies, M. I. Finley argues that we should continue to follow the eighteenth- and nineteenth-century usage, and restrict the term *colony* to only those implanted settlements characterized by (a) large-scale emigration from the homeland, (b) the appropriation of local lands through the subjugation of local peoples, (c) colonial control of the local labor force, or (d) formal political and economic control of the implanted settlement by the homeland or metropolis.[10] Central to Finley's model is the idea, drawn from European colonialism, that the implanted settlements dominate indigenous peoples, who are seen as "technically backward, small scale in their political organization, incapable of concerted action, as compared with their European conquerors. Above all they were…hopelessly outclassed in their ability to apply force."[11] Inequality and domination are thus inherent in every level of the model, so that the newly founded settlements are seen as parts of a chain of domination and dependency where homelands control colonies, while the colonies in turn control the indigenous host communities around them. As a result, Finley excludes a number of important historical and ethnographic cases from his definition of colonies because they do not reflect foreign domination over local communities.[12]

Although it is highly explicit and theoretically grounded in its considerations of political economy, Finley's model is nevertheless overly restrictive. By his own admission, the definitional requirements of homeland control, mass emigration, and colonial domination of the indigenous host communities exclude the implanted settlements of the eighth to sixth century B.C.: Greeks, the Phoenicians, Hellenistic settlements in former Persian lands, the Crusades, the Venetian Romania, the Genoese trading stations, Uganda, the Gold Coast, the Congo, Senegal, and the Ivory Coast.[13] The term *colony* is effectively limited to the international dominance relationships of European colonialism, and even then is restricted to a small number of European ventures such as the early stages of English and Spanish colonies in the Americas, and English or French "settler colonies" (*colonies de peuplement*) in Africa, for example, Kenya.

Clearly this model will not do. Any typology that excludes this many archaeological and historical cases needlessly multiplies analytical categories, and impedes rather than helps us in our goal of understanding the dynamics of ancient colonies. What is needed is a definition of colonies that subsumes, but is not limited to, European colonialism. A more neutral use of the term *colony* simply refers to a specific form of settlement, without assuming the kind of dominance hierarchy inherent in the concept of European colonialism, and without specifying the nature of social relations between the settlement and surrounding communities. For purposes of cross-cultural comparison, I suggest that a colony can be most usefully defined as follows:

an implanted settlement established by one society in either uninhabited territory or the territory of another society. The implanted settlement is established for long-term residence by all or part of the population and is both spatially and socially distinguishable from the communities of a host society. The settlement onset is marked by a distinct formal corporate identity as a community with cultural/ritual, economic, military, or political ties to its homeland, but the homeland need not politically dominate the implanted settlement.

The corporate nature of the foreign community and its formalized ties with its homeland, and with its host community, are key elements that provide an important distinction between colonies and episodes of migration by individuals or families. Note also that this definition treats the nature of power relations between the colony and the host community, and between the colony and its homeland as open issues to be to determined empirically, rather than assuming a priori that these are structured to fit in, as in the European colonialism model. By doing so, one is able to recognize the possibility that interregional interaction networks may be organized in a variety of ways; some colonies may dominate their host communities while others may not. The degree of homeland control over the colony is also something that may vary widely, even in the same colonial system, depending on local circumstances and power balances.[14] This reformulated definition has several advantages. First, it encompasses the sixteenth- to twentieth-century European expansion while also allowing us to compare a wide variety of ancient, non-Western, and precapitalist networks of colonies within a single general framework. Second, the recognition of variation in power relationships forces us to investigate the dynamics of historically specific interactional situations (that is, how the nature of relations worked between a particular colony and its host communities), while also attempting to identify the broader scale structural determinants of these relationships.

Colonies as Diasporas

By dropping the dominance assumptions of European colonialism, it becomes possible to recognize that there are multiple potential modes of power relations among colonies, homelands, host communities, and the specialists who act as intermediaries among them. This conceptual shift then poses the challenge of how to best describe and explain this variation. One of the most useful theoretical frameworks for the study of cross-cultural interaction is the trade diaspora model, developed by Abner Cohen in his analysis of relations between ethnically distinct enclaves of Hausa traders and their Yoruba host communities in West Africa.[15] Cohen defines trade diasporas as "interregional exchange networks composed of spatially dispersed specialized merchant groups which are culturally distinct, organizationally cohesive, and socially independent from their host communities while maintaining a high level of economic and social ties with related communities who define themselves in terms of the same general cultural identity."[16]

It is important to distinguish the very specific model of a trade diaspora from the more general notion in globalization studies of diasporas as transnational communities.[17] Trade diasporas arise in situations where culturally distinct groups are engaged in challenging communication and transportation conditions, and where centralized state institutions are ineffectively providing participants with either physical or economic security in long-distance exchanges. One strategy through which these difficulties can be overcome is for traders from one cohesive ethnic group to control all or most of the stages of trade in specific commodities. To do so effectively, the group must organize itself as a corporate entity capable of political action that can deal with external pressure from their host community or trading partners, ensure unified group action for common causes, and establish channels of communication and cooperation with members of the same group in other parts of the exchange network.

Members of the trading group move into new areas, settle down in market or transport centers along major trade routes, and specialize in exchange while maintaining a separate cultural identity from their host community. The foreigners attempt to maintain a monopoly of their particular trade specialization; this allows them to function as intermediaries or cross-cultural brokers between their host community and the outside world. The shared identity among different diaspora communities provides the framework for the communication, credit, and reliability necessary for the orderly long-term functioning of the exchange system. To allow for this ease of interaction between widely separated communities, diaspora organization is stable at the group level, but allows for substantial mobility among its members. The group has its own political organization that maintains order within the group and coordinates with other diaspora groups to maintain the diaspora's identity and economic "turf" in dealing with host communities. Often, the maintenance of this distinct political organization requires some level of judicial autonomy and mutual assistance between diaspora members as well.

Organizational factors alone are insufficient to hold the group together. Trade diasporas strongly emphasize their distinctive cultural identity as well, defining themselves as a moral community that acts as a group to enforce the conformity of individual members of the group to shared values and principles. According to Cohen, "The creation of a trading diaspora requires the mobilization of a variety of types of social relationships, the utilization of different kinds of myths, beliefs, norms, values, and motives, and the employment of various types of pressure and of sanctions. These different elements which are employed in the development of the diaspora are so interdependent that they tend to be seen in terms of an integrated ideological scheme which is related to the basic problems of man, his place in society and in the universe."[18]

An ideology of this type is necessary to build and maintain the cohesion of the diaspora and its effectiveness as a trade network despite the centrifugal forces of spatial dispersion and competition from host communities or other trade diasporas. For this reason, many of the best known trade diasporas are closely associated with "universal" civilizations or religions such as Confucianism, Hinduism, Islam, or Judaism.[19] In these kinds of interregional exchange systems, the most cohesive diaspora groups survive and prosper; groups that lose or lack a strong unifying ideology tend to fragment, lose the trade monopoly that is their raison d'être, and eventually merge with their host communities.[20]

Difference is the essence of a trade diaspora. The group defines its membership and scope of action by emphasizing its distinctive identity and exclusiveness relative to its host community. This deliberate separation is necessary to strengthen the diaspora's corporate identity; it also insures the diaspora's survival by preventing outsiders from entering the group and breaking their trade monopoly. Although most commonly defined through an ideology of shared descent or origin, diaspora identity can also be expressed through a variety of linguistic, religious, or other cultural criteria in which relative importance can shift as needed in order to maximize group distinctiveness. The group maintains the integrity of the interregional exchange network by trying to be as different as possible from its host community while at the same time emphasizing a shared cultural identity with sister diaspora communities. The trade diaspora's ethnicity can be seen as a deliberately invented and consciously maintained social identity, such that the members of the group are culturally distinct not only from their host community but even, on occasion, from their community of origin (as is the case with the Hausa in Yoruba communities).[21] Trade diasporas can be surprisingly long-lived as distinct ethnic communities. The extended maintenance of a separate cultural identity is especially likely to occur when it provides the diaspora with an economically advantageous trade link to its homeland.

Host communities allow diasporas to settle and accord them autonomy because the foreigners are useful to local rulers in several ways. In many agrarian or pastoral societies, exchange is viewed as a suspicious activity that is best left to outsiders or socially inferior groups within the polity.[22] Sponsoring and taxing trade diasporas provides an easy way for rulers in the host community to increase their own wealth without having to go through the conflict inherent in restructuring power relationships within their own community.[23] It is because strangers to the trade diaspora lack strong social ties with the majority of the host community that they have little choice but to be dependent on and, therefore, loyal to the local rulers. The key point to note here is that the social position of the diaspora is closely tied to local politics—specifically the degree of sociopolitical complexity and the nature of factionalism or competition in the host community.

A trade diaspora can have a wide range of possible relationships with other diaspora nodes, with its homeland, and especially with its host community. The three most important points along the continuum of diaspora-host relations are as follows: (a) marginal status, (b) social autonomy, and (c) in the extreme case, the diaspora can dominate the host community.

In some cases, the rulers of the host community treat the trade diaspora as a marginal or pariah group to be exploited at will. The foreign enclave's presence is only tolerated because of its usefulness to the host community. In these cases it is the host community that emphasizes the social separation of the diaspora group, defining the latter's autonomy more through restrictions than through rights. This marginal status was often characteristic of Jewish trade diasporas in medieval Europe,[24] Jains in India, or merchant groups in the Fulani-controlled Islamic state of Massina in the middle Niger region during the eighteenth and nineteenth centuries.[25] Although the Massina state reluctantly recognized the importance of exchange, it was seen as a low-status activity completely at odds with *Pulaaku*, the Fulani cultural ethos. As a result, virtually all exchange activities were carried out by non-Fulani such as the Dyula, Arabs, or Moors. These groups were tolerated but restricted in their activities, and were denied access to the state center at Massina.[26]

The second form of diaspora status is that of protected autonomy within the host community. This can be gained through the explicit granting of autonomous political status by the local rulers, as in the case of the Chinese trade diaspora in Southeast Asia. The Chinese trade diaspora was able to gain a high degree of autonomy in its various Southeast Asian host communities by being financially useful to local ruling elites. The Chinese had been long-distance traders throughout Southeast Asia for centuries, trading Chinese porcelain, cotton goods, and silk in return for pepper, nutmeg, and cinnamon. Ties to the homeland played an important role in establishing the autonomy of the overseas Chinese. The maritime experience of Chinese long-distance merchants and their monopoly on access to Chinese ports and goods were powerful incentives to local elites in Thailand, Indonesia, and the Philippines. These merchants were extended numerous trading monopolies, tax concessions, and exemptions from unpaid labor. In addition, the Chinese traders usually occupied special quarters set aside for them by the local rulers. In return, the Chinese diaspora provided local rulers with exotic prestige goods and other economic benefits of exchange such as customs taxes and loans when needed.[27] Chinese diaspora groups forged close alliances with local rulers and played key roles in the financial and administrative hierarchies of their host polities as tax farmers or other state officials. This client-community status benefited the Chinese, who were able to occupy a profitable, protected socio-economic niche. At the same time, the local rulers gained new sources of income and a group of subordinates whose dependence insured their loyalty.[28] Thus, trade diasporas such as the ethnic Chinese in Southeast Asia gained autonomy through the commercial advantages accrued from their close ties to the Chinese mainland, coupled with a strategy of political alliances with powerful local patrons.

At the extreme end of the range of variation in the organization of inter-regional exchange is the fairly unusual situation in which the trade diaspora actually controls its host community. The classic examples of this are the European trading post empires in Africa and Asia in the eighteenth and nineteenth centuries. The European trade diasporas established mercantile enclaves under their own military control while also using force to control the terms of trade with their host communities. This aggressive strategy was so successful that by the beginning of the nineteenth century, the English in India and the Dutch in Indonesia had effectively transformed their militarized trade diasporas into actual territorial empires.[29]

There is also a wide range of possible relationships among different nodes in the trade diaspora and between the diaspora and its homeland. One cannot assume that a foreign trading enclave represents a unified political entity controlled by its homeland or metropolis. For example, the Greek colonies in the Mediterranean, the Aegean, and the Black Sea during the later first millennium B.C. retained certain ideological ties with their mother cities, but were not necessarily dominated by them. At the same time, ties between colonies were weak or nonexistent, except in the broadest sense of a shared cultural identity. At the other end of the spectrum, diaspora nodes may be closely linked politically, as was the case in the Portuguese Estado da India, where the viceroy in Goa ruled over secondary diaspora nodes or colonies in Mozambique, Malacca, and Macao.

Given the extent of this variability in diaspora organization, and the degree to which it depends on the sociopolitical structure of the host communities, it should come as no surprise that trade diasporas do not remain static over time. Curtin points out that one of the most striking characteristics of trade diasporas is their tendency to work themselves out of business. Diasporas come into being because the differences between cultures in an interregional exchange network require the services of mediators. These middlemen become victims of their own success, however, and extended periods of mediation can reduce cross-cultural differences and hence the need for cross-cultural brokers.[30] When this happens, the diaspora loses its distinctive status as members of the host community take over the foreigners' position in the exchange network. At this point, several things can happen. In one common pattern, the trade diaspora can leave the host community and return to its homeland if the cultural ties between the two communities have remained sufficiently strong over time. This outcome was typical of medieval European trade diasporas, such as those connected with the Hanseatic League. These formal commercial enclaves were withdrawn from their host communities in places such as London by the end of the sixteenth century, as English merchants took over the trade. In a variation of this out-migration pattern, the trade diaspora may simply be expelled (regardless of whether they return to their ancestral home), as were the Indians from Uganda or the Jews from Spain.

In a second pattern, the trade diaspora may remain in the host community, but its members find new socioeconomic roles and remain as an ethnic minority. The classic example of this second pattern is the evolution of the Chinese trade diaspora in Southeast Asia from a protected community closely involved in international trade and local administration into a series of ethnic minorities involved in local exchange and manufacturing.[31]

In the third pattern, with the loss of its distinctive economic role, the trade diaspora can slowly disintegrate as a unique social group and be absorbed or assimilated into the host community.[32]

The trade diaspora concept thus provides a framework that allows for a tremendous range of variation in the organization of interregional interaction, in the strategies pursued by foreign trading enclaves and host elites, and in the developmental trajectories of these networks. Once we recognize that these different possibilities exist, how do we link them to specific historical or archaeological cases? From the examples discussed above, different forms of power configurations — within and between homelands, enclaves, and host communities — appear to have a marked influence on the relationship between a trade diaspora and its host community.

The military, political, and economic power of the trade diaspora or its parent community plays a key role in structuring interregional reaction. This is, of course, most clearly evident in the dominance of the militarized European trade diasporas over their Asian and African host communities in the eighteenth and nineteenth centuries. By contrast, when the homeland polity is either weak or nonexistent, then there is far more opportunity for negotiation between hosts and diasporas in the organization of interaction within the network.

When the baggage of colonialism is removed from the concept of "colonies," the latter emerge as highly flexible social entities in which organizational variability can best be understood through the trade diaspora model outlined above. The dominance relationships inherent in European colonialism apply to only a small subset of ethnohistorically documented relationships among colonies, homelands, and host communities in non-Western or precapitalist networks of interregional interaction. There is thus ample reason to believe that this kind of variability existed as well in the organization of colonies established by prehistoric state societies. Our task, then, is twofold: (a) to identify colonies in the archaeological record, and (b) to determine the organization of political and economic relations between these diasporas and their host communities, without assuming colonial dominance in advance.

The trade colonies established by early state societies can be considered as a particular kind of trade diaspora settlement. Both colonies and diasporas share a focus on trade and show tremendous variation in the forms of relations they can have with both their host communities and their homelands. The definitional differences between the colonies and diasporas mostly revolve around the degree of community cohesion or corporate identity and the extent to which the foreigners emphasize an ideology of distinctive cultural identity relative to the host population. I suggest here that for cross-cultural comparative purposes, however, trade colonies are most usefully seen as a territorially grounded form of trade diaspora settlement. Viewing exchange-oriented colonies as trade diasporas forces us to acknowledge in our models the potential for variation in relations among homelands, foreigners, and host communities. This flexibility is essential if we are to develop a general comparative model of colonies that can encompass both ethnographic and archaeological cases.

The identification of trade colonies or trade diasporas in the archaeological record is surprisingly difficult, not least because it is closely related to the problematic issue of recognizing ethnicity through material culture. We can identify as colonies those archaeological sites in which architecture, site plan, material culture assemblage, and behavioral patterning are identical to those of another region, but are located as spatially discrete occupations surrounded by settlements of the local culture. One would expect colonies to be founded as completely new settlements on previously unoccupied land. Alternatively, if founded in association with a preexisting settlement, a colony should show sharp architectural and artifactual discontinuities with both earlier occupations and contemporaneous indigenous residential areas. Artifactual similarities to the homeland should reflect a broad complex of material culture used in a variety of contexts, rather than being limited to a single category such as ceramics.

Robert Santley and his colleagues argue that the ethnic identity of the inhabitants in a colonial enclave should be expressed in material culture connected with two different levels of social inclusiveness—the enclave as a whole and the more restricted domestic level.[33] At the enclave-wide level, the identity of the foreigners is expressed and reinforced through public rituals; these are often centered on a ceremonial structure such as a church, temple, or mosque, where architecture generally incorporates the style or symbolic elements of the homeland. Common language, styles of dress, the wearing of particular badges or emblems, and burial customs are also enclave-wide ways to express the separate identity of foreigners. These practices are especially common because they provide highly visible identification of a person's ethnicity by others, both within and outside the group.[34]

At the domestic level, the members of an enclave generally live together in a geographically contiguous area, distinct from other parts of the host community. In the households of the foreign enclave, ethnicity will be expressed in culinary practices. Food preferences, preparation procedures, and the material culture associated with these practices should differ from local patterns in the host community while resembling the cultural practices of the homeland (although one might also expect to see eventual convergences in foreign and local cuisines in long-term colonial situations). In addition, the distinctive ethnic identity of the foreigners will often be reflected by the use of raw materials or styles from the homeland in the paraphernalia used for household rituals.[35]

It is important to consider alternative interpretations for the presence of foreign styles of material culture in the sites of a different culture, rather than automatically assuming that this material culture reflects the existence of a foreign enclave. The use of multiple criteria combined with contrastive patterning between the foreign and local assemblages is necessary to distinguish the actual presence of foreign settlers from (a) trade without a trade diaspora, or (b) emulation by groups of local elites who are simply adopting status-related aspects of foreign material culture (through either importation or imitation). Trade, emulation, and the presence of trade colonies or diasporas should leave different archaeological signatures. If interaction is limited to trade without the presence of a foreign enclave, then we would expect to see only portable trade items in the local settlement; foreign public and residential architecture would be absent, as would be evidence for foreign food preferences in spatially discrete contexts. If interaction consists of local elite emulation of foreign styles, we would expect to see these imports or imitations limited to high-status households, while lower-status groups retained local customs. In most cases, the elite households would show a distinction between the emulation of foreign styles in public contexts and the retention of local styles in domestic life.[36] Diachronic analyses can also distinguish a colonial enclave from a case of elite emulation; in the latter case one would expect to see the gradual appearance of foreign styles in elite contexts, rather than the sudden appearance of a complete range of foreign material culture as the archaeological signature of a colony.

Mesopotamian Colonies: The Uruk Expansion (circa 3700–3100 B.C.)

The earliest archaeologically identifiable network of colonies was established in the Near East during the fourth millennium B.C. Urban-centered state societies developed in southern Mesopotamia during the Uruk period in the mid-fourth millennium B.C.[37] Almost immediately, the economic sphere of the Uruk polities expanded to form an extensive interaction network connecting the southern alluvium with the less urbanized polities in the neighboring highlands areas of the Zagros Mountains, north Syria, and southeast Anatolia (see fig. 1).[38] A number of sites in these areas have been identified as Uruk trading colonies, apparently established to control trade and communication routes while extracting metals, semi-precious stones, lumber, or other commodities from the resource-rich highland zones, in what is apparently the world's earliest known colonial system. Sites with characteristic Uruk architecture, ceramics, and administrative technology (that is, seals, sealings, bullae, tokens, and numerical tablets) were established in the key routes through the Iranian Zagros,[39] on the Tigris River in northern Mesopotamia,[40] across the Habur headwaters region,[41] and up the Euphrates River into the Taurus highlands.[42] The Uruk expansion into Syria and Anatolia seems to have begun in the Middle Uruk period, probably circa 3700 B.C.,[43] and reached its fullest extent in the Late Uruk.[44] For reasons that we do not really understand, the Uruk expansion seems to have ended fairly abruptly circa 3100 B.C. with the abandonment or destruction of Uruk settlements in Syria, Anatolia, and the Zagros.

The south Mesopotamian colonies are quite distinctive as intrusive sites, established in the midst of local Iranian, Syrian, and southeast Anatolian cultures. Several different forms of Uruk material culture occurring together — notably ceramics, architecture, and administrative technology — serve to identify the Mesopotamian implanted settlements while distinguishing them from

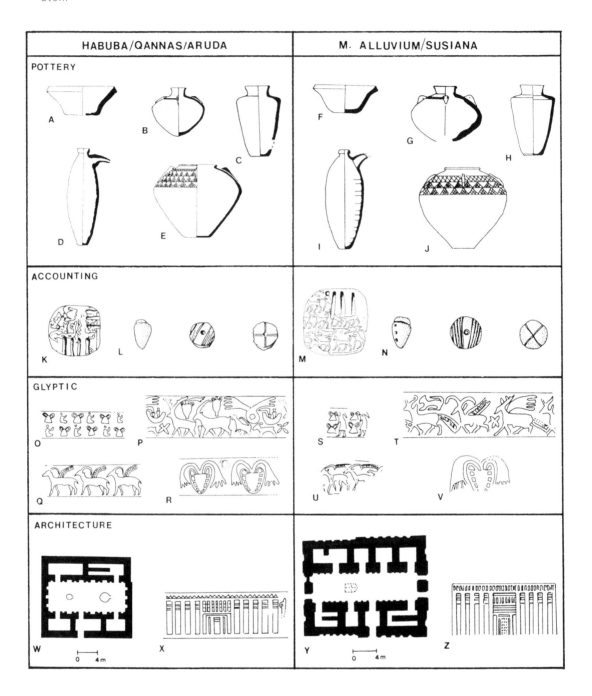

Fig. 2. Similarities in Uruk pottery, administrative technology, seal-design iconography, and public architecture, 4000–3000 B.C.

Left: artifacts from colonies such as Habuba Kabira, Qannas, and Jebel Aruda; *right:* artifacts from the southern Mesopotamian alluvium and the Susiana plain

contemporaneous local settlements.[45] Multiple criteria are necessary because ceramics alone are not a reliable indicator of ethnicity.[46]

Sites identified as Uruk colonies have a full range of Mesopotamian ceramic forms representing a wide set of functions. Local and indigenous ceramics tend to be rare or absent from these sites or parts of sites. The sites with the full repertoire of Uruk ceramic forms also have distinctive Uruk domestic or public and ritual architecture. The south Mesopotamian tripartite "middle hall" house with keyhole-shaped hearths and an associated court-yard characterizes implanted Uruk settlements.[47] Wall cone mosaic decoration is a second architectural element characteristic of the Uruk.[48] Similarly, niched facade temples are a distinctive Mesopotamian type of public build-ing.[49] A third distinctive feature of the Uruk-implanted settlements is the pres-ence of south Mesopotamian administrative technology such as cylinder seals, bullae, tokens, and clay tablets with numerical inscriptions used to monitor the mobilization, transportation, storage, and disbursement of goods.[50]

Based on these criteria, researchers have identified Uruk-implanted settle-ments at Godin in central western Iran;[51] at Brak and Nineveh in northern Mesopotamia;[52] and on the Syrian Euphrates at Qrayya, Habuba Kabira, and Jebel Aruda (fig. 2).[53] On the upper reaches of the Euphrates in Anatolia, excavations have identified Uruk implanted settlements at Hassek Höyük, and have suggested more tentatively that they may also be present at Samsat and Tepecik.[54]

These colonies seem to have been established on the major trade and communications routes leading up toward the main source areas of copper, lumber, and semiprecious stones in the Taurus Mountains of eastern Anatolia and the Zagros Mountains of Iran. Interaction between Mesopotamians and local societies took three different—and occasionally overlapping—forms: exchange, emulation, and the establishment of actual Uruk settlements in the territories of indigenous polities. The degree to which any one of these three interactional forms might have predominated in a given region probably var-ied depending on local conditions. In the areas closest to southern Meso-potamia proper, colonies such as Habuba Kabira or Tell Sheikh Hassan were large fortified settlements that apparently used coercion in a short-lived and ultimately unsuccessful effort to exert economic control over the sparsely populated local Syrian communities.[55] In more distant regions with larger populations, Uruk settlements such as Godin V or Hacınebi took the form of small "outposts" or "way stations" located inside the preexisting towns of local polities.[56]

In contrast with the apparent social isolation of the colonies at Habuba and Jebel Aruda, the large displays of local material culture in the Uruk outposts suggest that the latter interacted very closely with their host commu-nities. We have no evidence to suggest that these outposts dominated local economies through asymmetric exchange or coercion. Instead, the small numbers and vulnerable position of the Mesopotamians at Godin and other outposts meant that they could only survive by remaining on good terms with their more powerful indigenous neighbors. At the outermost edges of the Uruk interaction network, Mesopotamian material culture at sites such as Tepecik is so sparse that it becomes difficult to determine whether it reflects the actual presence of a Mesopotamian outpost or simply a process of emulation by a small subset of the local population.[57] These differences suggest that the organization of these settlements and the ways they interacted with their local neighbors varied markedly depending on a number of factors, most notably the distance from Mesopotamia, the size of the local population, and the degree of preexisting social complexity in the indigenous polities.[58]

The Uruk Mesopotamian Presence at Hacınebi, Turkey

Although Uruk "colonies" and "outposts" in Syria and Anatolia have been excavated, we know almost nothing about the organization of this interregional trade system or its impact on the political, social, and economic systems of the indigenous cultures in southeast Anatolia. Excavations from 1992 to 1997 at Hacınebi Tepe in southeast Turkey document the effects of Uruk Mesopotamian commercial expansion on local Anatolian polities.[59] Hacınebi is the ideal site to elucidate this problem, since it is an indigenous settlement strategically located near the Uruk enclaves on the Euphrates River trade route, and shows clear signs of contact with Mesopotamia during the Late Chalcolithic period (circa 3700–3200 B.C.). The evidence for an apparent Mesopotamian trading enclave in one corner of this Anatolian settlement, approximately 1,200 kilometers upstream from the city of Uruk, provides a rare opportunity to examine the nature of interaction between diasporas and host communities in the world's earliest known network of colonies.

Hacınebi is a 3.3 hectare mound located on the bluffs overlooking the east bank of the Euphrates River in Sanliurfa province, southeast Turkey (see figs. 1, 3). The site lies near the head of the main north-south riverine trade route linking Mesopotamia and Anatolia; it also occupies a strategic location on what has historically been the major east-west river crossing point at Birecik. The mound of Hacınebi is situated on an easily defensible east–west-oriented spur, which drops steeply down to the river on the west, and into deep canyons to the north and south. The Tigris-Euphrates survey project conducted by Guillermo Algaze first discovered Hacınebi and identified its main occupation as Late Chalcolithic, comprising both local southeast Anatolian Amuq F/G[60] and south Mesopotamian Uruk ceramic forms.[61] The only post-Chalcolithic ceramics noted at Hacınebi were Achaemenid-Hellenistic in date, circa fifth to second centuries B.C.

Excavations at Hacınebi have identified three main Late Chalcolithic occupation phases (fig. 4). Phases A and B1 date to the early fourth millennium B.C. and are characterized by local Anatolian chaff-tempered ceramics. Exposures of phase A and B1 occupations have found evidence of a possible fortification wall, monumental public architecture, large storage structures, long-distance exchange of copper and chlorite/steatite, on-site copper metallurgy, mortuary evidence for ascribed hierarchical social status, stamp seals,

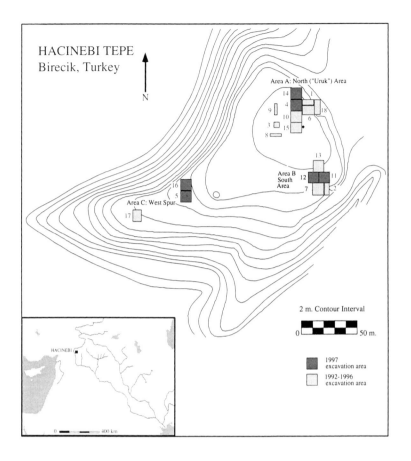

Hacınebi Tepe — Late Chalcolithic Relative Chronology

	Hacınebi	Kurban	Atatürk Dam Reservoir	Arslantepe	Amuq	Leilan	Tabqa Dam Reservoir	Southern Mesopotamia
3000 B.C.	EB I burials							
	(abandonment)						Habuba Kabira	Late Uruk
							Jebel Aruda	
		VIA	Hassek Karatut	VIA	G	IV		
							Sheikh Hassan	
3500 B.C.	B2							Middle Uruk
			VII	F	V		?	
	B1	VIB						
4000 B.C.	A							

Fig. 3. Topographic map of main excavation areas at Hacınebi, 1992–97

Fig. 4. Chronology for Hacınebi and selected other sites, 3000–4000 B.C.

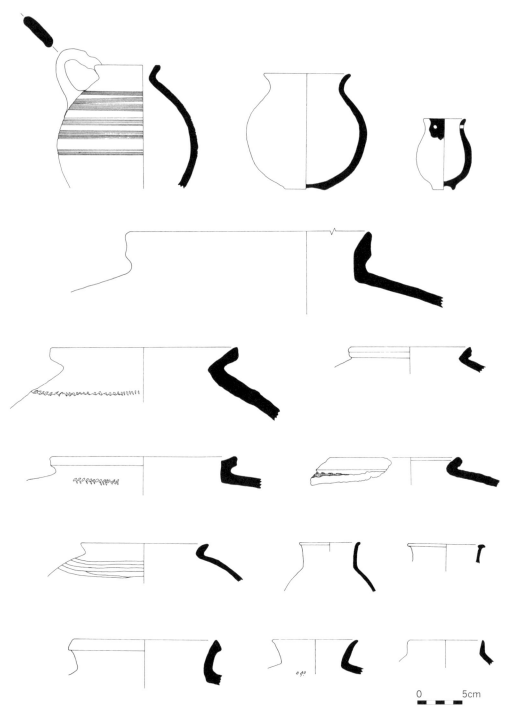

Fig. 5. Uruk Mesopotamian jar types, Hacınebi, 3700–3200 B.C.

and stamp seal impressions indicative of administrative activities.[62] These finds are consistent with the evidence from other sites such as Arslantepe in pointing to a fairly high level of social complexity in the local Late Chalcolithic cultures of southeast Anatolia even before the period of intensive contact with Uruk Mesopotamia.[63]

Late Chalcolithic phase B2 overlies phases A and B1, and shows complete stylistic continuity with them. In this later occupation, large concentrations of Uruk Mesopotamian material culture appear at Hacınebi. During phase B2 (circa 3700–3200 B.C.), a small Mesopotamian trading enclave seems to have been established in the northeast corner of this local Anatolian settlement. It is important to emphasize that the intrusive material neither replaces nor evolves out of the earlier Anatolian assemblage but instead appears alongside it as a second, parallel body of material culture. Two lines of evidence suggest that an Uruk Mesopotamian-implanted settlement was present at the site. First, the Mesopotamian artifacts are not just limited to ceramics but represent the full range of Uruk material culture used in both public and domestic contexts. Second, multiple classes of Uruk material culture occur in association with one another.

The full range of Uruk ceramic forms is present at Hacınebi. Stylistic analyses and radiocarbon dates both suggest that this material ranges from the Middle Uruk through the beginning of the Late Uruk period—circa 3700–3300 B.C.[64] Ceramic vessel form classes span the full range of functions, including those used for food preparation, serving, and storage. Predominant among these are beveled rim bowls, fine conical cups, crude conical cups, comb-incised strap-handled jars, low expanded-band rim jars, round rim jars, spouted jars, trays, and ladles (figs. 5, 6). Ware types and manufacturing techniques match southern Mesopotamian practices so that the majority of vessels are wheel-made, sand-tempered forms, while beveled rim bowls and trays are chaff tempered and manufactured by hand. The full range of Uruk forms of decoration are used, such as red slipping, appliqué bands, comb incision, and reserved slip. Finds of Uruk style kiln wasters and the preliminary results of instrumental neutron activation analysis all indicate that the Uruk style ceramics were manufactured on-site; the production of Uruk ceramics was contemporaneous with, but stylistically and technologically distinct from, the manufacture of the local Anatolian ceramic forms (fig. 7).

Uruk architecture is only indirectly attested at Hacınebi. No intact niched facade temples or middle room houses have been exposed as yet in phase B2 contexts; however, large numbers of ceramic wall cones—the uniquely Mesopotamian architectural decoration—have been found in trash deposits at the site (fig. 8).[65] Excavations in Mesopotamia proper and at colonies such as Habuba Kabira, Jebel Aruda, and Hassek Hüyük have shown that this architectural decoration was used on both public and domestic buildings in the Uruk period.[66]

An additional form of distinctively Mesopotamian material culture at

Fig. 6. Uruk Mesopotamian beveled rim bowls and conical
cups and bowls, Hacınebi, 3700–3200 B.C.

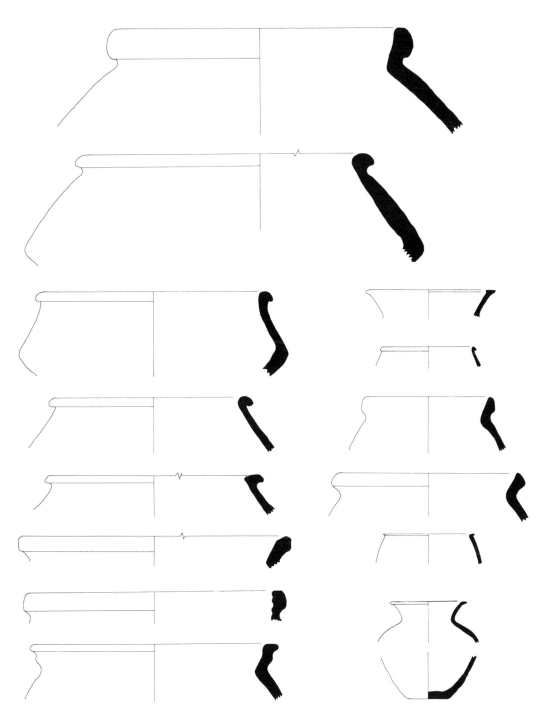

Fig. 7. Anatolian Late Chalcolithic jar types, Hacınebi, 3700–3200 B.C.

0   5cm

Fig. 8. Uruk Mesopotamian wall cones, Hacınebi, 3700–3200 B.C.

Fig. 10. Uruk Mesopotamian ceramic sickle fragment, Hacınebi, 3700–3200 B.C.

Fig. 9. Uruk Mesopotamian conical-headed copper pin, Hacınebi, 3700–3200 B.C.

Hacınebi is bitumen. Bitumen sources are common in southern Mesopotamia and the adjacent region of Khuzestan in southwest Iran, with one of the most widely used seepages at Hit on the Euphrates River. Bitumen was ubiquitous as a construction material, sealant, and raw material for a variety of functional or decorative objects in southern Mesopotamia, and has also been identified at Uruk colonies such as Habuba Kabira, Tell Sheikh Hassan, and Jerablus Tahtani.[67] Large amounts of this nonlocal petroleum-based raw material have also been found concentrated in phase B2 deposits associated with Uruk ceramics. Geochemical analyses have demonstrated that large amounts of the Hacınebi B2 bitumen derives from sources in the Uruk heartland of southern Mesopotamia and southwest Iran.[68] These clear interregional contrasts in bitumen availability and use raise the possibility that this material might have been either a trade good exported from Mesopotamia to southeast Anatolia, or else served as the packaging within which some other (as yet unidentified) trade good was transported.

Other distinctively Mesopotamian forms of material culture found at Hacınebi include personal ornaments, artifacts associated with commercial activities, and subsistence-related technology. A conical headed copper pin found in Uruk deposits at Hacınebi has an exact parallel in the Uruk colony at Tell Sheikh Hassan[69] and at southern sites such as Tello and Susa (fig. 9).[70] Cruciform grooved stone weights, known from the Uruk colony at Habuba Kabira[71] and Sheikh Hassan[72] are also present at Hacınebi. Finally, two examples of high-fired clay sickles have been found at Hacınebi (fig. 10). These tools are characteristic of fourth-millennium southern Mesopotamian artifacts in the Ubaid, Uruk, and Jemdet Nasr periods,[73] and have never, to this author's knowledge, been attested at any local Late Chalcolithic Anatolian settlements.

The northeast area of Hacınebi has yielded evidence for distinctively Mesopotamian administrative (sealing) systems. Mesopotamian record-keeping technology is easily recognizable in its use of cylinder seals as opposed to the Anatolian use of stamp seal technology. Local Anatolian-style stamp seals and seal impressions are present at Hacınebi in the earlier phases A and B1 and continue in use in phase B2. Phase B2 deposits in the northeast area of Hacınebi have yielded an almost complete range of standard Uruk administrative artifacts including jar sealings, jar stoppers, hollow clay ball or bullae filled with tokens, and a clay tablet—all bearing Uruk cylinder seal impressions, and all found in association with Uruk ceramics (fig. 11).[74] These record-keeping devices are common both at southern Mesopotamian urban sites such as Uruk[75] and at Uruk colonies such as Habuba Kabira, Jebel Aruda, Tell Sheikh Hassan, and Hassek Hüyük.[76]

Finally, behavioral patterning at Hacınebi is consistent with the artifactual evidence in matching the expected profile of a Mesopotamian colony. Animal bone remains can provide particularly strong evidence for the presence of a Mesopotamian enclave at Hacınebi, since food preferences and food preparation procedures are often very culture-specific.[77] The presence of such an

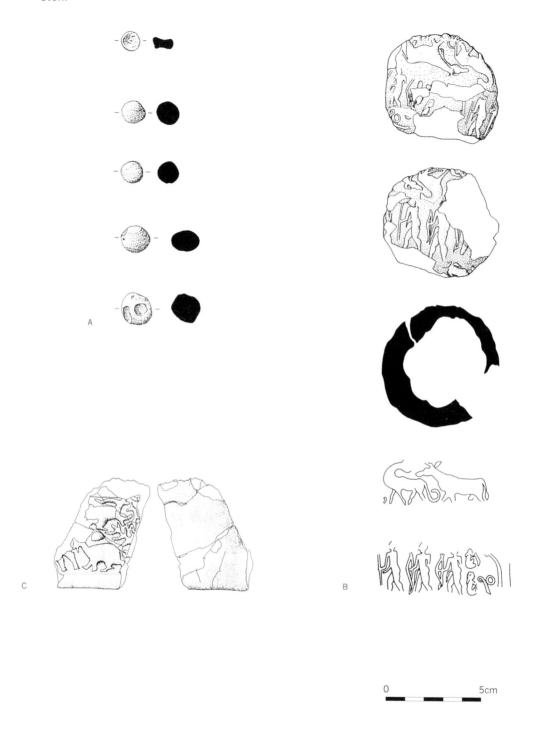

Fig. 11. Uruk Mesopotamian administrative technology, Hacınebi, 3700–3200 B.C.
A: unbaked clay tokens found in a cylinder seal-impressed hollow clay ball; B: two faces
and cross-section of a cylinder seal-impressed hollow clay ball (seal designs at top right);
C: cylinder seal-impressed tablet

enclave should be reflected by clear differences in food preferences, food preparation procedures, and possibly in butchery practices as well. Preliminary analyses show that major differences exist in the relative abundance of different animal species between those parts of Hacınebi with Uruk material culture and those where the local Anatolian assemblage predominates.[78] In Anatolian contexts caprids, mainly sheep and goats, form only about 50 percent of the sample. Pig is next in importance, at about 37 percent, and cattle third at 12 percent. This reflects a fairly diversified herding system. The unusually high proportion of pigs at Hacınebi is consistent with the pattern observed at other local Anatolian sites in the Euphrates valley. In a striking contrast to this pattern, Uruk contexts at Hacınebi show completely different food preferences; caprids form 85 percent of the sample, with only small amounts of pig and cattle present. This predominance of caprids fits very closely with what little is known about patterns of Uruk animal use at sites like Rubeideh and Farrukhabad in southern Mesopotamia and Khuzestan, where caprids range from 80 to 96 percent of the faunal assemblages.[79] In short, the faunal remains associated with Mesopotamian material culture match closely with known Mesopotamian food preferences and differ markedly from the animal bones associated with Anatolian contexts.

Taken together, the distinctively Mesopotamian ceramic, architectural, administrative, and other forms of material culture used in both public and domestic contexts at Hacınebi are completely consistent with both general criteria for the identification of colonies in the archaeological record,[80] and with the specific complex of material characteristic of Uruk colonies and settlements in the southern Mesopotamian homeland.[81]

Archaeological Correlates of the Colonial-Dominance and Trade Diaspora Models

The full range of Uruk material culture is not only present at Hacınebi, where it occurs together in deposits that are contemporaneous with, but spatially separate from Anatolian local Late Chalcolithic phase B2 deposits. These contrasting distributions of material culture at Hacınebi allow us to examine the organization of economic and political relations between the Mesopotamian colony and its host community. We have already noted that the variation in power relations between a trade diaspora and its host community can result in three different patterns of interaction: (a) diaspora marginality, (b) diaspora social autonomy, and (c) diaspora domination over its host community. Given the complexity of Uruk state societies and the size of the Uruk network of colonies, it would appear highly unlikely that they formed a socially marginal diaspora dominated by local host polities. We are left with two main options. The Uruk colonies might have dominated their host communities in an asymmetric power relationship along the lines of the European colonialist or Immanuel Wallerstein's world system models.[82] Alternatively, the Mesopotamian diaspora might have been a socially autonomous group, having an essential parity in economic and political relations with its Anatolian host community.[83] These two modalities in diaspora-host power relations should have distinctive archaeological correlates at Hacınebi.

If the Uruk enclave controlled the host community at Hacınebi along the lines of the colonial dominance model, one would expect to see the following archaeological correlates:

1. There should be evidence for Mesopotamian control over an asymmetric exchange system, as seen in the pattern of circulation of goods and the predominance of Mesopotamian administrative systems;
2. There should be evidence for a net outflow of subsistence and craft goods from the local settlement to the foreign enclave; and
3. There should be a high degree of complementarity in economic activities and exchange between the Uruk and the local host communities.

By contrast, if the Uruk enclave were a socially autonomous trade diaspora, one would expect to see the following as archaeological correlates:

1. Symmetric exchange relations, with no evidence for exclusive Mesopotamian economic or political control. Administrative artifacts should show evidence for both Mesopotamian and local control over the production, circulation, and consumption of commodities, or in degree of economic specialization;
2. There should be an essential parity in flows of subsistence and craft goods between the two communities; and
3. The Mesopotamian enclave should be largely self-sufficient in food and craft production. This would appear as the duplication of economic activities in both Mesopotamian and local Anatolian contexts.

There is no evidence for warfare or competition between the Uruk and Anatolian portions of the site. The phase B2 settlement shows no signs of warfare, fortifications, armaments, violent deaths, or sudden destruction events. Instead, a long series of superimposed occupational phases indicates that the Mesopotamian presence at the site was both peaceful and long-lived—extending for three hundred, and possibly, as long as five hundred years.

The Organization of Mesopotamian-Anatolian Trade at Hacınebi

Some of the best evidence for the organization of Mesopotamian-Anatolian interaction at Hacınebi comes from comparisons between contemporaneous deposits with overwhelmingly Mesopotamian material culture and those with mainly or exclusively local Late Chalcolithic Anatolian artifactual inventories. The complex of material culture and available evidence for food preferences from the two types of contexts strongly support the idea that an enclave of ethnically distinct Mesopotamians was present at the site. There is no evidence, however, that the Mesopotamians dominated their Anatolian host community. Instead, comparative analyses of ceramics, chipped stone, fauna, and record-keeping (administrative) artifacts from the Mesopotamian and local parts of Hacınebi suggest that the Uruk enclave was a socially and economically autonomous diaspora whose members raised their own food, produced their own crafts, and administered their own encapsulated exchange system.

Ceramics. Preliminary analyses of ceramics from the Uruk and local contexts show remarkable contrasts.[84] The Uruk and local contexts are generally trash deposits; that is, not in situ. The differences between the two contemporaneous sets of deposits indicate, however, that in at least some parts of the site, Uruk and local Anatolian ceramics were being used and then discarded separately.

A more detailed look shows that the differences go beyond the simple difference in cultural affiliation. The forms and dimensions of the ceramics also show clear contrasts in the functions or activities represented in the Uruk and Anatolian assemblages. In the Uruk deposits, over 90 percent of the ceramics are bowls—mainly beveled rim bowls. The Uruk bowls are not only more numerous, they are also much smaller than the Anatolian bowls. Most Uruk bowls have rim diameters between 8 and 22 centimeters, while most local bowls range from 25 to 40 centimeters. By contrast, the ceramic assemblage from the Local Anatolian deposits is much more evenly divided among bowls, jars, and the distinctive local "casserole" cooking vessels.

We can also see other important functional differences between the two samples. Cooking vessels, mainly casseroles, form about 21 percent of the ceramics in the Anatolian contexts. By contrast, local casseroles and Uruk strap-handled cooking pots together form less than 1 percent of the ceramics in the Uruk contexts. In short, the percentages of vessel forms and dimensions suggest that the Anatolian ceramics are a typical domestic assemblage used for food preparation, serving, and storage. Although storage and food preparation are represented in the Uruk deposits, the predominance of beveled rim bowls suggests that in addition to normal domestic activities some kind of highly specialized function was also taking place.

Bitumen. The presence and processing of bitumen, a petroleum-based raw material, points to additional differences between the Uruk and Anatolian parts of the site. As noted above bitumen occurs frequently at Uruk sites in southern Mesopotamia. At Hacınebi, bitumen occurs most frequently in association with Uruk material culture. Bitumen occurs in the three main forms that follow: as residues on ceramics (predominantly on Uruk forms), blocks, and shaped pieces—representing production debris, bulk storage, and finished products. All forms are far more common in Uruk contexts. Some of the bitumen residues on ceramics may reflect the use of this material as a waterproof sealant. The dribble patterns and locations of bitumen on many beveled rim bowls and in the spouts of conical cups suggest, however, that blocks of solid bitumen were being melted down and poured as an industrial activity in the midden in the Uruk contexts. There is no evidence for this activity in the Anatolian contexts. Chemical analyses of the bitumen by Dr. Jacques Connan of the French Elf Aquitaine Petroleum company,[85] and by Mark Schwartz of Northwestern University,[86] suggest that the Hacınebi bitumen is chemically identical to the bitumen from the Uruk colony at Habuba Kabira, and that both groups of samples are consistent with the composition of bitumen sources in the two main Uruk heartland areas of southern Mesopotamia and southwestern Iran. If this is correct, then the Hacınebi bitumen is the earliest Uruk trade good to be found in Anatolia.

In short, the ceramic and bitumen evidence suggest that the Mesopotamian enclave was engaged in some specialized activities that were not practiced by the local Anatolian host community. These differences should not, however, mask the overall pattern of two parallel economies in the Mesopotamian and Anatolian communities. A variety of artifact classes show that the people who generated the trash in Uruk and local contexts were engaged in similar types of activities, suggesting low levels of intracommunity exchange, and a high degree of socioeconomic autonomy in the Uruk enclave. This autonomy can be seen in the encapsulated nature of craft production, subsistence, and exchange-related administrative activities.

Chipped Stone Tool Production and Use. Patterns of chipped stone tool production and use suggest that the Uruk enclave at Hacınebi was characterized by a high degree of economic autonomy in both craft production and subsistence.[87] These show some interesting similarities and differences when compared to lithic use in the Anatolian areas of Hacınebi. Uruk deposits show clear evidence for stone tool manufacturing. The frequency of secondary flakes with large areas of cortex reflects early stages in the manufacture of large "Canaanean blades" made from a distinctive medium-banded cream-and-tan chert. The presence of this raw material and of secondary flakes in local Late Chalcolithic deposits as well suggests that blade tool manufacture took place concurrently in both Uruk and Anatolian parts of the site. Stone tool forms in the Uruk and Anatolian midden deposits suggest that both parts of the site were engaged in agricultural production. Many of the Canaanean blades show traces of bitumen hafting in the typical locations for sickle blades. Similarly, silica gloss, or "sickle sheen," is present on at least some blades from both areas. This is important because it suggests that the people who generated the midden in the Uruk contexts at Hacınebi were harvesting cereals. This stands in marked contrast to the Uruk colony of Habuba Kabira in Syria, where Dietrich Sürenhagen has suggested that the Uruk colonists were supplied with food by the local population.[88]

The same forms of stone tools were produced by both the Mesopotamian and Anatolian communities, Canaanean blades and simple blades from contexts with Mesopotamian material culture match the dimensions of these tool types in the Mesopotamian homeland while being significantly smaller than Canaanean and simple blades from Anatolian contexts.[89] These differences are consistent with ethnically specific contrasts in technological style between Mesopotamians and Anatolians at Hacınebi. [90]

Overall, the lithic evidence suggests three conclusions. First, both Anatolians and Mesopotamians at Hacınebi had access to the same raw materials. Second, both the Uruk and Anatolian areas were independently manufacturing parallel tool forms, although there may have been some ethnically distinctive differences in the technological styles they used to make particular blade types. Finally, both the Uruk and local areas were engaged in agricultural production.

Other Crafts. Other craft activities were also practiced in parallel by the Uruk and Mesopotamian communities. Ceramic spindle whorls are present in both areas, suggesting that both groups were weaving their own textiles.[91] Similarly, finds of Uruk-style kiln wasters indicate that the foreign enclave was manufacturing its own pottery, following southern Mesopotamian technological practices and stylistic conventions. A few minor variations have been noted in the ways that stylistic motifs were combined on Uruk ceramics at Hacınebi, perhaps reflecting the relative isolation of Uruk potters at Hacınebi from their homeland 1,200 kilometers to the south. Thus basic craft goods such as stone tools, ceramics, and textiles were all produced in parallel by both the Uruk and Anatolian communities. Spindle whorl styles show no differences between Uruk and local contexts.[92]

Administrative Technology. The Uruk administrative technology of cylinder seal use coexists with, but is separate from, the local stamp seals and sealings (see figs. 11, 12). Unused sealing clays are found in both Uruk and local contexts, confirming that each group monitored the movement of commodities. The two sealing systems differ in technology, iconography, function, and pathways of economic circulation. The Mesopotamian record-keeping system used cylinder seals, which were rolled over the wet clay sealing medium to produce a long, narrow continuous band of repeating images. Mesopotamian motifs stressed animal processions or work scenes depicting laborers engaged in agricultural or craft production. Uruk cylinder seals were impressed on hollow clay balls or bullae; on tablets; on mushroom-shaped clay jar stoppers; and, most frequently, on clay sealings affixed to the rim or exterior of ceramic vessels (fig. 12).

By contrast, the Anatolian system consisted of rectangular or round stamp seals, which created a single image each time the seal was pressed into the wet clay sealing. Anatolian seals almost always depicted lions and caprids in chase or hunt scenes.[93] The two systems were used for completely different functions. Anatolian stamp seal impressions at Hacınebi are found on sealings affixed to wooden boxes, packets of reed matting, leather bags, and cloth sacks; they never appear on ceramic vessels, tablets, jar stoppers, or bullae (fig. 13).

Most telling of all, a comparison of the administrative artifacts with the distribution of other classes of material culture reveals very low levels of

Fig. 12. Uruk Mesopotamian jar stoppers, Hacınebi, 3700–3200 B.C.
A, B: top views of two jar stoppers; *C, D:* top and side views showing the shape of the vessel
necks; *E, F:* obverse and reverse views of two jar stoppers showing the impressions of
the string and textiles used to cover the vessel mouth before the clay sealing was affixed

interaction among the Uruk and local spheres of exchange. This is important, because if Anatolians were delivering supplies as trade goods or tribute to the Mesopotamians, then we would expect to see the discarded local stamp sealings in Uruk Mesopotamian contexts. This is not the case; instead, Uruk-style cylinder-sealed artifacts used for record-keeping occur exclusively with Uruk-style ceramics, while local style stamp-sealed administrative artifacts are found almost always with local Anatolian ceramics. Out of more than one hundred local stamp seal impressions, only two have ever been found in deposits with Uruk ceramics and administrative technology. These few cases of Anatolian sealings in Uruk deposits are important because they confirm the contemporaneity of the two record-keeping systems while emphasizing that those systems were used to seal different goods that moved in separate economic spheres. The distribution of sealings suggests the operation of two autonomous, minimally interacting administrative systems monitoring separate sets of economic transactions, rather than the kinds of commodity flows to be expected if the Uruk colony were exercising political or economic dominance over its Anatolian host community.

Faunal Remains. The colonial domination model would imply that the local people supplied foreigners with meat; by contrast, if the autonomous diaspora model applies to Hacınebi, we would expect to see signs that the Uruk enclave had subsistence autonomy and raised its own animals. Analyses of body part distributions provide an effective means of determining whether the Uruk enclave was provisioned with animals. Generally, when a sheep or goat is butchered, the head and feet bones are removed and discarded. The body parts with the most meat on them are the forelimb and hindlimb. If the people in the Uruk enclave were receiving meat from elsewhere, then we would expect to see many limb bones, but very few head or foot bones. Since all of the main body parts are present, however, and since there is no clear predominance of the meat-rich limb bones, the available evidence suggests that the people on both the Uruk and local contexts were raising and butchering their own animals, and were not being provided with meat from any other part of the site.

Discussion and Conclusion
The spatial-functional analyses of material culture patterning at Hacınebi allow us to reconstruct several major aspects of identity and political economy in the interregional interaction network that linked the early complex societies of Mesopotamia, Anatolia, Syria, and Iran in the fourth millennium B.C. The data presented here are most consistent with the interpretation that (a) an ethnically distinct colony of Mesopotamians was, in fact, present at Hacınebi; and that (b) this colony was an autonomous trade diaspora that did not dominate the indigenous complex society with which it interacted. The heuristic value of the trade diaspora model as a way to conceptualize the relations between the Mesopotamians and their host community in the fourth millennium B.C. Near East suggests that this theoretical framework can be

Fig. 13. Anatolian Late Chalcolithic administrative technology, Hacınebi, 3700–3200 B.C.
A–F: stamp seal impressions from unbaked clay container sealings; *G:* face and cross-section of a square stamp seal, with seal impression

used cross-culturally in a more general model of variability in power relations within the networks that link homelands, colonies, host communities, and the specialist intermediaries who circulate among them.

A full range of Uruk Mesopotamian material culture is concentrated heavily in the northeast corner of the phase B2 settlement at Hacınebi. Two sets of criteria were proposed as ways to identify colonies as a general phenomenon,[94] and specifically, Uruk colonies,[95] in the archaeological record. The Hacınebi data meet both sets of criteria quite closely. The relatively sudden appearance of Mesopotamian material culture and the fact that it is apparently not limited to elite contexts all argue against an interpretation of this patterning as reflecting local elite emulation of Mesopotamian styles in material culture. One of the strongest arguments against the emulation model is the faunal evidence for distinctively Mesopotamian food preferences in contexts with Mesopotamian material culture, while Anatolian food preferences predominate in contexts with local Anatolian artifact assemblages. The most parsimonious interpretation of the Hacınebi evidence is that it represents the presence of a small group of ethnically distinct south Mesopotamians in one corner of this Syro-Anatolian settlement.

Spatial-functional comparisons of ceramics, lithics, fauna, and small finds between contexts with Mesopotamian material culture and those characterized by local Anatolian assemblages were used to evaluate whether the relationship between the Uruk colony at Hacınebi and its host community conformed to the inequalities expected under the European colonialist dominance model or the more symmetric power relationships of the autonomous trade diaspora model. The two models were tested by examining the degree of asymmetry in the exchange system, as seen in the pattern of circulation of goods, and the distribution of administrative or record-keeping artifacts. There was no evidence to suggest that the Anatolian host community supplied the Mesopotamian enclave with foodstuffs and craft goods either as trade items or as a tribute or taxation. The faunal and archaeobotanical evidence suggest that each group farmed its own crops and raised its own animals. In addition, each group produced its own stone tools, ceramics, and textiles.

Most telling of all is the distribution of the seal impressions as evidence for control over the storage, circulation, and consumption of goods. Each group maintained its own distinctive record-keeping system—the Mesopotamians using cylinder seals, while the local people relied on stamp seals. In an asymmetric system dominated by the Mesopotamians, one would expect to see large amounts of Anatolian stamp sealings in contexts with Uruk material culture, indicating that the local population was delivering commodities to the foreign enclave. Instead, the local stamp seals appear almost exclusively with Anatolian material culture, while the Uruk cylinder seal-impressed administrative artifacts occur only in Mesopotamian assemblages. We know that the two assemblages are contemporaneous by radiocarbon dating and by the presence of "crossovers"—small numbers of Uruk shards in local contexts and vice versa. The observed patterning, therefore, cannot be explained as being due to chronological differences.

The coexistence of both local and Uruk administrative artifacts suggests that both groups exercised some degree of control over the production, circulation, and consumption of commodities. The contrasting distributions of administrative artifacts indicate that the two communities had fairly autonomous economic and administrative spheres, operating in parallel and rarely interacting. There is no evidence for a net outflow of subsistence and craft goods from the local settlement to the foreign enclave. The Mesopotamian and Anatolian communities produced, exchanged, and consumed goods within their own encapsulated social domain. While some exchange no doubt took place between the two groups, the distribution patterns of administrative artifacts suggest that these exchanges were small scale and symmetric, rather than the large scale unequal transfers of commodities or preciosities as would be expected if applying the European colonialist dominance model. Finally, the lithic and faunal evidence that the Mesopotamian enclave was largely self-sufficient in food and craft production strongly suggests that the foreigners were an autonomous diaspora rather than a dominant colonial elite.

These two autonomous communities appear to have had a peaceful coexistence. There is no evidence for fortifications, warfare, or sudden violent destruction in any part of the phase B2 settlement at Hacınebi. Given the apparent small size of the Uruk community and the lack of evidence for either warfare or domination, it seems clear that the Mesopotamians were there at the sufferance of the local elites. Overall, the Uruk colonial enclave at Hacınebi best fits a model of an autonomous diaspora community, rather than a group of politically dominant foreigners, as would be expected in the European colonialist model. As this case study demonstrates, once we disentangle the more general social phenomenon of "colonies" from the highly specific European political-economical phenomenon of "colonialism," it becomes possible to generate more realistic models of cross-cultural interaction.

Notes

1. William Adams, "The First Colonial Empire: Egypt in Nubia, 3200–1200 B.C.," *Comparative Studies in Society and History* 26 (1984): 36–71; Guillermo Algaze, "Expansionary Dynamics of Some Early Pristine States," *American Anthropologist* 95 (1993): 304–33; Guillermo Algaze, *The Uruk World System: The Dynamics of Expansion of Early Mesopotamian Civilization* (Chicago: Univ. of Chicago Press, 1993); Timothy Champion, ed., *Centre and Periphery: Comparative Studies in Archaeology* (London: Unwin Hyman, 1989); Stephen Dyson, ed., *Comparative Studies in the Archaeology of Colonialism* (Oxford: British Archaeological Reports, 1985); and Michael Rowlands, Mogens Larsen, and Kristian Kristiansen, eds., *Centre and Periphery in the Ancient World* (Cambridge: Cambridge Univ. Press, 1987).

2. Algaze, "Expansionary Dynamics" (note 1).

3. Guillermo Algaze, "The Uruk Expansion: Cross-Cultural Exchange in Early

Mesopotamian Civilization," *Current Anthropology* 30 (1989): 571–608; Mitchell Allen, "The Mechanisms of Underdevelopment: An Ancient Mesopotamian Example," *Review: Journal of the Fernand Braudel Center for the Study of Economies, Historical Systems, and Civilizations* 15 (1992): 453–76; Marcella Frangipane and Alba Palmieri, "Urbanization in Perimesopotamian Areas: The Case of Eastern Anatolia," in Linda Manzanilla, ed., *Studies in the Neolithic and Urban Revolutions* (Oxford: British Archaeological Reports, 1987), 295–318; Alba Palmieri, "Eastern Anatolia and Early Mesopotamian Urbanization: Remarks on Changing Relations," in Mario Liverani, Alba Palmieri, and Renato Peroni, eds., *Studi di palentologia in onore di Salvatore M. Puglisi* (Rome: Università di Roma "La Sapienza," 1985), 191–213; and Dietrich Sürenhagen, "The Dry-Farming Belt: The Uruk Period and Subsequent Developments," in Harvey Weiss, ed., *The Origins of Cities in Dry Farming Syria and Mesopotamia in the Third Millennium B.C.* (Guilford, Conn.: Four Quarters, 1986), 7–43.

4. Abner Cohen, *Custom and Politics in Urban Africa: A Study of Hausa Migrants in Yoruba Towns* (Berkeley: Univ. of California Press, 1969); and Abner Cohen, "Cultural Strategies in the Organization of Trading Diasporas," in Claude Meillassoux, ed., *The Development of Indigenous Trade and Markets in West Africa: Studies Presented and Discussed at the Tenth International African Seminar at Fourah Bay College, Freetown, December 1969* (London: Oxford Univ. Press, 1971), 266–81.

5. David L. Sills, ed., *International Encyclopedia of the Social Sciences*, s.v. "colonialism" (entry by R. Emerson).

6. Jürgen Osterhammel, *Colonialism: A Theoretical Overview*, trans. Shelley L. Frisch (Princeton: Markus Wiener, 1997), 4.

7. Nicholas Dirks, "Introduction: Colonialism and Culture," in idem, ed., *Colonialism and Culture* (Ann Arbor: Univ. of Michigan Press, 1992), 1–25, esp. 3.

8. Edward Said, *Orientalism* (New York: Vintage, 1978).

9. "Colonialism" (note 5); and Georges Balandier, "La situation coloniale: Approche théorique," *Cahiers internationaux de sociologie* 11 (1951): 75.

10. M. I. Finley, "Colonies—An Attempt at a Typology," *Transactions of the Royal Historical Society*, 5th ser., 26 (1976): 184.

11. Finley, "Colonies" (note 10), 184.

12. Finley, "Colonies" (note 10), 177.

13. Finley, "Colonies" (note 10), 174–84.

14. Gil Stein, "Power and Distance in the Uruk Mesopotamian Colonial System" (paper presented at the annual meeting of the American Anthropological Association, Washington, D.C., 1993); and Gil Stein et al., "Southeast Anatolia before the Uruk Expansion: Preliminary Report on the 1997 Excavations at Hacınebi, Turkey," *Anatolica* 24 (1998): 143–93.

15. Cohen, "Cultural Strategies" (note 4), 266–67; and Philip Curtin, *Cross-Cultural Trade in World History* (Cambridge: Cambridge Univ. Press, 1984), 613.

16. Cohen, "Cultural Strategies" (note 4), 266–67.

17. See, for example, James Clifford, "Diasporas," *Cultural Anthropology* 9 (1994): 302–38.

18. Cohen, "Cultural Strategies" (note 4), 276.

19. Cohen, "Cultural Strategies" (note 4), 277.

20. Richard Warms, "Who Are the Merchants? Ethnic Identity and Trade in Western Mali," *Ethnic Groups* 8 (1990): 57–72.

21. See Cohen, "Cultural Strategies" (note 4), 271.

22. Victor Azarya, "Traders and the Center in Massina, Kong, and Samori's State," *International Journal of African Historical Studies* 13 (1980): 420–56.

23. Karl Yambert, "Alien Traders and Ruling Elites: The Overseas Chinese in Southeast Asia and the Indians in East Africa," *Ethnic Groups* 3 (1981): 173–98.

24. Curtin, *Cross-Cultural Trade* (note 15), 5.

25. Azarya, "Traders and the Center" (note 22).

26. Azarya, "Traders and the Center" (note 22), 443–44.

27. Yambert, "Alien Traders" (note 23), 180.

28. Yambert, "Alien Traders" (note 23), 181.

29. Curtin, *Cross-Cultural Trade* (note 15), 5.

30. Curtin, *Cross-Cultural Trade* (note 15), 3.

31. Yambert, "Alien Traders" (note 23).

32. Warms, "Who Are the Merchants?" (note 20).

33. Robert Santley, C. Yarborough, and B. Hall, "Enclaves, Ethnicity, and the Archaeological Record at Matacapan," in Réginald Auger et al., eds., *Ethnicity and Culture: Proceedings of the Eighteenth Annual Conference of the Archaeological Association of the University of Calgary* (Calgary: Archaeological Association, University of Calgary, 1987), 85–100.

34. Santley, Yarborough, and Hall, "Enclaves" (note 33), 87.

35. Santley, Yarborough, and Hall, "Enclaves" (note 33), 87–88.

36. Gil Stein, "Ethnicity, Exchange, and Emulation: Mesopotamian-Anatolian Interaction at Hacınebi, Turkey" (paper presented at the annual meeting of the Society for American Archaeology, Anaheim, 1994).

37. Robert McCormick Adams, *Heartland of Cities* (Chicago: Univ. of Chicago Press, 1981), 71; Gregory Johnson, *Local Exchange and Early State Development in Southwestern Iran* (Ann Arbor: Museum of Anthropology, University of Michigan, 1973); Hans Nissen, *The Early History of the Ancient Near East 9000–2000 B.C.* (Chicago: Univ. of Chicago Press, 1988); Susan Pollock, "Bureaucrats and Managers, Peasants and Pastoralists, Imperialists and Traders: Research on the Uruk and Jemdet Nasr Periods in Mesopotamia," *Journal of World Prehistory* 6 (1992): 297–336; and Henry Wright and Gregory Johnson, "Population, Exchange, and Early State Formation in Southwestern Iran," *American Anthropologist* 77 (1975): 267–89.

38. Algaze, "Expansionary Dynamics" (note 1); and Algaze, "Uruk World" (note 1).

39. Harvey Weiss and T. Cuyler Young, "The Merchants of Susa: Godin V and Plateau-Lowland Relations in the Late Fourth Millennium B.C.," *Iran* 13 (1975): 1–17.

40. Guillermo Algaze, "Habuba on the Tigris: Archaic Nineveh Reconsidered," *Journal of Near Eastern Studies* 45 (1986): 125–37.

41. Glenn Schwartz, "Excavations at Karatut Mevkii and Perspectives on the Uruk/Jemdet Nasr Expansion," *Akkadica* 56 (1988): 1–41.

42. Ufuk Esin, "Die kulturellen Beziehungen zwischen Östanatolien und Meso-potamien sowie Syrien anhand einiger Grabungs und Oberflaechenfunde aus dem oberen Euphrattal im 4. Jahrtausend v. Chr.," in Hans-Jörg Nissen and Johannes

Renger, eds., *Mesopotamien und seine Nachbarn: Politische und kulturelle Wechsel-beziehungen im alten Vorderasien vom 4. bis 1. Jahrtausend v. Chr* (Berlin: Dietrich Reimer, 1982), 1:13–21; Ufuk Esin, "Tepecik Excavations, 1974," *Keban Project 1974–75 Activities*, 1st ser., no. 7 (1982): 95–125; Frangipane and Palmieri, "Urbaniza-tion" (note 3), 297; and Sürenhagen, "Dry-Farming Belt" (note 3), 15.

43. Johannes Boese, "Excavations at Tell Sheikh Hassan, Preliminary Report on the Year 1987 Campaign in the Euphrates Valley," *Annales archéologiques arabes syri-ennes* 36/37 (1987): 67–100; Joan Oates and David Oates, "An Open Gate: Cities of the Fourth Millennium B.C.," *Cambridge Archaeological Journal* 7 (1997): 287–97; and Gil Stein et al., "Uruk Colonies and Anatolian Communities: An Interim Report on the 1992–1993 Excavations at Hacınebi, Turkey," *American Journal of Archaeology* 100 (1996): 205–60.

44. Sürenhagen, "Dry-Farming Belt" (note 3), 9.

45. Sürenhagen, "Dry-Farming Belt" (note 3), 9–13.

46. Geoffrey Emberling, "Ethnicity in Complex Societies: Archaeological Perspec-tives," *Journal of Archaeological Research* 5 (1997): 295–344; Carol Kramer, "Pots and Peoples," in Louis D. Levine and T. Culyer Young, eds., *Mountains and Lowlands: Essays in the Archaeology of Greater Mesopotamia* (Malibu: Undena, 1977), 91–112; and Santley, Yarborough, and Hall, "Enclaves" (note 33).

47. Sürenhagen, "Dry-Farming Belt" (note 3), 10.

48. Manfred Behm-Blancke, "Mosaikstifte aus der Uruk-Zeit am oberen Euphrat," *Istanbuler Mitteilungen* 39 (1989): 73–83; and Aliye Özten, "Two Pots Recovered in the Excavations at Samsat Belonging to the Late Chalcolithic Period," *Anadolu* 20 (1984): 261–69.

49. André Finet, "L'apport du Tell Kannas à l'histoire proche-orientale, de la fin du 4ᵉ millénaire à la moitié du 2ᵉ," in J. Cl. Margueron, ed., *Le Moyen Euphrate: Zone de contact et d'echanges* (Leiden: E. J. Brill, 1977), 107–15; and Gus van Driel and Carol van Driel-Murray, "Jebel Aruda 1977–1978," *Akkadica* 12 (1979): 2–28.

50. Hans Nissen, "The Emergence of Writing in the Ancient Near East," *Interdisci-plinary Science Reviews* 10 (1985): 349–61; Denise Schmandt-Besserat, "The Earliest Precursor of Writing," in C. C. Lamberg-Karlovsky, ed., *Hunters, Farmers, and Civiliza-tions: Old World Archaeology: Readings from* Scientific American (San Francisco: W. H. Freeman, 1979), 152–61; Denise Schmandt-Besserat, "From Tokens to Tablets: A Re-evaluation of the So-Called 'Numerical Tablets,'" *Visible Language* 15 (1981): 321–44; Gus van Driel, "Tablets from Jebel Aruda," in idem et al., eds., *Zikir Sumim: F. R. Kraus Festschrift* (Leiden: E. J. Brill, 1982), 12–25; and Gus van Driel, "Seals and Sealings from Jebel Aruda, 1974–1978," *Akkadica* 33 (1983): 34–62.

51. Weiss and Young, "Merchants of Susa" (note 39); and T. Cuyler Young, "Godin Tepe VI/V and Central Western Iran at the End of the Fourth Millennium," in Uwe Finkbeiner and Wolfgang Röllig, eds., *Gamdat Nasr: Period or Regional Style?* (Wies-baden: Ludwig Reichert, 1986), 212–28.

52. Algaze, "Habuba" (note 40); Schwartz, "Karatut Mevkii" (note 41); and Sürenhagen, "Dry-Farming Belt" (note 3).

53. Stephen Reimer, "Tell Qrayya on the Middle Euphrates," in Mitchell Rothman, ed., "Out of the Heartland: The Evolution of Complexity in Peripheral Mesopotamia

during the Uruk Period: Workshop Summary," *Paléorient* 15, no. 1 (1989): 284; Eva Strommenger, *Habuba Kabira: Eine Stadt vor 5000 Jahren: Ausgrabungen der Deutschen Orient-Gesellschaft am Euphrat in Habuba Kabira, Syrien* (Mainz am Rhein: Phillip von Zabern, 1980); and Gus van Driel and Carol van Driel-Murray, "Jebel Aruda, the 1982 Season of Excavation: Interim Report," *Akkadica* 33 (1983): 1–26.

54. Algaze, "Expansionary Dynamics" (note 1); Guillermo Algaze et al., "The Tigris-Euphrates Archaeological Reconnaissance Project: A Preliminary Report of the 1989–1990 Seasons," *Anatolica* 17 (1991): 175–240; Manfred Behm-Blancke, "Hassek Höyük: Eine Uruk Station im Grenzland zu Anatolien," *Nürnberger Blätter zur Archäologie* 8 (1992): 82–94; Manfred Behm-Blancke, "Die Ausgrabungen auf dem Hassek Höyük im Jahre 1982," *Kazı Sonuçları Toplantısı* 5 (1984): 163–68, 419–23; Manfred Behm-Blancke, "Die Ausgrabungen auf dem Hassek Höyük im Jahre 1985," *Kazı Sonuçları Toplantısı* 8 (1986): 139–47; and Esin, "Tepecik Excavations, 1974" (note 42).

55. Sürenhagen, "Dry-Farming Belt" (note 3).

56. Stein et al., "Uruk Colonies" (note 43); and Weiss and Young, "Merchants of Susa" (note 39).

57. Esin, "Tepecik Excavations, 1974" (note 42).

58. Gil Stein, "World Systems Theory and Alternative Modes of Interaction in the Archaeology of Culture Contact," in James Cusick, ed., *Studies in Culture Contact: Interaction, Culture Change, and Archaeology* (Carbondale: Center for Archaeological Investigations, Southern Illinois University, 1998), 220–55.

59. Stein, "World Systems" (note 58); Gil Stein and Adnan Mısır, "Hacınebi Excavations, 1992," *Kazı Sonuçları Toplantısı* 15 (1994): 131–52; Gil Stein and Adnan Mısır, "Excavations at Hacınebi Tepe, 1993," *Kazı Sonuçları Toplantısı* 16 (1995): 121–40; Gil Stein and Adnan Mısır, "1994 Excavations at Hacınebi Tepe," *Kazı Sonuçları Toplantısı* 17 (1996): 109–28; Stein et al., "Uruk Colonies" (note 43); Gil Stein et al., "Excavations at Hacınebi, Turkey — 1996: Preliminary Report," *Anatolica* 23 (1997): 111–71; Gil Stein et al., "Southeast Anatolia before the Uruk Expansion: Preliminary Report on the 1997 Excavations at Hacınebi, Turkey," *Anatolica* 24 (1998): 143–93; and Gil Stein et al., "Hacınebi, Turkey: Preliminary Report on the 1995 Excavations," *Anatolica* 22 (1996): 85–128.

60. Robert Braidwood and Linda Braidwood, *Excavations in the Plain of Antioch* (Chicago: Univ. of Chicago Press, 1960).

61. Algaze et al., "Tigris-Euphrates Archaeological Reconnaissance" (note 54).

62. Stein et al., "Southeast Anatolia" (note 59).

63. Marcella Frangipane, "Local Components in the Development of Centralized Societies in Syro-Anatolian Regions," in idem et al., eds., *Between the Rivers and Over the Mountains* (Rome: Università di Roma "La Sapienza," 1993), 133–61; and Stein et al., "Uruk Colonies" (note 43).

64. Susan Pollock and Cheryl Coursey, "Ceramics from Hacınebi Tepe: Chronology and Connections," *Anatolica* 21 (1995): 101–41; and Stein et al., "Uruk Colonies" (note 43).

65. See also Stein and Mısır, "Excavations at Hacınebi Tepe, 1993" (note 59).

66. Behm-Blancke, "Mosaikstifte" (note 48).

67. Edgar Peltenburg et al., "Jerablus-Tahtani, Syria, 1995: Preliminary Report," *Levant* 28 (1996): 1–25.

68. Mark Schwartz, David Hollander, and Gil Stein, "Reconstructing Mesopotamian Exchange Networks in the Fourth Millennium B.C.: Geochemical and Archaeological Analyses of Bitumen Artifacts from Hacınebi, Turkey," *Paléorient* 25, no. 1 (1999): 67–82.

69. Johannes Boese, *Ausgrabungen in Tell Sheikh Hassan*, vol. 1, *Vorläufige Berichte über die Grabungskampagnen 1984–1990 und 1992–1994* (Saarbrücken: Saarbrücker, 1995), 74.

70. Françoise Tallon, *Métallurgie Susienne I: De la Fondation de Suse au XVIIIᵉ avant J.-C.* (Paris: Editions de la Réunion des Musées Nationaux, 1987), entry nos. 934, 936, 937.

71. Olivier Rouault and Maria Grazia Masetti-Rouault, eds., *L'Eufrate e il tempo: La civiltà del medio Eufrate e della Gezira siriana* (Milan: Electa, 1993), pl. 148.

72. Boese, *Ausgrabungen* (note 69), 175.

73. Nancy L. Benco, "Manufacture and Use of Clay Sickles from the Uruk Mound, Abu Salabikh, Iraq," *Paléorient* 18, no. 1 (1992): 119–33.

74. Holly Pittman, "Administrative Evidence from Hacınebi Tepe: An Essay on the Global and the Local," *Paléorient* 25, no. 1 (1999): 43–50.

75. Hans Nissen, Peter Damerow, and Robert Englund, *Archaic Bookkeeping: Early Writing and Techniques of Economic Administration in the Ancient Near East* (Chicago: Univ. of Chicago Press, 1993).

76. In addition to the three articles by Behm-Blancke cited in note 54, see Boese, *Ausgrabungen* (note 69); Strommenger, *Habuba Kabira* (note 53); van Driel, "Tablets" (note 50); and van Driel, "Seals and Sealings" (note 50).

77. Lawrence W. McKee, "Delineating Ethnicity from the Garbage of Early Virginians: Faunal Remains from the Kingsmill Plantation Slave Quarter," *American Archaeology* 6 (1987): 31–39; and Pam J. Crabtree, "Zooarchaeology and Complex Societies: Some Uses of Faunal Analysis for the Study of Trade, Social Status, and Ethnicity," *Archaeological Method and Theory* 2 (1990): 155–205.

78. Gil Stein and Jeffrey Nicola, "Late Chalcolithic Faunal Remains from Hacınebi," in Gil Stein et al., "Uruk Colonies and Anatolian Communities: An Interim Report on the 1992–1993 Excavations at Hacınebi, Turkey," *American Journal of Archaeology* 100 (1996): 257–60; and Lauren Bigelow, "Zooarchaeological Investigations of Economic Organization and Ethnicity at Late Chalcolithic Hacınebi: A Preliminary Report," *Paléorient* 25, no. 1 (1999): 83–89.

79. Sebastian Payne, "Animal Bones from Tell Rubeidheh," in R. G. Killick, ed., *Tell Rubeidheh: An Uruk Village in the Jebel Hamrin* (Warminster, England: Aris & Phillip, 1988), 98–135; and Richard Redding, *Decision Making in Subsistence Herding of Sheep and Goats in the Middle East* (Ann Arbor, Mich.: University Microfilms, 1982).

80. Santley, Yarborough, and Hall, "Enclaves" (note 33).

81. Sürenhagen, "Dry-Farming Belt" (note 3).

82. Algaze, *Uruk World System* (note 1); and Immanuel Wallerstein, *Capitalist Agriculture and the Origins of the European World-Economy in the Sixteenth Century* (San Diego: Academic, 1974).

83. Stein, "World Systems" (note 58).

84. See the excavation reports by Stein and Mısır cited in note 59; and Stein, "World Systems" (note 58).

85. Jacques Connan, personal communication, 1995.

86. Schwartz et al., "Exchange Networks" (note 68).

87. Christopher Edens, "The Chipped Stone Industry at Hacınebi: Technological Styles and Social Identity," *Paléorient* 25, no. 1 (1999): 23–33.

88. Sürenhagen, "Dry-Farming Belt" (note 3), 22.

89. Christopher Edens, "Hacınebi Chipped Stone — 1995," *Anatolica* 22 (1996): 100–4; and Christopher Edens, "Chipped Stone," in Gil Stein et al., "Excavations at Hacınebi, Turkey — 1996: Preliminary Report," *Anatolica* 23 (1997): 124–27.

90. Heather Lechtman, "Style in Technology — Some Early Thoughts," in Heather Lechtman and Robert S. Merrill, eds., *Material Culture: Styles, Organization, and Dynamics of Technology* (Saint Paul: West Publishing, 1977), 3–20; and Rita Wright, "Technological Styles: Transforming a Natural Object into a Cultural Object," in Steven Lubar and David Kingery, eds., *History from Things: Essays on Material Culture* (Washington, D.C.: Smithsonian Institution Press, 1993), 242–69.

91. Stein, "Ethnicity" (note 36).

92. Kathryn Keith, "Spindle Whorls and Textile Production at Late Chalcolithic Hacınebi," in Gil Stein et al., "Excavations at Hacınebi, Turkey — 1996: Preliminary Report," *Anatolica* 23 (1997): 136–39.

93. Pittman, "Administrative Evidence" (note 74).

94. Santley, Yarborough, and Hall, "Enclaves" (note 33).

95. Sürenhagen, "Dry-Farming Belt" (note 3).

Greeks in Iberia:
Colonialism without Colonization

Adolfo J. Domínguez

For much of antiquity the Iberian Peninsula represented a peripheral and marginal region with respect to the major centers of the ancient Mediterranean world. As the "Far West" of the Mediterranean, Iberia served until Roman times as a source of numerous natural resources, which were drained from it and integrated into the economic systems of various neighboring cultures.[1] Phoenicians, Carthaginians, and Romans enjoyed the lion's share of economic advantages. By comparison, the Greeks never exerted any economic pressure on Iberia commensurate with that of other regional powers. Material traces of their activity, however, reflect the scale and intensity of their cultural influence (fig. 1). Paradoxically, although the Greek presence in Iberia can be generally defined as colonial in nature, one can hardly speak of colonies proper in the southeastern part of the peninsula where Greek influence was most strongly felt.

Since the term *colonialism* has had very different meanings at different times and according to various traditions, it is important to consider some basic definitions.[2] Peter van Dommelen's definition of the term *colonialism* offers a sound departure point: "the presence of one or more groups of foreign people in a region at some distance from their place of origin (the "colonizers"), and the existence of asymmetrical socioeconomic relationships of dominance or exploitation between the colonizing groups and the inhabitants of the colonized regions."[3] Scholars such as Edward Said who study colonization distinguish between imperialism and colonialism. Imperialism refers to "the practice, the theory and the attitudes of a dominating metropolitan center ruling a distant territory."[4] As a consequence of imperialism, colonialism involves "the implanting of settlements on distant territory."[5] For Said, the most salient features of imperialism and colonialism are the physical and ideological appropriations that they represent.

The model of modern European colonialism, however, is too restrictive when applied to many ancient contexts, as it often ignores shifts in the balance of power between homelands and colonies or between colonies and indigenous polities.[6] Most definitions of colonialism stress the dominance of the colonizers over the colonized through "the establishment and maintenance, for an extended time, of rule over an alien people that is separate from and subordinate to the ruling power."[7] A. D. King concludes that "in the simplest analysis, colonialism was a means by which the metropolitan power extended

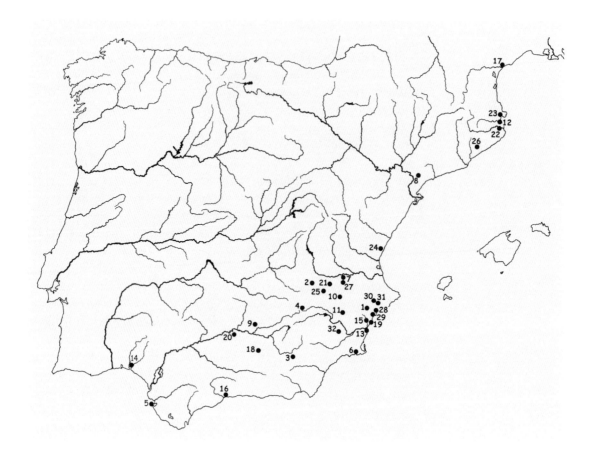

Fig. 1. Iberian Peninsula, 600–400 B.C.

1. Agost (Alicante)
2. Balazote (Albacete)
3. Baza (Granada)
4. Bogarra (Albacete)
5. Cadix
6. Carthago Nova
7. Casas de Juan Núñez (Albacete)
8. Castellet de Banyoles (Tivissa, Tarragona)
9. Cástulo (Linares, Jaén)
10. Cerro de los Santos (Albacete)
11. Coimbra del Barranco Ancho (Jumilla, Murcia)
12. Emporion (Ampurias, Gerona)
13. La Fonteta, (Guardamar del Segura, Alicante)
14. Huelva
15. Ilici (La Alcudia de Elche, Alicante)
16. Málaga

17. Pech Maho (Sigean, Aude)
18. El Pajarillo (Huelma, Jaén)
19. La Pícola (Santa Pola, Alicante)
20. Porcuna (Jaén)
21. Pozo Moro (Chinchilla, Albacete)
22. Puig de Sant'Andreu (Ullastret, Gerona)
23. Rhode (Rosas, Gerona)
24. Saguntum (Valencia)
25. El Salobral (Albacete)
26. Turó del Montgrós (El Brull, Barcelona)
27. Los Villares (Hoya Gonzalo, Albacete)
28. Illeta dels Banyets (Campello, Alicante)
29. Tossal de Manises (Alicante)
30. Alcoy (Alicante)
31. Benilloba (Alicante)
32. El Cigarralejo (Mula, Murcia)

its markets for manufactured goods and by which the colonies, in turn, supplied raw materials to the metropolis."[8] In this perspective, the economic character of the relationship prevails over the physical settlement of foreign peoples and introduces the issue of disparities in power between colonizer and colonized.[9] As will be revealed, colonialism can work as a powerful form of cultural hegemony rather than simply as political and economic sovereignty.[10]

Dominance and hegemony are often brought to the foreground in colonial contexts. Does colonialism necessitate the presence of colonizers to achieve its ends? The question is in part a problem of semantics. A critical issue is the reality of colonialism without the establishment of actual colonies, a reversal of Gil Stein's paradigm of "colonies without colonialism" (see Stein, this volume). The present case study posits a colonial relationship between Greeks and Iberians without clearly attested Greek settlements in Iberian territory and, therefore, draws a distinction between "colonialism" and "colonization" in the title.[11]

The Greeks who traded with various indigenous communities of the western Mediterranean developed relationships with these groups that were colonialist in character, although perhaps not so intensively as in other parts of the Greek colonial world such as Sicily, Magna Graecia, and the Black Sea. Dichotomies between Greek and Barbarian and between Self and Other,[12] so frequent in tales of Greek colonization, are on the whole lacking. The subordinate position or backward nature of indigenous peoples, one of the main features of colonialist discourse, is only occasionally alluded to in historical writing.[13] The notion of Greek cultural superiority is sometimes framed as a mission of "educating" the natives to teach them certain rites, however hybrid the result. It is very likely that a colonialist discourse arose in the Greek settlements in Iberia in much the same way that it did in other Greek colonial regions. Similarly, one can imagine that anticolonialist attitudes—indigenous resistance—may have developed in response to Greek action, but there are no textual accounts of such resistance.[14] The extant written sources provide little information that sheds light on the nature and extent of Greek-native interaction in this region.

Instead, we must rely mainly on the interpretation of the archaeological record in order to reveal the mechanisms of this interaction, in which indigenous peoples assumed, at least during certain periods, a subaltern role. The material evidence points to an alternative theory of Greek colonialism in Iberia and provides a basis for analyzing the main strategies promoted by Greek colonizers in their relations with the natives. Several elements of the physical record further suggest certain counterreactions to these strategies on the part of the indigenous populations. They reveal both "the effect of larger objective ideologies" and "their adaptation in practice, their moments of effective implementation and confidence as well as those of failure."[15] The archaeological evidence throws considerable light on the ways in which the local elites related to the Greeks and provides the only avenue for voiceless Iberians to tell their own story.[16]

Evidence for the existence of a Greek colonialist agenda in Iberia is clear. In the southeast of the Iberian Peninsula, the appearance of certain Greek cultural elements in the indigenous world indicates that colonial action there was intense. Among the most significant manifestations are stone sculptures reflecting Greek inspiration and thematic programs, an indigenous writing system based on the Greek alphabet, aspects of urban planning, as well as manufactured products (mainly pottery) originating from different Greek cities. Postcolonial theory offers a useful framework in which to consider the apparent Greek cultural hegemony and the collaborative, receptive, and resistive roles played by native elites.

In other parts of the Mediterranean where Greek foundations are well attested from as early as the eighth century B.C., the mechanisms by which these cities extended their influence over the surrounding indigenous environment can be studied. In the case of the southeast Iberian Peninsula, the very existence of Greek colonies has not been demonstrated. No contexts display the features that customarily define a Greek city: fortification walls, house plans, urban layout, or tomb typology. The application of such a traditional model of colonization based on the archaeological record can be misleading, as Robin Osborne has recently suggested.[17] As noted above, the extant written sources do not provide much information. Indeed, the most relevant testimony is that of Strabo (*Geographica* 3.4.6), where he writes about three tiny Massaliote townlets—what he refers to as *polichnia*—in the region, although he mentions only one of them, Hemeroskopeion, by name.

One of the first problems is to determine the reality of Greek presence when faced with the absence of actual colonial settlements in southeastern Iberia, a question that has been much debated in recent years.[18] During the period of Phocaean trade with Tartessos in the sixth century B.C., the Greeks founded a small city on the northeast coast of the peninsula at Emporion. From there, they began to explore and to give names to nearby coasts and territories. An important indication of the Greek colonialist attitude toward this region is the very name they gave to it. The Phoenicians had already applied the name *'ispanya* to the peninsula, a phenomenon that reflected Phoenician interests in the land.[19] The Greeks introduced a new name—Iberia—which has been interpreted in various ways.[20] The very process of naming can be viewed as "geographical violence" in Said's terms, a violence that is implicit in this act of appropriation.[21] The Greeks inaugurated a new kind of relationship with recently discovered lands by giving them new names and a new geographical identity. They appropriated the land for themselves and incorporated it into their notion of *oikoumene* (the universe), thus relocating it within a new conceptual framework. It is doubtful that the local inhabitants would have accepted the name "Iberian" at any time,[22] as opposed to one of its derivatives such as "Celtiberian," which seems to have been relatively successful at least in Roman imperial times.[23]

Beyond the generic divide between Greeks and "Barbarian Others," in Greek colonialist discourse the terms *Iberia* and *Iberian* play a role akin to that of the term *Indian* in Spanish colonialist discourse in America. As Jorge Klor de Alva observes, "'Indian' and similar labels, which erased or hid the cultural pluralism that existed behind the collective nouns, were imposed on the many contact-period groups because ethnic differences among them were considered irrelevant to the settlers' agendas. They were also imposed to simplify imperial administrative procedures and/or to weaken feelings of loyalty toward the corporate non-European communities."[24]

The names of most of the indigenous peoples living in Iberia before the arrival of the Romans were known, in some cases already as early as the sixth century B.C. Nevertheless, the Greeks always preferred the generic term *Iberians,* probably because, as Jorge Klor de Alva explains, they considered the differences among the various indigenous groups to be irrelevant. This allowed them to construct a single ethnic identity for the colonized, which led to the creation of a new image adapted to the interests of the colonizers, as Said has pointed out. This is expressed through the relationship established between the name of the country—arbitrarily called Iberia by the Greeks—and the name of the inhabitants, who were then dubbed Iberians. This terminology overlooked profound differences, both cultural and linguistic in nature, that existed among the local populations. The act of naming acquires a greater resonance when the Greek written sources are viewed as a literature of conquest and colonialism.

The wholescale appropriation of the territory was followed by the labeling of various localities and coastal landmarks with Greek names, which, in some instances, substitute the indigenous nomenclature.[25] Once the territory was deprived of its indigenous roots, Greek myths came to define the new landscape. The very existence of mythological accounts such as the Pillars of Herakles and the Garden of the Hesperides reaffirms the territorial appropriation. In later Hellenistic times, this appropriation was completed through the introduction of legends in which the ancestry of indigenous peoples and foundation of cities were attributed to traveling Greek heroes. Thus we observe three moments of the colonial process: the appropriation of indigenous identity by the application of names meaningful only to the Greeks; the relocation of Iberian topography into a Greek mythological framework; and the reidentification of indigenous peoples and cities as descendants of Greek heroes, a process that Irad Malkin has also observed in Etruria (see Malkin, in this volume).[26]

By contrast with the extensive evidence of toponymy and mythology, the relatively small quantity of Greek pottery dated to 600–550 B.C. recovered from the Iberian coast would suggest fairly limited commercial relations in the first moments of Greek contact.[27] It is only from the last third of the sixth century that a growing Greek cultural presence in the indigenous zones of coastal Iberia is observable, and then mainly in the southeastern part. This can be interpreted as a sign of "colonialist influence" exerted on the natives by Greek traders and intermediaries, but not through the establishment of permanent colonies. With the exception of cities such as Emporion and later Rhodes, established along the northeast coast of the Iberian Peninsula, no other Greek city is known to have existed in the rest of Spain.

Once the notion of the existence of Greek colonies in the area is discarded, two possibilities may account for the pattern of cultural elements visible in the material record: trade and emulation. Owing to the chances of survival and recovery, our knowledge of the trade in Greek products is almost wholly limited to pottery. Trade in Greek vases played an important role from the later sixth century, assuming greater importance throughout the fifth and fourth centuries (fig. 2). Although the participation of other commercial agents such as the Phoenicians cannot be discarded,[28] the scenario usually accepted involves Greek merchant activity based in the city of Emporion. Emulation is a phenomenon that is especially visible in adaptations and imitations of prestige goods used by local elites, including pottery and weapons, at different times in the fifth and fourth centuries. Iberian imitations of Greek ceramic shapes have been extensively studied in recent years. As R. Olmos observes, however, "the process of imitation is not a singular one ... it is frequently very complex and multidirectional."[29]

Trade and emulation alone are not sufficient to explain the pattern of cultural transformation evident in southeastern Iberia. Trade introduced new elements, above all Greek pottery, which was recontextualized as a marker of status among elite groups. The circulation of Greek pottery, however, is a phenomenon common to much of the Mediterranean and in itself does not explain the important changes that took place within indigenous communities both in Spain and elsewhere. Emulation would have played a certain role in the spread of new ideas and artistic styles. Native elites were instrumental because they benefited most from the introduction of Greek artistic models, which they adapted to reinforce their dominant social position. It remains to define, however, which were the models, how they arrived in Iberia, why they were accepted by the natives, and how prestige was attached to them. A variety of cultural elements visible in the material record do not appear to derive directly from colonization, trade, or emulation, although these were contributing factors. Rather, a more subtle process should be considered.

The changes that took place in the indigenous world of southeastern Iberia were accomplished by direct human agency, through contacts and relationships initiated between natives and foreign "colonizers." Although Greeks did not establish colonial settlements in the region, it is likely that they resided among indigenous populations, fostering trade by enlisting elites in a common cause. It is in this activity that a clear colonialist intent on the part of the Greeks is evident. Greek traders not only provided imported goods to indigenous communities but, above all, exerted pressure on them in order to guarantee a constant supply of raw materials and commodities. As noted above, one of the connotations of colonialism is "cultural hegemony" of the colonizers over the colonized. The introduction of Greek cultural practices through material artifacts and the visual arts worked as an instrument of this hegemony.

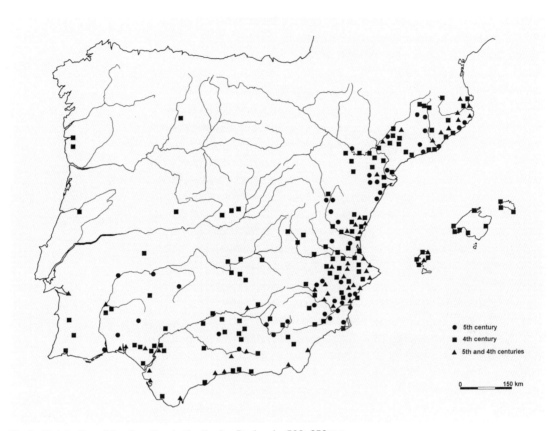

Fig. 2. Distribution of Greek pottery in the Iberian Peninsula, 500–350 B.C.

The posture of the Greeks vis-à-vis non-Greek populations in the Archaic period is not readily defined. The elaborate construction of their own ethnicity in contrast to that of foreigners doubtless implies a clear perception of their role and mission. Cultural objects brought by the Greeks were used by Iberians to reinforce a definition of themselves and to construct native social identity.[30] This is not to suggest that "Iberian ethnicity"—or, better still, the multiple "Iberian ethnicities"—were simply expressed through stone sculpture or a writing system of foreign derivation. Rather, these items, together with others that are not archaeologically visible, were used by Iberians in the process of redefining and shaping an identity that was markedly different from what had previously existed.[31] Ethnicity is a dialectical process that is not static but is "invented" or "culturally constructed."[32] As a consequence of new economic circumstances instigated by Greeks in search of trading opportunities, the indigenous communities of southeastern Iberia began to reorganize their internal affiliations, perhaps in order to better structure the territory they occupied. In this process are evident both the internal and external levels of identity definition, as framed by Richard Jenkins.[33] By means of internal definition, actors determine the limits of their groups, defining their nature and identity; through external definition, "Others" define those peoples according to both the perceived differences and their own vision. The naming of *ethne* is, as we have seen, one of the first steps in the creation of a new ethnic identity. The names of most of the ethnic groups that occupied the Iberian Peninsula were likely established during the sixth and fifth centuries. This naming marks the level of the internal definition, whereas the name given by the Greeks to the country and its inhabitants marks the external definition.

As part of the process of constructing ethnic identity, Iberian elites required new commodities and technology. Trade provided some of these commodities, while emulation facilitated the diffusion of new ideas and artistic representations throughout the indigenous world. In this way, both trade and emulation were responsible for the rise of an economically integrated area in southeastern Spain. This also encouraged the cultural integration of different territories that had not previously shared similar backgrounds and interests. Trade commodities and artistic models utilized by the Iberian aristocracy were not created locally; rather, they were introduced by Greek intermediaries as a means of obtaining and guaranteeing continued access to raw materials available in the region. The success of this enterprise was the success of Greek colonialism in Iberia, a colonialism without colonies.

Viewed from another perspective, Greek colonialism had to develop an alternative to the Phoenician relationship with Iberian elites.[34] Archaeological investigations have shown that the Phoenicians established important trading centers in the region as early as the seventh century B.C. The recently discovered Phoenician city at La Fonteta (Guardamar del Segura, Alicante) was founded in the late eighth or early seventh century. It was surrounded by an impressive city wall built about 650 B.C., which enclosed an area of 1.5 hectares. During the early phases of the settlement, Phoenician pottery was imported mainly from the Phoenician settlements on the south coast and especially from the Málaga region, as well as from other Phoenician centers, including Carthage. In time, the same style of pottery was manufactured in the native villages in the surrounding Sierra de Crevillente, such as Peña Negra. The center at La Fonteta, situated in a strategic area that incorporated the mouths of the Segura and Vinalopó Rivers, seems to have been responsible for the spread of Orientalizing influences both in the immediate hinterland and in the northernmost parts of the Iberian coast. About 550 B.C., Greek pottery (mainly Ionian cups) began to be imported, at which time the Phoenician settlement was peacefully abandoned.[35] Although this pottery may have been carried by Phoenician traders, the pattern seems to match that of imports at the contemporary Greek settlements at Emporion and Huelva, probably brought by Greek merchants.[36] Consequently, when Greeks began to show an interest in this region, the indigenous peoples were already familiar with the presence of foreign traders and settlers. Greeks never developed an occupation that was as intense and important as that developed by the Phoenicians some fifty or seventy-five years earlier. There is no evidence of Greek settlements comparable to the fortified site at La Fonteta in southeastern Iberia. It is not until the second half of the fifth century B.C. that a distinctive Greek influence on building techniques, especially at La Pícola (described below), is evident, and even then, the extent and nature of occupation is not conclusive.

Without full-fledged settlements, the Greeks had to develop effective collaborations with native leaders. Building on several centuries of profitable contact between Phoenicians and Iberians,[37] the Greeks exploited new commodities and technologies, which could be provided only by Greek merchants and artisans. These included stone sculpture, a system of writing, standardized weights and measures, novel building techniques, and the distribution of desired commodities, among which pottery is the most archaeologically visible. Once accepted, these items assumed a life of their own within a growing network of principalities comprising the entire southeast of the peninsula, as well as eastern Andalusia. In this network, the Greeks represented the last link in a complex chain of regional subsystems.[38]

The application of trade-diaspora models, as developed by Abner Cohen and Philip Curtin,[39] can lead to a better understanding of the relationship established between Greeks and Iberians. The pattern of "dispersed, but highly interrelated communities," organized "to co-ordinate the co-operation of its members in the common cause and establish channels of communication and mutual support with members from communities of the same ethnic group in neighboring localities who are engaged in the trading network" is appropriate to the ancient Iberian context.[40] The dealings of trade diasporas with host communities as well as the relations between different diaspora nodes are carried on in widely varying ways.[41] As Stein has argued, trading groups may develop relationships of "marginality," "autonomy," or "dominance" with their host communities.[42]

Greek relationships with indigenous communities in southeast Spain appear to conform most closely to the "diaspora marginality" modality, at least on a general level. Although it is possible that the Greeks were tolerated only because of their "usefulness to the host community," it is not likely that they were a marginal or pariah group, and in fact the opposite may well be true.[43] Clearly, the Greek presence does not fit the "diaspora autonomy" modality, which can be equated with the model of the *emporion*. The lack of any real Greek settlement in southeastern Iberia precludes the "diaspora dominance" modality. Instead, the evidence suggests a situation of "non-hegemonic contact," which is applicable to both Greek and Phoenician enterprises.[44] This is characterized by the existence of trade without foreign occupation and without the submission of the host community. If a model of "diaspora marginality" or "non-hegemonical contact" is accepted, it seems reasonable to conclude that the remains of this relationship cannot be of a monumental nature. Although pottery imports—not very abundant before mid-fifth century B.C.—gauge the existence of some trading activity, the indirect evidence of stone sculpture and writing indicate the deep impact that cultural contact had on the Iberians.

Stone Sculpture

Stone sculpture in Iberia was almost unknown before the arrival of the Phoenicians and Greeks; therefore, the beginnings of an indigenous sculptural tradition are generally attributed to colonial cultural influence. Iberian sculpture appears suddenly in the region comprising Upper Andalusia and the southeast Iberian Peninsula sometime in the second half of the sixth century B.C., perhaps in the last quarter. The earliest pieces known so far exhibit a clear and distinctive Oriental influence. This may be linked to the cultural influence exerted by the Phoenicians in these regions from at least the seventh century, with whom the Iberians were involved as trade partners.[45] A turning point is represented by the towerlike monument of Pozo Moro, which shows Oriental stylistic influences in the general outline of the monument and in the iconography of its relief decoration. The tomb on which the monument stood contained Greek pottery as grave offerings and is dated to the early fifth century B.C.[46]

The evidence of Phoenician influence that is obvious during the seventh and sixth centuries gives way to notably Greek influences sometime in the later sixth or earlier fifth century B.C., perhaps as a result of the general reshaping of Phoenician centers and interests at this time.[47] Some of the earliest pieces, such as the sphinxes of Bogarra and El Salobral, follow Greek iconographic models.[48] Greek influence is undeniable in the case of the sphinxes from Agost.[49] The function of these early sculptures was primarily funerary, although other purposes cannot be ruled out. Other sculptures crowning funerary monuments, like the pillar-stelae, are also related to similar Greek monuments.[50] This sculpture reached its maturity around the middle of the fifth century B.C., the probable date of the sculptural ensemble of Porcuna. This impressive ensemble was apparently destroyed not long after its construction, and its remains were carefully buried in trenches covered by stone slabs, perhaps not very far from the place in which it originally stood.[51]

At some point in the mid-fifth century B.C., a larger number of local workshops produced sculpture that reflected greater variety in style and quality. Much of the commentary about the quality of these pieces is subjective and departs from a "Helleno-centric" perspective. The extent to which the Iberian aristocrats who commissioned or used these sculptures were familiar with Greek originals is not known. The products of several contemporary workshops that were located not far from one another display rather different attitudes to Greek models. Classic examples are the two horsemen from Los Villares (figs. 3, 4) and the horse from Casas de Juan Núñez (fig. 5). These three pieces, all dating to the second half of the fifth century B.C. and found at sites approximately 15 kilometers apart, display significant stylistic differences, in terms of technique, overall composition, and iconographic detail. Of greater interest in this context are the messages implicit in the sculpture, rather than the formal qualities of the sculpture itself.

Such sculptural displays were used by an emerging Iberian society to underscore the prestige and power of social elites. The focus of this display was centered mainly on the grave and, as such, made direct reference to the ideology and status of the deceased buried beneath the sculptural monument. Prior to the middle of the sixth century B.C., indigenous groups did not use monumental sculpture as a means of ideological expression. Whether such sculpture arose independently in Iberia or whether it owed its inspiration to external stimuli have been moot points. From a colonialist perspective, however, such sculpture begins to acquire a different meaning. The indigenous societies later in the sixth century were undergoing important changes in their system of political and territorial organization. Villages gave way to urban nuclei. Within this evolving political structure, community leaders required new ways of expressing their power and prestige, acquired in part as a result of trading activities and other forms of economic interaction with the Greeks. This process built on the pattern of earlier relationships with Phoenician settlers. It was precisely at this time—that is, the later sixth or early fifth century B.C.—that the indigenous world of southeastern Iberia and eastern Andalusia was experiencing profound changes leading toward urban organization, fueled by the Greek, and earlier Phoenician, need for resources. Iberian sculpture is, therefore, a by-product of a colonial exchange between Greeks and Iberians, a hybrid form involving Greek taste and technology in a totally new cultural context.[52]

To explain the process of transmission, one argument favors the existence of a series of indigenous sculptural workshops in which the participation of Greek artisans trained under Greek masters is postulated. In this scenario, Greek sculptors directly influenced both technology and iconographic composition. These workshops, however, made both imitations and adaptations of subjects taken from the Greek repertory but retooled them to serve the interests of the indigenous upper class. Iberian workshops did not make Greek sculpture. They produced a local style aimed at Iberian princes. Animals known in the Iberian landscape—bulls, horses, stags, wolves—as well as unknown animals and mythological creatures, such as lions, sphinxes, griffins, sirens, and bulls with human heads, became the instruments by which an Iberian elite ideology and identity was communicated. The technological process of rendering abstract concepts through concrete figures is, nonetheless, typically Greek.[53] The Iberian prince who ordered the more than forty scenes on the Porcuna ensemble was making use of a new technology put into the service of an ideology, which, although not new, was now expressed through a new medium and iconography (fig. 6). Whereas the form and technique are clearly indebted to Greek sculptural traditions, the overall result and iconography are clearly local. Indigenous ideas were communicated through Greek forms of expression.

Iberian sculpture is the result of the activity of many workshops, which, for the most part, had a limited regional distribution. It seems likely that some of these workshops, such as those of Porcuna and Agost, may have included craftsmen trained by Greek masters. Others may have arisen without any

Fig. 3. *Horseman, No. 1*
Los Villares, 450 B.C., stone, H: 165 cm (65 in.), L: 141 cm (55½ in.)
Albacete, Museo de Albacete

Fig. 4. *Horseman, No. 2*
Los Villares, ca. 410 B.C., stone, H: 100 cm (39⅜ in.),
L: 126 cm (49⅝ in.)
Albacete, Museo de Albacete

Fig. 5. *Horse*
Casas de Juan Núñez, ca. 450–400 B.C., stone, H: 75 cm
(29½ in.), L: 132 cm (52 in.)
Albacete, Museo de Albacete

Fig. 6. *Combat between Warrior and Griffin*
Porcuna, ca. 450 B.C., stone, H: 63.5 cm (25 in.), L: 84 cm (33⅛ in.)
Jaén, Museo Provincial de Jaén

direct involvement of Greek artisans and may explain the great diversity in style of Iberian sculpture. The number of new workshops that were established in the course of the fifth century B.C. and the increased demand for such sculpture suggests the likely presence of sculptors trained in Greek sculptural traditions. In the case of the Casas de Juan Núñez and Los Villares sculptures mentioned above, the three equestrian statues exhibit significant stylistic differences, despite the fact that they are more or less contemporary and come from the same vicinity (see figs. 3–5). These workshops contributed to the creation of a distinctly "Iberian style" that integrated various elements derived from Greek sculptural traditions. This could have been achieved without the actual intervention of Greek masters.[54]

The use of sculptural monuments in Iberian contexts must also be considered in the light of the dynamics of the indigenous societies themselves.

Simply put, one cannot envisage a Greek trader wandering throughout Iberia and offering sculpture to local chieftains. Imitation and emulation played an important role in the acceptance of such cultural practices. The new demand for sculpture necessitated a continuous training of artisans in workshops, which may have involved foreign input. Whereas some princes may have been satisfied with sculpture of lesser quality, others sought the best they could afford. It was this demand that created a hierarchy among the different sculptural centers. Indeed, there may have been some competition between various local chieftains for access and control of the superior product.[55]

Critical in this discussion is the afterlife of such monumental sculpture. Initially a flourishing art form throughout the fifth century B.C., locally manufactured "Greek-style" sculpture suffered a similar fate: in all of the regions in which it had developed, Iberian sculpture was destroyed or abandoned. To judge from the best preserved contexts, it appears that many of the monuments had already been destroyed at the beginning of the fourth century B.C. and the remnants were reused in various cemeteries. Other early sculptures appear to have been demolished and not reused. It is clear, nevertheless, that sculpture continued to be produced during the fourth century both in cemeteries and in sanctuaries,[56] and these later examples display firsthand knowledge of Greek originals.

I have argued elsewhere that the pattern of destruction of Iberian sculpture may have taken place during a period of instability, possibly in reaction to manifestations of luxury of the Archaic Iberian aristocracies.[57] The phenomenon must be seen in terms of a new type of civic space in which those sculptures had lost their earlier meaning once different symbols of power came to be preferred.[58] P. Rouillard suggests that Greek cultural features were only partially integrated by the Iberians,[59] which may imply resistance by the colonized against the colonizers, undoubtedly accompanied by similar counterreactions less visible in the archaeological record.

Within the new cities, the upper echelons of Iberian society now shared power that was previously exerted by the narrow circle of the prince and his family. The earlier statues, which served as a reminder of the ideological basis of the power they had exerted, had to disappear. They were either intentionally destroyed or were simply neglected until the monuments collapsed, and were often reused unceremoniously as basic construction material. In the closely interrelated world of ancient Iberia, the reaction spread rapidly. The fall of the Archaic principalities was accompanied by irreversible damage to Hellenized sculptures.

That this process represents indigenous resistance is quite clear. Whereas economically the Iberian world remained stable, there was a great deal of social flux.[60] Emerging social structures sought out new ways to represent identity and power, and turned away from the model represented by Hellenized sculpture. This was not so much a reaction against Greek goods or traders, since from the beginning of the fourth century B.C. the quantity of the Greek imports in the Iberian Peninsula increased considerably, while Iberian imitations of Greek pottery shapes were also more abundant.[61] Sculpture, which was not in the strictest sense a Greek product, represented something more meaningful, since the fallen Archaic aristocracies had represented their power through it.

From the very beginning, sculpture in Iberia represented something foreign, and its fate was intimately linked to that of the groups who used it. The subsequent rejection of sculpture implies that the ideological messages implicit in it were also considered alien and foreign. If there was an indigenous anticolonialist discourse, it is most clearly visible in the fate of Hellenized sculpture. Whereas in other colonialist contexts, such as Roman Gaul, sculpture seems to have been used in a "subversive" way,[62] in Iberia the opposite seems true, since sculpture was, at first, enthusiastically accepted by the indigenous elites. The eventual reaction to it by indigenous non-elites may be attributed to the fact that it was an instrument of power of foreign imposition. As Thomas has pointed out, "the logic of colonial expansion makes it almost inevitable that collaboration and compromise with an indigenous elite, or with the population of one region within a colonized country, will engender resistance and hostility on the part of subaltern groups or traditional enemies in other regions." The fate of Hellenized sculpture in Iberia provides a classic case of such resistance.[63]

Writing

During the middle and later first millennium B.C., the Iberian world was a literate one. The main writing system, with more than 1,500 known texts, is generically referred to as "Iberian script," in which two variants can be distinguished. It is a semisyllabic system, perhaps derived from the old Tartessian script used in the southwest of the peninsula between the seventh (even as early as the eighth) and the fifth centuries B.C.[64] The oldest written documents thus far known probably date to the fifth century B.C.[65]

In addition to these two systems, both of which arose from preexisting writing traditions in Iberia, there is a third script, conventionally known as the Greco-Iberian alphabet or Contestan script, named after Contestania, the region where it is almost exclusively found. Greco-Iberian script was "simply an adaptation of the Ionian alphabet of Asia Minor ... used by the Phocaean Greeks who founded Massilia and Ampurias, to represent the phonetic inventory of the Iberian language."[66] This alphabet was developed in Contestania and must have arisen before 450 B.C., perhaps as early as the second quarter of the fifth century B.C. The oldest documents so far known, however, belong to the fourth century B.C. The number of extant texts is small: seven lead tablets and some nineteen scratched inscriptions on pottery (fig. 7).[67]

In addition to graffiti on pottery, which are for the most part marks of ownership or personal names, the lead tablets refer to commercial transactions. Similar lead tablets were commonly used by Greek merchants to record or document commercial transactions and instructions, and it seems likely that the Iberians learned how to use these from Greek traders.[68] The use of writing by

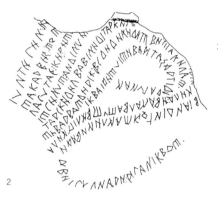

0   5cm

Fig. 7. Iberian texts written in the Greco-Iberian alphabet
(1) Lead tablet, La Serreta, 400–350 B.C.; (2) lead tablet, El
Cigarralejo, 400–350 B.C.; (3) lead tablet, Saguntum,
400–350 B.C.; (4) graffitti on the foot of Attic black-glaze
bowl, 350 B.C.; (5) lead tablet, Coimbra del Barranco Ancho,
400–350 B.C.

Fig. 8. Greek commercial texts
(1) Lead tablet, Ampurias, 525–500 B.C.; (2) lead tablet,
Pech Maho, 450–400 B.C.

the Iberians to render their own language argues for the intervention of Greeks in southeastern Iberia, before 450 B.C., as commercial and cultural agents. Moreover, the origin and development of the Greco-Iberian alphabet is contemporary with the rise of Hellenized Iberian sculpture. Greek colonialist enterprise, consequently, introduced changes in the Iberian world needed to foster the commercial collaboration with the indigenous population. This collaboration was indispensable for the Greeks and, at the same time, was manipulated as a defining element by the emerging Iberian aristocracy.

Recent studies by J. de Hoz have concluded that the Iberian language was the mother tongue of only a restricted area within what we know as the Iberian world. It was undoubtedly the native language of the Contestan region and, very probably, of regions in eastern Andalusia (Oretans and Bastetans), as well as perhaps of the northern neighbors of the Contestans, the Edetans.[69] Two points are worth stressing. First, a common language can now be added to the economic and cultural relationship between southeastern Iberia and Upper Andalusia already discussed. Second, the distribution of texts written in the Greco-Iberian alphabet points to the importance of the coast and to the main axis of penetration into the interior of the Peninsula. It underlines, once more, Greek interests in this part of Iberia.

Through an alphabetic script foreign to local traditions, the Greeks promoted an instrument of trade that was profitable for Greek merchants. The use of the Greek alphabet to transmit the Iberian language introduced new types of documents whose main beneficiaries were the Greeks. As the acceptance or rejection of writing is optional,[70] the Iberian adoption of a wholly foreign system and its subsequent development made them full participants, whether willingly or unwillingly, in a Greek colonialist enterprise.

Greek lead tablets recently discovered at Emporion (modern Ampurias) and Pech Maho demonstrate that commercial collaborations between Greeks and Iberians were established from at least the later sixth century B.C. in Saguntum (lead letter from Emporion) and during the second third of the fifth century B.C. in the region of Narbonne (lead tablet from Pech Maho) (fig. 8).[71] De Hoz may be correct in considering the Iberians as the primary middlemen in Greece's trade with the western Mediterranean,[72] a situation best witnessed in the region of southeastern Iberia and eastern Andalusia. Thus, the Greeks can be envisaged not only as the instigators of a system of colonial trade in the core of the Iberian world but also as those who exploited Iberians in their commercial activities along the remainder of the Iberian coastline. If this scenario is accepted, the local Iberian princes benefited in wealth, prestige, and power by supporting this colonialist system.

Although trade was the priority activity of the Greeks, it became a central feature of Iberian economic life, to judge from the archaeological evidence and the later existence of true Iberian commercial documents.[73] The use of a Greek system of writing, which lasted for at least two centuries, also implies mechanisms for teaching, learning, and dissemination through a relatively wide territory, and bilingualism.[74] This process can be understood only from a colonialist perspective, in which the acquisition of raw materials valuable to the colonizer is facilitated by the cultural hegemony exerted over the colonized. Although composed of different peoples, this cultural milieu shared the same language, the same commercial interests, and a similar way of symbolizing political power through the use of stone sculpture. The spread of writing in this part of Iberia relied more heavily on mutual commercial interests rather than direct political control.[75]

Writing in Iberia follows a pattern similar to that of monumental sculpture. The classical Iberian script, also referred to as "northeastern" or "Levantine,"[76] was increasingly used during the fourth century B.C., usually in the same places in which texts in Greco-Iberian alphabet appeared. During the third century, this script completely superseded both the Greco-Iberian alphabet and the "southern" Iberian script. Curiously, Iberian script represents a step backward in the development of writing because it is a semisyllabic system, which also retained some conventions inherited from the old Tartessian script. Why the Iberian script was so enthusiastically embraced is not well understood, particularly because it was more complicated and difficult to adapt to Iberian phonetics than the Greco-Iberian alphabet. Perhaps the success of this script involved factors not strictly linguistic. Iberians may have looked on Iberian script as a system of their own, whereas the Greco-Iberian alphabet was foreign. In the wave of rejection of certain foreign cultural elements representative of Greek colonialism, it is possible that this alphabet, which was never very popular, lost its prestige. It appears that from the third century B.C., Iberian script was one of the key elements in the rise of a new Iberian identity now comprising not only southeastern Iberia and Upper Andalusia but also the rest of the Mediterranean fringe, even southern France.[77] This script and the lingua franca that it represented were to embrace all the territory where "Iberian culture" was developed. The decline of the Greco-Iberian alphabet was contemporary with the decline of Greek trade in southeast Iberia, which was progressively replaced by other merchants, primarily Punic.

Architecture and Building Techniques

In general, what is known of domestic architecture in Iberian towns owes little to Greek models. With the exception of the examples discussed below, the internal arrangement of habitations does not appear to derive from Hellenic prototypes. A slight Greek influence can perhaps be detected in the relative regularity of the layout of certain Iberian towns, but this is far from clear.[78] The fortifications of Iberian towns undoubtedly represented important collective enterprises, which demanded strong political organization to mobilize resources. With few exceptions, however, direct Greek intervention cannot be established.[79] Some cases of influence, almost always in the vicinity of Emporion, have been noted. These include Puig de Sant'Andreu (Ullastret, Gerona), where Greek fortification techniques can be observed during the fourth and third centuries B.C.[80] At Turó del Montgrós (El Brull, Barcelona), a fourth-century B.C. wall shows some Greek influence.[81] The third-century B.C. entrance gate flanked by two pentagonal towers at Castellet de Banyoles (Tivissa, Tarragona) also finds parallels in the Greek world;[82] there are, perhaps, several more cases.[83] In general, Greek architectural technology had a limited impact and does not seem to have modified, in any significant way, indigenous building traditions.[84] Moreover, the few examples noted above are later than the phenomena of sculpture and writing and clearly derive from the regional influence of the Greek commercial establishment at Emporion.

In terms of overall architectural layout and fortifications, significant Greek characteristics can be observed only at the site of La Pícola (Santa Pola, Alicante), recently excavated and published (fig. 9). Santa Pola was in ancient times the Portus Ilicitanus, the maritime outlet of the important town at La Alcudia de Elche (ancient Ilici). Next to the ancient beach, a tiny settlement was established around 430 B.C. Its construction was more or less quadrangular, 60 meters to the side, and it was surrounded by a complete defensive system composed of a wall, a berm, a scarp with an outer wall, a wet ditch, and a counterscarp, covering an area more than 12 meters wide. It has been argued that these fortifications are similar to those found in Emporion as well as Athens. The settlement was apparently planned on the basis of an orthogonal grid with straight streets and standardized houses. Its plan is symmetrical and the regular layouts of streets and houses was built according to a module based on a foot measuring 29.7 or 30 centimeters. Only about 10 percent of the ceramics and $2\frac{1}{2}$ percent of the transport amphorae found in the town are Greek, factors that may exclude a wholly Greek character for the settlement. The planning of the site and its construction, however, were possibly entrusted to a Greek architect. The site was abandoned around 350 B.C.[85]

The case of La Pícola reveals a number of idiosyncratic features: its relationship to Ilici (La Alcudia de Elche), which functioned as the center of southern Contestania; the Greek character of its construction, but its occupation by Iberians; and the variety of Greek imports, despite their paucity in relation to local material. All these features make La Pícola the closest thing to a Greek settlement known in Iberia, outside Emporion and Rhodes. Nevertheless, La Pícola is not a truly Greek establishment. In its 3,350 square meters of usable surface (that is, not counting the space occupied by the defensive works), no more than eighty-four houses, each of 20 square meters, could have existed—a lesser figure if there was a central square (see fig. 9). La Pícola is best interpreted as a center dependent on Iberian authorities from Ilici, its harbor and marketplace perhaps frequented or controlled by Greek traders. It is significant that the native princes chose a Greek architect, or an individual trained in a Greek environment, to design the town in the second half of the fifth century B.C.[86] It is in this period that Hellenized sculpture reached its height (Ilici was one of the most important centers for sculpture) and Contestan communities adopted a Greek alphabet.

La Pícola provides an excellent example of Greek architectural design that native princes put to the service of trade, to their own advantage. These facili-

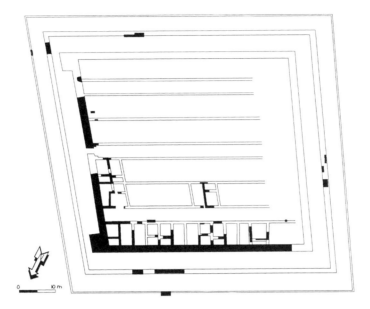

Fig. 9. Plan of La Pícola

ties are meaningful only against the backdrop of a commercial relationship that did not require the existence of politically independent Greek centers. La Pícola, therefore, may be considered as a sign of the success of colonialist politics, in which foreign concerns convinced indigenous elites to place at their disposal those elements that would facilitate the exploitation of the raw materials of southeastern Iberia and eastern Andalusia. It is reasonable to imagine that some Greeks — a diaspora — may have resided in La Pícola. In such a scenario a foreign minority in La Pícola may have controlled the settlement in order to carry out their trading activities. In this case, La Pícola could have functioned as a vector of Greek colonialism, but was not a true colony. The proximity of La Pícola not only to Elche but also to a number of other native centers located around the mouths of the Vinalopó and Segura Rivers, suggests the presence of a trading center frequented or controlled by Greek merchants who offered prestige and economic importance to the local elites. Similar situations occur in other places and times.[87]

Conclusion

From the later fifth century until the mid-fourth century B.C., Greeks based at Emporion undertook a broad colonialist enterprise that affected much of the coast of the Iberian Peninsula. Their activity was most deep-rooted and lasting in the southeastern regions of the peninsula and eastern Andalusia, where a Greek colonialist discourse was established; in time, it was integrated into Roman imperialist discourses. It originated in Greek attitudes to Iberia that took shape in the fifth century B.C., when native elites were subordinate to Greek demands. The Greeks developed a form of colonialism based not on the foundation of a network of colonies but above all on the stimulation and satisfaction of new needs among elite members of competing indigenous communities. The lack of true Greek colonies outside Emporion and Rhodes led to a colonialist strategy of collaboration with the indigenous populations to secure a ready supply of raw materials and other commodities. In order to compensate for the fact that they could not effectively apply military strength, the Greeks had to rely on negotiation with the natives. The materialization of this relationship can be seen in the technology required to make ideologically meaningful stone sculptures, as well as in writing and in standards of weights. These practices represent a form of colonialism without colonization.

Colonial action relied mainly on the trade in commodities, both raw materials and prestige goods, introduced by the Greeks at a time when the indigenous societies were undergoing a process of profound sociopolitical transformation. Indigenous elites were receptive to certain Greek cultural elements and used them to help shape and define a new Iberian identity. The indigenous elites were particularly receptive to foreign items that had no precedent in local tradition, especially images in stone sculpture that expressed dynastic tales of power, as well as the Greco-Iberian script, used to further manage trade. Their attraction to these novelties played into Greek hands. Through technology and writing, the Greeks shaped and manipulated a new and advantageous economic order.

Greek colonialist enterprise in southeastern Iberia reached its height in the second half of the fifth century B.C. Although the Iberians no doubt acted autonomously and molded Greek contributions to local tastes, the Greeks were the instigators of the process. The many workshops producing indigenous sculpture for Iberian aristocrats reflect the uninterrupted influence of Greek techniques and iconography. A Greek architect or Greek-trained master builder was involved in the construction of the small, fortified precinct at La Pícola, within the territory of the indigenous city at La Alcudia de Elche. Important public works were built at Emporion and its economic relationship with Cadix seems clear.[88] Much of the Attic pottery and other imported commodities found in Iberia were distributed from Emporion. It was, consequently, a key center within a commercial network comprising all the western Mediterranean, with possible direct links to mainland Greek cities such as Athens.

As in other colonial contexts, the local reaction to the strategies described above shifted over time. Despite the inclination of Iberians to emulate or imitate Greek material and artistic culture, there are also clear signs of rejection. This is particularly the case in the later fifth and early fourth centuries B.C., when sculptural monuments suffered neglect and destruction. At this same time, Iberian script became increasingly popular and the Greco-Iberian alphabet was discarded. The Iberian world experienced important transformations as new aristocratic states emerged. There was a conscious resistance to the models imposed by outsiders, a process that goes hand in hand with the rise of new economic and social structures within the native world.

The Greek response appears to have been focused and to a certain extent targeted. Whereas sculpture of Greek style was on the wane, imported Greek pottery, especially Attic, is found in greater quantity and may represent a new marker of prestige among local ruling circles. Coastal centers, and perhaps some inland settlements, were the focus of trade with the Greeks. This situation lasted until the mid-fourth century B.C., at which time the general situation in the western Mediterranean changed and Greek colonial presence was increasingly replaced or subsumed by Carthaginian imperialism.

In this overview we lack, of course, the narratives of the colonizers and the colonized. On the analogy of foundations like Massalia, it is possible to imagine that in Emporion a colonialist discourse was developed. The exact process and mechanism of this remain difficult to establish. Perhaps there is a clue in the reference by Strabo to the tiny Greek settlements or *polichnia*, as well as the spread of the worship of Artemis Ephesia. Curiously, however, the meager references in the extant literary sources referring to how the Greeks saw themselves in Iberia do not always correspond with the archaeological evidence. As a consequence, Greek colonialism in Iberia, characterized by an almost total absence of colonies, must be analyzed through the material record and from a theoretical perspective that can appraise both the indigenous and foreign perspectives. At a time when many studies analyze contact between indigenous populations and Greeks, we sometimes tend to lose sight of the mechanisms of interaction by which colonialist strategies were established. By analyzing the evidence of interactions and the manner in which colonial influence was received, integrated, or rejected, we are able to bring to the fore the contradictions of Greek colonialism and to understand better its successes and shortcomings.

Notes

1. For a review of the classical sources that refer to the exploitation of natural resources on the Iberian Peninsula, see Adolf Schulten, *Geografía y etnografía antiguas de la Península Ibérica* (Madrid: Consejo Superior de Investigaciones Científicas, 1963). The main Greek interest in southwest Iberia (Tartessos) was silver, already alluded to by Herodotus (*History* 1.163, 4.152). At Huelva the remains of furnaces for the extraction of silver from the mineral ore are contemporary with the earliest Greek presence there; see J. Fernández Jurado, "Aspectos de la minería y la metalurgia en la protohistoria de Huelva," *Huelva arqueológica* 10–11 (1988–89): 177–214. Silver mining is not attested in southeast Iberia until the fourth century. The region around Cástulo (Linares, Jaén) was one of the richest mining districts of ancient Spain, as shown by recent survey work; see Claude Domergue and G. Tamain, "Note sur le district minier de Linares-La Carolina (Jaén, Espagne) dans l'antiquité," in *Mélanges de*

préhistoire, d'archéocivilisation, et d'ethnologie offerts à André Varagnac (Paris: SEVPEN, 1971), 199–229. Mining was also important in the mountainous region, known as Sierra Morena, along the upper valley of the Guadalquivir River; see Claude Domergue, *Catalogue des mines et des fonderies antiques de la péninsule ibérique* (Madrid: Diffusion de Boccard, 1987), chart 2. On products such as salt and textiles (flax, esparto grass), see A. J. Domínguez, "Reinterpretación de los testimonios acerca de la presencia griega en el Sudeste peninsular y Levante en época arcaica," in *Homenaje a Luis Siret (1934–1984)* (Seville: Consejería de Cultura de la Junta de Andalucía, 1986), 601–11. Wine production during the later seventh century in Alt de Benimaquia (Denia, Valencia) is well attested; see C. Gómez, P. Guerin, and G. Pérez, "Temoignage d'une production de vin dans l'Espagne préromaine," in Marie-Claire Amouretti and Jean-Pierre Brun, eds., *La production du vin et de l'huile en Méditerranée* (Paris: Diffusion de Boccard, 1993), 379–95. For wine produced during 450–400 B.C. in La Quéjola (San Pedro, Albacete), see J. Blánquez, "El poblado ibérico de La Quéjola," *Patina* 6 (1993): 99–107.

2. See J. Jorge Klor de Alva, "The Postcolonization of the (Latin) American Experience: A Reconsideration of 'Colonialism,' 'Postcolonialism,' and 'Mestizaje,'" in Gyan Prakash, ed., *After Colonialism: Imperial Histories and Postcolonial Displacements* (Princeton: Princeton Univ. Press, 1995), 241–75.

3. Peter van Dommelen, "Colonial Constructs: Colonialism and Archaeology in the Mediterranean," *World Archaeology* 28 (1997): 305–23, esp. 306.

4. Edward W. Said, *Culture and Imperialism* (New York: Knopf, 1994), 9.

5. Said, *Culture and Imperialism* (note 4), 9.

6. See Gil Stein, in this volume.

7. David L. Sills, ed., *International Encyclopedia of the Social Sciences*, s.v. "colonialism" (entry by R. Emerson); cited in Anthony D. King, *Urbanism, Colonialism, and the World-Economy: Cultural and Spatial Foundations of the World Urban System* (London: Routledge, 1990), 46–47.

8. King, *Urbanism* (note 7), 49.

9. Susan Frankenstein, *Arqueología del colonialismo: El impacto fenicio y griego en el sur de la Península Ibérica y el suroeste de Alemanía* (Barcelona: Crítica, 1997), x.

10. Nathan Reingold and Marc Rothenberg, "Introduction," in idem, eds., *Scientific Colonialism: A Cross-Cultural Comparison* (Washington, D.C.: Smithsonian Institution Press, 1987), vi–xiii.

11. This is in contrast to a number of studies that have proposed to give the same value to both terms or even to substitute colonialism for colonization; see, for instance, H. Lühty, "Colonization and the Making of Mankind," in George H. Nadel and Perry Curtis, eds., *Imperialism and Colonialism* (New York: Macmillan, 1964), 28–29; and Frankenstein, *Arqueología* (note 9), ix. Thus, I adhere to the idea recently defended by Jane Webster, for whom "'colonialism' generally denotes all instances of direct political control of a people by a foreign state, irrespective of the number of settlers present"; see Jane Webster, "Roman Imperialism and the 'Post Imperial Age,'" in Jane Webster and Nicholas J. Cooper, eds., *Roman Imperialism: Post-Colonial Perspectives* (Leicester: Univ. of Leicester, 1996), 5.

12. Gyan Prakash, "Introduction: After Colonialism," in idem, ed., *After Colonial-*

ism: Imperial Histories and Postcolonial Displacements (Princeton: Princeton Univ. Press, 1995), 3–17.

13. For example, Strabo, *Geographica* 3.4.8. The manner in which the Greeks transmitted their cult of Artemis Ephesia to the Iberians, and how Iberians were taught to sacrifice in the Greek way (Strabo, *Geographica* 4.1.5), has been interpreted in various ways; see Irad Malkin, "Missionaires païens dans la Gaule grecque," in idem, ed., *La France et la Méditerranée: Vingt-sept siècles d'interdépendance* (Leiden: E. J. Brill, 1990), 42–52. It must be stressed, however, that one of the primary literary sources, Strabo's *Geographica*, represents more the Roman view than the Greek. For a discussion on the lack of a Greek, as opposed to a Roman, colonialist discourse in Strabo, see A. J. Domínguez, "Reflexiones acerca de la sociedad hispana reflejada en la *Geografía* de Estrabón," *Lucentum* 3 (1984): 210–18; A. J. Domínguez, "Los romanos e Iberia como tema histórico en la *Geografía* de Estrabón," in *Actas del II Congreso andaluz de estudios clásicos: Antequera, Málaga, 24-26 de mayo, 1984* (Málaga: Delegación de Málaga de la Sociedad Española de Estudios Clásicos, 1987–94), 1:177–83; and D. Plácido, "Estrabón III: El territorio hispano, la geografía griega y el imperialismo romano," *Habis* 18–19 (1987–88): 243–56.

14. Similarly, the mechanisms developed in recent years to analyze Western colonial discourse might be fruitfully applied to an analysis of the ancient indigenous populations of Iberia; see Robert J. C. Young, *Colonial Desire: Hybridity in Theory, Culture, and Race* (London: Routledge, 1995), esp. 159–60, on the use of literary texts, travel writings, memoirs, and academic studies, and the construction of the Other.

15. Nicholas Thomas, *Colonialism's Culture: Anthropology, Travel, and Government* (Princeton: Princeton Univ. Press, 1994), 60.

16. Compare Young, *Colonial Desire* (note 14), 162.

17. Robin Osborne, "Early Greek Colonization? The Nature of Greek Settlement in the West," in Nick Fisher and Hans van Wees, eds., *Archaic Greece: New Approaches and New Evidence* (London: Duckworth, 1998), 251–69, 264, writes, "What I have tried to do . . . is to undermine confidence that the archaeology distinguishes clearly between the nature of the settlements we have come to call 'colonies' and the nature of those settlements for which scholars cast about for an alternative term."

18. See Brian B. Shefton, "Greeks and Greek Imports in the South of the Iberian Peninsula: The Archaeological Evidence," in Hans Georg Niemeyer, ed., *Phönizier im Westen: Die Beiträge des Internationalen Symposiums über 'Die phönizische Expansion im westlichen Mittelmeerraum' in Köln vom 24. bis 27. April 1979* (Mainz am Rhein: Phillip von Zabern, 1982), 337–70; and Domínguez, "Reinterpretación de los testimonios" (note 1).

19. Jesús-Luis Cunchillos and José-Ángel Zamora, *Gramática fenicia elemental* (Madrid: Consejo Superior de Investigaciones Científicas, 1997), 141–54.

20. A. J. Domínguez, "Los términos 'Iberia' e 'Iberos' en las fuentes greco-latinas: Estudio acerca de su origen y ámbito de aplicación," *Lucentum* 2 (1983): 203–24.

21. Said, *Culture* (note 4), 225.

22. Domínguez, "Los términos" (note 20).

23. Francisco Burillo Mozoto, *Los celtíberos: Etnias y estados* (Barcelona: Crítica, 1998), 51–55.

24. Klor de Alva, "Postcolonization" (note 2), 248–49.

25. P. Jacob, "Notes sur la toponimie grecque de la côte méditerranéenne de l'Espagne antique," *Ktema* 10 (1985): 247–71.

26. A. J. Domínguez, "Más allá de Heracles: De la Iberia real a la recreación de una Iberia griega," in Paloma Cabrera and Carmen Sánchez, eds., *Los griegos en España: Tras las huellas de Heracles* (Madrid: Ministerio de Educación y Cultura, 1998), 44–65, 439–48.

27. Shefton, "Greeks and Greek Imports" (note 18), 353–64; Pierre Rouillard, *Les grecs et la péninsule ibérique du VIIIᵉ au IVᵉ siècle avant Jésus-Christ* (Talence, France: Université de Bordeaux III, 1991), 113–17; Paloma Cabrera, "Greek Trade in Iberia: The Extent of Interaction," *Oxford Journal of Archaeology* 17 (1998): 191–206, esp. 194–99; and A. J. Domínguez and Carmen Sánchez, *Greek Pottery from the Iberian Peninsula: Archaic and Classical Periods* (Leiden: E. J. Brill, 2001), 88–89.

28. See Shefton, "Greeks and Greek Imports" (note 18); and, most recently, Sarah P. Morris and John K. Papadopoulos, "Phoenicians and the Corinthian Pottery Industry," in Renate Rolle and Karin Schmidt, eds., *Archäologische Studien in Kontaktzonen der antiken Welt* (Göttingen: Vandenhoeck & Ruprecht, 1998), 251–62.

29. Ricardo Olmos, "Original Elements and Mediterranean Stimuli in Iberian Pottery: The Case of Elche," *Mediterranean Archaeology* 2 (1989): 101–9, esp. 104. In my opinion, however, imitations of pottery forms were developed quite independently from any direct Greek influence exerted over the Iberians; see A. J. Domínguez, "Hellenisation in Iberia? The Reception of Greek Products and Influences by the Iberians," in Gocha R. Tsetskhladze, ed., *Ancient Greeks East and West* (Leiden: E. J. Brill, 1999), 301–29, esp. 313–16.

30. Admittedly, there is no single definition of ethnicity. For my purposes here, ethnicity can be defined simply as "self-conscious identification with a particular social group at least partly based on a specific locality or origin"; see Stephen Shennan, "Introduction: Archaeological Approaches to Cultural Identity," in idem, ed., *Archaeological Approaches to Cultural Identity* (London: Unwin Hyman, 1989), 1–32, esp. 14.

31. Compare Shennan, "Introduction" (note 30), 16. On the process of ethnic definition in the Iberian world, see the general remarks by Arturo Ruiz and Manuel Molinos, *Los iberos: Análisis arqueológico de un proceso histórico* (Barcelona: Crítica, 1993), 240–46.

32. Richard Jenkins, *Rethinking Ethnicity: Arguments and Explorations* (London: Sage, 1997), 13–14, 18–19. See also Werner Sollors, "Introduction: The Invention of Ethnicity," in idem, ed., *The Invention of Ethnicity* (New York: Oxford Univ. Press, 1989), ix–xx; and, most recently, Siân Jones, *The Archaeology of Ethnicity: Constructing Identities in the Past and Present* (London: Routledge, 1997). On culturally constructed ethnicities elsewhere in the Mediterranean, see Jonathan M. Hall, *Ethnic Identity in Greek Antiquity* (Cambridge: Cambridge Univ. Press, 1997); and John K. Papadopoulos, "Phantom Euboians," *Journal of Mediterranean Archaeology* 10 (1997): 191–219, esp. 203–7.

33. Jenkins, *Rethinking Ethnicity* (note 32), 53.

34. On the nature of Phoenician trade in the Mediterranean coast of the Iberian

Peninsula, see María Eugenia Aubet, *Tiro y las colonias fenicias de Occidente*, rev. ed. (Barcelona: Ediciones Bellaterra, 1994), 290–93.

35. Alfredo González Prats, Antonio García Menarguez, and Elisa Ruiz Segura, eds., "La Fonteta: Una ciudad fenicia en Occidente," *Revista de arqueología* 190 (1997): 8–13; Alfredo González Prats, "Las cerámicas fenicias de la provincia de Alicante," and Alfredo González Prats et al., "La Fonteta, 1997: Memoria preliminar de la segunda campaña de excavaciones ordinarias en la ciudad fenicia de la desembocadura del río Segura, Guardamar (Alicante)," in Alfredo González Prats, ed., *La cerámica fenicia en Occidente: Centros de producción y áreas de comercio* (Alicante: Instituto de Cultura Juan Gil-Albert, 1999), 111–28, 257–301; and Rafael Azuar et al., "El asentamiento orientalizante e ibérico antiguo de 'La Rábita,' Guardamar del Segura (Alicante), avance de las excavaciones 1996–1998," *Trabajos de prehistoria* 52, no. 2 (1998): 1–17.

36. Paloma Cabrera, "El comercio foceo en Huelva: Cronología y fisonomía," *Huelva arqueológica* 10–11 (1988–89): 41–100; Cabrera, "Greek Trade" (note 27); and Domínguez, "Reinterpretación de los testimonios" (note 1). On the topic of the carriers of various commodities, including pottery, see, most recently, Morris and Papadopoulos, "Phoenicians" (note 28).

37. It also seems clear that the Phoenicians had benefited from preexisting trading networks controlled by the Iberians, thus further establishing close relationships; see Aubet, *Tiro y las colonias* (note 34), 303–4.

38. A. J. Domínguez, "Mecanismos, rutas y agentes comerciales en las relaciones económicas entre griegos e indígenas en el interior peninsular," *Estudis d'història econòmica* (1993): 39–74.

39. Abner Cohen, "Cultural Strategies in the Organization of Trading Diasporas," in Claude Meillassoux, ed., *The Development of Indigenous Trade and Markets in West Africa: Studies Presented and Discussed at the Tenth International African Seminar at Fourah Bay College, Freetown, December 1969* (London: Oxford Univ. Press, 1971), 266–81; and Philip D. Curtin, *Cross-Cultural Trade in World History* (Cambridge: Cambridge Univ. Press, 1984), 1–14.

40. Cohen, "Cultural Strategies" (note 39), 266–67.

41. Curtin, *Cross-Cultural Trade* (note 39) has dealt extensively with many of these different relationships.

42. See Gil Stein, in this volume.

43. On the relationships between host communities and minority groups, see Curtin, *Cross-Cultural Trade* (note 39), 5–6; and the general observations in Fredrik Barth, "Introduction," in idem, ed., *Ethnic Groups and Boundaries: The Social Organization of Culture Difference* (Boston: Little, Brown, 1969), 9–49, esp. 38–41.

44. J. Alvar, "El problema de la precolonización en la gestación de la polis," in Domingo Plácido et al., eds., *Imágenes de la polis* (Madrid: Ediciones Clásicas, 1997), 19–33; and J. Alvar, "Los fenicios en Occidente," in José M. Blázquez et al., *Fenicios y cartagineses en el Mediterráneo* (Madrid: Cátedra, 1999), 311–447, esp. 330–39.

45. Aubet, *Tiro y las colonias* (note 34), 303–4.

46. Martín Almagro-Gorbea, "La iberización de las zonas orientales de la Meseta," *Ampurias* 38–40 (1976–78): 93–156, esp. 111–12; Martín Almagro-Gorbea, "Los relieves mitológicos orientalizantes de Pozo Moro," *Trabajos de prehistoria* 35

(1978): 251–78; Martín Almagro-Gorbea, "Pozo Moro y el influjo fenicio en el período orientalizante de la Península Ibérica," *Rivista di studi fenici* 10 (1982): 231–72; and Martín Almagro-Gorbea, "Pozo Moro: El monumento orientalizante su contexto socio-cultural y sus paralelos en la arquitectura funeraria ibérica," *Madrider Mitteilungen* 24 (1983): 184.

47. This process has been referred to by some scholars as the "sixth-century crisis," and it implies profound changes throughout the western Phoenician world; see Aubet, *Tiro y las colonias* (note 34), 293–96; and Alvar, "Los fenicios" (note 44), 404–15.

48. Teresa Chapa, "Las esfinges en la plástica ibérica," *Trabajos de prehistoria* 37 (1980): 309–44, esp. 317–19.

49. Chapa, "Las esfinges" (note 48), 314–15; and Teresa Chapa, *Influjos griegos en la escultura zoomorfa ibérica* (Madrid: Consejo Superior de Investigaciones Científicas, 1986), 115–16, 121–22, 189–90 (note also the bull with human face from Balazote).

50. Martín Almagro-Gorbea, "Pilares-estela ibéricos," in *Homenaje al Prof. Martín Almagro Basch* (Madrid: Ministerio de Cultura, 1983), 3:7–20.

51. Juan Agustín González, *Escultura ibérica de Cerrillo Blanco: Porcuna, Jaén* (Jaén: Diputación Provincial de Jaén, 1986), 17–23; on this ensemble, see also Iván Negueruela, *Los monumentos escultóricos ibéricos del Cerrillo de Porcuna, Jaén: Estudio sobre su estructura interna, agrupamientos e interpretación* (Madrid: Ministerio de Cultura, 1990).

52. The Iberian elites found in Hellenic taste a means of reproducing their own systems of social relationships; see Ruiz and Molinos, *Los iberos* (note 31), 214–15. See further the general comments on the transformation of objects in cultural contexts in Nicholas Thomas, *Entangled Objects: Exchange, Material Culture and Colonialism in the Pacific* (Cambridge: Harvard Univ. Press, 1991), 87; and Nicholas Thomas, "The Case of the Misplaced Ponchos: Speculations concerning the History of Cloth in Polynesia," *Journal of Material Culture* 4 (1999): 5–20.

53. Ricardo Olmos, "Original Elements and Mediterranean Stimuli in Iberian Pottery: Part 2," *Mediterranean Archaeology* 3 (1990): 7–25, esp. 19.

54. See, for instance, the case of the Lady of Elche, P. León, "Impresiones desde la plástica griega," in Ricardo Olmos and Trinidad Tortosa, eds., *La Dama de Elche: Lecturas desde la diversidad* (Madrid: AGEPASA, 1997), 125–32.

55. Here Thomas's comments on the "musket economy" in the southern Marquesas are relevant, particularly the manner in which local chiefs attempted to monopolize a given foreign commodity of power and prestige; see Thomas, *Entangled Objects* (note 52); and Thomas, *Colonialism's Culture* (note 15), 101–2.

56. The use of sculpture in Iberian cemeteries of the fourth century, both inside and outside the tomb, is known in cemeteries such as Baza and Coimbra del Barranco Ancho; see F. Presedo Velo, "La Dama de Baza," *Trabajos de prehistoria* 30 (1973): 151–206; and José García Cano, "El pilar estela de Coimbra del Barranco Ancho (Jumilla, Murcia)," *Revista de estudios ibéricos* 1 (1994): 173–201. On Iberian sanctuaries with sculpture during the fourth century B.C., see Monica Ruiz, *Los exvotos del santuario ibérico del Cerro de los Santos* (Albacete: Instituto de Estudios Albacetenses, 1989); and Manuel Molinos, *El santuario heroico de El Pajarillo (Huelma, Jaén)* (Jaén: Universidad de Jaén, 1998).

57. A. J. Domínguez, "La escultura animalística contestana como exponente del proceso de helenización del territorio," in Francisco Burillo, ed., *Arqueología espacial: Coloquio sobre distribución y relaciones entre los asentamientos, Teruel, 27 al 29 de septiembre 1984*, vol. 4, *Del bronce final a epoca ibérica* (Teruel: Colegio Universitario de Teruel, 1984), 141–60; and Francisco Burillo, "Aportaciones y comentarios," in Teresa Chapa, *Influjos griegos en la escultura zoomorfa ibérica* (Madrid: Consejo Superior de Investigaciones Científicas, 1986), 311–26, esp. 324–25.

58. Domínguez, "Reinterpretación de los testimonios" (note 1). Other scholars prefer to see this as a simple abandonment and neglect of those monuments rather than as an active destruction reflecting ideological change; see Teresa Chapa, "La destrucción de la escultura funeraria ibérica," *Trabajos de prehistoria* 50 (1993): 185–95.

59. Pierre Rouillard, "Tombe, sculpture et durée chez les iberes," *Revue des études anciennes* 78 (1986): 339–49, esp. 349: "un élément exogène pour l'essentiel, la sculpture, et qui fut significant un temps dans les nécropoles ibériques en l'est plus. Trés tôt, au IVe siècle, il n'a plus été sémantisé, ou n'a pas été resémantise."

60. This is shown, for example, in a recent sociological study on the use of weapons by the Iberians: Fernando Quesada, *El armamento ibérico: Estudio tipológico, geográfico, funcional, social y simbólico de las armas en la cultura ibérica (siglos VI–I a.C.)* (Montagnac, France: Monique Mergoil, 1997), 611–15.

61. Rouillard, *Les grecs* (note 27), 123–26. For Iberian imitations, see Virginia Page, B. de Griño, Ricardo Olmos, and Carmen Sánchez, *Imitaciones de influjo griego en la cerámica ibérica de Valencia, Alicante y Murcia* (Madrid: Consejo Superior de Investigaciones Científicas, Instituto Antonio de Nebrija, 1984); Virginia Page, "Imitaciones ibéricas de cráteras y copas áticas en la provincia de Murcia," and J. Pereira and Carmen Sánchez, "Imitaciones ibéricas de vasos áticos en Andalucía," in Marina Picazo and Enric Sanmartí i Grego, eds., *Ceràmiques gregues i hel·lenístiques a la Península ibèrica* (Barcelona: Institut de Prehistòria y Arqueologia, Diputació de Barcelona, 1985), 71–81, 87–100; Virginia Page, "Las imitacionas ibéricas de las ceràmicas griegas," in Juan Pérez, ed., *El mundo ibérico: Una nueva imaginen en Los Albores del año 2000* (Toledo: Junta de Comunidades Castilla-La Mancha, 1995), 145–51; and Carmen Sánchez, "Greek Vases for Iberian Princes," in *Hoi Archaioi Hellenes sten Hispania: Sta ichne tou Herakle = Los griegos en España: Tras las huellas de Heracles*, exh. cat. (Madrid: Ministerio de Educación y Cultura, Secretaría de Cultura, 1998), 511–20, esp. 515–16.

62. Jane Webster, "Necessary Comparisons: A Post-Colonial Approach to Religious Syncretism in the Roman Provinces," *World Archaeology* 28 (1997): 324–38, esp. 327.

63. Thomas, *Entangled Objects* (note 52); and Thomas, *Colonialism's Culture* (note 15), 171.

64. J. de Hoz, "La lengua y la escritura ibéricas, y las lenguas de los íberos," in Jürgen Untermann and Francisco Villar, eds., *Lengua y cultura en la Hispania prerromana: Actas V coloquio sobre lenguas y culturas prerromanas de la Península Ibérica* (Salamanca: Universidad de Salamanca, 1993), 635–66, esp. 638–44; and Javier Velaza, *Epigrafía y lengua ibéricas* (Madrid: Arco, 1996), 18–20.

65. M. Lejeune, "Rencontres de l'alphabet grec avec les langues barbares au cours du 1er millénaire avant Jésus-Christ," in *Modes de contacts et processus de*

transformation dans les sociétés anciennes: Actes du colloque de Cortone, 24–30 mai 1981 (Pisa: Scuola Normale Superiore, 1983), 738; and De Hoz, "La lengua" (note 64), 659–60.

66. J. de Hoz, "La escritura greco-ibérica," *Veleia* 2–3 (1985–86): 285–98; and J. de Hoz, "Western Greek Epigraphy and Graeco-Iberian Writing," in *Hoi Archaioi Hellenes sten Hispania: Sta ichne tou Herakle = Los griegos en España: Tras las huellas de Heracles,* exh. cat. (Madrid: Ministerio de Educación y Cultura, Secretaría de Cultura, 1998), 503–10, esp. 507.

67. De Hoz, "La escritura" (note 66); and de Hoz, "Western Greek Epigraphy" (note 66).

68. J. de Hoz, "Escritura e influencia clásica en los pueblos prerromanos de la península," *Archivo español de arqueología* 52 (1979): 227–50, esp. 232–37.

69. De Hoz, "La lengua" (note 64), 659.

70. Lejeune, "Rencontres de l'alphabet" (note 65), 739; and Greg Woolf, "Power and the Spread of Writing in the West," in Alan Bowman and Greg Woolf, eds., *Literacy and Power in the Ancient World* (Cambridge: Cambridge Univ. Press, 1994), 84–98.

71. Enric Sanmartí and R. A. Santiago, "Une lettre grecque sur plomb trouvée à Emporion (Fouilles, 1985)," *Zeitschrift für Papyrologie und Epigraphie* 68 (1987): 119–27; and Michel Lejeune, Jean Pouilloux, and Yves Solier, "Etrusque et ionien archaïques sur un plomb de Pech Maho (Aude)," *Revue archéologique de Narbonnaise* 21 (1988): 19–59.

72. De Hoz, "La lengua" (note 64), 659.

73. Enric Sanmarti, "Una carta en lengua ibérica, escrita sobre plomo, procedente de Emporion," *Revue archéologique de Narbonnaise* 21 (1988): 95–113.

74. Lejeune, "Rencontres de l'alphabet" (note 65), 739–40.

75. Woolf has argued that in southern Gaul, for instance, writing may have been one means of signaling ethnic differences between the competing Iberian and Celtic populations; see Woolf, "Power" (note 70), 88–89. It is conceivable that the late appearance of Gallo-Greek may reflect a deliberate rejection of the culture of both Iberians and Massiliote Greeks.

76. De Hoz, "La lengua" (note 64), 662.

77. See, most recently, Eric Gailledrat, *Les ibères de l'ebre à l'Hérault: VIe–IVe siècles avant Jésus-Christ* (Lattes, France: Association pour la Recherche Archéologique en Languedoc Oriental, 1997), 27–55.

78. See Pierre Rouillard, "Les fortifications préromaines de l'aire ibériques," in *La fortification dans l'histoire du monde grec: Actes du colloque international—La fortification et sa place dans l'histoire politique, culturelle et sociale du monde grec* (Paris: Editions du Centre National de la Recherche Scientificque, 1986), 213–19; and Pierre Moret, *Les fortifications ibériques: De la fin de l'âge du bronze à la conquête romaine* (Madrid: Casa de Velázquez, 1996), 267–68.

79. Rouillard, "Les fortifications préromaines" (note 78); and Moret, *Les fortifications ibériques* (note 78), 214–18.

80. Pierre Moret, "Les fortifications grecques et leur influence dans la péninsule ibérique," *Les dossiers d'archéologie* 179 (1993): 50–51; and Moret, *Les fortifications ibériques* (note 78), 374–78.

81. Moret, "Les fortifications grecques" (note 80), 50; and Moret, *Les fortifications ibériques* (note 78), 383–85.

82. Moret, "Les fortifications grecques" (note 80), 51; and Moret, *Les fortifications ibériques* (note 78), 416–18.

83. R. Pallarés et al., "Cataluña: Sistemas ibero-griegos de defensa," *Revista de arqueología* 65 (1986): 42–52; and F. Gracia, "Poliorcética griega y fortificaciones ibéricas," in *La guerra en la antigüedad: Una aproximación al origen de los ejércitos en Hispania* (Madrid: Ministerio de Defensa, 1997), 165–83.

84. Moret, *Les fortifications ibériques* (note 78), 221–22.

85. Pierre Moret et al., "The Fortified Settlement of La Picola (Santa Pola, Alicante) and the Greek Influence in Southeast Spain," in Barry Cunliffe and S. J. Keay, eds., *Social Complexity and the Development of Towns in Iberia: From the Copper Age to the Second Century* A.D. (Oxford: Oxford Univ. Press, 1995), 109–25; Pierre Moret et al., "La Picola (Santa Pola): Un asentamiento fortificado de los siglos V y IV a.C. en el litoral alicantino," in *Actas del XXIII Congreso nacional de arqueología, Elche, 1995* (Elche: Ayuntamiento de Elche, 1996), 1:401–6; Alain Badie and Pierre Moret, "Métrologie et organisation modulaire de l'espace au Vᵉ siècle avant Jésus-Christ sur le site ibérique de La Picola (Santa Pola, Alicante)," *Pallas* 46 (1997): 31–46; Moret, *Les fortifications ibériques* (note 78), 488–90; and Alain Badie et al., *Le site antique de La Picola à Santa Pola, Alicante, Espagne* (Paris: Éditions Recherche sur les Civilisations, 2000).

86. Badié and Moret, "Métrologie" (note 85), 40–41, state, "La Picola est somme toute l'expression hybride d'un contact prolongé entre deux cultures méditerranéennes, le reflet en terre ibère de l'architecture grecque occidentale."

87. Compare, especially, the case of the Hueda in West Africa with respect to foreign traders; see the cogent arguments in K. G. Kelly, "The Archaeology of African-European Interaction: Investigating the Social Roles of Trade, Traders, and the Use of Space in the Seventeenth- and Eighteenth-Century Hueda Kingdom, Republic of Bénin," *World Archaeology* 28 (1997): 351–69, esp. 355–56:

> Rather than being exclusively focused on the material or economic aspect of trade goods, the Hueda gave equal importance to the management of the symbolic asset of multiple European presences that were not in positions of hegemony over the traditional Hueda elite. Indeed, trade cannot be seen simply as the addition of new materials into an existing corpus of material goods: at Savi, we see that trade items were adopted and incorporated into Hueda society, and were assigned values and meanings consistent with the Hueda cultural system.

See also Kenneth Kelly, in this volume. A somewhat similar situation seems to have developed in Tripolitania in Roman times; see Mark Grahame, "Rome without Romanization: Cultural Change in the Pre-Desert of Tripolitania (First–Third Centuries A.D.)," *Oxford Journal of Archaeology* 17 (1998): 93–111, esp. 105–6.

88. M. P. García-Bellido, "Las relaciones económicas entre Massalia, Emporion y Gades a través de la moneda," *Huelva arqueológica* 13 (1994): 115–49; and Cabrera, "Greek Trade" (note 27), 201–2.

Indigenous Responses to Colonial Encounters on the West African Coast: Hueda and Dahomey from the Seventeenth through Nineteenth Century

Kenneth Kelly

African states in the Bight of Benin engaged in trade with European nations from the 1660s, and continued to do so for nearly 250 years. Trading with Europe was widespread among coastal African groups during this era, yet the trading circumstances enjoyed by the nations of Hueda and Dahomey, and imposed on their European partners, were unique along the African coast. The remarkable degree to which the European trading presence was regulated and manipulated by African elites evokes a complexity in African-European interaction that is quite unexpected when considered in the light of the common (and simplistic) extrapolation of late-nineteenth- and early-twentieth-century African-European interactions into earlier time periods.

The responses to European encounters described below indicate a significant and sophisticated African understanding of the potential benefits and costs to coastal states of sustained trade with European nations. Historical and archaeological data are used in conjunction to generate insights into the unusual historical, political, and environmental setting of trade between the Hueda state (circa 1660–1727), and its successor state, Dahomey, which replaced Hueda in 1727 as the preeminent trading nation in the region. This continued until Dahomey was conquered by the French in the last years of the nineteenth century. The unique developments seen on the coast of Benin can be attributed in large part to the presence of representatives of multiple European trading nations. This contrasts with the trading situations found in virtually all other settings on the African coast, where a single European nation enjoyed exclusive trading rights and privileges along a relatively limited segment of coast. In most cases this meant that one European nation engaged with one African nation or polity, and vice versa. Hueda and Dahomey, however, maintained a trading environment that facilitated and encouraged the presence of trading representatives from several European nations at the same time.[1] This unique arrangement permitted the Hueda and later Dahomey to better profit from European trade and to minimize the threat posed by European traders to continued Hueda autonomy.[2] The investigation of the consequences of these actions for Africans and Europeans can be furthered by elaborating on the strategies utilized by the Hueda, and by using archaeological evidence from Savi, the Hueda capital, coupled with historical documents. Archaeological and historical data pertaining to Ouidah, the Dahomean town that succeeded Savi, facilitates the examination of active strategies adopted by Dahomey to manage the continued presence of representatives of European trading nations and Dahomean responses to the changing economic circumstances of the late nineteenth century. Comparisons with the results of historical archaeology conducted at Elmina enhance the appreciation of the unique setting at Savi and Ouidah,[3] as well as an understanding of the complexity of African-European interaction in general.

This analysis develops a theoretical perspective that recognizes the inherent historicity of European-African intercultural interaction and acknowledges the creative and ongoing renegotiation of the contact setting. Precolonial African-European interactions differed significantly from those characterizing the aftermath of the late-nineteenth-century "scramble for Africa." In order to understand the sensible choices made by Africans and Europeans, one must accept that in the same way that objects can be "entangled,"[4] and thus take on very different meanings in different settings, so too can the exchanges themselves. Thus, while traded objects can be very important for what they are and what they mean, the meanings assigned to the *trade partners* involved may be of equal importance. The context of the intercultural interactions between Europeans and Africans in the Bight of Benin changed repeatedly throughout the more than three hundred years of trade and colonization. While we necessarily tend to look back on African-European interaction and see the results through the lens of the *longue durée*, in which the colonization of Africa by Europeans seems inevitable, there is an alternative perspective. It is perhaps possible to gain a better understanding of the social processes involved in negotiating intercultural interaction among various groups of Africans and representatives of different European nations by placing emphasis on the events (*événements*) and the *conjoncture*, to use the *Annales* terms that describe timescales of lived experience.[5] One must remember that the actions of individual European traders, and African merchants, elites, and commoners were informed not by vast overarching stretches of depersonalized history but by their own experiences. Their actions made sense to them in terms of what they knew.

Comparison with other West African trading situations, specifically that occurring at Elmina, Ghana, brings to the fore the broader ramifications of exploring African-European interaction at Savi and Ouidah from a perspective that focuses on the importance of the negotiated meaning of trade and traders (fig. 1). At Elmina, in dramatic contrast to Savi and Ouidah, the strength of African control over the trade arena diminished rapidly at the hands of Portuguese, then Dutch, and finally British traders, with the result that African sensibilities were at least outwardly changed in ways that

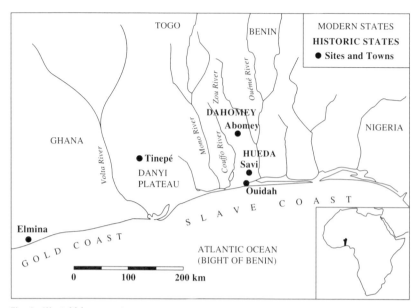

Fig. 1. West African coast

anticipated, or perhaps facilitated, the imposition of colonial authority and the development of a "creolized" population. In contrast to the situation at Elmina, the Hueda and Fon of Dahomey exhibit relatively little indication of significant European impact on their cultures. At the same time, however, the novel cultural expressions of the nineteenth-century immigrant Afro-Brazilians of Ouidah can profitably be contrasted with that of the creolized "Anglo-Fanti" of Elmina.[6]

Intercultural Interaction, Agency, and Archaeology

Much of what we know about the active role of African creativity in their interactions with Europeans is derived from critical readings of primary accounts by European traders, travelers, and emissaries.[7] Through the careful investigation of these sources, it is possible to discern a perspective that better reflects the choices of the active participants. Yet no matter how complex and comprehensive the interpretation of European-authored documents, these initial observations are fundamentally the product of outsiders. Archaeological evidence, which is the material residue of African (and European) behaviors, provides another perspective from which to investigate the ways that intercultural interaction was explored and conceived by African participants. Although archaeological data do not clearly provide the details of individual actions as documents can do, archaeology demonstrates the cumulative effects of behavior. In effect, archaeology provides evidence of aggregate strategies explored by individuals and groups who, except in extraordinary circumstances, remain anonymous. These aggregate past actions, while not able to "speak for themselves," are amenable to interpretation from a critical perspective. They constitute an alternate pathway through which to discern the conscious and unconscious actions of those who were motivated to reach specific ends or outcomes.

How do we know that interaction and trade were occurring at Savi, or for that matter, at Elmina? In both of these settings the trade in enslaved Africans was a significant component of the economic interaction; however, it has been suggested that with so little direct archaeological evidence of the trade in slaves, archaeology seriously underrepresents the scope and scale of the slave trade. The strength of any archaeology conducted on periods for which we have good historical context is that it affords us the luxury to be concerned with more than simply defining interactions. Instead, it allows us the opportunity to move outside the perspective handed to us by contemporary observers, and to attempt to understand interactions from a setting that foregrounds the agency of otherwise muted people.

The impact of the slave trade on African societies cannot be read in lists of baubles and tallies of trinkets. Indeed, many of the trade goods provided by Europeans were perishable, such as cloth, or consumable, such as liquor or tobacco. Items that were not so transient, such as firearms or iron, were also highly desirable commodities, subject to rapid dispersal through trade, or to curation. Furthermore, the material trappings of an African economy based on slavery, while not clearly understood at the present, cannot be expected to be manifest in piles of shackles and structures designed for confinement. Rather, the impact and scale of the slave trade must be teased out of changes in settlement pattern, the rise of politically centralized complex societies, and the establishment of new trade routes. Thus while the rise of Savi, Elmina, and a host of other coastal trade towns speak to one manifestation of the slave trade, other African sites must also be included to develop our understanding of the range of African reactions to change. In addition to these coastal trade centers, the archaeological exploration of the African response to the slave trade can also be read at sites such as Tinepé, a small village on the Danyi Plateau of Togo (see fig. 1 for location). Here, small-scale earthworks surrounding an isolated village defy explanation until oral traditions that link their construction to threats in the past from a huge, marauding "man-eating" snake are considered. When the snake, a metaphor for slave-raiding caravans, is further combined with archaeological evidence of hiding places, the impact of the slave trade can be read without reference to artifacts of conquest and capture.[8]

The nature of the data explored must be viewed broadly using all manner of material evidence for archaeological interpretation. Thus, in addition to the investigation and analysis of artifacts and structures, spatial organization and the construction of landscapes must also be included. All of these categories of material evidence are capable of manipulation by individuals or groups, whether intentionally or unintentionally. They may not all be artifacts or "objects," but they are all entangled in various webs of meaning.[9] By recognizing the potential to communicate, which is inherent in all kinds of human action, the detailed study and interpretation of the material evidence of past actions can expose us to the ways that social interactions were perceived and controlled by people caught up in new circumstances. Material evidence recovered from the Bight of Benin and compared with Elmina facilitates an understanding of the social processes that occurred during more than two hundred years of sustained intercultural contact and commerce primarily involving Africans and Europeans.

The Setting

The accounts of European travelers and traders document the presence of the Hueda and Dahomey states in the Bight of Benin region from at least 1660 to the end of the nineteenth century.[10] In contrast to Gold Coast trade destinations, such as Elmina where the Portuguese, and subsequently the Dutch, had maintained a trade castle since the late fifteenth century, European traders did not begin to frequent the Bight of Benin until the mid-seventeenth century.[11] There were several reasons for this: first and foremost, the primary motivation for the first two centuries of European trade in West Africa was the acquisition of gold, a commodity that could be obtained from the Fanti hinterland at Elmina, and not in the Bight of Benin. Second, the Atlantic shore of the Gold Coast offered numerous, well-protected inlets and bays, along with rocky promontories well suited to the construction of defensible European trading posts, whereas the Bight of Benin offered no such protected anchorages or castle sites. Thus it was not until the demand for a new commodity — the human cargo available in the Bight of Benin — escalated in the early seventeenth century, that the region that would become known as the "Slave Coast" became a regular destination of Europeans.

The middle of the seventeenth century ushered in a new era for the peoples of the Bight of Benin. In Brazil, the Caribbean, and the southeastern portion of North America plantation economies were beginning to expand, and with them the desire for enslaved Africans to provide the necessary labor. The growth of the Atlantic slave trade presented new opportunities and risks for the polities in the Bight of Benin. The introduction of new trading relations on the previously little-visited and impoverished coast overturned existing power relations, with the result that the Hueda, who had previously been subject to Allada, an interior state, found themselves in the key position to profit from the slave trade. The power associated with access to wealthy trading partners enabled the Hueda to throw off the yoke of Allada domination and become established as an autonomous political and economic power by about 1660.[12] At this time, the Hueda state enters into European written histories.[13]

Through sophisticated control and manipulation of multiple European trading partners,[14] the Hueda maintained their political autonomy for about sixty years. They ultimately lost their independence not at the hands of

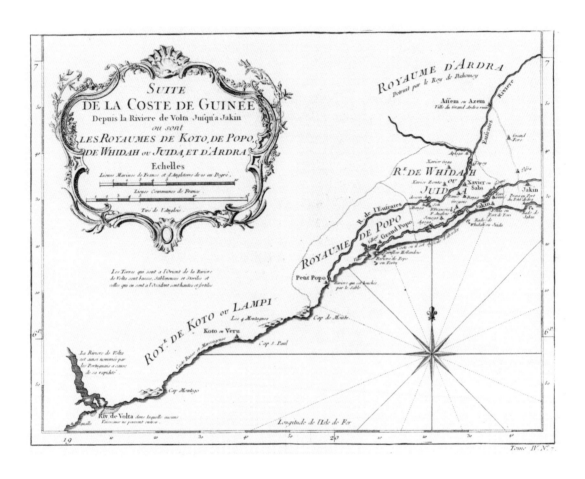

Fig. 2. Allada (Ardra) and Hueda (Whidah) Kingdoms of
the Slave Coast, Bight of Benin, ca. 1725

European colonists but through defeat by Dahomey, a rising power in the interior of the Bight of Benin.[15] Dahomey's growth, at the expense of neighboring countries, was due to the recognition by King Agadja (reigned 1708–32) that wealth and power were available to those who controlled trade with Europeans.[16] To this end, Dahomey began a military campaign aimed at securing access to the unfettered trade opportunities of the coast by first conquering Allada in 1724, and then Hueda in 1727.[17] With the Dahomean conquest of the Hueda, the European trading establishments decamped from Savi and relocated at Glewhe (modern Ouidah), closer to the coast, yet still some 3 kilometers inland from the shore (fig. 2). Dahomey continued the Hueda precedent of actively managing European trade opportunities by restricting European establishments to the town of Glewhe, and forbidding Europeans from visiting Abomey, the capital town of Dahomey.[18] Like Hueda, Dahomey actively encouraged the presence of multiple European trading nations. As before, the slave trade was central to the interactions between Europeans and Dahomey. Indeed, the slave trade remained important to Dahomey well after the official cessation of the slave trade instigated by the Danes, British, and Americans in the first decade of the nineteenth century, and continued after emancipation in British colonies in 1834–38. Gradually, as the legal slave trade to the French and Spanish islands and Brazil waned in the first half of the nineteenth century, so-called legitimate trade became increasingly important. Legitimate trade involved the production of agricultural products, particularly palm nuts and oil, by Africans for export and consumption in the European industrial economies.[19] For a variety of reasons, the Dahomean leadership never embraced legitimate trade to the same extent as they had the slave trade.

Archaeological and Historical Research

The histories of the towns of Savi and Ouidah, and their relationship to powerful African states as well as to their multiple European trading partners, provide an excellent context for the investigation of a series of anthropological questions. Foremost among these are the processes by which cultural transformations take place in settings of intercultural interaction,[20] and the way material culture plays a role in these transformations. An understanding of the ways in which African elites managed and negotiated the contradictions inherent in the presence of potentially controlling outsider traders provides an important corrective to the uncritical perspective that simply transplants the colonial experience of the late nineteenth and early twentieth centuries into earlier settings (fig. 3).[21] It is also important to study the ways in which economic opportunities for both Hueda and Dahomey were expressed in political change, and ultimately, the manner in which intercultural interaction resulted in an evolutionary trajectory for coastal people, from a tributary relationship to other African polities, through autonomy and independence, to eventual colonial administration. Investigating these questions at Savi and Ouidah is particularly interesting since there exists a sizable comparative data

Fig. 3. *Couronnement du roi de Juida,* 1700s [Europeans and Africans at the coronation of the Hueda king]
Probably from, or after an illustration in, Jean Baptiste Labat, *Voyage du chevalier Des Marchais en Guinée, isles voisines, et à Cayenne, fait en 1725, 1726 et 1727,* 2d ed. (Amsterdam: aux dépens de la Compagnie, 1731)

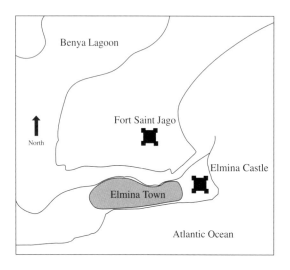

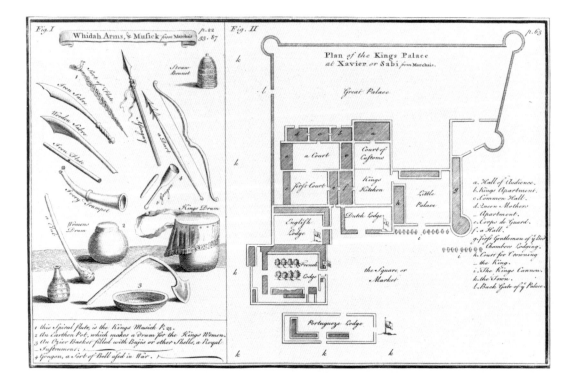

Fig. 4. Fort Saint Jago, Elmina Castle, and Elmina Town, 1400–1900
After Christopher R. DeCorse, "Culture Contact, Continuity, and Change
on the Gold Coast: A.D. 1400–1900," *African Archaeological Review* 10
(1992): 177

**Fig. 5. Engraving showing, at right, European trading lodges associated
with the Hueda palace complex at Savi, 1700s**

set from Elmina, Ghana. Elmina is the only other setting of significant and sustained African-European interaction that has been investigated from an archaeological as well as a historical perspective.[22] As the subject of intensive archaeological excavations directed by Christopher DeCorse, Elmina provides a setting that is remarkable for its broad similarities—and for its significant contrasts—to the experience of the Bight of Benin.[23] The two settings of Elmina and Hueda-Dahomey therefore permit the use of archaeological data including the use of space, architecture, and artifacts to investigate the indigenous responses to the precolonial and colonial encounters between Africans and Europeans.

It is essential to recognize and value important details provided by documentary evidence that would appear to be unavailable in any other fashion. Yet the archaeological data from Savi and from Elmina, even if considered without supporting written records, could stand alone to describe the unique and different processes of intercultural interaction that occurred in each setting. The messages materialized at Elmina and Savi by the location and construction of the European establishments are clear.[24] At Elmina, the castle stands at the end of a promontory forming the protected bay in which trading ships could anchor, safe under the guns of the castle (fig. 4). Furthermore, the imposing castle and its hilltop outlier (Fort Saint Jago) clearly command the entire setting where the Fanti town was located. At Savi, the European lodges were located within the precinct of the Hueda palace surrounded by ditches, and architecturally less imposing than the palace structures (fig. 5).[25] Not only were these trading lodges exposed to constant surveillance by the Hueda, they were isolated inland, separated from the sea and European support, by some 10 kilometers of track passing through several marshes and lagoons before arriving at the shore (see fig. 2).[26] The spatial arrangement and scale of European establishments alone demonstrate that substantially different social interactions were occurring at the two locations.

The range and numbers of artifacts recovered from excavations at Elmina and Savi in late-seventeenth- and early-eighteenth-century contexts further demonstrate that distinct processes were operating in each setting. Excavations at each site clearly show the significant presence of Europeans and European trade. Excavations throughout Savi have recovered small quantities of imported and locally manufactured tobacco pipes at nearly every location. Since European pipes are not durable artifacts, their widespread distribution points to the continued importation and availability of foreign goods throughout the five or more decades of Savi's heyday. The presence of local pipes, however, also signifies the strength of external trade as tobacco and smoking were not present in West Africa before the arrival of Europeans.[27] Indeed, the ubiquity of pipes at Savi demonstrates that Hueda people had broad access to at least some forms of imported goods, such as tobacco. Although European and Asian ceramics, glassware, and beads have been recovered from Savi as well, they are not distributed with the same frequency across the site. There is good reason, therefore, to believe that European imports were not supplementing or transforming many facets of Hueda culture, except perhaps in the elite district surrounding the palace site where their use may have had very specific ideological roles.[28]

In contrast to the relative paucity of imported artifacts at Savi, excavation at Elmina shows an acceptance of the material trappings associated with Europeans. While artifacts imported by European traders make up less than 10 percent of the total from Savi, they constitute closer to 50 percent of the assemblage at Elmina. It is important, however, that these artifacts not be interpreted as demonstrating the Europeanization of the Elmina residents. Rather, DeCorse has argued convincingly that the archaeological data reveal the process of cultural continuity or resistance, with Elminans remaining "African" in terms of their core beliefs or worldview.[29] The residents of Elmina were not becoming Europeanized, and yet they were undergoing "creolization," gradually making themselves into a unique and distinct cultural entity. This suggestion that Elminans were becoming something different than either the Europeans or the traditional Fanti can be supported by the analysis of multiple classes of archaeological data, including artifacts, burials, and architecture and spatial arrangements. Artifacts from Elmina suggest the process of material augmentation, not replacement, with imported goods being accepted, frequently in traditional ways, into daily life.[30] Burials also suggest the notion of supplementation; they are located in traditional settings, beneath the floors of houses, yet they incorporate imported material goods in place of traditional grave offerings. The incorporation of new forms when the old ones are still present creates a distinction that cannot be denied either in the past, or now in the present, between the "traditional" way of doing things, and the "new" or "modern" way. It can therefore be argued that the presence and use of new materials demonstrates modernity.

Architecture is one area where DeCorse believes that new ideas were adopted that were fundamentally different from local Fanti traditions. Archaeological finds demonstrate that many of the buildings in the Dutch period (1637–1871) of Elmina Town are built of dressed stone, a technique that is not present in the traditional Fanti hinterland of Elmina or in the earlier period town. Architectural evidence also suggests that the houses in the town that grew up around the Elmina castle were built with flat roofs, perhaps in imitation of the flat roofs on the castle constructed by the Dutch.[31] These transformations in the built environment indicate the materialization of difference between Elminans and other local Fanti people. When we also consider that imported artifacts were used in ways that may be "traditional" in terms of foodways or burial, we must also be aware of the messages communicated by those imported goods. For example, the intended, unspoken messages sent and received by individuals sharing food from Chinese and European bowls in a stone-built house with a flat roof may have contextualized very different social meanings than those meanings associated with sharing food from earthenware bowls in a traditional earth-and-wood house with a thatched roof. I would argue that residents of Elmina made conscious decisions to use

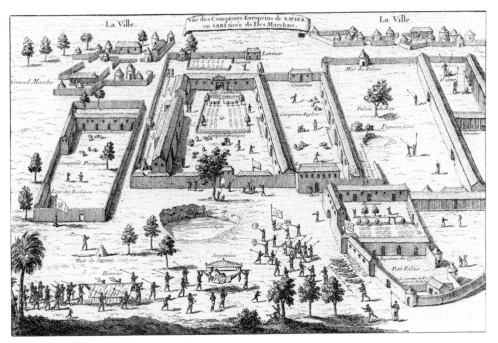

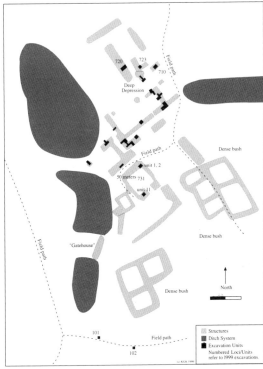

Fig. 6. *Vue des comptoirs Europeans de Xavier ou Sabis orée de Des Marchais,* 1700s [European trading lodges at Savi, adjacent to the Hueda palace complex]
Probably from, or after an illustration in, Jean Baptiste Labat, *Voyage du chevalier Des Marchais en Guinée, isles voisines, et à Cayenne, fait en 1725, 1726 et 1727,* 2d ed. (Amsterdam: aux dépens de la Compagnie, 1731)

Fig. 7. Hueda palace complex indicating structural mounds and excavation locations

these new materials precisely because of their "entangled" nature, and for the messages their use communicated that set them apart from the Fanti and others of the hinterland.

At Savi, architectural remains have been much more elusive than at Elmina, due in large part to the very different construction techniques. At Elmina, many structures were built with stone foundations and walls, whereas at Savi, all structures appear to have been built in the same fashion still current, with coursed earthen walls built directly on the ground, and without any foundation trenching. If architectural changes at Elmina do embody new notions of belonging and difference, we can see that Hueda sensibilities regarding architecture and the built environment did not undergo any significant changes as a result of European interaction. Data from Savi are limited, as the only structures that have been clearly identified and excavated to date are from the elite precinct, and these also present some unique occurrences of imported materials used in highly symbolic ways.[32] Indeed, the incorporation of Europeans into the palace complex at Savi is indicative of local incorporation and control over outsiders, albeit in a traditional, African manner (figs. 6, 7). Although commoner housing has not yet been located and exposed, it is highly likely — given the information from the elite district — that it would exhibit no transformations. Unfortunately, burial data, so important for identifying change and continuity in worldview at Elmina, have not been recovered from Savi.

There remains an additional line of evidence to further our understanding of how the arrival of Europeans impacted the Hueda people. There is little archaeological evidence to suggest that Savi existed as a major settlement before European trade began. Virtually every excavated context at Savi has some indication of European trade, whether the object is a bead, pipe fragment, shard of glass, or other imported wares. This lack of demonstrably pre-slave trade context strongly suggests that Savi grew to its prominence rapidly, and only after the Hueda achieved their independence from Allada in the 1660s. The formation of this new state and the rise to new levels of socio-political complexity appear to be responses to the pressures, and opportunities, of increased African-European interaction.[33] The difference between this scenario and what occurred at Elmina is that Elmina owed its existence to the establishment of the Portuguese fort, whereas Savi grew up with the incorporation of the Europeans within a traditional framework.

Dahomey and Ouidah in the Eighteenth Century: A Different Use of Space
Archaeological evidence demonstrates the continuation, and reinterpretation, of the unique intercultural interactions that occurred following the Dahomean conquest of Savi. The eighteenth century was a period of significant European demand for captives and also a period of considerable uncertainty for Dahomey. The Dahomean response to this uncertainty is apparent in their continued manipulation of the European presence. Dahomey's conquest of the coast and the Hueda state helped to facilitate their rise to the

status of a regional power, and yet they were not able to secure themselves as the dominant polity in the Bight of Benin region. A characteristic underlying all Dahomean actions throughout the eighteenth century and even into the nineteenth century was that despite repeated attempts to alter the situation, they remained a polity tributary to Oyo in the Nigerian interior.[34]

The Dahomean desire to ensure independence and complete autonomy is represented in the details of their relationship with European traders. In complete contrast to the Hueda, who incorporated the Europeans into the symbolic structure of the capital town, the Dahomean plan initially involved the isolation of the Europeans in an easily manageable cluster. Following the destruction of Savi, the Europeans retired to their now somewhat fortified trading warehouses at Glewhe, some 3 kilometers inland from the sea. Here the Europeans were isolated, each in their forts, located about 300 meters from one another (fig. 8). There was little, if any, permanent African settlement surrounding their establishments at this time, unlike the situation at Elmina. Limited excavation and archaeological survey in the quarters surrounding the locations of the European forts indicate the slow growth of African settlement. The lack of seventeenth- and early-eighteenth-century artifacts identified in the earthen walls of existing homes in the neighborhood of the English and Portuguese forts demonstrates that little or no occupation occurred until later in the eighteenth century.[35] This illustrates the dramatic contrast between Ouidah and Savi, and also Elmina, where African settlement was thick outside the walls of the castle.

Later in the eighteenth century, when the continued restriction of European traders to Ouidah attracted African settlement to the economically active areas surrounding the forts, the Dahomean rulers installed a powerful state official, called the Yovogan, to regulate trade and activities of the Europeans.[36] No archaeological work has been conducted in the region where the Yovogan is believed to have resided, although the study of a map of 1776 provides some interesting insights into how the Yovogan's presence structured spatial organization at Ouidah. In these illustrations (figs. 9, 10), the Yovogan's compound can be seen lying directly to the north of the English fort, and centered between the French and Portuguese establishments. This location is significant for demonstrating its ability to symbolically block European access to the interior. Similarly, the location of a Dahomean military camp, directly north of the French fort, conveys the same message. Interestingly, the area occupied by the Yovogan's compound in the late eighteenth and early nineteenth centuries is today the location of several other symbolically important components of the modern town, including the Catholic cathedral, the Python Temple (the location of the primary shrine to Dangbe, the serpent deity, present at least since the 1720s), and the police station. While one cannot be certain that this was a conscious decision, the suggestion bears consideration, as there is widespread precedent for the claiming of symbolic capital by placing significant structures in particular locations.

Fig. 8. *Vue sud ouest de Williams fort ou du Fort Guillaume à Juida,* 1700s
[the English fort, Ouidah]
Probably from, or after an illustration in, Jean Baptiste Labat, *Voyage du chevalier Des Marchais en Guinée, isles voisines, et à Cayenne, fait en 1725, 1726 et 1727,* 2d ed. (Amsterdam: aux dépens de la Compagnie, 1731)

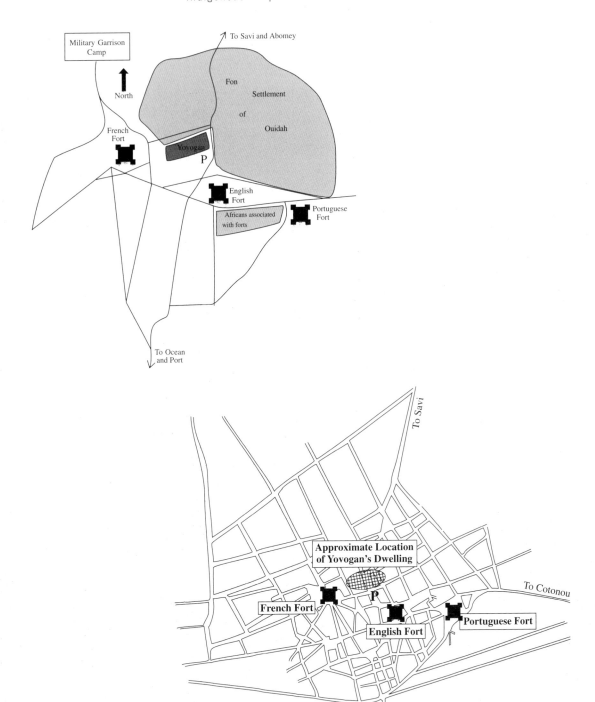

Fig. 9. Arrangement of European forts, African settlements, the military garrison, and the Yovognan's residence, 1776

P indicates the location of the Python Temple
After a map by the abbé Bullet reproduced in Simone Berbain, *Le comptoir français de Juda (Ouidah) au XVIIIe siécle* (Paris: Larose, 1942), pl. III

Fig. 10. European forts and Yovogan's dwelling, 1776

P indicates the location of the Python Temple; sites are superimposed on a modern street plan of Ouidah

Architecture as Evidence of Cultural Transformation

When considering archaeological and historical evidence for architecture at Elmina, DeCorse suggested that the town adjacent to the castle walls was qualitatively different from indigenous Fanti architecture used at other coastal settlements in the area. The limited survey and excavations undertaken within the town of Ouidah offer nothing to suggest a similar pattern of architectural transformation exhibited by local Africans. Indeed, there is nothing to suggest any innovation or other changes in Ouidah architecture throughout the eighteenth century and into the nineteenth century, despite increased wealth, opportunities for "Atlantic Creole" populations to develop, and participation in the Atlantic trade.[37] The first indications of architectural transformation within the town of Ouidah probably occur in the mid- to late nineteenth century, and are due to the growing numbers and importance of the Afro-Brazilians. The Afro-Brazilian community owes its origin to two sources: first, elements of the Afro-Brazilian community are descendant from Francisco Felix de Souza, a Brazilian slave trader who, during the first half of the nineteenth century, rose to a level of importance in Dahomey as Yovogan, surpassed only by the king himself. The second source is the return and settlement of Africans enslaved in Brazil, who had obtained their freedom and returned to Africa.[38] From these two sources a local community developed that remains distinct in a number of ways. Afro-Brazilians are predominantly Catholic, and have been so since the nineteenth century. They are characterized by distinct foodways that incorporate a number of Brazilian elements in their cuisine. Furthermore, their architecture is highly distinctive, incorporating a variety of styles and design elements that are unique to the Afro-Brazilians, and significant in the archaeological identification and interpretation of their presence and role in society. Particularly notable among these architectural features is the frequent presence of a second story.

The map of Ouidah shows the distribution of Afro-Brazilian architectural elements across the town (fig. 11). They are clustered in two discrete areas: the quarter today called Brésil and the neighboring Maro, and the quarter called Fonsaramè. In the absence of historical documentation that might tell us the economic importance of the Afro-Brazilian community, the size and scale of the architecture alone is sufficient to call attention to the structures. The concordance of location and style, where Afro-Brazilian detailing is found on structures that are clearly residences, as well as on buildings with commercial purpose, provides direct evidence of the economic importance of the Afro-Brazilians.

The contrast between the architectural style of traditional structures and the image put forth by the Afro-Brazilian buildings is readily apparent.[39] Afro-Brazilian houses are characterized by a contained plan, with rooms opening onto an enclosed veranda encircling the core of the structure. Thus one can remain inside the structure and still move from room to room. This is very different from traditional architecture where rooms generally open directly to the outside, with no hallways or internal passageways (figs. 12, 13).

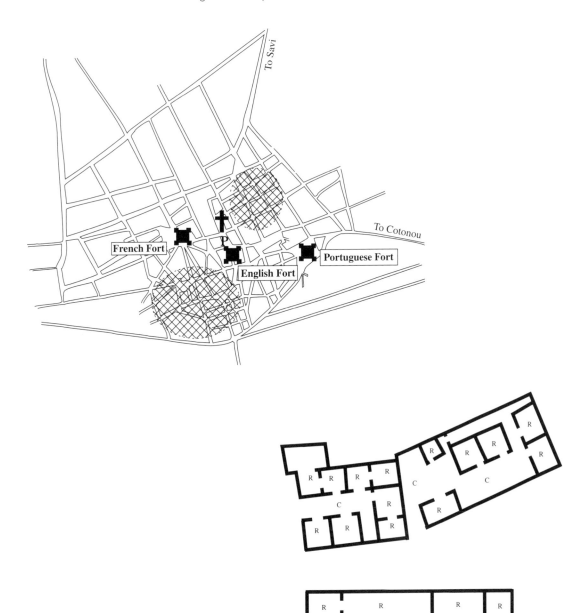

Fig. 11. Ouidah, late 1800s–mid-1900s
Cross-hatching indicates areas of greatest Afro-Brazilian concentration; cross indicates the location of the Catholic cathedral

Fig. 12. Contrasting floor plans of traditional Fon housing (above) and Afro-Brazilian housing (below)
After Alain Sinou, *Le comptoir de Ouidah: Une ville africaine singulière* (Paris: Éditions Karthala, 1995), 48, 117

Fig. 13. Afro-Brazilian villa in Ouidah, 1999

In this case one can pass from one room to the next only by going outside into the compound and entering through the next door. Notions of architectural appropriateness demonstrate a significant cultural transformation from traditional notions of space and proxemics to a new interpretation of space and the built environment.

At Ouidah this transformation in housing is due to the emigration of a new population, culturally distinct from the local Fon and Hueda people. Thus the evidence that is present for a form of creolization is somewhat deceptive. Certainly creolization was occurring, but it was not (at least in the late nineteenth and early twentieth centuries) the transformation of indigenous cultural forms; instead, it was the highly visible creolization of a new elite population. In this, the circumstances at Ouidah differ considerably from those at Elmina. The Elmina data demonstrate the transformation of a generalized Fanti culture into a distinctive Elmina culture, creolized perhaps through sustained contact with Portuguese, then Dutch, and finally British traders. What may further influence the difference between the two settings is the degree of control exerted by the culturally distinct "protocolonial" settlers. At Elmina, the Europeans demonstrated their ability to influence the Fanti through force, whereas at Ouidah, the Afro-Brazilian population was never "in charge," although some members were very important politically and economically. Thus archaeology presents evidence for the development of a distinctive African population at Elmina as far back as the seventeenth century, whereas the development of a culturally distinctive population in Ouidah relied on the immigration of people from Brazil, and their rise to economic prominence. Furthermore, it is important to keep in mind that the Afro-Brazilian colonial immigration was motivated not so much by monetary gain as by settlement and return, hence the expression of a greater visibility to assert their presence, naturalizing themselves to Ouidah.

Archaeology and Colonial Encounters in the Precolonial World

The sustained encounters between Europeans and Africans on the West African Coast frequently involved trade, exploitation, and establishment of permanent fortified garrisons defending mercantile interests. The Europeans did likewise. Yet the archaeological manifestations of these contact situations are apparently highly variable: in some regions, a great deal of cultural transformation or creolization occurred, while in other regions participating in the Atlantic trade little or no change can be discerned, at least when measured by the yardstick of material culture. In still others, what appears to have been significant trade and contact has left little evidence behind. Why do we see these differences and how can we explain them? The answer to the first question is relatively easy: we see these differences because we are looking for them. Archaeologists working on contact situations in Africa have seen their research demonstrate that simplistic notions of acculturation and domination derived from the early-twentieth-century period of direct European administration do not apply to the earlier centuries of interaction (if indeed such notions of acculturation have any validity). It is more difficult to explain this variation, although there are at least one or two significant variables. There have been only two large-scale archaeological projects investigating the process of cultural transformation in coastal West Africa during the period of the Atlantic trade, so our results are necessarily preliminary. Archaeological research on this topic is in its infancy, and, therefore, we lack an adequate comparative base. It is not at all surprising that observations from Elmina should differ from those at Savi/Ouidah. Perhaps it is more interesting that they differ so much, while having so much in common.

One of the most significant factors influencing long-term outcomes in each region is the specific circumstance surrounding the establishment of the initial European trade center. When, in the 1480s, the Portuguese began construction of their Elmina castle, they set the stage for all subsequent interactions with the local Fanti. Likewise, when the Hueda required the traders of many nationalities to settle within Savi, they too structured all the interaction to come. Thus, strategic decisions made by unknown Hueda officials, and the precedent set for subsequent Dahomean policy, were crucial. It is not known to what extent that decision was informed by knowledge of the interactions elsewhere on the coast; however, we can speculate that the Hueda policy, so at odds with virtually all other trade settings on the West African coast, must have been formed with some understanding of the potential consequences of their actions. Existing coastal trade networks would certainly have facilitated such knowledge.[40] The Hueda and Dahomey states were able to ensure their continued autonomy by playing various European traders off of one another. In compelling the Europeans to locate themselves at a considerable distance from the sea, the long-term weakness of the European presence could be maintained.

The role of the Afro-Brazilian community in precipitating change at Ouidah is also interesting. It is suggested that significant cultural transformation of the sort seen at Elmina in the seventeenth century did not occur until at least the middle of the nineteenth century in Ouidah, at which time it coincided with the rise to prominence of Afro-Brazilian émigrés. This transformation may be associated with the emulation of a new group of high-status people entangled in webs of social, political, and economic life, just as at Elmina there are suggestions that some of the transformations within Fanti settlements may be due to emulation of the Dutch. While these are intriguing suggestions, at this point we cannot be certain of the outcome. Only additional research will significantly further our understanding of the continuing social processes on the West African coast. Christopher DeCorse and his students are in the middle of a long-term project investigating the Fanti hinterland of Elmina and neighboring towns, and this will provide a richer base for comparisons between town and country. Other essential work has been conducted in the interior of Ghana at the northern boundary of the forest, investigating settlement complexes spanning more than five hundred years of change from pre-European times, through the imposition of colonial administration in the twentieth century.[41] Studies such as these are essential for understanding how the European impact may have manifested itself differently in the interior. Equally important, we await the results of work that will hopefully one day be conducted at yet other important sites elsewhere along the West African coast, such as Bunce Island in Sierra Leone. It is abundantly clear that complex cultural interactions such as those characterizing the precolonial and colonial period on the West African coast must be appreciated in all their rich variability. The interactions explored by different European and African polities were informed by the views held by the individuals involved in trade and contact, and it is the change and transformations in those views that we should seek.

It remains clear that in whatever context, be it the sustained and imposed European presence typifying Elmina and other coastal castles, the more tenuous toehold provided at the pleasure of African elites as at Savi, or the responses of interior societies to both the perceived and real threats of the slave trade, archaeology and the study of material culture can inform us of the ways in which different groups of people chose to interact. The Hueda, Fanti, or any other of the hundreds of ethnic or social groups who entered into new relationships as a result of the arrival of Europeans along the African coast each made conscious decisions about how to engage these novel situations. These choices and the societal transformations attendant on the exercise of chosen strategies were materialized in both intentional and unintentional ways through the expression of material culture.

Regardless of the strategies exercised by Europeans or Africans, the colonial juggernaut, foreshadowed by the establishment of trade castles and ending with the establishment of colonial governments in the late nineteenth century, was driven by commerce and commodities and generally not by settlement and the establishment of colonial production. New and challenging interpretations of colonialism must be expected in light of this significant contrast to many other well-known colonial encounters of the Columbian era. Archaeological and historical research in West Africa thus offers a unique opportunity for investigating the processes of cultural transformation in settings characterized by indigenous autonomy, power, and agency, rather than the wholesale imposition of new and dominant societies. As is demonstrated by the archaeological record of Elmina, Savi, and other West African settings, the direction and manifestations of those cultural transformations vary according to the histories and the activities of each group.

Notes

The research at Savi and Ouidah would not have been possible without the encouragement of Professor Merrick Posnansky of the University of California, Los Angeles and Professors Alexis Adandé and Elisée Soumonni of the Université nationale du Bénin. The cooperation and support of the Ministry of Cultural Patrimony, Republic of Bénin, and the staff of the Museum of History in Ouidah is gratefully acknowledged.

This research has been supported financially in part by the UCLA Department of Anthropology, the UCLA Institute of Archaeology, a Fulbright grant, the University Research Expeditions Program (UREP) of the University of California, and the University of South Carolina College of Liberal Arts. The comments and suggestions offered by Claire Lyons, Richard Lindstrom, John Papadopoulos, and Cécile Kelly have improved the paper considerably, although any errors or omissions are my own. I thank Claire Lyons for inviting me to participate in the Fourth World Archaeological Congress in Cape Town, South Africa.

1. For a detailed history of Hueda and Dahomey from documentary sources, see Robin Law, *The Slave Coast of West Africa, 1550–1750: The Impact of the Atlantic Slave Trade on an African Society* (Oxford: Clarendon, 1991).

2. Kenneth G. Kelly, "The Archaeology of African-European Interaction: Investigating the Social Roles of Trade, Traders, and the Use of Space in the Seventeenth- and Eighteenth-Century Hueda Kingdom, Republic of Bénin," *World Archaeology* 28 (1997): 77–95.

3. Christopher R. DeCorse, "Culture Contact and Change in West Africa," in James G. Cusick, ed., *Studies in Culture Contact: Interaction, Culture Change, and Archaeology* (Carbondale: Center for Archaeological Investigations, Southern Illinois University, 1998).

4. Nicholas Thomas, *Entangled Objects: Exchange, Material Culture, and Colonialism in the Pacific* (Cambridge: Harvard Univ. Press, 1991).

5. John Bintliff, ed., *The Annales School and Archaeology* (Leicester: Leicester Univ. Press, 1991); Kenneth G. Kelly, "African History/African Archaeology: Towards an Understanding of the Social Consequences of European/African Trade in West Africa," *Journal of Archaeological Method and Theory* 4 (1997): 353–66; and A. Bernard Knapp, ed., *Archaeology, Annales, and Ethnohistory* (Cambridge: Cambridge Univ. Press, 1992).

6. Larry W. Yarak, "West African Coastal Slavery in the Nineteenth Century: The Case of the Afro-European Slaveowners of Elmina," *Ethnohistory* 36 (1989): 44–60.

7. Law, *Slave Coast* (note 1).

8. Kenneth G. Kelly, "The African Diaspora from the Ground Up: The Importance of Historical Archaeology for Diaspora Studies" (paper presented at the conference "La ruta del esclavo en Hispanoamerica," San Jose, Costa Rica, 1999).

9. Thomas, *Entangled Objects* (note 4).

10. François de Medeiros, ed., *Peuples du Golfe du Bénin* (Paris: Éditions Karthala, 1984).

11. Law, *Slave Coast* (note 1).

12. Kenneth G. Kelly, "Long Distance Trade and State Formation: The Archaeology of the Hueda State, Bénin, West Africa" (paper presented at the Fourteenth Biennial Conference of the Society for Africanist Archaeologists, Syracuse, New York, 1998).

13. Law, *Slave Coast* (note 1).

14. Kelly, "African-European Interaction" (note 2).

15. Robin Law, *Correspondence from the Royal African Company's Factories at Offra and Whydah on the Slave Coast of West Africa in the Public Record Office, London, 1678–93* (Edinburgh: Centre of African Studies, Edinburgh University, 1990);

Law, *Slave Coast* (note 1); and David Ross, "The Dahomean Middleman System, 1727–c. 1818," *Journal of African History* 28 (1987): 357–75.

16. David Henige and Marion Johnson, "Agaja and the Slave Trade: Another Look at the Evidence," *History in Africa* 3 (1976): 91–126; Law, *Slave Coast* (note 1); and David Ross, "The Anti-Slave Trade Theme in Dahoman History: An Examination of the Evidence," *History in Africa* 9 (1982): 263–71. See I. A. Akinjogbin, *Dahomey and Its Neighbors, 1708–1818* (Cambridge: Cambridge Univ. Press, 1967), for the alternate view that Agadja was in fact attempting to eradicate the slave trade.

17. Ross, "Middleman System" (note 15).

18. Ross, "Middleman System" (note 15), 369.

19. Robin Law, "Introduction," in idem, ed., *From Slave Trade to "Legitimate" Commerce: The Commercial Transition in Nineteenth-Century West Africa* (Cambridge: Cambridge Univ. Press, 1995), 1–31.

20. Edward M. Schortman and Patricia A. Urban, eds., *Resources, Power, and Interregional Interaction* (New York: Plenum, 1992).

21. Compare Michael Dietler, "Consumption, Agency, and Cultural Entanglement: Theoretical Implications of a Mediterranean Colonial Encounter," in James G. Cusick, ed., *Studies in Culture Contact: Interaction, Culture Change, and Archaeology* (Carbondale: Center for Archaeological Investigations, Southern Illinois University, 1998).

22. Christopher R. DeCorse, *An Archaeology of Elmina: Africans and Europeans on the Gold Coast, 1400–1900* (Washington, D.C.: Smithsonian Institution Press, 2001); Christopher R. DeCorse, "Culture Contact, Continuity, and Change on the Gold Coast: A.D. 1400–1900," *African Archaeological Review* 10 (1992): 163–96; and Yarak, "Coastal Slavery" (note 6).

23. DeCorse, "Culture Contact" (note 3).

24. Elizabeth de Marrais, Luis Jaime Castillo, and Timothy Earle, "Ideology, Materialization, and Power Strategies," *Current Anthropology* 37 (1996): 15–31.

25. Kelly, "African-European Interaction" (note 2).

26. Law, "Introduction" (note 19), 1–31.

27. John Edward Philips, "African Smoking Pipes," *Journal of African History* 24 (1983): 303–19.

28. Kenneth G. Kelly, "Transformation and Continuity in Savi, a West African Trade Town: An Archaeological Investigation of Culture Change on the Coast of Bénin during the Seventeenth and Eighteenth Centuries" (Ph.D. diss., University of California, Los Angeles, 1995); and Kelly, "African-European Interaction" (note 2).

29. DeCorse, "Culture Contact" (note 3).

30. DeCorse, *An Archaeology of Elmina* (note 22); and DeCorse, "Culture Contact" (note 3).

31. DeCorse, "Culture Contact" (note 3).

32. Kelly, "African-European Interaction" (note 2).

33. Kelly, "Long Distance" (note 12).

34. Law, *Slave Coast* (note 1).

35. Kenneth G. Kelly, "Preliminary Historic Archaeological Research at Ouidah, Bénin" (paper presented at the Eleventh Biennial Conference of the Society for Africanist

Archaeologists, University of California, Los Angeles, 1992).

36. Law, *Slave Coast* (note 1).

37. Ira Berlin, "From Creole to African: Atlantic Creoles and the Origins of African-American Society in Mainland North America," *William and Mary Quarterly* 53 (1996): 251–88; and Peter Mark, "The Evolution of 'Portuguese' Identity: Luso-Africans on the Upper Guinea Coast from the Sixteenth to the Early Nineteenth Century," *Journal of African History* 40 (1999): 173–91.

38. Jerry Michael Turner, "Les Brésiliens — The Impact of Former Brazilian Slaves upon Dahomey" (Ph.D. diss., Boston University, 1974).

39. See Peter Mark, "'Portuguese' Architecture and Luso-African Identity in Senegambia and Guinea, 1730–1890," *History in Africa* 23 (1996): 179–96, for a similar discussion in reference to Senegambia.

40. Robin Law, "Between the Sea and the Lagoons: The Interaction of Maritime and Inland Navigation on the Precolonial Slave Coast," *Cahiers d'études africaines* 29 (1989): 209–37.

41. Ann B. Stahl, "The Archaeology of Global Encounters Viewed from Banda, Ghana," *African Archaeology Review* 16 (1999): 5.

Ambiguous Matters:
Colonialism and Local Identities
in Punic Sardinia

Peter van Dommelen

The term *colonial* is widely used in Mediterranean archaeology to describe situations in which the archaeological and historical evidence shows people living in clearly distinct settlements in a "foreign" region or enclave at some distance from their place of origin. The situation most often referred to in these terms is the Greek presence in southern Italy and Sicily from the eighth century B.C. onward. The prominence of the Greek cities even gave this region the name of Magna Graecia. Other cases are the Roman occupation of the Mediterranean and northwestern Europe, the Phoenician settlements in the central and western Mediterranean, and the Greek presence on the shores of the Black Sea. While these may be less well known, they should certainly not be regarded as somehow "less colonial."

The colonial terminology commonly used to refer to these situations has never been questioned, because the abundant archaeological evidence clearly shows a sharp contrast between the local cultures of, for instance, the Italian and Spanish mainland and the Greek or Phoenician presence in these regions. The arrival of both Greeks and Phoenicians in the western Mediterranean is moreover well documented by numerous classical authors who have written extensively about the foundation of new cities in foreign countries, explicitly labeling these as *coloniae*. It is because the colonial terminology appeared to provide a coherent and transparent framework for studying a wide variety of loosely related situations, colonialism has become a well-established and prominent feature of Mediterranean and classical archaeology and ancient history.

Colonial Implications

Despite numerous assumptions and suggestions to the contrary, it does not follow from the obvious association between the ancient and modern words that the meanings and connotations of colonial terminology must be identical: colonialism in (early) modern times is commonly associated with violence, political domination, and economic exploitation of indigenous peoples, but the ancient terms primarily referred to absence from home and being in a foreign country. While the Latin term *colonia* denotes a settlement deliberately established elsewhere, which is admittedly akin to modern usage, its Greek equivalent *apoikía* literally means "away from home." Neither of these

terms implies violent occupation or exploitation of the region involved —
although they do not exclude it either. The association of the Roman notion
of imperium with modern concepts of imperialism is similarly misleading,
because the former basically denotes "power to command" in a generic sense,
with particular reference to administrative and military authority,[1] while
the latter is usually regarded as a specific historical, strictly early modern,
phenomenon.[2]

Given the absence of reflection on colonial terminologies and the lack of
theoretical discussion of colonialism in Mediterranean archaeology, it does
not come as a surprise that the impact of modern connotations and catego-
rizations on representations of ancient colonial situations has been considerable, as recent reviews have shown.[3] In this essay, I therefore intend to discuss
the implications of the term *colonial* in ancient colonial situations and to
review it in the light of modern debates on colonial representations. Subsequently, I shall elaborate these ideas in the specific colonial situations of
the Mediterranean island of Sardinia under Carthaginian and Roman domination, drawing on detailed archaeological evidence for the Classical and
Hellenistic periods.

Understanding Colonial Societies

Representations of ancient Mediterranean colonialism have been heavily
influenced by modern colonial situations in the late-nineteenth- and early-
twentieth-century Mediterranean and elsewhere.[4] The British and French
colonial authorities in particular were quick to point out the similarities
between the Roman domination of the Mediterranean and their own occupation of the Levant and the Maghreb, and to justify their own occupation
with reference to their Roman "predecessors."[5] The French colonial army in
Algeria, for instance, not only took the initiative for the restoration of numerous Roman monuments in the country but also used these as models for their
own memorials.[6] At the same time, contemporary colonial experiences largely
shaped representations of ancient colonialism. For instance, the British historian T. R. S. Broughton clearly expressed contemporary colonialist ideas when
he wrote about the "native populations" of the Mediterranean that "it is
doubtful if they had remained untouched by foreign influence whether they
would have evolved any advanced political or social organization."[7] Both this
statement and the French construction of a direct historical connection
between the Roman and modern occupation of the Maghreb bear witness to a
clear sense of (modern) colonial superiority that was projected onto the past.

In more recent years, this one-sided view has been broadened to include
the local inhabitants of colonized regions. Although Marcel Bénabou argued
as early as 1976 in *La résistance africaine à la romanisation* that the North
African people played an active part in the shaping of society and economy of
Roman North Africa,[8] the idea of a substantial indigenous contribution has
only in recent years started to find its way into Mediterranean and Classical
archaeology. The changing views of the Greek colonization of southern Italy

are a case in point, because until recently there has been more attention to the relationships between the various colonial foundations and their "mother-cities" in Greece than to the regional context of indigenous settlement and local social organization—which is of course a valid research goal in itself, but not one that sheds much light on specific colonial situations.[9] With regard to the earliest Greek foundation of Pithekoussai in the Bay of Naples, for example, academic debate has tended to focus on the collaboration between colonizing Euboean Greeks and Phoenicians and on the role of the Euboeans in the early stages of Greek colonialism.[10] Even when contacts with indigenous inhabitants of the Italian peninsula have been considered, attention has still tended to focus on the Etruscans rather than on the local inhabitants of western Campania.[11] There has, on the whole, been remarkably little attention in discussions of Pithekoussai for the wealth of data on indigenous Iron Age settlement and burials in the Campanian hinterland of the Bay of Naples—which in turn are primarily discussed in their indigenous context.[12] Even in a rare discussion of Pithekoussai in its regional Campanian context, the emphasis is entirely on the Greek impact on the indigenous inhabitants of Campania: in the end, the latter are still not seen as contributing to the colonial situation in any substantial way.[13]

Recognizing that both colonizers and colonized make up a colonial situation still does not, however, adequately address the issue of their mutual relationships. As it was pointed out in response to Bénabou's study, emphasizing the ways in which indigenous resistance against colonial domination shapes the colonial situation actually underscores the leading role of the colonizers, because such a view is ultimately based on the principle of colonial primacy.[14] As a consequence, the "colonial divide" is effectively reified as the principal characteristic of colonial situations and the relationships between the two constituents are no longer the object of study, because they are a priori assumed to be antagonistic.

From a theoretical point of view, such a binary representation of colonial society is flawed in several respects. The most important one is the underlying holistic notion of culture, which reduces colonial situations to a clash between two autonomous but isolated entities. In the first place, there is no room for human agency in these mechanistic views of contact and acculturation, because social groups and social practice are determined by the overarching culture. In the second place, each of the two opposing sides of a colonial situation is assumed to possess an intrinsic and irreducible essence in which the cultural identity of each group is grounded. In this view, colonial—or indigenous—objects fully retain their "original" meaning as a colonial—or indigenous—product, regardless of their context. From this perspective, for instance, distributions of imported Greek vessels in southern Italian and Sicilian contexts have often been regarded as literally "measuring" the degree of "Hellenization" of the indigenous culture.[15] Both this view and the associated approach, however, run counter to current notions of the meaning of material culture as actively constructed by groups of people interacting in specific contexts.[16] Nor are they in keeping with recent ethnographic observations of material culture in (early) modern contexts, which, for instance, have shown that imported Western objects were perceived and used in the nineteenth- and twentieth-century Pacific in ways that were not necessarily related to Western ideas about these items.[17] Despite common assumptions of the opposite, Greek imports in south Italian cemeteries, therefore, do not necessarily denote Greek culture, as has been demonstrated for imported Euboean pottery in a variety of places in the Mediterranean.[18] The Greek imports found in combination with unusually "un-Greek" burial customs at Morgantina (Sicily) similarly show that Greek objects and customs had been integrated in local traditions and conventions, as can also be deduced from the settlement evidence.[19] The meaning and significance of the Greek objects must consequently be sought in the *local* web of meanings that was spun around local and imported material culture in the indigenous setting.

These theoretical arguments against dualist representations of colonial situations as defined by a clear-cut colonial divide find firm support in concrete historical and ethnographic evidence, which shows that colonial situations were not as neatly organized as conventional views suggest. Although the contrast between colonial and indigenous was usually well marked, not all inhabitants of a colonized region could be unambiguously categorized as either colonial or indigenous, as the essentialist perspective would have it. Other divisions of society along the lines of gender, class, or profession cut across the colonial divide.[20] Even the terms *colonial* and *indigenous* are less straightforward than they might seem, because they can be defined in more than one way: people of colonial descent whose families have lived in the colony for several generations, for instance, undermine essentialist classifications, because they qualify for either category, being "native" in a literal sense and colonial in terms of their origins.

In recent history, the Algerian town of Annaba has provided a fine example of the ways in which distinctions between indigenous and colonial notions of identity can be obscured. Although the French colonizers evidently brought about major changes in the regional demography when they established the town under the name of Bône in 1832, census documents of the late nineteenth century show a remarkably varied situation where colonization had given rise to anything but a homogenous French society.[21] The evidence shows that the inhabitants of Annaba consisted of more groups than just French colonizers and colonized Algerians, as there were substantial numbers of Arab-speaking Jews and Europeans of other than French nationality. Furthermore, while the Algerians and Jews largely made up the permanently settled community of the town and most Europeans, including the French, tended to stay only limited periods for administrative or commercial jobs, there was also a group of people of French descent who resided permanently in Annaba. To complicate matters further, large numbers of south Italian and Maltese men stayed in the town on a seasonal basis. In time, this situation became still more complex, as ever more people were born and raised in

Fig. 1. Henri Dormoy
L'Algérie, 1830–1930: Pays de grande production agricole [poster celebrating agricultural production in colonial Algeria, with colonial farmer overseeing indigenous workers]
Éditions publicitaires Henri Dormoy
Paris, 1929, lithograph on backing, 113 × 80 cm (44½ × 31½ in.)
Los Angeles, Getty Research Institute

Annaba, no matter their descent, while the overall number of inhabitants remained stable: by the 1930s, nearly everyone in Annaba was "native" in a literal sense.

It is in this context that the terms *pied noir* and *évolué* were coined (fig. 1).[22] Although both terms referred to people born and raised in French North Africa and educated according to French norms, often in France itself, they suggested a substantial difference between the two, as the former indicated French descent and the latter a local North African background. The significance of these terms is precisely that they tried to impose a distinction between these groups of people, whose intermediate situations were in reality quite similar, since neither was entirely colonial nor fully indigenous.

While the specific situation of French North Africa is first and foremost part of modern Western colonialism, it nevertheless has a bearing on ancient colonial situations. Its relevance resides in the contrast between, on the one hand, the inevitably complex reality of colonial situations as in Annaba, and on the other hand, the attempts of the people actually living in these conditions to construct their own identity in relation to one another and to the colonial context. It also underscores the problematic distinction between colonial and indigenous. Although French North Africa surely cannot be taken as a general model for ancient colonial situations because of the obvious and fundamental discrepancies between modern and ancient colonialism, it does suggest that even obvious differences as observed in the material culture of, for instance, the Greek colonies and Italic settlements of south Italy should not be taken at face value. More particularly, the differences need not necessarily be interpreted in terms of a divided colonial society — especially since the emphasis on the colonial divide may well be a recent Western notion itself.

Postcolonial Theory and Colonial Ambivalence

Contrasts between reality and representation as observed in Annaba stand at the heart of the postcolonial critique of Western colonialism, which claims that cultural representations of a colonial situation matter just as much as the daily economic reality in the colonized area.[23] Considerations of representation and discourse have gained academic ground since Edward Said demonstrated in his seminal study *Orientalism* how Western domination over the Middle East was as much grounded in literary and historical representations as in military and economic power.[24] In Said's wake, the aspirations of postcolonial theory go, therefore, well beyond the literary realm.

In practice, however, many postcolonial studies of (early) modern Western imperialism focus rather narrowly on the analysis of literary representations of colonial situations and tend to overlook the historical and cultural contexts of these representations. This lack of historical contextualization, in fact, seriously undermines many postcolonial analyses of nineteenth-century literature and artwork.[25] Postcolonial theory need not be ahistorical or oriented solely toward literature, as a growing number of anthropological and historical studies demonstrate.[26] These show how "culture" and representation in general have been an integral part of Western colonialism in early modern Africa and Asia. They explicitly underpin the postcolonial claim that colonial domination is more than just a matter of economic exploitation and political or military power. They also make it clear that all forms of representation can be analyzed in order to understand how they contributed to the construction and maintenance of colonial domination. Underlying this approach is an understanding of power and discourse as advocated by Foucault and Said, which regards discourse as a practice that takes place in, and which is very much part of, a given social context.[27] It follows from this view that studying the material conditions of discourse and representations has just as much to say about the social context as an analysis of the discourse itself.

Despite the obvious archaeological relevance of this point, postcolonial theory has not had any significant follow-up in archaeology. The few archaeological studies that have been inspired by postcolonial theory have remained restricted to the analysis of contemporary archaeological writing about colonial situations in the past, thus adhering to the literature and discourse-oriented approach.[28] A good example is the discussion of the impact of T. J. Dunbabin's own experiences of the British "imperial present" on his representation of the "ancient past" of Greek colonialism in southern Italy as described in his landmark publication, *The Western Greeks*.[29] What is conspicuously lacking in archaeology at large, however, are discussions of concrete colonial situations in the past that are informed by postcolonial notions and insights or the historical and ethnographic explorations of recent and contemporary colonialism.

This reluctance is likely to stem from the admittedly problematic issue of whether observations and conclusions regarding modern Western colonialism can be transposed to premodern contexts. This is an issue that has not received much attention in postcolonial studies in general, partly because these have little diachronic interest and partly because they lack historical contextualization. It is clearly a problem that cannot easily be resolved, because of the inherently situated nature of colonial situations and colonial discourse. While there are many aspects of modern colonialism that are peculiar to the age of capitalism and modernity, postcolonial theory has both perspectives and insights to offer that are more generally, if not universally valid — and that consequently are relevant to studies of ancient colonialism. The significance of the cultural dimension for colonial situations represents, for instance, one of the major general principles of postcolonial studies, which goes beyond particular temporal and spatial contexts, as is demonstrated by its relevance to a wide variety of early modern and contemporary colonial situations.[30] Other features, however, are more specific and cannot automatically be transposed to other periods or places. The emphasis on racism in late-nineteenth-century Western colonial representations is a case in point:[31] since racism seems to have been much less prominent in earlier periods, many of the postcolonial conclusions about racist representations must be seen as period-specific and are hardly relevant to ancient colonialism.[32] It is precisely at this point that cross-cultural comparison has a role to play, since comparison of different colonial situations can help to identify the structural elements and particular conditions of various instances of colonialism. Careful consideration of the pertinence of postcolonial notions is, consequently, a necessary prerequisite for considering ancient or more generally premodern colonialism.

This holds, in particular, for the twin notions of ambiguity and ambivalence, which have been brought to the fore by the postcolonial theoretician Homi Bhabha as the key to an understanding of the contrast between reality and representation as observed in the colonial Maghreb, as they draw attention to "the more complex cultural and political boundaries that exist on the cusp of these often opposed political spheres."[33] While the contrast itself is likely to constitute a recurrent, if not universal, feature of colonial situations, as there will always be some communities or groups who "fit" neither "side" of the alleged colonial divide,[34] Bhabha's interpretation of these notions may well be exclusive to modern colonialism, as he draws heavily on psychoanalytical insights into Western society. In his view, ambivalence and ambiguity capture the tension between, on the one hand, the Western ambition to "civilize the natives" and to transform them to their own image, and on the other hand, the wish to maintain the differences with the colonized: in Bhabha's words, the colonial Other had to be *"almost the same, but not quite."*[35] The absence of any notion of a "civilizing mission" in antiquity, however, seriously undermines the relevance of this view for ancient colonialism, as there are no indications in ancient texts of any urge to "improve" the inhabitants of the colonized regions and to transform them to colonial standards. The absence of ancient equivalents of modern missionaries and schools for literally educating the natives is worthwhile noting, because they constitute critical features of modern Western colonialism.[36] Even if ancient accounts of "barbarians" show that a sense of Greek and Roman superiority did exist, this does in no way resemble Western ideas about "educating the natives" as a moral colonial duty.[37] Greek colonialism was, in fact, inspired by wholly other concerns, and it was accordingly represented in quite different terms.[38]

Of a rather different order is Bhabha's observation that stereotypes are instrumental in emphasizing the difference of the colonial Other by constructing exaggerated representations such as "the lazy native." According to Bhabha, exaggeration is a necessary aspect of such stereotypes, which "must always be in *excess* of what can be empirically proved or logically construed."[39] For the same reason, stereotypes need constant reassertion in order to become widely shared. Crucial, however, is the ambivalence that the stereotype *might* be true. The wider significance of Bhabha's claim is that expressions such as "the lazy native" should not be understood literally—they usually were not, as is demonstrated by the widespread use of "natives" as a workforce—but rather that they underscore the contrast between the indigenous inhabitants and the colonizers, who regarded themselves as modern and industrious. In this view, stereotyping is understood as a way of classifying or categorizing the social reality people live in. As such it is a common and, indeed, necessary element of constructing and perceiving identities.[40] Given the inherent complexity and confusion of colonial situations, I would argue that stereotypes in this broad sense should be regarded as a common and recurrent feature of colonial encounters, although the *content* of the stereotypes is necessarily of a historically specific nature.

As argued by Bhabha in a somewhat different way, ambiguity is then the necessary companion of stereotypes, because reality inevitably fails to conform to these—often binary—classifications. It is, therefore, only Bhabha's interpretation of ambiguity in terms of racism and the Western *mission civilisatrice* that is strictly modern and is entirely appropriate for his discussion of modern colonialism. Ambiguity and stereotyping in themselves need not be racist and indeed have only become so with the increasing emphasis on race in the late nineteenth century. In a more generic and not necessarily racist sense, both ambiguity and stereotyping can therefore be regarded as recurring features of colonial situations, including premodern ones in the ancient Mediterranean.

The relevance of all of this for archaeologists lies in the implications that these considerations have for the study of the relationships between the colonizing and the colonized inhabitants of a given region: if stereotypes and ambiguity can be expected to contribute to the construction of identities in a colonial situation, then these notions must be taken into account in archaeological and historical interpretations of developments such as the imitation of colonial material culture by colonized indigenous communities. More specifically, these considerations amount to a critical review of the interpretation of material culture in colonial situations: What does it mean in terms of the self-representation of the communities involved when colonial objects are incorporated in an indigenous context or even replace traditional local products? Bhabha's remarks about mimicry and ambivalence cannot be ignored, because they add an entirely new dimension to conventional interpretations: the usually tacit assumption that the adoption of colonial (material) culture by the inhabitants of a colonized region marks the transformation of indigenous to colonial society—or even its substitution—seems astoundingly simplistic in the light of Bhabha's comments and ethnographic observations about the connotations and implications carried by colonial and indigenous culture.

Given the inherent complexities of colonial situations and the range of colonial and indigenous nuances that can be expected, there clearly is a case for reconsidering modern conventional representations of colonialism in the ancient Mediterranean and for focusing archaeological discussion on the concrete evidence of specific colonial situations. I shall therefore concentrate on the Mediterranean island of Sardinia where in the course of a few centuries the local inhabitants of the west central region faced both Carthaginian and Roman colonial intervention.

Colonialism and Settlement in Punic Sardinia

Punic settlement on Sardinia developed from the previously established Phoenician foundations on the southern and western coasts of the island and initially remained confined to a limited number of small circumscribed areas such as headlands or enclosed coastal plains. They were part of a much wider network that covered most of the western Mediterranean and was especially strong in North Africa, western Sicily, Sardinia, southern Spain, and the Balearic Islands.[41] The loosely shared cultural background of these regions and their Phoenician origins are generally referred to as "Punic." The city of Carthage was economically and culturally dominant in this network; therefore, it is possible to trace a specifically "Carthaginian" influence throughout the Punic world of the western Mediterranean. In Sardinia, colonial settlement initially — until the late fifth century B.C. — comprised only a limited number of nucleated colonial establishments, which moreover remained confined to rather isolated coastal headlands and small islands. They coexisted with a large number of dispersed indigenous settlements in the interior of the island, but contacts between the inhabitants of these colonial and indigenous settlements seem to have been occasional.[42]

This situation began to change dramatically by the end of the fifth century B.C., when a rapidly increasing number of sites with a new, ostensibly colonial appearance was established throughout the inland regions of southern Sardinia. Reliable evidence of this kind has so far been recorded only in Sardinia and on Ibiza, but there are indications of similar developments in the North African hinterland of Carthage, which suggest a major reorganization of the entire Carthaginian colonial network. As documented by excavations and surface collections in various regions of Sardinia, this development resulted in a substantial variety of colonial settlements, ranging from major colonial cities to small isolated farmsteads.[43] In the particular region of west central Sardinia, the former were represented by the city of Tharros, which had been founded on the remote San Marco headland in the Phoenician period (fig. 2). A slightly different category of colonial settlement, was made up by the two minor towns of Othoca and Neapolis. Like Tharros, they were substantial nucleated settlements, but in contrast to this city, they were situated farther inland and had been established in the late Phoenician and early Punic periods (seventh–sixth centuries B.C.). The large numbers of small- and medium-sized isolated rural sites established after the fifth century B.C. constitute a third type of colonial settlement, which, unlike the previous ones, can be found throughout the region, both in the low-lying wetlands around the bay of Oristano and further inland in the Campidano plain.[44] Intensive field surveying in the southern Arborèa by the Leiden-Glasgow Riu Mannu project has shown that these small rural sites mostly represent single farmsteads, in which the inhabitants worked the surrounding land and participated in both local and wider colonial exchange networks.[45] As the remarkable concentration of these sites in the wetlands of the southern Arborèa demonstrates, colonial settlement was also rather unevenly distributed within this region.

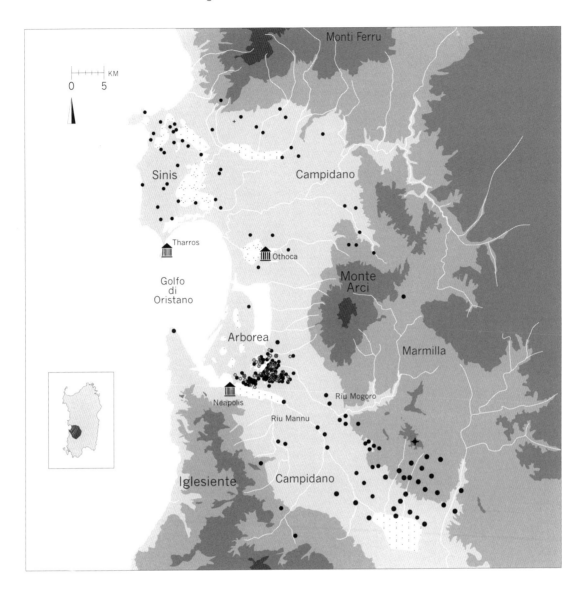

Fig. 2. West central Sardinia

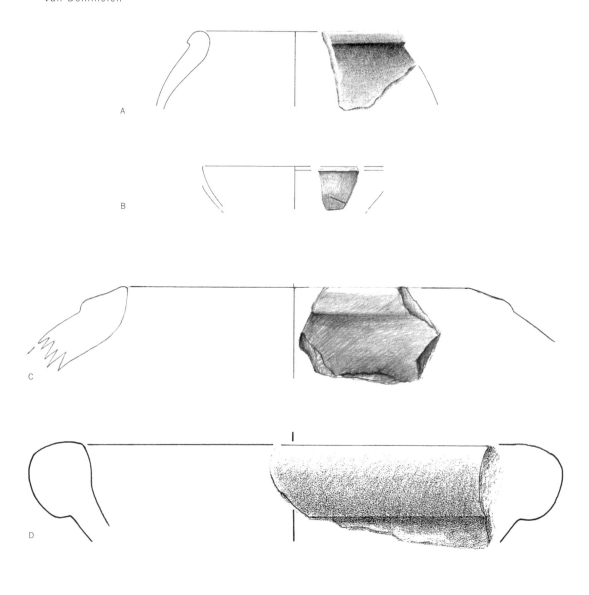

Fig. 3. Punic pottery locally produced in west central Sardinia (area of the Riu Mannu estuary)
A: Punic neckless transport amphora (type Bartoloni D), 300–200 B.C., Diam: 14 cm (5½ in.);
B: Punic neckless transport amphora (type Bartoloni D), 400–200 B.C., Diam: 14 cm (5½ in.);
C: Punic open bowl (type via Brenta VI), 400–200 B.C., 17 cm (6⅝ in.); D: Punic deep bowl
(type via Brenta III), 400–200 B.C., Diam: 20 cm (7⅞ in.)

Both the farms and the towns qualify as "colonial" settlement, because they were thoroughly Punic in appearance, even if most of the domestic pottery and amphorae were locally produced. Vessel types and decorations of all local products met Punic standards and can often be distinguished from imported products only on the basis of the local fabric (fig. 3). Construction and appearance of the settlements themselves nevertheless marked the difference with indigenous Sardinian settlement most obviously, because the red tiles and regular mud-brick walls of the Punic farms were completely unlike the so-called *nuraghi* that had characterized Sardinian settlement for many centuries. The latter are conical stone towers built of large irregular blocks of local stone, usually granite or basalt. Rising several tens of meters high, they usually consisted of two stories and a rooftop balcony connected by staircases built within the massive walls. The strong correlations between the spread of colonial settlement in the interior of southern Sardinia and the abandonment of *nuraghi* in the same regions, while those in the northern parts of the island continued to be inhabited, have conventionally been interpreted in terms of military conquest and occupation. Remarks of classical authors about Carthaginian military expeditions to Sardinia have supported the representation of a classic colonial situation in which the indigenous inhabitants of southern Sardinia were completely assimilated to the dominant colonial Punic culture.[46]

Colonial Ambivalence in West Central Sardinia

It is precisely the complete replacement of indigenous Sardinian material culture with its Punic counterpart that raises doubts about the meanings of the label "colonial" in the context of Punic Sardinia. As the differentiation of colonial settlement within the single region of west central Sardinia already suggests, the apparent colonial uniformity of the regional archaeological record for the Punic period breaks down at close scrutiny: whereas colonial settlement in the interior of the Campidano plain and Marmilla hills was dispersed and closely associated with abandoned *nuraghi*, the coastal area adjacent to the Gulf of Oristano presented a centralized settlement pattern that evolved around the colonial towns of Neapolis and Tharros and ignored all traces of previous occupation.[47] The Carthaginian takeover of the region resulted, therefore, not in one single coherent colonial settlement pattern but gave rise to two quite different cultural landscapes in the coastal zones of the Arborèa and in the interior of the Campidano plain and Marmilla hills. Both may be termed colonial. This suggests that the people who occupied these sites in the fourth century B.C. and later perceived the surrounding landscape and its previous inhabitants in rather different ways, even if they used similar kinds of material culture. The identification of "nuraghic" features in the rituals, which were celebrated in a shrine installed in an abandoned *nuraghe* of the Marmilla hills, moreover, suggests that colonial settlement somehow seems to have been "less colonial" in the interior of west central Sardinia than in the coastal area.[48]

The uniformity of the term *colonial* is yet further undermined when these two landscapes are considered in their wider regional context: the towns of Neapolis and Othoca in particular were not only the focal points of rural settlement in the Arborèa coastal zone, but together with Tharros, they also constituted the colonial and urban core of west central Sardinia. Both towns were nevertheless appreciably different from Tharros, which possessed all conventional urban features such as monumental architecture, the *tophet* sanctuary[49] and heavy fortifications (fig. 4).[50] Neapolis, by contrast, has not yielded evidence of monumental constructions, architectural decorations in stone or terra-cotta or, most significantly, of a *tophet* sanctuary, which was the prime indicator of urban status in the Phoenician-Punic world of the central Mediterranean. A comparison of the cemeteries of both places confirms the superior status of Tharros, which boasted many lavish rock-cut chamber tombs, while the necropolises of Neapolis consisted of simple trench graves or, at best, of slightly more elaborate "pseudo-chamber" burials. These burial customs side Neapolis with its rural hinterland, as trench and "pseudo-chamber" burials were the norm in the rural cemeteries of both the coastal and inland areas.[51]

The position of Neapolis in west central Sardinia is best exemplified by its function as a central place in the southern Arborèa, where it must have constituted the principal place of reference for several hundreds of farms. The many transport amphorae found in what was presumably the port of the town, and the abundance of imported fine wares and amphorae throughout the region, stress the function of Neapolis as a distribution center and consequently set the town apart from other rural settlement in west central Sardinia. Yet, there remains a strong rural connotation to these economic activities, as agricultural products must have constituted the bulk of the transports. This contrasts sharply with the primarily artisanal and commercial significance of Tharros, where specialized products such as scarabs, amulets of precious stone, jewelry, stone stelae, incense burners, masks, and domestic utensils were manufactured. Many of these products found their way to the Punic world elsewhere in the western Mediterranean, while some products such as stone mortars and large decorated bowls were distributed in Sardinia itself (fig. 5).[52] Neapolis, by contrast, produced primarily, if not exclusively, plain domestic wares and transport amphorae, which were locally in widespread use. The only exception to this picture is the production of ceramic votive statuettes in Neapolis. Even these figurines were exclusively manufactured for local use, however, as the bulk of them have been found in a healing sanctuary near Neapolis and a limited number of specimens come from small shrines elsewhere in the southern Arborèa. These statuettes signal the difference between Tharros and Neapolis in a powerful and significant way, because the mold-made figurines produced in Tharros closely adhered to common Punic and Hellenistic standards, while the ones produced in Neapolis were considerably different in appearance and material, even if they still fitted in general Punic categories of votive statuary (fig. 6).[53]

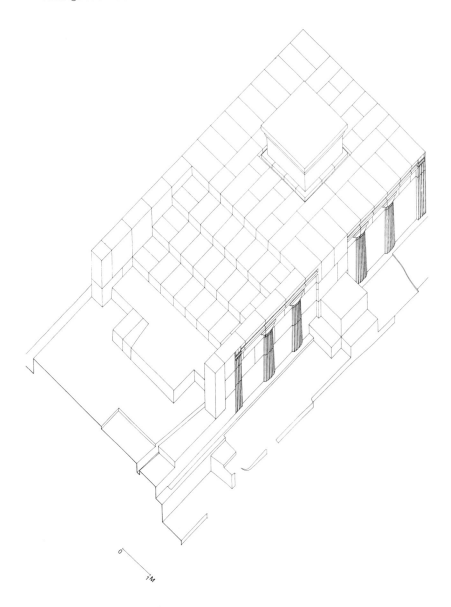

Fig. 4. Axonometric reconstruction of the so-called temple of the Doric semi-columns, possibly dedicated to Melqart, Tharros, 400–300 B.C.
After Enrico Acquaro, "Tharros tra Fenicia e Cartagine," in *Atti del 2. Congresso internazionale di studi fenici e punici* (Rome: Consiglio Nazionale delle Ricerche, 1991), vol. 2, fig. 8

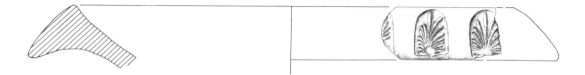

Fig. 5. Decorated Punic bowl, Tharros, 300–200 B.C.,
Diam.: 29 cm (11⅜ in.)

Fig. 6. Terra-cotta figurines
Left: Neapolis, 400–200 B.C., H: 15 cm (5⅞ in.);
right: Tharros, 400–200 B.C., H: 18 cm (7⅛ in.)

Neapolis thus occupied an ambivalent position in west central Sardinia as a colonial settlement that was both rural and urban. Neapolis was urban in the sense that it acted as a central place in the coastal landscape of rural settlements, but compared to Tharros and other major colonial cities it showed distinctively rural traits—and as a central place, it was actually an integral part of the rural settlement pattern. The principal economic activities carried out in Neapolis—manufacture and trade—similarly were in themselves not rural but were, nevertheless, a function of its rural hinterland. Neapolis defied not only the functionalist and economic categories of regional organization but has also provided evidence of an ambivalent identity in various other aspects. The ambivalence is most evident in the contrast between Neapolis and Tharros, which has most explicitly been defined in terms of an opposition between an urban-based "high culture" and a rural "popular culture": whereas the former connected the principal Punic cities of the Mediterranean and gave them a shared Hellenistic appearance, the latter characterized colonial settlement in the interior of Sardinia. The locally produced statuettes of Neapolis, therefore, embody the rural appearance of this town with respect to Tharros and the Punic world in general.[54] Yet, from a Sardinian perspective, Neapolis was only relatively different from Tharros and represented the wider Punic world and its Hellenistic culture in Sardinia, if only because of its role as a distribution center of imported (colonial) products. In many respects, Neapolis can thus be seen as the Sardinian equivalent of the Algerian *évolué* by being *"almost the same* [as the Carthaginian colonizers], *but not quite."*[55]

The three words "but not quite" are particularly relevant to the Sardinian situation, because they help explain the rapid transformation of settlement and culture to colonial standards in the southern regions of the island. If Punic settlement in these areas was less thoroughly and less uniformly colonial than it is usually assumed to have been, my interpretation of this process is that the indigenous inhabitants were not utterly assimilated and "deculturalized" as, for instance, Giovanni Lilliu would have it.[56] My view is that they on the contrary were able to retain and express a distinct sense of identity, even if they had to do so by taking recourse to new—Punic—material culture. The persistent occurrence of certain "indigenous" elements such as the association of settlement sites with *nuraghi* and the inclusion of certain "indigenous" rituals in "colonial" cults in fact demonstrates that colonial culture in the interior of Sardinia developed some subtle but yet noticeably distinct traits. This does not mean that indigenous culture was somehow preserved "in disguise," because people did after all replace their traditions with Punic customs; it shows, however, that the transformation process was not a one-way imposition of colonial norms. Local differences between the inhabitants of the coastal wetlands and those of the hills or those of the Phoenician foundations were transformed but also were preserved as variations *within* a broad colonial category.[57]

Roman Stereotypes of Sardinian Identities

In the aftermath of the First Punic War between Carthage and Rome (264–241 B.C.), Carthage had to cede its western Sicilian territories to Rome and subsequently lost control over Sardinia in the wake of a mercenary revolt. In a move that even an author as pro-Roman as Polybius defined as fraudulent (3.28.1–4), Rome seized the occasion and sent in troops who occupied Sardinia in 237 B.C. The island was formally incorporated into the Roman Republic in 227 B.C., when the *provincia Sardiniae et Corsicae* was created, and it was directly administered by the Roman consuls and their representatives. Roman rule would last nearly seven centuries, and it would eventually transform the lives and traditions of the Sardinians in a profound way. Most of these changes, however, which are conventionally captured by the term "romanization," took place in the Imperial period, when the major cities were reorganized according to Roman standards, *villae* were built in the countryside, and an extensive road system was laid out across the island.[58]

The first two centuries of Republican rule were, in fact, characterized by a remarkable absence of a visible Roman presence and by a strong continuity of Punic cultural traditions in both urban and rural contexts. Throughout the second century and in most cases well into the first century B.C., the Punic language and alphabet remained in official use, Punic institutions such as the *suffetes*[59] continued to hold sway, and neo-Punic architectural styles were adopted for new public architecture in all the major cities of the island, including Karales (Cagliari), which had become the principal Roman stronghold on Sardinia.[60] In the countryside, too, Punic material culture continued to be produced and used in both domestic and ritual contexts, as is shown, for instance, by the detailed surface collections of the Riu Mannu survey. The persistence of Punic burial customs in both rural and urban cemeteries shows that cultural continuity pervaded all dimensions and layers of Sardinian society. Continued contacts of various sorts between Sardinia and North Africa are also demonstrated by the presence of imports from the latter region, which include both amphorae and fine wares.[61] Most of all it is the persistence of the rituals celebrated at the *tophet* sanctuaries outside the major Punic cities until well into the first century B.C. that particularly underscores the deep roots of Punic culture in Sardinia and the strong Punic focus of Sardinian society under the first centuries of Roman rule, as these rituals went back to the very foundation of these cities in the early years of Phoenician colonialism.

In this light, Cicero's taunt (*Pro Scauro* 19, 45) about Sardinians being "sons of Africa" ("*Africa ipsa parens illa Sardiniae*") seems to make perfect sense, as he referred to an association between Punic Sardinia and Punic North Africa that must have been obvious for anyone familiar with the regions. Given the fact that Cicero was speaking in defense of M. Aemilius Scaurus, a former praetor in Sardinia who was accused of corruption and extortion, it may be evident, however, that the expression should not be taken as an objective historical observation. To a Roman audience, the phrase in fact carried no doubt negative connotations and defined the Sardinians at the very least as being obviously not Italian—as the provincial status of the island also confirmed.

In reality, the situation of the late third and second centuries B.C. was far less straightforward than suggested by Cicero's remark, if only because the northern half of the island had never been dominated by Carthage—with the exception of an isolated enclave around Olbia on the northeast coast.[62] In these regions, the Sardinians had never adopted Punic material culture at any scale, adhering instead to their ancestral customs and traditions of nuraghic origin. It was, in fact, these tribal groups who, according to Roman sources, resisted the Roman occupation of Sardinia most fiercely and who continued to rebel throughout the second century B.C.[63] As Sardinians were also referred to as *"Sardi pelliti"* (skin-clad Sardinians) and *"mastrucati latrunculi"* (brigands dressed in sheepskin: Cicero, *De provinciis consularibus* 15),[64] Cicero's Roman audience must have been aware of these alternative representations of the island and its inhabitants that ignored any Punic reference.

These conflicting views, which are exclusively Roman, or colonial views, demonstrate two points in particular. First, they illustrate the process of stereotyping at work and make patently clear that stereotypes need not be rigorous, consistent, or logical. The main effect of such stereotypical views is the classification of Sardinia in straightforward terms: as argued above, they serve to come to grips with an unfamiliar reality and to make intelligible a world that in many ways was quite different from the Roman one. As Bhabha has observed with regard to modern stereotypes, such views remain at least superficially plausible, because their effect relies on the exaggeration of otherwise undisputed features. The association of "skin-clad mountain tribes" and fierce military resistance was after all a widely accepted truism in Roman representations,[65] and the repeated celebration of triumphs *de Sardeis* had made the Sardinian resistance a tangible reality even in Rome.[66] Moreover, it is in the contradictions between the Roman representations of Sardinian identities that the ambivalent connotations of Punic culture in Roman Republican Sardinia emerge, as they do not recognize the Punic traditions of southern Sardinia as Sardinian but instead associated them with their colonial North African origins. By the same token, they ascribed military resistance exclusively to the "mountain tribes" of northern Sardinia, even if the largest and potentially most threatening revolt occurred in the Punic south in 217 B.C.; nor are they affected by the reality of widespread resistance of the Punic inhabitants in southern Sardinia.[67] These ambiguities were necessarily ignored by the Roman representations, as they would have otherwise undermined the clear-cut stereotypes.

It is precisely this ambivalence that is critical for understanding Punic identity in Roman Republican Sardinia, because in the new colonial situation the Punic inhabitants of southern Sardinia cannot be labeled in conventional terms as either "colonial" or "indigenous." This dichotomy is elusive because it is based on the essentialist assumption that meanings and origins are fixed

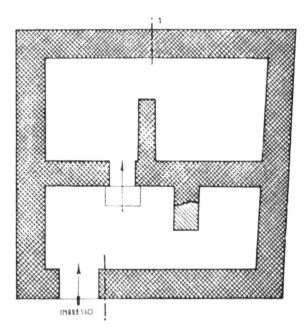

Fig. 7. Plan of house excavated near *nuraghe* Marfudi, Barumini
After Giovanni Lilliu, "Barumini (Cagliari) . . . ," *Notizie degli scavi di antichità* 7 (1946): fig. 6

and inextricably attached to certain objects. The use of Punic material culture in Republican Sardinia demonstrates, in fact, that Punic-style objects, imports, and customs were increasingly associated with long-abandoned "nuraghic" monuments and specific traditions equally going back to precolonial times. This point is well made by the case of *nuraghe* Marfudi (Barumini), which is situated in the eastern Marmilla hills of west central Sardinia (see fig. 2). Having been abandoned as a settlement at some point in the Late Bronze Age, the *nuraghe* was for centuries only sporadically frequented: it was only well into the Republican period that the monument was again regularly used, possibly for storage of agricultural produce. More significantly, however, was the construction of a rectangular house at a distance of some 20 meters from the monument (fig. 7). It was built of small rough stones and mud, and it was covered with a tiled roof. The floor consisted of bricks. The finds include both imported so-called Campanian black glaze pottery and local Punic-style jugs and bowls, which suggest a foundation date of the early to mid-second century B.C. Both the house and the *nuraghe* remained in use until the mid- to late second century A.D. Some 125 meters northwest of the *nuraghe* and the house, a small cemetery has been recorded, where several burials in a simple trench or stone coffin have been brought to light. It covers roughly the same time span.[68]

Not unlike the Punic sanctuary at Cuccuru s'Arriu (Cabras), which was installed in an abandoned well-sanctuary in the northern Campidano,[69] it is the long period of abandonment and the different usage made of the monument that rule out continuous indigenous presence at *nuraghe* Marfudi. The shift in settlement from the *nuraghe* to the nearby house is perhaps the most meaningful feature of the site, because it combines the colonial Punic-style way of living with the monumental location into a type of settlement that is uniquely Sardinian. Since it is from the hybrid combination of both "Punic" and "nuraghic" elements that the ambivalent nature of this type of settlement stems and with it its resistance against rigid classifications as either colonial or indigenous, I suggest that it should be understood in specifically local terms as "local" and "Sardinian" as opposed to "Roman" or "Punic" or "nuraghic."[70] The observation that Punic reuse of *nuraghi* first occurred in the fourth century B.C. but that the hybrid combination with houses seems to be a later development furthermore underscores the specifically local nature of the phenomenon.

Conclusion: Constructing Colonial Society

The Sardinian case study underscores the complexity of colonial situations in much the same way as theoretical considerations and ethnographic observations have undercut the colonial divide as an absolute opposition. They effectively undermine conventional dualist representations of colonialism. The Sardinian case also demonstrates that this complexity can be observed in the archaeological record, if the opposition between colonial and indigenous is not accepted at face value and if the implications of subtle variations in the use of material culture are taken into consideration. Particularly relevant for an archaeological analysis of colonial situations is the postcolonial emphasis on the cultural dimension of colonialism, because it argues that the cultural remains of the archaeological record played a critical part in colonial situations. A postcolonial perspective thus helps to overcome the notorious difficulties of detecting events as military conquest.

With regard to the term *colonial*, this study of Punic and Roman Republican Sardinia provides ample and concrete support for the theoretically inspired doubts about its uniformity and meanings, as close scrutiny of the archaeological record has demonstrated that the label "colonial culture" captures a variety of slightly different realities. This not only undermines dualist views of colonialism but also runs counter to essentialist representations in which colonial or indigenous objects carry an absolute "original" meaning. The different manifestations of "colonial culture" in the interior of west central Sardinia and the ambivalent position of Neapolis in particular suggest that "colonial" should be seen as a relative term. This does not, however, minimize the actual Carthaginian political and economic dominance in southern Sardinia, since the archaeological record incontestably shows its profound impact on the local inhabitants. The evidence also shows, however, how these people tried to come to terms with the new reality imposed on them and how they made sense of it—which was not necessarily along Carthaginian lines.

Homi Bhabha's notion of "hybridization" captures these processes well, because it emphasizes that the outcome of the appropriation of "colonial" (material) culture in local colonized contexts is a primarily *local* process.[71] At the same time, it also stresses that the outcome cannot be seen as a purely local achievement, because it respects the limits of the hegemonic colonial culture.[72] A distinction must consequently be made between the meanings of "colonial culture" in the colonized regions and in the country of origin, even if there is little or no physical difference between concrete objects. In any colonial situation, therefore, "colonial society" should largely and primarily be seen in specifically local terms. In west central Sardinia, this paradox is most clearly exemplified by Neapolis, which in Sardinian terms was "colonial" but which from a Carthaginian point of view must have appeared as a Sardinian rather than Carthaginian settlement.

As may be evident from the discussion of Sardinia under both Carthaginian and Roman rule, ambivalence is in many ways the key to an appreciation of the subtle nuances and shifts over time that denote local self-identifications and perceptions of material culture and cultural identity in west central Sardinia in the Classical and Hellenistic periods. While the two different colonial situations certainly had an impact on these variations, they were no less indebted to existing local traditions of various kinds and origins.

My conclusion from these arguments is not that the term *colonial* should be avoided, because colonialism is and was the principal characteristic of the contexts I have discussed and it certainly is not my intention to deny or minimize its impact on colonized regions. I do wish to call for more caution, however, when using the term and most of all for an awareness of the inherent subtle variations and outright contradictions of the terms. To sum up, I want to reiterate two cardinal points of postcolonial theory that appear to me to be particularly relevant for archaeologists: in the first place, that the implications of the term *colonial* can be appreciated only if the cultural dimension of colonialism is regarded in conjunction with the "hard reality" of economic exploitation and military occupation. Second, given the local roots of "colonial culture" in any specific context, colonialism should be considered as much a local phenomenon as a supraregional process.

Notes

This essay has benefited much from discussions during the "Archaeology of Colonialism" session at the Fourth World Archaeological Congress in Cape Town, South Africa, as well as from comments by Claire Lyons and John Papadopoulos and by Michael Given of the University of Glasgow. I gratefully acknowledge their helpful suggestions and comments.

1. The "spatial" connotation of the term, as in "empire," is a later development and actually refers to the area over which the power is exercised; see P. G. W. Glare, ed., *Oxford Latin Dictionary*, s.v. "imperium."

2. Erich S. Gruen, *The Hellenistic World and the Coming of Rome* (Berkeley: Univ.

of California Press, 1984), 273–78; and Marc Ferro, *Histoire des colonisations: Des conquêtes aux indépendances, XIIIᵉ–XXᵉ siècle* (Paris: Seuil, 1994), 13–41.

3. Bruce Trigger, "Alternative Archaeologies: Nationalist, Colonialist, Imperialist," *Man*, n.s., 19 (1984): 355–70; Peter van Dommelen, "Colonial Constructs: Colonialism and Archaeology in the Mediterranean," *World Archaeology* 28 (1997): 305–23; Franco de Angelis, "Ancient Past, Imperial Present: The British Empire in T. J. Dunbabin's *The Western Greeks*," *Antiquity* 72 (1998): 539–49; and Michael Given, "Inventing the Eteocypriots: Imperialist Archaeology and the Manipulation of Ethnic Identity," *Journal of Mediterranean Archaeology* 11 (1998): 3–29.

4. Van Dommelen, "Colonial Constructs" (note 3), 306–8.

5. D. Mattingly, "From One Imperialism to Another: Imperialism in the Maghreb," in Jane Webster and Nicholas J. Cooper, eds., *Roman Imperialism: Post-Colonial Perspectives* (Leicester: School of Archaeological Studies, University of Leicester, 1996), 49–69.

6. Monique Dondin-Payre, "*L'exercitus Africae* inspiratrice de l'armée française d'Afrique: *Ense et aratro*," *Antiquités africaines* 27 (1991): 141–49.

7. T. Robert S. Broughton, *The Romanization of Africa Proconsularis* (Baltimore: Johns Hopkins Press, 1929), 6.

8. Marcel Bénabou, *La résistance africaine à la romanisation* (Paris: F. Maspéro, 1976).

9. For example, see A. J. Graham, *Colony and Mother City in Ancient Greece* (Manchester: Manchester Univ. Press, 1964).

10. Compare David Ridgway, *The First Western Greeks* (Cambridge: Cambridge Univ. Press, 1992), 111–20.

11. Ridgway, *First Western Greeks* (note 10), 139–44; and Irad Malkin, *The Returns of Odysseus: Colonization and Ethnicity* (Berkeley: Univ. of California Press, 1998), 156–77.

12. M. Cuozzo, "Patterns of Organisation and Funerary Customs in the Cemetery of Pontecagnano (Salerno) during the Orientalising Period," *Journal of European Archaeology* 2 (1994): 263–98. See now, however, M. Cuozzo, "Orizzonti teorici e interpretativi, tra percorsi di matrice francese, archeologia post-processuale e tendenze italiane: Considerazioni e indirizzi di ricerca per lo studio delle necropoli," in Nicola Terrenato, ed., *Archeologia teorica: X Ciclo di lezioni sulla ricerca applicata in archeologia: Certosa di Pantignano (Siena), 9–14 agosto 1999* (Florence: Edizioni all'Insegna del Giglio, 2000), 323–60.

13. Ridgway, *First Western Greeks* (note 10), 121–29.

14. Yvon Thébert, "Romanisation et déromanisation en Afrique: Histoire décolonisée ou histoire inversée?" *Annales, économies, sociétés, civilisations* 33 (1978): 65–82.

15. See, for example, the overviews presented by Dinu Adamesteanu, "Greeks and Natives in Basilicata," and Francesco D'Andria, "Greek Influence in the Adriatic: Fifty Years after Beaumont," in Jean-Paul Descoeudres, ed., *Greek Colonists and Native Populations* (Oxford: Clarendon, 1990), 143–50, 281–90. Compare, however, C. Antonaccio, "Urbanism at Archaic Morgantina," in Helle Damgaard Andersen, H. Horsnæs, and A. Rathje, eds., *Urbanization in the Mediterranean in the Ninth to Sixth*

Centuries B.C. (Copenhagen: Museum Tusculanum Press, 1997), 167–93, esp. 170–72; and Robert Leighton, *Sicily before History: An Archaeological Survey from the Palaeolithic to the Iron Age* (London: Duckworth, 1999), 219–22.

16. Daniel Miller, *Modernity, an Ethnographic Approach: Dualism and Mass Consumption in Trinidad* (Providence, R.I.: Berg, 1994).

17. Nicholas Thomas, *Entangled Objects: Exchange, Material Culture, and Colonialism in the Pacific* (Cambridge: Harvard Univ. Press, 1991), 83–124.

18. Sarah P. Morris, "Bearing Greek Gifts: Euboean Pottery on Sardinia," in Miriam S. Balmuth and Robert H. Tykot, eds., *Sardinian and Aegean Chronology: Towards the Resolution of Relative and Absolute Dating in the Mediterranean* (Oxford: Oxbow, 1998), 361–62; John K. Papadopoulos, "Phantom Euboians," *Journal of Mediterranean Archaeology* 10 (1997): 191–219; and John K. Papadopoulos, "Archaeology, Myth-History, and the Tyranny of the Text: Chalkidike, Torone and Thucydides," *Oxford Journal of Archaeology* 18 (1999): 377–94.

19. Claire L. Lyons, "Sikel Burials at Morgantina: Defining Social and Ethnic Identities," in Robert Leighton, ed., *Early Societies in Sicily: New Developments in Archaeological Research* (London: Accordia Research Centre, University of London, 1996), 177–88; and Antonaccio, "Urbanism" (note 15), 172–80.

20. Ann Stoler, "Rethinking Colonial Categories: European Communities and the Boundaries of Rule," *Comparative Studies in Society and History* 31 (1989): 134–61.

21. David Prochaska, *Making Algeria French: Colonialism in Bône, 1870–1920* (Cambridge: Cambridge Univ. Press, 1990), 62–93.

22. Prochaska, *Making Algeria French* (note 21), 206–29. Note that the poster I reproduce here as figure 1 celebrates agricultural and rural life in colonial Algeria. It also reasserts the binary representation of colonial society, with the colonial farmer overseeing the work of the indigenous workers, even though most of the land was farmed by *pied noirs*, who were as "native" as their indigenous workers.

23. Ania Loomba, *Colonialism-Postcolonialism* (London: Routledge, 1998), 104–83.

24. Edward Said, *Orientalism* (New York: Vintage, 1978).

25. L. Turner, "Consuming Colonialism," *Critique of Anthropology* 15 (1995): 203–12.

26. For example, Jean Comaroff and John Comaroff, *Of Revelation and Revolution*, vol. 1, *Christianity, Colonialism, and Consciousness in South Africa* (Chicago: Univ. of Chicago Press, 1991); and Roger Keesing, "Colonial and Counter-Colonial Discourse in Melanesia," *Critique of Anthropology* 14 (1994): 41–58.

27. Said, *Orientalism* (note 24), 93–96; Michel Foucault, "Afterword: The Subject and Power," in Hubert L. Dreyfus and Paul Rabinow, *Michel Foucault: Beyond Structuralism and Hermeneutics* (Brighton: Harvester, 1982), 208–26, esp. 216–19.

28. See, for example, Trigger, "Alternative Archaeologies" (note 3); and Webster and Cooper, *Roman Imperialism* (note 5).

29. Thomas J. Dunbabin, *The Western Greeks: The History of Sicily and South Italy from the Foundation of the Greek Colonies to 480 B.C.* (Oxford: Clarendon, 1948); de Angelis, "Ancient Past" (note 3); and compare Given, "Inventing the Eteo-cypriots" (note 3) on ancient Cyprus.

30. Nicholas Thomas, *Colonialism's Culture: Anthropology, Travel, and Government* (Cambridge: Polity, 1994), 33–65.

31. Loomba, *Colonialism* (note 23), 124–33; and Nicholas Thomas, *In Oceania: Visions, Artifacts, Histories* (Durham: Duke Univ. Press, 1997), 133–55.

32. Thomas, *Colonialism's Culture* (note 30), 53–54.

33. Homi Bhabha, "The Other Question: Stereotype, Discrimination, and the Discourse of Colonialism," in idem, *The Location of Culture* (London: Routledge, 1994), 66–84, 173.

34. Stoler, "Rethinking" (note 20).

35. Homi Bhabha, "Of Mimicry and Men: The Ambivalence of Colonial Discourse," in idem, *The Location of Culture* (London: Routledge, 1994), 85–92, esp. 86, author's emphasis.

36. Peter Pels, "The Anthropology of Colonialism: Culture, History, and the Emergence of Western Governmentality," *Annual Review of Anthropology* 26 (1997): 163–83, esp. 171–72.

37. Compare Greg Woolf, "The Formation of Roman Provincial Cultures," in Jeannot Metzler et al., eds., *Integration in the Early Roman West: The Role of Culture and Ideology* (Luxembourg: Musée National d'Histoire et d'Art, 1995), 9–18, esp. 15–16; and compare Emma Dench, *From Barbarians to New Men: Greek, Roman, and Modern Perceptions of Peoples of the Central Apennines* (Oxford: Clarendon, 1995), 72–80.

38. Carol Dougherty, *The Poetics of Colonization: From City to Text in Archaic Greece* (New York: Oxford Univ. Press, 1993).

39. Bhabha, "The Other Question" (note 33), 66, author's emphasis.

40. M. MacDonald, "The Construction of Difference: An Anthropological Approach to Stereotypes," in Sharon MacDonald, ed., *Inside European Identities: Ethnography in Western Europe* (Providence, R.I.: Berg, 1993), 219–36.

41. María Eugenia Aubet, *The Phoenicians and the West: Politics, Colonies, and Trade*, trans. Mary Turton (Cambridge: Cambridge Univ. Press, 1993), 185–276.

42. Carlo Tronchetti, "Sardaigne," in Véronique Krings, ed., *La civilisation phénicienne et punique: Manuel de recherche* (Leiden: E. J. Brill, 1995), 712–42, esp. 712–28.

43. Tronchetti, "Sardaigne" (note 42), 728–40.

44. Van Dommelen, "Punic Persistence: Colonialism and Cultural Identity in Roman Sardinia," in Ray Laurence and Joanne Berry, eds., *Cultural Identity in the Roman Empire* (London: Routledge, 1998), 25–48.

45. M. Annis, Peter van Dommelen, and P. van de Velde, "Rural Settlement and Socio-Political Organization: The *Riu Mannu* Survey Project, Sardinia," *BABESCH: Bulletin Antieke Beschaving* 70 (1995): 133–52.

46. Ferruccio Barreca, *La civiltà fenicio-punica in Sardegna* (Sassari: Delfino, 1986), 31–40; and Giovanni Lilliu, "Ancora una riflessione sulle guerre cartaginesi per la conquista della Sardegna," *Rendiconti (Accademia nazionale dei Lincei, Classe di scienze morali, storiche e filologiche)*, 9th ser., 3 (1992): 17–35.

47. Van Dommelen, "Colonial Constructs" (note 3), 313–14; and Peter van Dommelen, *On Colonial Grounds: A Comparative Study of Colonialism and Rural Settlement in First Millennium B.C. West Central Sardinia* (Leiden: Faculty of Archaeology, University of Leiden, 1998), 150–51.

48. Caterina Lilliu, "Un culto di età punico-romana al nuraghe Genna Maria di Villanovaforru," in Caterina Lilliu et al., *Genna Maria II, 1: Il deposito votivo del mastio e del cortile* (Cagliari: Stef, 1993), 11–39.

49. A *tophet* was a characteristic feature of the major Phoenician settlements in the central Mediterranean and can best be described as an open-air, enclosed sanctuary situated at the northern edge of the settlement area. *Tophets* received the ashes of young children, who had presumably died before initiation. The urns also contained small grave goods as jewelry. While the precise nature of the rituals performed in this area is unknown, it is evident that they were of prime importance for a city, as the *tophet* was among the earliest established features of each Phoenician settlement in the central Mediterranean and the sacred area was never enlarged—despite continuous use—until the Roman period. It has therefore been suggested that the *tophet* was associated with the urban nature and civic independence of these Phoenician settlements; see Barreca, *La civiltà* (note 46), 108–23; Aubet, *The Phoenicians* (note 41), 215–21; and van Dommelen, *Colonial Grounds* (note 47), 82–83.

50. Barreca, *La civiltà* (note 46), 55–68.

51. Raimondo Zucca, *Neapolis e il suo territorio* (Oristano: Editrice S'Alvure, 1987).

52. Sabatino Moscati, *Le officine di Tharros* (Rome: Università degli Studi di Roma, 1987); and L. Manfredi, "I bacini decorati punici di Tharros," in *Atti del II Congresso internazionale di studi fenici e punici, Roma, 9–14 novembre 1987* (Rome: Consiglio Nazionale delle Ricerche, 1991), 1011–18.

53. Sabatino Moscati, "Tra cartaginesi e romani: Artigianato in Sardegna dal IV a.C. al II d.C.," *Memorie (Accademia nazionale dei Lincei, Classe di scienze morali, storiche e filologiche)*, 9th ser., 3, no. 3 (1992): 1–103, esp. 65–72; and van Dommelen, "Colonial Constructs" (note 3), 315–18.

54. Moscati, "Tra cartaginesi e romani" (note 53), 99–101.

55. Bhabha, "Mimicry" (note 35), 86.

56. Giovanni Lilliu, *La civiltà dei Sardi: Dal paleolitico all'età dei nuraghi*, 3d ed. (Turin: Nuova ERI, 1988), 472.

57. Van Dommelen, *Colonial Grounds* (note 47), 115–59.

58. Piero Meloni, *La Sardegna romana*, 2d ed. (Sassari, Italy: Chiarella, 1990), 97–138; Peter van Dommelen, "Cultural Imaginings: Punic Tradition and Local Identity in Roman Republican Sardinia," in S. J. Keay and Nicola Terrenato, eds., *Italy and the West: Comparative Issues in Romanization* (Oxford: Oxbow, 2001), 68–84.

59. The *suffetes* were the highest officials in a Phoenician and Punic city and were, in many respects, including their limited period of office (usually one year), comparable to the Roman consuls or Greek *archontes*; see Barreca, *La civiltà* (note 46), 91.

60. Sandro Filippo Bondì, "Le sopravvivenze puniche nella Sardegna romana," in Sandro Filippo Bondì and Massimo Guidetti, eds., *Dalle origini alla fine dell'età bizantina* (Milan: Jaca, 1987), 205–11.

61. Van Dommelen, "Punic Persistence" (note 44), 34–40.

62. A. Sanciu, "Insediamenti rustici d'età tardo-repubblicana nell'agro di Olbia," in Mustapha Khanoussi, Paola Ruggeri, and Cinzia Vismara, eds., *L'Africa romana: Atti del XII Convegno di studio, Olbia, 12–15 dicembre 1996* (Olbia: Editrice

Democratica Sarda, 1998), 777–99.

63. Meloni, *La Sardegna romana* (note 58), 71–83.

64. For *Sardi pelliti*, see Livy, *Ab urbe condita* 23.32.10; for *mastrucati latrunculi*, see Cicero, *De provinciis consularibus* 15.

65. Dench, *Barbarians* (note 37), 73–80.

66. Meloni, *La Sardegna romana* (note 58), 43–83.

67. Van Dommelen, "Punic Persistence" (note 44), 41–42.

68. Giovanni Lilliu, "Barumini (Cagliari): Saggi stratigrafici presso i nuraghi di Su Nuraxi e Marfudi, 'Vicus' di S. Lussorio e necropoli romana di su Luargi," *Notizie degli scavi di antichità* 7 (1946): 175–207, esp. 183–95.

69. Van Dommelen, "Cultural Imaginings" (note 58), 75–80.

70. Van Dommelen, "Cultural Imaginings" (note 58), 80–82.

71. See van Dommelen, "Colonial Constructs" (note 3), 319.

72. Keesing, "Counter-Colonial" (note 26).

Part II

Ideologies

A Colonial Middle Ground: Greek, Etruscan, and Local Elites in the Bay of Naples

Irad Malkin

As they did at the end of the Bronze Age, mainland Greeks of the late ninth century B.C. sailed beyond the island of Ithaca, the home of Homer's Odysseus and the westernmost Greek community in the *Iliad* and the *Odyssey*. They made trade and guest-friendship contacts along the coasts of Epirus (modern northwestern Greece and Albania) and across the Straits of Otranto to Apulia. By the early eighth century B.C., the Greeks sailed the coasts of western Italy. These protocolonial contacts were followed by settlements in the Bay of Naples, first on the island of Pithekoussai (Ischia) in about 770–750 B.C. and then at Kymē (Cumae) on the mainland of Campania. These settlements or trade posts are considered the first "colonial" establishments in the West, in what would come to be called Magna Graecia, or Greater Greece.

The local inhabitants encountered by the Greeks in this area of the Bay of Naples were not politically organized in strong city-states but in loosely confederated, internally hierarchical chiefdoms. For their part, Greek settlers were either uninterested in or incapable of coordinating a program of territorial expansion. It was an open-ended situation, where local Italic elites had relations with foreigners from the mainland and the eastern Mediterranean as well as with their northern neighbors, the Etruscans.

In assessing the encounter of peoples and cultures in Campania, the least fruitful approach is one current in much of the scholarship concerning the question of the "Other." In the disciplines of cultural studies and history, a binary model of alterity, *l'image de l'autre,* and of "Self vs. Other" has dominated the field, sometimes cleverly inverting the order of what is Self and what is Other, but basically retaining a bipolar categorization. A different theoretical model, that of the "Middle Ground," is preferred, because it evokes the intricacies of colonial encounters and the dynamic new cultural creations that resulted.

Defined in terms of seventeenth- and eighteenth-century colonization that occurred in the North American Great Lakes region, Middle Ground theory can be usefully applied to the world of early Greek colonization. Comparison of historical colonization in North America and medieval Europe with the ancient Greek situation in the western Mediterranean reveals similarities in structures and social dynamics, and underscores the formative, co-optative, and normative aspects of the colonial experience. These dynamics apply to the sending societies (mother cities), the settlers, and the local cultures with which they came into contact. The maritime perspective (ship to shore) that is characteristic of the Greek and Etruscan presence in Campania and the pattern of "peripheral sitings" of myths were significant factors in establishing a Middle Ground of cultural mediation and accommodation.

In addition, this paper considers artifacts and texts that reflect "mythic" articulations of collective identities in order to argue for an emergence of a mediating culture. This culture, marked by transcultural images and values, inflected concrete contacts and actual settlement. The figure of Odysseus well represents such a transcultural icon and arbiter of the Middle Ground among Greeks, Etruscans, and local elites of central Italy.[1] The qualities that made the mythic framework of Odysseus attractive to inhabitants of the region of Pithekoussai and Kymē can be viewed in terms of the iconographic representations of his exploits, the Etruscan adoption of Euboian alphabetic script, the role of the *symposion* (wine drinking party) among local elites, and the development of mediating genealogies.

The term *Middle Ground* was coined by Richard White to describe the encounters between Native Americans and Europeans in the Great Lakes Region of North America between the years 1650 and 1815. White is interested in how individuals of different cultural backgrounds reached accommodation and constructed a common, mutually comprehensible world. This construction was frequently the result of mutual misrepresentation of values and practices, sometimes involving behavior according to values one thought the "other side" shared, although this was mistaken or simplistic.

> On the Middle Ground diverse peoples adjust their differences through what amounts to a process of creative, and often expedient, misunderstandings. People try to persuade others who are different from them by appealing to what they perceive to be the values and practices of those others. They often misinterpret and distort both the values and the practices of those they deal with, but from these misunderstandings arise new meanings and through them new practices — the shared meanings and practices of the Middle Ground.[2]

The Middle Ground is not only a social metaphor but also the physical space "in between" and "within which" people(s) interact. The worlds of the colonists and the natives "melted at the edges,"[3] and it was not always clear whether their way of doing things was "French" or "Algonquian." For long periods of time and in areas where total coercion was neither possible nor even aimed at, mutual reliance for specific ends was de rigueur. One may note that a similar situation, with no coercive authority, existed in Campania. White observes that as individuals applied cultural expectations and conventions to new situations, the very act of application caused a change in culture, eventually resulting in a shift of conventions. A similar process is identified by Solange Alberro with regard to "how the Spanish ceased being Spanish" in Mexico.[4]

Colonial settlers, seeking out the cultural premises of others in order to achieve desired ends, looked for "congruencies," such as casting an Indian in the role of a Christian prophet or interpreting the independence of women as "prostitution." Indigenous communities were, no doubt, engaged in parallel processes of cultural translation. While the monotheistic filters of Spanish Christianity were less receptive to cross-cultural accommodations, in the case of the Greek/Etruscan Middle Ground, the identification of shared heroic genealogies served to promote mutually beneficial social and political alliances. For the Greek Odysseus to become the Etruscan Utuse was both possible and desirable.

The concept of the Middle Ground is appealing also because it forces us to examine the traditional "Greek-native" problem beyond the notion of "acculturation," another popular but unilateral anthropological model that has been used to explain the transformation (Hellenization, Europeanization) of indigenous cultures in colonial contexts. The Middle Ground "is not acculturation under a new name. As commonly used, acculturation describes a process in which one group becomes more like another by borrowing discrete cultural traits."[5] As the Subcommittee on Acculturation of the American Social Science Research Council defined acculturation in 1936, it involves "those phenomena which result when groups of individuals having different cultures come into continuous first-hand contact, with subsequent changes in the original culture-patterns of either or both groups."[6] This is a rather nuanced definition that can be deployed quite constructively in any number of contact situations. Too often, however, it is understood as one superior culture pouring itself from its own overflowing cups into the empty containers of the receiving, inferior culture. Some discussions of "Hellenization" bear this mark.[7]

In the sense of common terrain, the actual lands where people met and interacted, the Middle Ground is both a "center" and a "periphery." The Campanian hinterlands were a colonial frontier, peripheral in relation to early Greek colonizing settlements like offshore Pithekoussai and coastal Kymē. It was also a periphery in relation to the powerful "one-over" Etruscan civilization established mostly to the north of Campania and Latium; Etruscans were also resident in Campania as guest-friends, traders, and immigrants. In general, nonterritorial colonization (that is, one not conquering, displacing, or subjugating natives) often stimulates economic and cultural interaction in the areas "facing" settlement, areas of encounter and exchange, not annexation. But it also constitutes a stimulus for the "one-over" civilization, as in the modern instances of the British in Hong Kong, the Portuguese in Dao and Goa, and numerous other cases. Campania may have been a periphery for both Greeks and Etruscans, but it was a shared periphery and hence a Middle Ground for both, creating a context of mediation and cultural permeability, a new "center."[8]

A Middle Ground of accommodation was facilitated in Campania because for long periods of time Greeks, Etruscans, and local elites could neither dictate to nor ignore one another. The circumstances for the success of the

Campanian Middle Ground are the same as those of early Greek colonization in other areas. Unlike the contemporary Near East, the western Mediterranean was free of empires and centrally organized kingdoms. It was a vacuum where slight edges and advantages mattered a great deal; where maritime capabilities, flexible social frameworks, and a shared aristocratic ethos opened the way for original and responsive cultural creations.

The Middle Ground could become an effective area of mediation in Campania because there was no compelling authority and no side could achieve its ends through sheer force. Before the significant territorial expansion of the Greek colonies in south Italy and Sicily in the seventh century B.C., early-eighth-century colonization implied a different colonial outlook, one of touching and tapping rather than grabbing and possessing. Mid-eighth-century colonization in the West was more a legacy of protocolonial trade contacts than a precursor of strategic territorial expansion. This does not mean, however, that expansion was not ultimately on the minds of colonists. The frontier should not be perceived naively, as if territorial ambitions were entirely dormant.

Here the term *colonial frontier* needs clarification. The Greek colonial perspective was a maritime one, from shore to land. The border "line" was the coast and the rest was an open-ended frontier rolling to the hinterland. It is difficult to assess, however, how seriously the realization of the potential this frontier played on the minds of colonists of the first generation. A century later, at expansionist Sicilian Gela or especially at Libyan Cyrene, it seems evident that the colonists did not regard their "charter" in terms of a point within the colonial space. The Cyrenaean colonists, for example, rather ambitiously saw all of Libya as their land of colonization, a point made explicit in the various foundation stories and oracular prophecies of the colony.[9] Cyrene, however, was founded after more than a century of Greek colonization in the Mediterranean and no other mainland city competed for Libyan territories. Greek Libya was basically colonized from Cyrene, a situation very different from Magna Graecia, where numerous colonial groups vied with one another. In short, whether or not Greeks harbored expansionary ambitions, the reality of eighth-century B.C. Campania, which was thickly settled by various well-armed Italic tribes, was that of accommodation rather than expansion.

As Robert Bartlett notes with regard to the colonization of Europe during the Middle Ages, colonization frequently proceeds by three often overlapping means: expropriation, assimilation, and the discovery of new ecological and trading niches.[10] Offshore islands, promontories, and coastal areas can provide such a niche, especially when there is a marked difference between maritime and nonmaritime civilizations. Many are familiar with the poetic articulation of this in book 9 of the *Odyssey* when Odysseus speaks of an ideal colony site, an empty island facing the extremely rich land of the wild Cyclopes, who "do not possess ships."[11] Nonmaritime civilizations (notwithstanding fishermen who make a living from the sea but do not use it as a bridge to distant shores) may consider as irrelevant and peripheral the kind of sites — offshore islands, capes, and promontories — valued by a maritime civilization.

In the context of such encounters, the coast may thus become a Middle Ground, an aspect emphasized by Greg Dening in *Islands and Beaches* with regard to the colonization of the Marquesas Islands.[12] From an archaeological point of view, it now seems clearer, for example, that such a situation existed in the Crimea and Black Sea region during the seventh and sixth centuries.[13] Similarly, the notion of the coast as a new colonial and ecological niche is nicely illustrated by Greek-Phocaean colonization in southern France and Iberia.[14] The coastal Middle Ground constituted a new niche of material and cultural contact, successfully operating in a nonthreatening environment, where trading opportunities outweighed fears of Etruscan piracy.[15]

The Greek colonial Middle Ground owed much of its success to the flexibility of founding Greek institutions, constituting in their ensemble a new polis, independent from its mother city. As Jean Bérard notes, this represents a salient difference between ancient and modern colonialism. In the instance of "France over-seas," the state regards the colonists of Algeria as its own citizens.[16] Medieval colonization in Europe developed what Robert Bartlett calls "international, legal forms or blueprints which could generate new structures quite independently of an encompassing political matrix."[17] The inherent "frontier" situation promised success and independent initiatives. Meager control and direction by monarchies and central hierarchies encouraged colonization. Conversely, when kings and central government grew stronger, their energy turned to fighting one another rather than colonizing the frontiers of Europe. Perhaps something similar happened when Chalkis and Eretria turned against each other during the so-called Lelantine War. Effectively, both had ceased their involvement in colonization since the early seventh century. The situation in ancient Greece differed in respect to regime and religion, but was similar in the dynamics implied by the relative independence of colonies, an independence that itself functioned as an impetus for more initiatives and new foundations.

The colonial Middle Ground was the area in which an independent society was deliberately created, inventing and forming itself as a political community (city-state). Here another comparison with the medieval town-colony may be enlightening. In the High Middle Ages towns were often founded through charters (for example, *Stadtrechte* or *fueros*), constituting what Bartlett calls "a picture, a set of norms that could be adapted to, rather than swamped by, local institutions." Archaic Greeks had no legally defined blueprints, nor were their new city-states officially chartered in the medieval sense. Like the city-colonies of the European Middle Ages, however, they rapidly created a "normative and self-defining quality" often replicated or imitated among new foundations. Such imitative processes could take place either laterally, with one colony looking over its shoulder at what the other was doing (such as a Corinthian colony in Sicily observing the foundation of a Chalkidian colony), or more "prismatically" and hierarchically, through the agency of an active mother city, such as Miletus or Chalkis, learning quickly from its own numerous and relatively contemporary new foundations.

The colonial Middle Ground functioned, therefore, both in relation to so-called natives and in relation to the settlers themselves. There was also, however, a Middle Ground in relation to the mother cities. The colonial undertaking often constituted a resolution of a crisis of integration and homogenization of the sending society. I have argued elsewhere that by sending out colonists, the mother city was also founding or refounding itself.[18] Political stasis, dissatisfied aristocrats, poor people or younger sons hoping for a *kleros* of their own (with its political and social implications), entire "marked" groups, and others were vying for a place in the world of emergent poleis. Colonization was a solution for both. The mother city could consolidate itself as a political unit (colonization being tantamount to a reestablishment of the social order at home) and the colony could achieve coherence and independence, but without losing its mother-city "identity." Colonists retained, for example, the right to share in the sacrifices at home, a salient feature of archaic citizenship.[19]

Finally, the creation of such normative and self-defining qualities functioned dynamically (both informing the situations and being invented and improved through them) especially in the case of mixed colonies. For example, when Himera was founded by Zancle (Messana) in about 649 B.C., it was settled by many Chalkidians, but also by the exiled Myletidai from Syracuse (a Dorian city). The language of Himera resulted in a mixture of Doric and Chalkidic, but the *nomima* (the calendar, social division, magistracies, and so on) that prevailed were Chalkidian.[20] These two kinds of Middle Ground, the linguistic and the customary-legal, serve as an excellent illustration for the way the Middle Ground operates internally. The colonial Middle Ground produced a linguistic mixture because language was neutral, not an object of a priori decision (unlike certain cases of modern nationalism). By contrast, because settlers needed to live from the outset according to an established sacred calendar or social division (*nomima*), no gradualist mixture was possible. Deliberate, express decisions, arbitrating and mediating the social and religious order, had to be made, and newcomers needed to be co-opted into the formative Middle Ground.

This Greek Middle Ground, because it was "internally" dynamic and adaptable, was attractive to non-Greeks, especially to the Etruscans. The relative ease with which "foundation norms" were created and mutually copied, coupled with an aristocratic ethos that flourished side by side with an emerging civic one, explains both the success of these settlements and their attractiveness to city-state societies in the making, such as the Etruscans.

The extent to which Etruscans adopted Greek institutions has been debated by others.[21] What is of most interest here is the functioning of the Middle Ground in terms of the interaction and occasional adoption of Greek narrative frameworks that provide the terms for constructing collective identities. In addition to the flexible and open-ended nature of their emergent social and political institutions and common aristocratic ethos, it was the "alphabetic" quality of Greek myth that facilitated the transmission of ideas and stories to local elites. Like the spread of the alphabet—a system devoid of ethnic symbolism—narrative frameworks could be transplanted and adopted without being overly constricted by local connotations.[22]

It has been suggested that the Etruscans adopted both the Greek alphabet and Greek myths from Euboian Greeks who traded and settled in Pithekoussai and Kymē.[23] Neither letterforms nor myths privileged any ethnic entity. What made it possible for Greeks to ascribe their heroic genealogies to others was precisely the quality that made them attractive to others. Greeks did not regard the heroic genealogies as Greek; they were simply heroic.[24] Their genealogies and narrative framework involved—like the *Odyssey*—various *xenoi* (I avoid the English word "foreigners," which has a strong ethnic connotation), regardless of ethnic ascriptions. The heroes were not "Greek," and the *xenoi* with whom they were involved in the myths were not "non-Greek." Thus the heroes of what we call "Greek" mythology provided a blueprint of personal-aristocratic origins that was easily extended to other communities.

Counterintuitively, one notes a striking prominence of mythic and even cultic identification of Greek heroes not in the central foci of colonization and settlement but in peripheral, frontier areas. From the Greek perspective we note a total lack of jealousy: Herakles, Odysseus, Menelaos, Diomedes, Philoctetes, and others were freely "given away." These heroes were not considered founders of colonies, at least not before the fifth century, for both historical and mythic-religious reasons. From a historical point of view, colonists focused their attention on the human history of the colonial center, on the actions of the first colonists. The initial generation of colonists, headed by the founder, constituted a "beginning" and hence an existence and identity. Settlers were proud of their exploits as colonists, and their historical founders were regarded as having performed larger-than-life deeds. Colonial history was heroic in perspective and historical in application, a new phenomenon in what we call Greek history. Such features are not uncommon in other colonizations. In the case of European colonization during the High Middle Ages, for example the English in the Celtic world, the Germans in eastern Europe, the Spanish and their Reconquest, and the Crusaders in the eastern Mediterranean, all celebrated the "first coming of the conquerors, the heroic military pioneer, and the superhuman exploits of the new men."[25] Although revolving around historical deeds, colonial *ktiseis* (foundation stories) contained a strong mythological flavor, and a heroic cult was accorded to the dead founder, buried in the colony's agora (fig. 1).[26]

With such self-centered magnification of the generation of first settlers and emphasis on narratives of departure, consultation at Delphi, and acts of settlement and conquest, men of the first few generations had a keen awareness of their youthful origins and exploits. The stories they would tell themselves were often exaggerated, but—unlike the common fallacy—their myths did contain significant kernels of truth. What they spoke about was history. By contrast, the invention of mythological associations, connected with colonial centers (such as Kroton's adoption of Herakles as *Utistes* [founder]), occurred

Fig. 1. Heroon at Paestum, 600–500 B.C.
From John Griffiths Pedley, *Paestum: Greeks and Romans in Southern Italy* (New York: Thames & Hudson, 1990), fig. 11

after some two centuries of colonial history had passed, when Italian colonies felt less secure and wished to be *en par* with the ancient cities of Greece.[27]

For the early periods of settlement, however, the great epic heroes did not legitimate possession of sites, nor were their stories connected to the foci of settlement. Rather, they were connected "peripherally" to the Middle Ground. What heroes such as Menelaos and Odysseus did was to mediate for the colonists the topography and ethnography of what they could see (or suspect) from their settlement. Colonization implied a sense of novelty, juxtaposed with what preexisted in the land. Since both the sites and the peoples encountered by Greek settlers had already been there since they arrived, they—not the colonists themselves—came to be associated with mythic heroes. Menelaos had already been at "the port of Menelaos" in North Africa (at the edges of Cyrenaean territory); royal houses in Epirus or Italy were "descendants" of Odysseus; the inhabitants of the land were "originally" Trojan refugees, Cretan soldiers of Minos, or ancient Arkadian migrants. Mythic topography and ethnography started as peripheral and thus shaped the Middle Ground.[28]

We shall see that during the protocolonial and early colonial periods, when Campania was an unthreatened Middle Ground, the adoption of heroic mythological frameworks was flexible and attractive. The situation of encounter in the frontier zone of the Middle Ground was helpful. Not one, but two maritime, trading, and colonizing peoples — Greeks and Etruscans — were present in Campania, but not antagonistically (at least not at first). Phoenicians also were in residence, but probably as trade partners more than as colonists. The similarity of their situations, both *xenoi* in relation to the local towns and elites, apparently facilitated the transmission of outlooks and attitudes. More Etruscans than Greeks had already settled among these elites. What is notable is that because these Etruscans were living in closer proximity to the Greeks of Kymē and Pithekoussai than to the Etruscan centers of Latium and Etruria (much farther to the north), they were susceptible to Greek ideas. Like the Greeks, they too were newcomers and the nature of their coming was similar: maritime contact with peoples less interested in the sea. It is therefore likely that Greek cultural notions were transmitted to local elites not only directly by Greeks but also via local Etruscan residents who were open to Greek ideas through their own contacts with the colonists of Pithekoussai and Kymē.

Nobody in Campania was an "absolute other" in terms of the binary-oppositional model. Campanians and Etruscans were not alien barbarians living in a hitherto unrecognized terrain. They occupied a composite land, where Greeks, Etruscans, Phoenicians, and local indigenous communities, whether individually as traders, artisans, or migrants, or collectively, in the form of colonies or nuclei of resident communities. It is unclear if the Greeks even saw themselves collectively as "Greeks" so early on, or if they did, whether that sense of ethnic identity constituted a meaningful difference. Campania was not the Spanish New World and the Greeks were not Spanish conquistadores. The way for a Middle Ground was opened by several factors. Polytheistic religion and myth were accommodating, and no antagonistic "missionizing" (Christianization) took place. No one community was threatened by direct domination at the outset. There was a similarity of the "maritime-perspective" between Greek and Etruscan cultures as well as a similarity of interests and attractions. The colonial situation was less constrained and, therefore, open to novelty and change.

Odysseus, Campania, and the Etruscans

The protocolonial situation along the southern and western shores of Italy already implies lively contacts and familiarity among the traders that sailed these coasts.[29] This is evidenced from eighth-century Greek artifacts imported especially from Euboea that have been discovered in both Etruria and Latium.[30] The evidence seems to indicate maritime trading along the coast and, particularly, around the areas of the river mouths: the Picentino (Pontecagnano), the Volturno (Capua), and the Tiber (Veii).[31] Functioning both as a permanent settlement and as an *emporion*, or trading station, the founding of Pithekoussai around 770–750 B.C., followed by Kymē about the same time or a generation later, transformed the situation into a colonial one. I will avoid the debates around the precise nature of the colonial enterprises of these "first western Greeks," as David Ridgway terms them.[32] What matters here are the implications for the colonial context in relation to the Campanian Middle Ground, where we find evidence for mutual contacts among Greek, Etruscan, and local Italic elites, such as at Pontecagnano. An Etruscan aristocracy was resident here and later in Naples and Capua,[33] and it has plausibly been argued that Pithekoussai was responsible for some of the correspondences of material culture.[34] Pithekoussai's influence as a trading post seems evident among the Opicians of Campania where Greek Middle Geometric and Late Geometric pottery has been found in the necropolises (especially in the Sarno Valley): oinochoai, kotylai and cups of the Aetos 666, chevron, and Thapsos types.[35] In Kymē, the well-known Fondo Artaico tomb, a rich and aristocratic assemblage of about 730–720 B.C., contained an Etruscan shield that holds a cauldron with the cremated remains of the deceased. Fifty-two metal objects, including gold, silver, and electrum, accompanied the burial. The tomb indicates significant Etruscan influence or, as Ingrid Strøm argues, perhaps an Etruscan was actually interred there.[36] Giorgio Buchner, Pithekoussai's major excavator, claims that clasps found in the tomb illustrate that personal ornaments used by Greeks in Pithekoussai and Kymē in the second half of the eighth century "were *identical* to those used in Etruria and Latium" (author's emphasis).[37]

It is generally agreed that the new Greek presence provided the Etruscans with unprecedented social, cultural, and political stimuli.[38] This was not, of course, a one-sided affair. As Bruno D'Agostino emphasizes, the Etruscans themselves appear to have been frequenting the coasts of Campania via the sea, and Michel Gras has argued for the expansion of Etruscan contacts all the way to the eastern Aegean (note especially Lemnos, where what may be an Etruscan inscription of the early sixth century was discovered).[39] The criss-crossing of contemporary contacts and influences is notable. For example, in the Etruscan orbit the transition from Villanovan IIB to the Orientalizing Period is contemporary with the first tombs at Pithekoussai.[40] Dedications of Etruscan objects in the Panhellenic Greek sanctuaries are significant, pointing either to direct Etruscan contacts or to Greek *xenia* relations that considered such contacts to be very important.[41] Two bronze helmets, probably from Tarquinia, were dedicated in Olympia and Delphi in the first half of the eighth century.[42] Between 750 and 700 B.C., more varied Etruscan dedications were discovered (spear points, shields, fibulae, and various personal ornaments) at the sanctuaries of Dodona, Perachora, and Samos, and one awaits publication of two Etruscan fibulae found in Chalkis, one of the two mother cities of Pithekoussai.[43] Nevertheless, however we interpret the precise nature of such objects, it is clear that the Etruscans formed a notable part of the Greek experience during the whole of the eighth century.

Several groups are likely candidates for advancing contacts with the Etruscans, including emigrant Phokaians from Asia Minor, the Greek colony of Sybaris in south Italy, or various individual initiatives. The account of the

Bakchiad Demaratos, an exiled Corinthian aristocrat who came to Etruscan Tarquinia with three artists and fathered Rome's legendary king Tarquinius Priscus, may provide some indication of this.[44] The story of Demaratos combines both immigration of a nobleman and that of artisans, and is a good example of another route of the formation of the Middle Ground: individual migration and integration. In this early time frame of the eighth century, much emphasis has been given to Euboians setting out from the major cities of Chalkis and Eretria, the historical founders of Pithekoussai and Kymē.[45]

It was during the second half of the eighth century B.C. that the evidence for Euboian-Etruscan contacts is most prominent. During this period, the Etruscans adopted the Euboian alphabet, learning it from the Euboian settlers of Pithekoussai and Kymē.[46] By about 700 B.C., the alphabet was already shaped by the special needs of Etruscan phonetics. Alphabetic script was perceived as having intrinsic importance and as a marker of status. The Marsiliana d'Albegna tablets recording an entire Greek alphabet sequence, for example, were placed in a cauldron inside a tomb dating to about 675–650 B.C. Walter Burkert has convincingly stressed the role of individual "teachers," who disseminated the North Semitic alphabet among Greeks.[47] It seems reasonable that in Italy something similar was happening, this time involving Greek teachers. Their standing may have been like the individual craftsmen and potters who worked among the Etruscans and who were probably responsible for the rapid dissemination of Greek-style pottery. Such teachers, both craftsmen and script professionals, were most likely also responsible for another cultural innovation: the spread of motifs from the Greek epics.

The famous Aristonothos krater, dated to the second quarter of the seventh century B.C., displays a popular epic motif: Odysseus blinding the Cyclops Polyphemos (fig. 2). It was probably made by a Greek artist who settled in Etruscan Caere, signing his name to the rim in Euboian characters.[48] Adapting his style to suit the local taste — a taste that admired things Greek — Aristonothos chose among the epic images one that appeared to Etruscan eyes as quintessentially Greek. The krater implies an adoption of a Greek elite practice of drinking together, the *symposion*. As at Greek *symposia*, the krater was placed in the center from which the banquet participants could draw wine. The symposiasts may have viewed the pictures painted on it, and their conversation must have turned to the stories it illustrated. One side shows a naval warfare, while the other depicts Odysseus and his companions putting out the single eye of Polyphemos. When compared with contemporary representations of the blinding of Polyphemos, this scene "agrees most closely with the *Odyssey*."[49] The same may be said of a contemporary painted pithos (650–625 B.C.), which illustrates Odysseus and his companions blinding a seated Polyphemos, with an enormous wine jug in the center of the scene.[50]

The Aristonothos krater demonstrates how, by the second quarter of the seventh century B.C., writing, lifestyle, and epic content combined to spread the Odysseus motif among the Etruscans, expressed in the most popular painted narrative scene from the *Odyssey*. This would be the most economical interpretation of the Polyphemos episode.[51] It has also been claimed that the scene implies that a local Etruscan princeps saw himself, on the model of the heroic origins of a Greek *genos*, as a descendant of Odysseus (with the naval scene indicating Etruscan "piratical" activity).[52] The Euboian characters of the inscription provide a pointer to the identity of one of the agents of cultural dissemination. The visual iconography itself, whether it is interpreted through Greek or Etruscan eyes (or perhaps *because* it can be readily viewed from either perspective) offers a telling example of the efficacy of myth as a cultural intermediary.

Cyclops scenes represent the earliest iconography of Odysseus in extant Greek vase painting, appearing between 670 and 650 B.C. Some scholars, such as Walter Burkert, find the identification with the Cyclopea of the ninth book of the *Odyssey* problematic. Since it is known that the Cyclops is a common folk motif, its appearance on 10 seventh-century vases does not have to be linked with the *Odyssey*;[53] however, this is not the point. The Cyclops may very well have been a general folk motif, on which the Homeric epic was drawn. The generic blinding of a giant and the particular story of the blinding of the Cyclops Polyphemos must have coalesced at some point. A Greek of the mid-seventh century B.C. observing the scene on figured vases such as the Eleusis amphora or the Aristonothos krater would have recognized them as depicting the narrative-specific *Odyssey* scene. What matters in the world of the Greek-Etruscan Middle Ground is the seventh-century B.C. association that the painting evoked.[54]

The sympotic association of the Aristonothos krater reminds us of the sympotic context of the so-called Nestor's cup at Pithekoussai, dated to one century earlier (fig. 3). It was found in a tomb of a young boy, who died at about the age of twelve and was buried around 720 B.C. His parents may have been among the first generation of colonists. The promise of the new society marred by personal tragedy,[55] the dead boy was accorded an adult burial and in his tomb were placed vases used for an adult *symposion*, including kraters for wine mixing, rare in Pithekoussai.[56] One small inscribed cup has become famous among experts of Homer and of early Greek epigraphy and historians of Greek colonization. The cup (probably a Rhodian *kotylē*) bears a verse inscription in three retrograde lines (one either prose or iambic trimeter, two hexameters), with the words and phrases separated.[57] The verses are written in the alphabet of Euboian Chalkis.[58] The grave goods are particularly rich and may indicate that the boy belonged to a wealthy, aristocratic family, perhaps well-to-do merchants. From the inscription it has been inferred that the cup's owner and his family were possibly Euboian or at least literate in Euboian Greek:[59] "I am the cup of Nestor, a joy to drink from [or "Nestor had a fine drinking cup"], but anyone drinking from this cup will immediately be struck with desire for lovely-crowned Aphrodite."[60]

In the present context I will only state my view of the cup, without entering into a full discussion of the complex issues it raises.[61] The inscribed verses

Fig. 2. Aristonothos krater
Caere, 680–670 B.C., H: 36 cm (14⅛ in.), Diam.: 32 cm (12⅝ in.)
Rome, Musei Capitolini

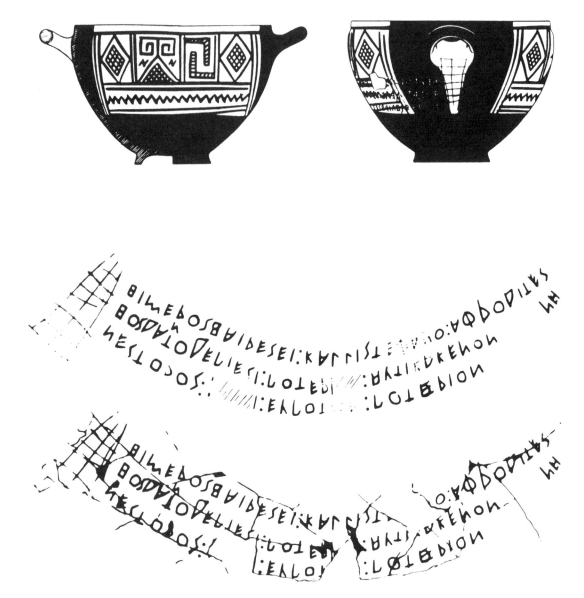

Fig. 3. Drawing of so-called Nestor's cup and its inscription
From Giovanni Pugliese Carratelli, ed., *Magna Grecia: Il Mediterraneo,
le metropoleis e la fondazione delle colonie* (Milan: Electa, 1985), fig. 343

exhibit maturity, sophistication, and a sense of literary saturation. They play jokingly on an allusion to the famous Nestor's cup in the *Iliad*,[62] a heavy, ornate metal vessel. The lines indicate an acquaintance with the details of the *Iliad* description, which includes a digression on the venerable cup of the old counselor. The Nestor's cup at Pithekoussai demonstrates familiarity not just with a specific episode of the *Iliad* but with particular textual details from it. It assumes existing knowledge of Homer's epics—not necessarily the texts as we have them, but perhaps something rather close were known and recited along with a host of pre- and post-Iliadic poems, including the various songs of return (*Nostoi*).

This cup was used in the communal experience of the *symposion*; therefore, the Homeric allusion was meaningful to a wider circle than the immediate family that buried the child. As noted above for the later Aristonothos krater, the Nestor's cup also assumes familiarity with epic on the part of the entire sympotic group, namely the generation of the boy's parents, around 750 B.C. or perhaps a little earlier. It is also safe to infer knowledge of Odysseus, a major hero in the Homeric epics. As we shall see, Odysseus was regarded by Greeks as an ancestor and a ruler of the Etruscans, and his name appears in fifth-century Etruscan inscriptions as Utuse. The implied knowledge of Homeric motifs so early among the Euboians of Pithekoussai should, therefore, be considered significant for the role of the hero as mediator among Greek colonists, the lands they inhabited, and the populations they encountered.[63]

A "sympotic lifestyle" is evidenced materially among both Greeks and Etruscans during the second half of the eighth century B.C.,[64] thus serving as one of the social forms of mediating the Middle Ground. Communal drinking among the Etruscan and Italic elite may not have been identical to the *symposion* of Greek aristocracy as we know it from later sources, but one may not disregard the evidence for the ensemble of sympotic objects that reconfigure local practices along Greek terms (fig. 4).[65] Sympotic gatherings may have provided an occasion for the exchange of gifts and prestige goods of the sort discovered in Greek and Etruscan princely tombs, thereby consolidating hierarchies of status and political power.[66] Dating to the latter part of the eighth century B.C., such princely tombs have been unearthed in Kymē, Etruria, and Latium. Contemporary with these are also the princely tombs at Euboian Eretria and at Paphos and Salamis in Cyprus, about which it has been observed that the salient features of the burials and the tomb inventories were inspired by Homeric descriptions, notably the funeral of Patroklos.[67] Similar influences may have affected the Etruscans, or at least the forms that their aristocratic burials took.[68]

Due to the egalitarian and reciprocal nature of the *symposion*, it provides a means of transmission for images and ideas, especially when these are compatible with the heroic lifestyle it represents. The *symposion* of the second half of the eighth century B.C. was "Homeric" both in content and form. As the songs of Phemios and Demodokos in the *Odyssey* illustrate, the subject of poetry sung in *symposia* was often tales of return, *Nostoi*. During the eighth and seventh centuries B.C. Greek and Etruscan elites underwent a process of mutual familiarization through the discovery of complementary ideas and lifestyles.[69] Both Greeks and Etruscans reclined at Homeric-style *symposia* and drank from *sympotic* cups bearing Homeric motifs expressed either through inscribed verses (Nestor's cup) or through painted Homeric scenes like "Odysseus blinding Polyphemos." Transport amphorae filled with wine, such as one discovered at Pithekoussai with a seal showing Ajax carrying Achilles (circa 700 B.C.), must have reached Etruscan customers (fig. 5).[70] Odysseus in particular, believed by Greeks of circa 700 B.C. to have been the progenitor of the Etruscans, would have played a special role as a "mediating hero" in the encounter with a non-Greek aristocratic culture that led a similar lifestyle, drank from the same cups, and hosted occasions of guest-friendship exchange.

At the end of Hesiod's *Theogony,* one finds the following verses: "And Circe the daughter of Helios, Hyperion's son, loved steadfast Odysseus and bare Agrios and Latinos who was faultless and strong.... And they ruled over the famous Tyrsenoi, very far off in the recess of the holy islands."[71] The passage forms an element in the earliest pattern of the Greek application of *Nostoi* genealogies to non-Greek peoples. It mentions neither particular cities nor Greeks, and seems to address a protocolonial horizon. It probably reflects Euboian images current one or two generations before Hesiod, who is deliberately archaizing here, since by his time Euboian colonial activity was at its acme. Hesiod represents himself in the *Works and Days* as having visited Euboian Chalkis, where he won a trophy in the funeral games of Amphidamas.[72] The authenticity of the *Theogony* lines has been contested, although a case can be made in their favor. Suffice it to say that by the sixth century B.C. there developed an alternative model to Etruscan origins, of which our poet seems unaware.[73]

Odysseus is a protocolonist who, like Herakles, explores and leaves descendants behind, but does not settle. His Italian sons, Latinos (ancestor of the Latins) and Agrios (who, as his name suggests, represents the wild hinterland peoples), are apparently personifications of the protocolonial imagination, as seen from the perspective of the maritime explorers and from new centers of Greek colonization on the island of Pithekoussai or the coast of Kymē in the Bay of Naples. It is important to note that the verses do not refer to the ethnography of direct and familiar contact, that is, to the peoples living immediately across from Pithekoussai and Kymē on the mainland. These were at once too familiar and, therefore, distinct and differentiated, for a generalized appellation. Rather, the Latins and Agrioi denote a peripheral vision, looking to what lies beyond the region of direct contact through commerce and colonization. This is another case of an ethnographic periphery to which a *Nostoi*-genealogy was applied, rather than to the peoples with whom Greek colonists came into face-to-face contact. Odysseus, in particular, was well suited for the "Beyond" and the "wild."

Perhaps because the Greeks consistently provided non-Greeks with a *Nostoi*-genealogy, such genealogies paradoxically became popular among

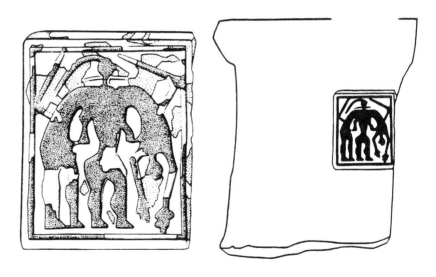

Fig. 4. Wall-painting with *symposion* scene from the Tomb of the Diver, Poseidonia, ca. 480 B.C.
From John Griffiths Pedley, *Paestum: Greeks and Romans in Southern Italy* (New York: Thames & Hudson, 1990), pl. 8

Fig. 5. Greek geometric seal impression on an amphora neck: Ajax carrying the body of Achilles, Ischia Pithekoussai, ca. 700 B.C.
Left: detailed drawing; *right:* schematic drawing
From Giorgio Buchner, "Pithekoussai: Oldest Greek Colony in the West," *Expedition* 8, no. 4 (1966): 11

Fig. 6. Fair copy: Tomba dell'Orco II (detail of wall painting of Odysseus, *UTUZTE*, blinding the cyclops Polyphemos, *CUCLU*, Tarquinia, ca. 366–330 B.C.)
Italy (Tarquinia), 1908, watercolor on watercolor paper, 78 × 113 cm (30¾ × 44½ in.)
Copenhagen, Ny Carlsberg Glyptotek

non-Greek peoples. Not worried about direct colonial control by Greek colonies, local Italic peoples would not have seen in Greek "ethnic" myths implications of territorial expansion or cultural domination. Since no Etruscan city faced the Greeks settlers of Pithekoussai and Kymē, the Etruscans would have been less threatened than others.

The Hesiodic verses connect the *Nostos* of Odysseus with the ethnography of the most distinct Italian civilization encountered by Greeks.[74] Odysseus functions within a typical Greek "ethnographic" model of defining others: the heroic genealogy. We have no idea whether initially the Etruscans welcomed this or whether or not Greeks cared if they did. The Etruscans apparently adopted the hero, just as they did other figures of Greek mythology. In the Etruscan language, Odysseus's name appears as "Utuse" (fig. 6), a "transliteration" that clearly points to the linguistic identity of the Greeks responsible for introducing Odysseus: the Euboians (note that the alternative Doric-

Corinthian form, Olytteus, eventually became Ulysses).[75] Since we do not have direct information concerning how the Etruscans themselves understood Odysseus in this period, we should attempt to evaluate to what extent Odysseus's connection with them was a one-sided, Greek idea. Thus far we have noted a context for the legitimacy of the question: Hesiod's text, written probably about 700 B.C.; Greek mythological motifs—Odysseus included—on painted vases available to the Etruscans; the matrix, archaeologically established, of close commercial and cultural contacts between Etruscans and the Euboians of Pithekoussai and Kymē during the second half of the eighth century B.C. and even earlier; our knowledge, based on the Nestor's cup of Pithekoussai, that those Euboians knew some Homer; and the Etruscan adoption of the Euboian alphabet in general and of the Euboian form of Odysseus's name, "Utuse," in particular.

It is time to enlarge the Etruscan and local contexts. Already noted is the familiarity of the settlers of Pithekoussai with Homeric motifs. The geographical context of cultural communication between Euboians and the Etruscans may help us assess why Odysseus may have been significant to the latter. By 650 B.C. the Etruscans were already a major influence in Campania.[76] Capua, for example, the most celebrated of Campanian cities that later also boasted of another Nestor's cup,[77] had known an unbroken development since the ninth century B.C. The same Euboian pottery found at Pithekoussai occurs at Capua and several other Etruscanized centers. There are other examples of Etruscan influence, such as at Nola and Pompeii where Strabo mentions a period of Etruscan control,[78] although these may have originally been Greek foundations that were later "Italicized."[79]

Local communities and their elite leaders, sometimes mixed with Etruscans, are particularly significant in mediating the Middle Ground. Pontecagnano (Picentia), on the river Picentino, best illustrates the intermixture of indigenous peoples, Etruscans, and Greeks. Its cemeteries show a sequence, as in Etruria, continuing since the ninth century B.C. Particularly rich tombs of around the year 700 B.C. have been discovered that also seem to evidence links with coastal areas.[80] In the pottery types, strong Euboian influence is evident. Imported pottery provides an interesting indication of circulation, whereas locally made Greek pottery as well as typically Greek decorations on local and hybrid shapes indicate the cultural Euboian spread and influence. Bruno D'Agostino cites the example of black-glazed skyphoi that had mostly disappeared elsewhere in Greece, but were still being produced in Euboia (Middle Geometric II) when they appear in Pontecagnano. Such pots indicate direct and close trade contacts that likely served as a vehicle for more profound cultural exchanges.[81]

Relations between Greeks and Etruscans must have been relatively good at this time, although this would later change. One should not be influenced by historical teleology when discussing Greek-Etruscan relations in the eighth century B.C.: "l'histoire n'est pas la tragédie. Pour comprendre le réel historique, il faut parfois ne pas connaître la fin."[82] In contrast to the conflicts of the sixth and fifth centuries B.C. (the Etruscan defeats in the wars with Kymē in 525–524, 506, and 504 B.C.,[83] and the intervention of Syracuse in 474 B.C.), Greek-Etruscan relations during the eighth and seventh centuries seem to have been mutually unthreatening and beneficial. There were a wide variety of Greek settlers: captives, traders, metics, craftsmen, aristocratic guest-friends, political exiles, and the like.[84] Even in the sixth century relations and points of contact between the two groups intensified as small communities of Greeks inhabited Etruscan ports such as Gravisca and Pyrgi.[85]

The colonial situation lent itself to the imposition of mythic genealogies onto new lands and newly encountered peoples. Greek myths of origins and travel seeped into Etruscan culture, perhaps among guest-friends, together with the wine drunk at aristocratic *symposia*. It also reached the Etruscans through other aspects of contact and adoption of Greek culture: art, artisans, and alphabet teachers. In short, the same colonizing need, the same situation of strangers penetrating new lands shared by both Etruscans and Greeks, enhanced the attractions of the Greek legends as meaningful and applicable.

To widen the perspective for a moment, one should note that in late-Classical and Hellenistic sources Odysseus became Etruscanized. He was connected with particular Etruscan sites and accorded a founder-hero worship (on a Greek model) as the founder of Etruscan Cortona. Viewed through the eyes of Greek protocolonists as the progenitor of the "Tyrsenoi," he is no longer primarily connected with Campania, although he can still be vaguely linked with Pithekoussai,[86] or portrayed as having landed in Kymē after his stay with Circe.[87] Aside from visual representations, our first source to provide an Etruscan story is Theopompos.[88] Odysseus returns home to find that his wife has been unfaithful. He leaves Ithaca again, sails to Tyrrhenia, and founds the city of Gortynaia (Cortona, above Lake Trasimene). Odysseus dies in the city he founded and, like any other Greek *oikist*, is worshiped by the citizens. The story seems compatible with a fragment of the Aristotelian *Constitution of the Ithakesians*,[89] in which Odysseus departs for Italy after he accomplished his return to Ithaca. Another fragment,[90] an epitaph for the heroes who partici-pated in the Trojan War, relates two epigrams about Odysseus's burial in Tyrrhenia. Finally, Lycophron, mixing together various traditions about the Italian-Etruscan stories of Odysseus, recounts that Odysseus died in Ithaca and his ashes were sent to Gortynaia: "Perge, hill of the Tyrrhenians [Monte Perge, near Cortona?], shall receive his ashes in the land of Gortyn."[91] The mention of an Etruscan cult points to a reality of interrelations between the Etruscans and the hero, which goes beyond the myth-making processes. Cult points to a liv-ing reality, shared by audiences different from those of the aristocratic poets. Quite obviously, the cult was an *oikist* cult, providing a symbol of common orientation, collective identity, and a perception of "Beginning" and origins.[92] In Italy and Sicily in particular, *oikist* cults had special prominence and seem to have provided the conceptual framework for imitation by other peoples, such as the Etruscans and, later, the Romans. By the fifth century B.C. it seems that identity and ethnic origins could be perceived mostly in Greek terms.

By the Hellenistic era, Odysseus's role expanded from that of a city founder to a leader of the entire Etruscan migration and settlement in Italy. Lycophron, perhaps following Timaios, speaks of Odysseus in such terms. He refers to him obliquely as "nanos" (short in stature): the "nanos who in his wanderings explored all the nooks of sea and land, will join Aineas with a friendly army."[93] This finds confirmation in Hellanikos,[94] who says that Nanas led Pelasgians from Thessaly, sailed to the river Spines (at the head of the Adriatic), and went on to take Kroton. This is probably Etruscan Cortona, where Odysseus was independently identified as a founder and as a cult recipient.

In hindsight, it seems amazing how many peoples have co-opted the Greek myth of the Trojan War and *Nostoi* poems as the framework for their own origin-myths and ethnic definitions. One may justifiably ask why there was no reverse situation of Greeks adopting narrative frameworks of local ethnic origins. Why did Etruscans adopt Odysseus and why did Greeks not adopt Etruscan heroes? The phrasing of the question is itself problematic. Once Etruscans adopt Odysseus, his story is no longer "Greek." A simplistic "acculturation model," perceiving of cultural adoption as if pouring from a full cup to an empty one, is not operative here. Once poured, the liquid is no longer the same. Odysseus and the Etruscans may be understood better in terms of a new, cultural Middle Ground. In Greek terms, too, Odysseus has changed and metamorphosed. From a Homeric hero whose adventure story deliberately is given no real geographical and ethnographical coordinates, he comes to be connected in the colonial world with distinct peoples and topographical locales, such as the "Cape of the Sirens"[95] or the "Mountain of Circe."[96] At the same time, it is apparent that no equivalent Etruscan hero played a similar part in a Greek Middle Ground. To return to the pouring metaphor, the Middle Ground was like a wine krater; cups of wine stock and water would be poured into it and the resulting mixture was "wine" fit for the *symposion*. In Campania the wine stock part of the mixture had a definite Greek flavor, even though it was no longer "the same."

Perhaps Greek myths had more authority. In later periods, as Elias Bickerman suggests, other nations accepted Greek definitions of their own identity because of the perceived "scientific" aspect of the Greek outlook. Everyone had myths; but Greek myths were also "accounts" — the result of "investigations" — and these usually disregarded what natives had to say about themselves.[97] Thucydides, for example, says that although the Sikans of Sicily claim to be autochthonous, "the truth as it is found to be" (ἡ ἀλήθεια εὑρίσκεται), is that they were Iberians who migrated to Sicily.[98] In a later period, probably after the sixth century B.C., the Etruscans seem to have adopted the Greek "scientific" theory of their Lydian — not Odyssean — origins. They did not give up on Odysseus, however; he quickly became their migration leader.

Bickerman's model applies to the Classical and Hellenistic periods. What was the situation earlier, before the rise of logography and history? A function similar to that of the later Greek "myth-science" was probably fulfilled in the early Archaic period by epic poetry. They were Great Epics, sung, alluded to, represented in paintings, and recounted at *symposia*. The Etruscans apparently had nothing equivalent. Their power, beauty, and heroic ethos transcended the "Greek" sphere.

This may just be a case where, following Anthony Smith, "the fuller *ethne* set the pace for the empty ones."[99] The *origins-mentalité* of nations is oddly susceptible to the stranger's opinion, similar to the curious psychological disposition to succumb to snobbery—one of the most potent and underrated forces in social history. Such susceptibility is recognition of one's inferiority. By appropriating the stranger's myths and other cultural achievements, however, one can accept and even transform one's status. In antiquity some Hellenized Jews made claims that Greek philosophers stole their wisdom from the Hebrew sages, just as certain contemporary African Americans claim that the wisdom of the "West" is of African origin. The myth of the colonizer is adopted by the colonized, but with a twist. The Romans likewise adopted the entire framework of the Greek origin myth but carved their independent niche by choosing the Trojan side. This is how Odysseus was integrated in Italy, whether as progenitor (Hesiod) or, according to one of the Odyssey sequels, during his subsequent travels after the first return. The Etruscans, a "people" whose political and cultural identity was being formed at the time of the encounter with Greek and Phoenician civilizations, were also formulating ideas of who they were. It was in such contexts that they adopted the story of Utuse, Odysseus.

We can thus see the emergence of a Middle Ground in Campania, a frontier zone for both Greeks and Etruscans, an area where they mixed with local elites and where Greek mythic frameworks were being disseminated, transformed, and appropriated. Campania was an area of mediation where a new "colonial" culture—not one of cultural "imperialism" but one of accommodation—emerged. This Middle Ground could emerge because the colonial situation was not threatening to either party. The Middle Ground was articulated, among other means, through myths of Greek *Nostoi* origins, and succeeded because such origins were not perceived to be exclusively "Greek" to begin with. The *Odyssey* and its related myths were something Greeks could offer as a cultural "commodity" in a multifaceted system of exchange.[100] People, apparently, liked the story, and it is not too difficult to understand why.

Notes

1. Irad Malkin, *The Returns of Odysseus: Colonization and Ethnicity* (Berkeley: Univ. of California Press, 1998).

2. Richard White, *The Middle Ground: Indians, Empires, and Republics in the Great Lakes Region, 1650–1815* (Cambridge: Cambridge Univ. Press, 1991), x.

3. White, *Middle Ground* (note 2), 50.

4. Solange Alberro, *Les espagnols dans le Mexique colonial: Histoire d'une acculturation* (Paris: Armand Colin, 1992), 9–16.

5. White, *Middle Ground* (note 2), x.

6. See Kerwin Lee Klein, "Reclaiming the 'F' Word, or Being and Becoming Postwestern," *Pacific Historical Review* 65 (1996): 179–217, esp. 191.

7. As noted by Kathryn Lomas, "The Greeks in the West and the Hellenization of Italy," in Anton Powell, ed., *The Greek World* (London: Routledge, 1995), 347–67.

8. On "center" and "periphery" in archaeological theory, see Michael Rowlands, Mogens Larsen, and Kristian Kristiansen, eds., *Centre and Periphery in the Ancient World* (Cambridge: Cambridge Univ. Press, 1987); and Timothy C. Champion, ed., *Centre and Periphery: Comparative Studies in Archaeology* (London: Routledge, 1995).

9. Irad Malkin, *Myth and Territory in the Spartan Mediterranean* (Cambridge: Cambridge Univ. Press, 1994), 169–74.

10. Robert Bartlett, *The Making of Europe: Conquest, Colonization, and Cultural Change, 950–1350* (Princeton: Princeton Univ. Press, 1993), 303.

11. Homer, *Odyssey* 9.125.

12. Greg Dening, *Islands and Beaches: Discourse on a Silent Land: Marquesas, 1774–1880* (Honolulu: Univ. Press of Hawaii, 1980).

13. Gocha R. Tsetskhladze, "Greek Colonisation of the Black Sea Area: Stages, Models, and Native Population," in idem, ed., *The Greek Colonisation of the Black Sea Area: Historical Interpretation of Archaeology* (Stuttgart: Franz Steiner, 1998), 9–68.

14. Recently Michel Bats, "Marseille archaïque: Étrusques et phocéens en Méditerranée nord-occidentale," *Mélanges de l'École française de Rome: Antiquité* 110 (1998): 609–33.

15. Margherita Giuffrida Ientile, *La pirateria tirrenica: Momenti e fortuna* (Rome: Giorgio Bretschneider, 1983).

16. Jean Bérard, *L'expansion et la colonisation grecques, jusqu'aux guerres médiques* (Paris: Aubier, 1960), 12–15.

17. Bartlett, *Making of Europe* (note 10), 309.

18. Irad Malkin, "Inside and Outside: Colonization and the Formation of the Mother City," in Bruno D'Agostino and David Ridgway, eds., *Apoikia: I più antichi insediamenti greci d'Occidente: Funzioni e modi dell'organizzazione politica e sociale: Scritti in onore di Giorgio Buchner* (Naples: Istituto Universitario Orientale, 1994), 1–9.

19. A. J. Graham, "Argos, Cnossus, Tylissus, and Religious Relations," in idem, *Colony and Mother City in Ancient Greece*, 2d ed. (Chicago: Ares, 1983), 154–65.

20. Thucydides, *History of the Peloponnesian War* 6.5.1.

21. Mario Torelli presents a useful summary of the recent bibliography in "The Encounter with the Etruscans," in Giovanni Pugliese Carratelli, ed., *The Greek World: Art and Civilization in Magna Graecia and Sicily* (New York: Rizzoli, 1996), 567–76.

22. Compare Bartlett, *Making of Europe* (note 10), 311.

23. Mauro Cristofani, *L'arte degli etruschi: Produzione e consumo* (Turin: Einaudi, 1978), 33; and David Ridgway, *The First Western Greeks* (Cambridge: Cambridge Univ. Press, 1992), 89–90.

24. Robert Drews, *The Greek Accounts of Eastern History* (Washington, D.C.: Center for Hellenic Studies, 1973), 4–19; and Jean Rudhardt, "De l'attitude des grecs à l'égard des religions étrangers," *Revue de l'histoire des religions* 209 (1992): 219–38.

25. Bartlett, *Making of Europe* (note 10), 85.

26. Irad Malkin, *Religion and Colonization in Ancient Greece* (Leiden: E. J. Brill, 1987), pt. 2.

27. Malkin, *Myth and Territory* (note 9), 133–39.

28. See also P. Fabre, "Les grecs et la connaissance de l'Occident" (Ph.D. diss., Université Charles-de-Gaulle Lille III, 1991); Dominique Briquel, *Les pélasges en Italie: Recherches sur l'histoire de la légende* (Rome: École Française de Rome, 1984); and Dominique Briquel, "Le regard des grecs sur l'Italie indigène," in *Crise et transformation des sociétés archaïques de l'Italie antique au Ve siècle av. J.-C.: Actes de la table ronde* (Rome: École Française de Rome, 1990), 165–88.

29. For example, see the information provided in the section, by David Ridgway, entitled "'Cycladic' Cups at Veii," in David Ridgway and Francesca R. Ridgway, eds., *Italy before the Romans: The Iron Age, Orientalizing and Etruscan Periods* (London: Academic, 1979), 113–24. For the down-dating of the pendent semicircle skyphoi, see Jean-Paul Descoeudres and Rosalinde Kearsley, "Greek Pottery at Veii: Another Look," *Annual of the British School at Athens* 78 (1983): 9–53; Rosalinde Kearsley, *The Pendent Semi-Circle Skyphos: A Study of Its Development and Chronology and an Examination of It as Evidence for Euboean Activity at Al Mina* (London: Institute of Classical Studies, University of London, 1989), 126–28; R. Ross Holloway, *The Archaeology of Early Rome and Latium* (London: Routledge, 1994), 46; and F.-W. von Hase, "Ägäische, griechische, und vorderorientalische Einflüsse auf das tyrrhenische Mittelitalien," in Monika zu Erbach, ed., *Beiträge zur Urnenfelderzeit nördlich und südlich der Alpen: Ergebnisse eines Kolloquiums* (Bonn: Dr. Rudolf Habelt, 1995), 239–86, esp. 248–52. For David Ridgway's revised approach, see Ridgway, *First Western Greeks* (note 23), 131; and Judith Toms, "The Relative Chronology of the Villanovan Cemetery of Quattro Fontanili at Veii," *Annali: Sezione di archeologia e storia antica* 8 (1986): 41–97. For "precolonial" Greek imports, see Gianni Bailo Modesti and Patrizia Gastaldi, eds., *Prima di Pithecusa: I più antichi materiali greci del golfo di Salerno*, exh. cat. (Naples: Arte, 1999).

30. Bruno D'Agostino, "I paesi greci di provenienza dei coloni e le loro relazioni con il Mediterraneo occidentale," in Giovanni Pugliese Carratelli, ed., *Magna Grecia: Prolegomeni* (Milan: Electa, 1985), 209–44.

31. Georges Vallet et al., *La céramique grecque ou de tradition grecque au VIIIe siècle en Italie centrale et méridionale* (Naples: Centre Jean Bérard, 1982); Descoeudres and Kearsley, "Greek Pottery" (note 29), 9–53; and David Ridgway, Francesca Boitani, and A. Deriu, "Provenance and Firing Techniques of Geometric Pottery from Veii: A Mössbauer Investigation," *Annual of the British School at Athens* 80 (1985): 139–50. Particularly rich in metal minerals is the area between Caere and Tarquinia and in western Etruria, Populonia, and the island of Elba.

32. Ridgway, *First Western Greeks* (note 23).

33. Gilda Bartoloni, *La cultura villanoviana: All'inizio della storia etrusca* (Rome: La Nuova Italia Scientifica, 1989); and Bruno D'Agostino, "Le genti della Campania antica," in Giovanni Pugliese Carratelli, ed., *The Greek World: Art and Civilization in Magna Graecia and Sicily* (New York: Rizzoli, 1996), 531–89. D'Agostino interprets the evidence from the grave as if the local populations in Campania included many Opicians practicing inhumations.

34. Giorgio Buchner, "Early Orientalizing: Aspects of the Euboean Connection," in David Ridgway and Francesca R. Ridgway, eds., *Italy before the Romans: The Iron Age, Orientalizing and Etruscan Periods* (London: Academic, 1979), 133.

35. Bruno D'Agostino, "Le necropoli protostoriche della Valle del Sarno: La ceramica di tipo greco," *Annali: Sezione di archeologia e storia antica* 1 (1979): 59–75; and Bruno D'Agostino, "La ceramica greca o di tradizione greca nell'VIII secolo in Italia Meridionale," in Georges Vallet et al., *La céramique grecque ou de tradition grecque au VIIIᵉ siècle en Italie centrale et méridionale* (Naples: Centre Jean Bérard, 1982), 55–67. The small number of Chevron cups creates difficulties in determining the chronology. See the table in Ridgway, *First Western Greeks* (note 23), 132.

36. M. W. Frederiksen, "The Etruscans in Campania," in David Ridgway and Francesca R. Ridgway, eds., *Italy before the Romans: The Iron Age, Orientalizing and Etruscan Periods* (London: Academic, 1979), 290; C. Albore Livadie, "Remarques sur un group de tombes de Cumes," *Cahiers du Centre Jean Bérard* 2 (1975): 53–58; Buchner, "Early Orientalizing" (note 34), 129–144, esp. 130–31, 138, in opposition to Ingrid Strøm, *Problems Concerning the Origin and Early Development of the Etruscan Orientalizing Style* (Odense: Odense Universitetsforlag, 1971), 47, 59 ff., 98 ff.; and Ingrid Strøm, "Relations between Etruria and Campania around 700 B.C.," in Jean-Paul Descoeudres, ed., *Greek Colonists and Native Populations* (Oxford: Clarendon, 1990), 87–97, esp. 90. See also Torelli, "Encounter" (note 21), 567.

37. Buchner, "Early Orientalizing" (note 34), 133, author's emphasis; in opposition to Strøm, "Relations" (note 36), 90. See J. N. Coldstream, "Mixed Marriages at the Frontiers of the Early Greek World," *Oxford Journal of Archaeology* 12, no. 1 (1993): 89–107, esp. 90–95, for the likelihood of mixed marriages between Greek colonists and Etruscan women, perhaps attested to by the presence of ritual "spiral amphorae" in female tombs. Coldstream's paper overlooks much of the earlier discussion; see A. J. Graham, "Religion, Women and Greek Colonization," *Atti: Centro ricerche e documentazione sull'antichità classica* 11 (1984): 293–314.

38. For example, see Cristofani, *L'arte degli etruschi* (note 23).

39. See Michel Gras, *Trafics tyrrhéniens archaïques* (Rome: École Française de Rome, 1985), chap. 11, and esp. 630–31.

40. Bruno D'Agostino, "Relations between Campania, Southern Etruria, and the Aegean in the Eighth Century," in Jean-Paul Descoeudres, ed., *Greek Colonists and Native Populations* (Oxford: Clarendon, 1990), 73–85, esp. 77.

41. I am particularly grateful to Bruno D'Agostino for the following references. See von Hase, "Ägäische, griechische, und vorderorientalische" (note 29); and F.-W. von Hase, "Présences étrusques et italiques dans les sanctuaires grecs (VIIIᵉ–VIIᵉ siècle av. J.-C.)," in Françoise Gaultier and Dominique Briquel, eds., *Les plus religieux des hommes: État de la recherche sur la religion étrusque: Actes du colloque international, Galeries nationals du Grand Palais, 17–19 novembre 1992* (Paris: Documentation Française, 1997), 293–323. Compare David Ridgway, "La presenza etrusca nella Campania Meridionale," in Patrizia Gastaldi and Guglielmo Maetzke, eds., *La presenza etrusca nella Campania Meridionale: Atti delle giornate di studio, Salerno-Pontecagnano, 16–18 novembre 1990* (Florence: Leo S. Olschki, 1994), 513–16.

42. K. Kilian, "Zwei italische Kammhelme aus Griechenland," in *Études delphiques*

(Athens: École Francaise d'Athènes, 1977), 429–42, dates the helmets closer to 800 B.C.; and von Hase, "Présences étrusques et italiques" (note 41), 253 n. 24, places them in the first half of the eighth century B.C.

43. Hans-Volkmar Hermann, "Altitalisches und etruskisches in Olympia: Neue Funde und Forschungen," *Annuario della Scuola archeologica di Atene e delle missioni italiane in Oriente*, n.s., 45 (1983): 271–94.

44. Polybius, *Histories* 6.11a.7; Pliny, *Natural History* 35.43, 152; Dionysius of Halicarnassus, *Roman Antiquities* 3.46.3–5. Compare Alan Blakeway, "'Demaratus': A Study in Some Aspects of the Earliest Hellenization of Latium and Etruria," *Journal of Hellenic Studies* 25 (1935): 129–49; and Domenico Musti, "Etruria e Lazio arcaico nella tradizione (Demarato, Tarquinio, Mezenzio)," in Mauro Cristofani, ed., *Etruria e Lazio arcaico: Atti dell'incontro di studio, 10–11 novembre 1986* (Rome: Consiglio Nazionale delle Ricerche, 1987); and Ridgway, *First Western Greeks* (note 23), 143.

45. See Michel Bats and Bruno D'Agostino, eds., *Euboica: L'Eubea e la presenza euboica in Calcidica e in Occidente: Atti del convegno internazionale di Napoli, 13–16 novembre 1996* (Naples: Centre Jean Bérard, 1998).

46. Lilian Hamilton Jeffery, *The Local Scripts of Archaic Greece: A Study of the Origin of the Greek Alphabet and Its Development from the Eighth to the Fifth Centuries B.C.*, rev. ed. (Oxford: Clarendon, 1990), 236–37; and Mauro Cristofani, "Sull'origine e la diffusione dell'alfabeto etrusco," *Aufstieg und Niedergang der römischen Welt* 1 (1972): 466–89; compare Ridgway, *First Western Greeks* (note 23), 141.

47. Walter Burkert, *The Orientalizing Revolution: Near Eastern Influence on Greek Culture in the Early Archaic Age*, trans. Walter Burkert and Margaret E. Pinder (Cambridge, Mass.: Harvard Univ. Press, 1992), 28–33; compare Barry B. Powell, *Homer and the Origin of the Greek Alphabet* (Cambridge: Cambridge Univ. Press, 1991), 123–80.

48. Gudrun Ahlberg-Cornell, *Myth and Epos in Early Greek Art: Representation and Interpretation* (Jonsered, Sweden: Paul Åströms, 1992), 94–95. For other representations of scenes from the Homeric epics in Etruscan art, see G. Colonna, "Riflessi dell'epos greco nell'arte degli etruschi," in *L'epos greco in occidente: Atti del diciannovesimo convegno di studi sulla Magna Grecia, Taranto, 7–12 ottobre 1979* (Taranto, Italy: Istituto per la Storia e l'Archeologia della Magna Grecia, 1980), 303–20; and Françoise-Hélène Massa-Pairault, *Iconologia e politica nell'Italia antica: Roma, Lazio, Etruria dal VII al I secolo a.C.* (Milan: Longanesi, 1992), 19–23. Early depictions of the Polyphemos story on a Caeretan hydria and on two Etruscan ivory pyxides are listed in *Lexicon Iconographicum Mythologiae Classicae*, s.v. "Odysseus/Uthuze," nos. 57, 60–62. See also Bernard Andreae and Claudio Parisi Presicce, eds., *Ulisse: Il mito e la memoria*, exh. cat. (Rome: Progetti Museali, 1996), 42–51, 120–33.

49. See Anthony Snodgrass, *Homer and the Artists: Text and Picture in Early Greek Art* (Cambridge: Cambridge Univ. Press, 1998), 88–98, for arguments for and against Homeric influence. His notion of "influence" is closely textual (see below, note 54).

50. Marion True and Kenneth Hamma, eds., *A Passion for Antiquities: Ancient Art from the Collection of Barbara and Lawrence Fleischman* (Malibu: J. Paul Getty Museum, 1994), 182–86; and Snodgrass, *Homer and the Artists* (note 49), fig. 38.

51. Compare Emma Dench, *From Barbarians to New Men: Greek, Roman and*

Modern Perceptions of Peoples of the Central Apennines (Oxford: Clarendon, 1995), 39; and Jeffery, *Local Scripts* (note 46), 239.

52. Massa-Pairault, *Iconologia e politica* (note 48), 19–20; and Torelli, "Encounter" (note 21), 568.

53. W. Burkert, "The Making of Homer in the Sixth Century B.C.: Rhapsodes versus Stesichoros," *Papers on the Amasis Painter and His World* (Malibu: J. Paul Getty Museum, 1987), 43–62. Compare Oskar Hackman, "Die Polyphemsage in der Volksüberlieferung" (Ph.D. diss., Frenckellska, Helsinki, 1904); J. Glen, "The Polyphemos Folktale and Homer's Kyklopeia," *Transactions of the American Philological Association* 102 (1971): 133–81; Claude Calame, "La légende du Cyclope dans le folklore européen et extra-européen: Un jeu de transformations narratives," *Études de lettres*, 3d ser., 10, no. 2 (1977): 45–79; and R. Mondi, "The Homeric Cyclopes: Folktale, Tradition, and Theme," *Transactions of the American Philological Association* 113 (1983): 17–38.

54. See the remarks of Anthony M. Snodgrass, *An Archaeology of Greece: The Present State and Future Scope of a Discipline* (Berkeley: Univ. of California Press, 1987), 140–41; and Snodgrass, *Homer and the Artists* (note 49), 88–98. Compare H. Alan Shapiro, *Myth into Art: Poet and Painter in Classical Greece* (London: Routledge, 1994), 49–55. Even without inscriptions, we can resolve the matter by looking for unambiguous attributes of the *Odyssey*. The Eleusis amphora (circa 670 B.C.) shows Polyphemos with some interesting peculiarities: the Cyclops is sitting rather than lying down, the stake is driven into his eye horizontally rather than from the top, and he is holding in his hand the wine cup that Odysseus offered him (earlier, in the *Odyssey*). The identifying features, especially the wine cup, are "textual details." The painter condenses the action and "quotes" the wine cup. On a sixth-century B.C. Lakonian vase a third element is being synchronized: the wine cup is shown, Polyphemos holds in each of his hands a leg of one of Odysseus's companions, and at the same time the stake is being driven into his eye(s).

55. For the sympotic (and empathetic) interpretation of the burial, see Oswyn Murray, "Nestor's Cup and the Origins of the Greek Symposium," in Bruno D'Agostino and David Ridgway, eds., *Apoikia: I più antichi insediamenti greci d'Occidente: Funzioni e modi dell'organizzazione politica e sociale: Scritti in onore di Giorgio Buchner* (Naples: Istituto Universitario Orientale, 1994), 47–54.

56. Ridgway, *First Western Greeks* (note 23), 57.

57. Giorgio Buchner and C. F. Russo, "La coppa di Nestore e un'iscrizione metrica da Pithecusa dell'VIII secolo a.C.," *Rendiconti (Accademia nazionale dei Lincei, Classe di scienze morali, storiche e filologiche)*, 8th ser., 10 (1955): 215–34; R. Cantarella, "He Megale Hellas ῾Η μεγάλη ῾Ελλάς," in *La città e il suo territorio: Atti del settimo convegno di studi sulla Magna Grecia, Taranto, 8–12 ottobre 1967* (Naples: Arte, 1968), 11–28, 41; Ridgway, *First Western Greeks* (note 23), 55–57; Murray, "Nestor's Cup" (note 55); and in opposition to Georg Danek, "Der Nestorbecher von Ischia, epische Zitiertechnik und das Symposion," *Wiener Studien* 107/108 (1994–95): 29–44. For the meter of the first line and a comparison with the text of the *Iliad*, see Carlo Ferdinando Russo, "Nota testuale e iliadica," in Giorgio Buchner and David Ridgway, *Pithekoussai: Testo* (Rome: Giorgio Bretschneider, 1993), 746–47; and compare F. Hansen, "The

Story of the Sailor Who Went Inland," in Linda Dégh, Henry Glassie, and Felix J. Oinas, eds., *Folklore Today: A Festschrift for Richard M. Dorson* (Bloomington: Research Center for Language and Semiotic Studies, Indiana University, 1976), 221–30, 235–40. For an overview, see Powell, *Homer* (note 47), 163–67; and Kevin Robb, *Literacy and Paideia in Ancient Greece* (New York: Oxford Univ. Press, 1994), 45–48.

58. Jeffery, *Local Scripts* (note 46), 235–36; and compare Margherita Guarducci, *Epigrafia greca*, vol. 1, *Caratteri e storia della disciplina, la scrittura greca dalle origini all'età imperiale* (Rome: Istituto Poligrafico dello Stato, 1967), 226–27.

59. Ridgway, *First Western Greeks* (note 23), 116. For a convenient description of the excavation, see Ridgway, *First Western Greeks* (note 23), chap. 4. For a discussion of possible, partial Levantine origins of the family, see Ridgway, *First Western Greeks* (note 23), 111–18. The argument ("partly non-Greek" or the ambiguous "Levantine extraction") is somewhat speculative. Ridgway's reliance on settlement patterns (promontories and offshore islands) as "startlingly reminiscent" of Phoenicians is blind to the fact that this is the consistent pattern for all maritime colonizations. Accordingly, the Crusader's colonies of Acre or Atlit, or the British colony at Hong Kong could similarly be interpreted "as if they . . . had Phoenician advice." The semitic inscription on amphora 571 is not directly tied to the Rhodian *kotylē* (Nestor's cup), which was not necessarily brought to Pithekoussai by Phoenicians passing through Rhodes. Without addressing the general question of Phoenicians (or Arameans) in Pithekoussai, the fact remains that the inscription on the cup is in Euboian Greek.

60. The first line seems comparable to inscribed titles of ownership, found on drinking vessels. The restored word is $\epsilon[\mu]\acute{\iota}$ or $\epsilon\iota[\mu]\acute{\iota}$; see P. A. Hansen, "Pithecusan Humour: The Interpretation of 'Nestor's Cup' Reconsidered," *Glotta* 54 (1976): 25–43; Powell, *Homer* (note 47), 164; and Murray, "Nestor's Cup" (note 55), 28.

61. Malkin, *Returns of Odysseus* (note 1), 157–60; and Murray, "Nestor's Cup" (note 55).

62. Homer, *Iliad* 2.632–37; compare Homer, *Odyssey* 3.51–53, 63.

63. Christopher Faraone, "Taking the 'Nestor's Cup' Seriously: Erotic Magic and Conditional Curses in the Earliest Inscribed Hexameters," *Classical Antiquity* 15 (1996): 77–112, acknowledges the sympotic context but claims that the three lines of the inscription (apart from the "owners assertion") contain the formula for a magical spell designed to work as an aphrodisiac. Hence Faraone is less certain about "Nestor" (simply a name?). I still believe an allusion is there: the line is set apart from what Faraone regards as a formula; a double entendre works well with varieties of formulae; and Campania knew other Nestor's cups in later periods (see below, note 77).

64. This is the general conclusion of A. Rathje, "The Adoption of the Homeric Banquet in Central Italy in the Orientalizing Period," in Oswyn Murray, ed., *Sympotica: A Symposium on the Symposion* (Oxford: Clarendon, 1990), 279–88.

65. Murray, "Nestor's Cup" (note 55); compare Pauline Schmitt Pantel, *La cité au banquet: Histoire des repas publics dans les cités grecques* (Rome: École Française de Rome, 1992), 46–48. For the funerary context of the Etruscan *symposion*, see Oswyn Murray, "Death and the Symposion," *Annali: Sezione di archeologia e storia antica* 10 (1988): 239–58; and compare G. Bartoloni, M. Cataldi, and F. Zevi, "Aspetti dell'ideologia funeraria nella necropoli di Castel di Decima," in Gherardo Gnoli and Jean-

Pierre Vernant, eds., *La mort, les morts dans les sociétés anciennes* (Cambridge: Cambridge Univ. Press, 1982), 257–73.

66. Bruno D'Agostino, "Tombe 'principesche' dell'orientalizzante antico da Pontecagnano," *Monumenti antichi: Serie miscellanea* 2 (1977): 1–110; and compare Holloway, *Archaeology of Early Rome* (note 29), 156–60.

67. John N. Coldstream, *Geometric Greece* (London: E. Benn, 1977), 349–51; and Ridgway, *First Western Greeks* (note 23), 138.

68. Ridgway, *First Western Greeks* (note 23), 138.

69. D'Agostino, "Tombe 'principesche'" (note 66).

70. Ahlberg-Cornell, *Myth and Epos* (note 48), 288, fig. 46b; and John K. Papadopoulos, "Early Iron Age Potters' Marks in the Aegean," *Hesperia* 63 (1994): 437–507, esp. 453 (C5), 470–71, 483–85 with plate 117e, points also to the probable use of the same stamp on a plaque at the Heraion at Samos.

71. Hesiod, *Work and Days* 1011–18.

72. Hesiod, *Work and Days* 654.

73. Martin West's strongest argument against authenticity, that Greeks had no real awareness of Etruscans before the sixth century B.C., is patently wrong. See Hesiod, *Theogony*, trans. and ed. Martin L. West (Oxford: Clarendon, 1966), commentary, ad loc.; and Malkin, *Returns of Odysseus* (note 1), 180–91.

74. For the advanced level of Etruscan city development, see Renato Peroni, "Communità e insediamento in Italia fra età del bronzo e prima età del ferro," *Storia di Roma* [Turin] 1 (1988): 7–38. By contrast, Latium in the eighth century B.C. seems to have been made up of villages, federated around sanctuaries. Centers do not emerge until the second half of the eighth century B.C. See *La formazione della città nel Lazio: Seminario tenuto a Roma, 24–26 giugno 1977, Dialoghi di archeologia*, 2d ser., 2 (1980): 1–234; A. Guidi, "An Application of the Rank-Size Rule to Protohistoric Settlements in the Middle Tyrrhenian Area," in Caroline Malone and Simon Stoddart, eds., *Papers in Italian Archaeology 4: The Cambridge Conference* (Oxford: British Archaeological Reports, 1985), 217–42; and G. Colonna, "I latini e gli altri popoli del Lazio," in Giovanni Pugliese Carratelli, ed., *Italia omnium terrarum alumna: La civiltà dei Veneti, Reti, Liguri, Celti, Piceni, Umbri, Latini, Campanie Iapigi* (Milan: Libri Scheiwiller, 1988), 411–530.

75. Compare Cristofani, "Sull'origine e la diffusione" (note 46); Cristofani, *L'arte degli Etruschi* (note 23); Mauro Cristofani, "Recent Advances in Etruscan Epigraphy and Language," in David Ridgway and Francesca R. Ridgway, eds., *Italy before the Romans: The Iron Age, Orientalizing and Etruscan Periods* (London: Academic, 1979), 373–412; Mauro Cristofani, "I greci in Etruria," in *Modes de contacts et processus de transformation dans les sociétés anciennes: Actes du colloque de Cortone, 24–30 mai 1981* (Pisa: Scuola Normale Superiore, 1983), 239–55; Colonna, "Riflessi dell'epos greco" (note 48); F. Delpino, "L'ellenizzazione dell'Etruria villanoviana: Sui rapporti tra Grecia ed Etruria fra IX e VIII sec. a.C.," in *Secondo Congresso internazionale etrusco, Firenze, 26 maggio–2 giugno 1985* (Rome: Giorgio Bretschneider, 1989), 105–16; Carlo De Simone, *Die griechischen Entlehnungen im Etruskischen*, 2 vols. (Wiesbaden: Harrassowitz, 1968–70); Frederiksen, "The Etruscans" (note 36); and Ridgway, "La presenza etrusca" (note 41). The form Olytteus (eventually Ulysses) may

have had its origins in Corinth, arriving in Latium probably via Messapia.

76. Martin Frederiksen, *Campania,* ed. Nicholas Purcell (London: British School at Rome, 1984), 117–29; Patrizia Gastaldi and Guglielmo Maetzke, eds., *La presenza etrusca nella Campania Meridionale: Atti delle giornate di studio, Salerno-Pontecagnano, 16–18 novembre 1990* (Florence: Leo S. Olschki, 1994); Mauro Cristofani, "Presenze etrusche tra Stabia e Pontecagnano," *Atti e memorie della Società Magna Grecia,* 3d ser., 1 (1992): 61–66; and G. Colonna, "Etruschi a Pitecusa nell'orientalizzante antico," in Alfredina Storchi Marino, ed., *L'incidenza dell'antico: Studi in memoria di Ettore Lepore,* vol. 1, *Atti del convegno internazionale, Anacapri, 24–28 marzo 1991* (Naples: Luciano, 1995–96), 325–42.

77. Athenaeus, *Deipnosophistae* 466e–489c, esp. 477b. See also Eustathius, *Ad Iliadem* 11.635.

78. Strabo, *Geographica* 5.247. See Frederiksen, "The Etruscans" (note 36), 297.

79. Kathryn Lomas, *Rome and the Western Greeks, 350 B.C.–A.D. 200: Conquest and Acculturation in Southern Italy* (London: Routledge, 1993), 28–30.

80. See D'Agostino, "Relations" (note 40), for previous references to his important work; compare Frederiksen, "The Etruscans" (note 36), 279; Annette Rathje, "Oriental Imports in Etruria in the Eighth and Seventh Centuries B.C.: Their Origins and Implications," in David Ridgway and Francesca R. Ridgway, eds., *Italy before the Romans: The Iron Age, Orientalizing and Etruscan Periods* (London: Academic, 1979), 152 ff.; Pliny, *Natural History* 3.5.70; and M. Cuozzo, "Patterns of Organization and Funerary Customs in the Cemetery of Pontecagnano (Salerno) during the Orientalizing Period," *Journal of European Archaeology* 2 (1994): 263–96.

81. D'Agostino, "Relations" (note 40), 78–80.

82. Pierre Vidal-Naquet, "Les juifs de la France et l'assimilation," in idem, *Les juifs, la mémoire et le présent,* vol. 1 (Paris: F. Maspero, 1981), 88.

83. Dionysius of Halicarnassus, *Antiquitates Romanae* 7.6.1–2.

84. Frederiksen, "The Etruscans" (note 36), 290.

85. Francesca R. Serra Ridgway, "Etruscans, Greeks, Carthaginians: The Sanctuary at Pyrgi," in Jean-Paul Descoeudres, ed., *Greek Colonists and Native Populations* (Oxford: Clarendon, 1990), 511–30; Mario Torelli, "Il santuario greco di Gravisca," *La parola del Passato,* no. 177 (1977): 398–458; and Mario Torelli, "Gravisca," in Giuseppe Nenci and Georges Vallet, gen. eds., *Bibliografia topografica della colonizzazione greca in Italia e nelle isole tirreniche* (Pisa: Scuola Normale Superiore, 1977–), 8:172–76.

86. Lycophron, *Alexandra* 688–93, with schol. on 688. See also the review of the evidence in D. Briquel, "Remarques sur les traditions de Nostoi en Italie: L'example de la légende d'Ulysse en Etrurie," *Acta Classica Universitatis Scientiarum Debreceniensis* 34–35 (1999): 235–52. His approach, denying Mycenaean precedents and stressing archaic *xenia* contacts, is similar to mine.

87. Pseudo-Scymnus, *Ad Nicomedem regem* 225–41.

88. For Theopompus, see Felix Jacoby, *Fragmente der griechischen Historiker,* 115 F 354 = schol. Lyc. 806. For further discussion, see L. Braccesi, "Cortona e la leggenda di Ulisse," in Giorgio Bonamente and Filippo Coarelli, eds., *Assisi e gli Umbri nell'antichità: Atti del convegno internazionale, Assisi, 18–21 dicembre 1991* (Assisi: Società Editrice Minerva, 1996), 127–38.

89. Aristotle, frag. 507 Rose = Plutarch, *Quaestiones Graecae* 14.

90. Pseudo-Aristotle, *Peplos* 640 Rose 12, 13.

91. Lycophron, *Alexandra* 795, 807; and E. D. Phillips, "Odysseus in Italy," *Journal of Hellenic Studies* 73 (1953): 53–67, esp. 65.

92. Malkin, *Religion and Colonization* (note 26).

93. Lycophron, *Alexandra* 1242–5. For Odysseus being short, see Homer, *Iliad* 3.193; Homer, *Odyssey* 6.230; Phillips, "Odysseus" (note 91), 60–61; Nicholas M. Horsfall, "Some Problems in the Aeneas Legend," *Classical Quarterly*, 2d ser., 29 (1979): 372–90, esp. 381; Geneviève Dury-Moyaers, *Énée et Lavinium: À propos des découvertes archéologiques récentes* (Brussels: Latomus, 1981), 65–72; and J. Poucet, "Énée et Lavinium," *Revue belge de philologie et d'histoire* 61 (1983): 148–59.

94. For Hellanikos, see Felix Jacoby, *Fragmente der griechischen Historiker*, 4 F 323a.

95. See Hesiod, *Catalogue of Women* 47 (= Schol., Apollonius Rhodius, *Argonautica* 4.892). Strabo, *Geographica* 5.247, with *de mir. ausc.* 103, which speaks of regular sacrifices that took place there. Compare Luisa Breglia Pulci Doria, *Dalla Magna Grecia a Cos: Ricerche di storia antica* (Naples: Luciano, 1996). Compare Strabo, *Geographica* 1.22–23, 6.258; Ptolemy, *Geographica* 3.1.79; Eustathius, *Ad Odysseiam* 1709; Virgil, *Aeneid* 864; Pomponius Mela, *De chorographia* 2.4.9; Pliny, *Natural History* 3.62; and C. Julius Solinus, *Collectanea rerum memorabilium* 2.22. Naples (Parthenope): Strabo, *Geographica* 1.26, with F. Raviola, "La tradizione letteraria su Parthenope," *Hesperìa: Studi sulla grecità di occidente* 1 (1990): 19–60. Keukosia: Lycophron, *Alexandra* 722, with schol.; and Strabo, *Geographica* 6.252.

96. See Theophrastus, *Historia plantarum* 5.8.3, who says it is the belief of the *enchorioi* who point out the grave of Odysseus's companion, Elpenor. Compare Pliny, *Natural History* 15.119; Cicero, *De natura deorum* 3.48; compare *Corpus Inscriptorium Latinarum* 10.6422; compare Pseudo-Scylax, *Periplous* 8; Aristotle, *Ventorum situs et nomina* 973b; Pseudo-Aristotle, *De mirabilibus auscultationibus* 78, 835b33; Pseudo-Scymnus, *Ad Nicomedem regem* 224–25; Strabo, *Geographica* 5.232; and Varro ap. Servius, *Ad Aeneam* 3.386.

97. Compare Dench, *Barbarians* (note 51), 35; and E. J. Bickerman, "Origines gentium," *Classical Philology* 47 (1952): 65–81.

98. Thucydides, *History of the Peloponnesian War* 6.2.2.

99. Anthony D. Smith, *The Ethnic Origins of Nations* (Oxford: Basil Blackwell, 1986), 178; and A. Appadurai, "The Past as a Scarce Resource," *Man,* n.s., 16 (1981): 201–19.

100. In answer to the question, "What had Greece to offer (the Etruscans) in return (for metals, etc.)?" David Ridgway adopts Coldstream's idea that Greeks gave Cyprus in the late eighth century B.C. the "greatest gift" in the form of the Homeric epics; see Ridgway, *First Western Greeks* (note 23), 138. He goes on to say that the Euboians had done the same for the Etruscans: "Could not the Nestor kotyle, the Ajax and Achilles seal impression and aspects of the burial rite at Pithekoussai have equally momentous implications for the circulation of the Homeric poems in the West?"

Colonizing Cloth: Interpreting the Material Culture of Nineteenth-Century Oceania

Nicholas Thomas

I f all social and historical analysis can or should involve the study of transformation, inquiry into colonialism cannot avoid doing so. Colonialism is not domination but the effort to produce relations of dominance, to produce social orders that have not previously existed. In many different modalities, it is oriented toward incorporation, exploitation, assimilation, and reform; however, these operations are understood, they are transformative ones, ones that typically entail not only new forms of government and economic exchange but new perceptions of space and time, new habits, and new modes of embodiment as well.

Material cultures and technologies are central to the transformative work of colonialism. Everyone knows that colonial power has generally depended on the superior military capacities of colonizers. I am not concerned with the degree to which this commonsense understanding is adequate or not. Furthermore, I do not want to pursue a question I have addressed in earlier writing, of the ways in which novel objects are, in fact, not self-evidently attractive to indigenous peoples, but may be valued because they are assimilated in certain ways to prior categories and hierarchies. Instead, attention should be turned to a more variable and nebulous sense in which objects may be intimately linked with the transformative workings of colonialism. This sense is nebulous partly because it rests on the inherent ambiguity that characterizes the workings of objects in social life. Objects are, on the one hand, things that carry properties, things that carry certain efficacies that follow from their material qualities and their histories; on the other hand, objects are mutable entities that are susceptible to redefinition, and radical redefinition at that. If we emphasize the second of these dimensions, we imply that things are primarily passive, that they are subject to recontextualization, that they merely mediate transformations in which they play no particular role in constituting.

This essay starts from a contrary premise, that it may be productive to explore the ways in which objects actively "text" their contexts. This is not intended as a theoretical axiom, which suggests that physical matter actually possesses social agency;[1] instead, my interest is in drawing attention to ways in which objects, and artifacts in particular, do not only mediate but also empower and render visible efforts of cultural transformation. In colonial histories, this leads one to emphasize not unequal exchange, the appeal of new commodities, or the recontextualizations associated with mutual appropriations, but rather the ways in which the adoption of particular objects can amount to the invention of a new way of being in the world. My examples relate to the use of cloth, and perhaps all I am saying, no doubt in an overelaborate way, is that colonialism, and here specifically conversion to Christianity, involved dressing differently. What I seek to demonstrate, however, is that one particular novel form of dress had specific values and effects, which followed from the ways in which they simultaneously resembled and departed from prior practice. The point is not that new garments were acceptable because they had material affinities with earlier indigenous forms, but that they were effective and appealing insofar as they extended and departed from those forms.

The example employed here is drawn from the history of bark cloth and missionary-imported cloth in the Pacific. The visual and artifactual evidence for the shifts is in a sense everywhere—late-nineteenth-century photographs show some people dressed in bark cloth while others are dressed in manufactured cloth, and Gauguin's paintings notoriously depict Tahitian women in "Mother Hubbards," the missionary gowns that, it has often been presumed, aimed to stifle native sensuality—but specific documentation is frustratingly thin. Certain missionaries who were sufficiently interested in bark cloth to collect it in quantity, and who were actively engaged in importing cloth, had little to say about either the uses of the former or the process through which the latter was adopted. This essay is, therefore, in the loosest sense, an archaeological effort in that it attempts to reconstruct social and cultural processes from material evidence that is perforce scanty and ambiguous. Its material evidence is drawn mainly from museum collections; it draws on the fragmentary documentation that contextualizes its objects, but attempts to use those objects, as it were, to contextualize themselves. In a methodological sense, this is patently problematic, but may exemplify the way in which poorly documented museum objects can be mobilized to inform inquiry into the archaeology of colonialism. At least, what is problematic in this procedure recapitulates what is problematic in artifactual history itself: it is never clear whether artifacts are actively contextualizing, or just being contextualized; the problem is not only that of the analyst but also of those who used the artifacts and were caught up in the histories and prior uses of the objects.

Bark Cloth in Polynesia

Bark cloth is one of the material forms of Oceanian peoples and, to adopt the term of an old-fashioned comparative ethnology, one of the cultural traits that manifests the affinities of peoples across the region.[2] It was produced all the way from insular Southeast Asia to Hawaii and Rapa Nui (or Easter Island). Although there were significant tapa traditions around coastal New Guinea, and even in the non-Austronesian interior, as well as in parts of the Solomon Islands, and in southern Vanuatu, Pacific bark cloth is associated above all with Polynesia, where its production and use were nearly pervasive.

The cloth, beaten from soaked strips of the bark of various ficus and paper mulberry trees, was made by women nearly everywhere, although it does not necessarily follow that it was defined as "women's wealth." While much of the cloth was undecorated, much was also stained, rubbed, stenciled, stamped, or painted. Decoration often featured elaborate, optically dynamic nonfigurative designs, some of which consisted of dense geometric motifs and others of more open patterns and freehand elements. The material was used in garments and various artifacts, and in rituals associated with hierarchy and reproductive exchange. There were various types and grades, ranging from heavy waterproofed clothes for common wear to very fine white tissue (often compared by early writers to muslin), which was monopolized by members of the elite. Although typically made and circulated simply in the form of sheets of cloth that were wrapped around the body, bundled, or extended in long strips, tapa was also sometimes used in figurative constructions, presumed to represent ancestral deities, notably in the Cook Islands, the Marquesas, and Rapa Nui (fig. 1).

The ritual significance of bark cloth related to identifications with the skin, which can be seen as "natural" associations, insofar as the bark is the skin of the tree. Such identifications are certainly attested to by fragments of Tahitian folklore, such as the report that the avaro tree "was the shadow of the god A-varo.... Persons approaching it irreverently were supposed soon to become afflicted with blotches over the skin, resembling the spots on the bark of the tree."[3] What is more systematically fundamental, however, is the functional affinity between skin and cloth; both wrapped the body, preventing the uncontrolled dissemination of sacredness (*tapu*), which could be injurious; additional wrappings were frequently required under conditions of peculiar ritual intensity or exposure, such as childbirth, bloodletting rituals, and death.[4] Certainly bark cloth also marked the often dangerous sacredness of a person or site. Mortuary places, the bodies of high-ranking people, and particular sacred artifacts, such as carvings of gods, were all wrapped in tapa (fig. 2). Had an eighteenth-century Tahitian priest been transported through time and space to encounter one of Christo's wrapped landscapes or buildings, he would not have found the work difficult to interpret.

In Fiji, Tonga, and Samoa, the making of bark cloth has never been abandoned. Tapa is still widely produced for huge presentations around events such as marriages, funerals, and celebrations associated with families of chiefs; it also features in contexts such as national and church diplomacy. Through familial connections tapa is exported in considerable quantities for use among the Polynesia diasporas in New Zealand, the United States, and Australia; it is also sold to tourists. In central and eastern Polynesia, that is, in the Cook Islands, the Society Islands, the Marquesas, and Hawaii, however, tapa production ceased at some point in the nineteenth century; perhaps as early as the 1820s or 1830s in Tahiti, and later in the nineteenth century in most island groups.

Even in those parts of western Polynesia where tapa is still extensively produced, its use as clothing has been long abandoned, except in particular

Fig. 1. Francesco Bartolozzi (Italian, 1727–1815), after John Webber (British, 1750–93)
A Young Woman of Otaheite [*Tahiti*], *Bringing a Present*
From James Cook and James King, *A Voyage to the Pacific Ocean*... (London: printed by
W. & A. Strahan, for G. Nicol & T. Cadell, 1784), pl. 27 (in atlas)

Fig. 2. William Byrne (British, 1743–1805), after John Webber (British, 1750–93)
The Body of Tee, a Chief, as Preserved after Death, in Otaheite [*Tahiti*]
From James Cook and James King, *A Voyage to the Pacific Ocean* . . . (London: printed by
W. & A. Strahan, for G. Nicol & T. Cadell, 1784), pl. in atlas

ceremonial contexts and in various cultural performances. Hence it is partly misleading to speak of persistence in the West and abandonment in the East, since in both places a more diverse pattern of shifts have actually taken place, involving continuity in some domains, discontinuity in others, and new spheres of circulation, such as tourist markets.

Misplaced and Migrant Ponchos

This history of the changing uses of indigenous and introduced textiles is intimately linked with the history of conversion to Christianity in the Pacific. Missionaries everywhere encouraged girls and women to participate in sewing classes and to produce garments, which conformed to the missionaries' standards of modesty, particularly for the purposes of attending church. There is now extensive literature on the ways evangelism was not limited to changing religious beliefs, but entailed at the same time a far wider conversion of "social habits" of work, residence, conjugality, and gender roles (figs. 3, 4).[5] Christianity not only brought new forms of worship and new beliefs; missionaries attempted at the very least to impose new ideas of work, a new calendar, and a new sense of the body. Sewing was important not only in itself but because its discipline entailed the new way of being in the world that the missionaries sought to render pervasive. Yet we cannot suppose that the Pacific Islander women who took up sewing understood the practice in the same way that the missionaries did, nor that they were necessarily transformed in the way that the missionaries desired. The values of these new habits, modes of dress, and forms of worship for Samoans, Tahitians, and others have to be investigated. We do not know what was received simply because we know what was being offered.

The most important Protestant mission in Oceania was, of course, the London Missionary Society (LMS), which began work in Tahiti in 1797 and extended its efforts westward from there to the Cook Islands, Samoa, Niue, and elsewhere in the first decades of the nineteenth century.[6] In all these places progress was initially slow, but indigenous elites, as well as individual converts, were gradually brought over to the cause. The great majority of Tahitians were nominally Christian by the 1820s, and by 1850, Christianity was well established also through most of western Polynesia. The popular demonization of missionaries has obscured the point that evangelization was effected, to a very substantial degree, not by white missionaries but by Polynesian teachers and catechists. Although they were not, until much later, fully ordained ministers, Tahitians, and later Cook Islanders and Samoans, were frequently deposited by missionary ships and left to deal with hostile situations as best they could, generally without the trade goods and other resources that gave the white missionaries some nebulous measure of prestige. Even when a mission was led by a white missionary and his wife, they were often accompanied by several Polynesian families, on whom much of the fraught business of cultural negotiation and intervention presumably fell.

Not only was Tahiti the first base of LMS activity in the Pacific, it also

Fig. 3. Beatrice Grimshaw (Irish, 1870–1953)
The New Woman in Niue
From Beatrice Grimshaw, *In the Strange South Seas*
(London: Hutchinson, 1907), 214

Fig. 4. Charles Gustave Spitz (French Polynesian, 1857–94)
Family group in front of thatched house, Tahiti
Tahiti, ca. 1890–95, albumen print, 20 × 24 cm (7⅞ × 9½ in.)
Los Angeles, Getty Research Institute

happened to be one of very few places in which there was any type of upper-body clothing. Throughout Oceania, indigenous dress consisted in loin-cloths, waist-wraps, belts, and skirts of various kinds; although flax and feather capes were made by Maori and Hawaiians, the chest was generally routinely uncovered, except in Tahiti, where early observers such as James Cook and George Forster described garments like ponchos (*tiputa*), consisting simply of long rectangular pieces of cloth, bearing a slit or hole through which the head was inserted.[7]

> Their clothing are either of Cloth or matting or several differen[t] sorts the dress of both men and women are much same which is a peice of Cloth or Matting wrapped two or three times round their waste…another peice or sometimes two or three, about 2 yards or 2½ yards long with a hole in the middle thro which they put their heads, this hangs over their shoulders down behind and before and is tied round their waste with a long peice of thin Cloth and being open at the sides gives free liberty to their arms.[8]

Although these poncholike garments were worn by both women and men, they were not so ubiquitous as to be remarked on by many observers, and the only early illustration of a *tiputa* is one being worn by a chief.[9] There is no definite information suggesting that *tiputa* were worn only by persons of high rank, but people of lower relative status were generally required to bare their chests in the presence of those more sacred; therefore, it may accordingly be assumed that only those of high status routinely wore garments of this kind. A type of poncho was also worn in the precontact or at least the early-contact period in the Cook Islands; extant examples are often described as the dresses of high-born individuals, and are elaborately perforated with small diamond-shaped cuts, motifs associated in Cook Islands carving with sacred ceremonial adzes and the presence of deities. Simon Kooijman points out that this does not mean that commoners did not wear *tiputa*; theirs, if they existed, were probably more basic and undecorated, and never attracted the interest of collectors.[10]

At the time of the Cook voyages, Tahitian bark cloths in general were either undecorated, stained, or decorated in a minimal way, with circular motifs, stamped in red or black with the end of a cut bamboo. By 1792, however, a new style emerged, involving direct printing with leaves and ferns: "they imprint sprigs and leaves on the cloth by wetting them with this juice, and impressing them on the cloth according to their fancy."[11] Reasonably enough, Kooijman suggests that this was stimulated by printed trade cloth that was presumably introduced during the Cook voyages. Some examples feature just a few leaves, while others combine stamped ferns with painted botanical motifs within a clearly defined diamond-shaped area.

If Tahitian ponchos underwent local changes in the late eighteenth and early nineteenth centuries, the question of their uses and identities becomes, soon afterward, a great deal more complicated. There are many examples in museums that are decorated not with these stamped botanical motifs but with designs that are unmistakably western Polynesian. Some of these are accordingly attributed to Samoa, Niue, or the Cook Islands, although others are said to be Tahitian, and even provenanced to collectors who visited Tahiti but not western Polynesia. If most of these pieces have simply been misprovenanced, it is possible that some are more anomalous, acquired in Tahiti, but plainly bearing western Polynesian patterns. If the particular origins and histories of many specific *tiputa* will remain obscure, the larger picture is clear: the Tahitian teachers who constituted the missionary vanguard in Samoa somehow managed to get the Samoans to adopt garments of this type, and that from the early 1830s to the 1860s, or perhaps later, they were made and worn by Christian Samoans, Niueans, and possibly Tongans. In the Cook Islands older autochthonous poncho types were partially replaced by neotraditional varieties associated with Tahitian missionary influence (fig. 5).[12] As imported cloth became more widely available, it came to be locally preferred. By the time islanders were being extensively photographed, nearly all of them wore European garments, except on occasions when "traditional dress" was required. The journals of the enterprising John Williams, notable for their ethnographic acuity as well as their evangelical and imperialistic zeal, enable us to make some sense of the question of precisely why a change of dress might have constituted an issue during the early phases of the conversion process in Samoa.

Thanks to the French voyager Louis-Antoine de Bougainville and many writers since, Tahiti has the reputation of being an "island of love," while Samoa, after Derek Freeman, is taken in contrast to have been a somewhat repressed place. Based on the experiences of the Tahitian teachers Williams deposited on Upolo in 1830, these images might be reversed: the Tahitians preached restraint while the Samoans paraded their sexual license. The important point is not that the Tahitians were reputedly shocked by Samoan sexuality, nor that exhibitionism and orgiastic ceremonies loom large in Williams's account of heathen Samoan mores; rather, it is that Tahitian teachers and Samoans alike evidently understood their differences in terms of the exposure and the display of the body, and played on those differences, in their missionary efforts and reactive mockery, respectively.

When Williams returned to Samoa in 1832, he inquired of the Tahitian teachers whether "they had not taught them [the Samoans] to make their nice white Tahitian cloth" (incidentally thereby indicating that the bark cloth appealed to the missionaries because of its plain and chaste associations, associations that are hardly likely to have been present in Tahitians' minds).

They said they themselves had made a great deal for the Chiefs but they could not get the women to learn. They were so intolerably lazy. They liked the cloth very well to put round their middles but they could not induce them to cover their persons of which they are exceedingly proud especially their breasts which are generally very large. They are continually wishing the teachers wives to lay aside their garments &

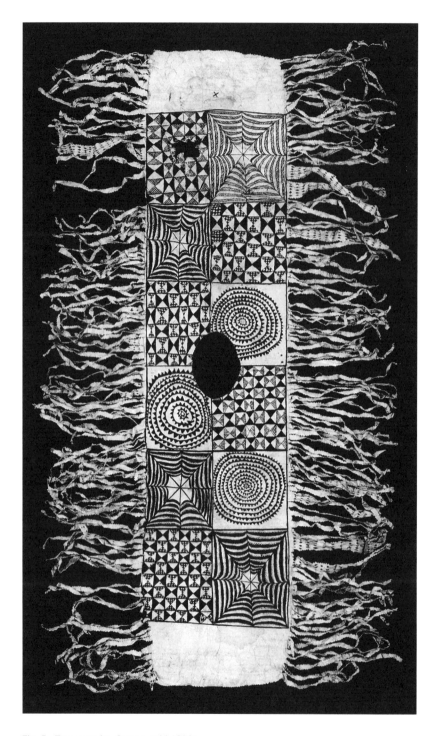

Fig. 5. Tapa poncho, Samoa, mid-1800s
Wellington, Museum of New Zealand Te Papa Tongarewa

"faasamoa" do as the Samoa ladies do, gird a shaggy mat round their loins as low down as they can tuck up the corner in order to expose the whole front & side of the left thigh anoint themselves beautifully with scented oil, tinge themselves with turmeric put a string of blue beads round their neck & then faariaria [make a display] walk about to show themselves. You will have, they say, all the *Manaia* the handsome young men of the town loving you then.[13]

Elsewhere Williams reported that a young European whom he considered "respectable" had initially been troubled by women removing their mats and exposing their genitals; his shy response prompted others to do the same and dance before him, "desiring him not to be bashful or angry it was Faa Samoa or Samoa fashion."[14] It appears, in other words, as though Samoans, and Samoan women in particular, were responding assertively to Tahitian and European foreigners alike, insistently displaying their bodies, insisting on the pleasure of self-decoration, and on the value of these practices as Samoan practices.

Even in 1832, however, this was not a sustained or consistent line of resistance. Williams had learned even as he was approaching Upolu and Savaii the second time that many of the people had turned to Christianity. This would seem an extraordinary development, if one understood Christianity as a European system that perforce had to be imposed by some powerful force of white missionaries. Still it is clear that Williams happened to bring the Tahitian teachers at a highly fortuitous moment, when a high chief and priest had recently been assassinated, when the warrior-chief Malietoa, with whom Williams, in effect, formed an alliance, was in the ascendancy.[15] The Samoan enthusiasm for Christianity at this moment thus seems to have had little to do with the concerns of the LMS, and Williams himself well understood that a plethora of motivations were at play, not least the fairly obvious interest in the acquisition of European wealth in various forms. Here again, we need to do more than merely note that islanders wanted guns or cloth, but ask what guns and cloth represented to them, and what guns and cloth enabled them to do.

It is notable that in Samoa, unlike neighboring Tonga, Tahiti, and the Cook Islands, bark cloth was not routinely used in ordinary garments. Dress consisted instead of several kinds of simple leaf skirts, and in a variety of grades of mats. The latter may have been held in place by bark cloth belts, but sheets of bark cloth themselves were not worn, except in exceptional ritual circumstances. The bride, for instance, wore a large piece of white *siapo* underneath her fine mats, and this piece was stained with blood when she was ritually deflowered. The strong associations that bark cloth had with sanctity, and with ritually marked or dangerous conditions, elsewhere in Polynesia, can only have been intensified in Samoa. Here, it had fewer quotidian uses, although it is important to acknowledge that tapa was also used in household screens and in a few other situations, which were presumably not marked by peculiar sacredness.

It is striking that, if Williams's reports are to be credited, Samoan chiefs discoursing on the merits of Christianity seem to have suggested that the religion was true because English people were visibly strong, and were visibly equipped with fine things, especially clothes. He reported that one said, "Only look at the English people. They have noble ships while we have only canoes. They have strong beautiful clothes of various colours while we have only ti leaves. They have sharp knives while we have only a bamboo to cut with."[16] Earlier, the chief Fauea, crucial as a go-between, had argued, "And you can see...that their God is superior to ours. They are clothed from the head down to the feet and we are naked."[17] Although Williams probably embellished these quotations (as he certainly did in his published account of the Pacific missions), it is unlikely that they were simply concocted.[18] The suggestion that some spiritual condition is "proved" by the efficacy and the well-being of the people associated with a certain religion is very much in conformity with Polynesian rhetoric and ways of thinking. It is, at any rate, interesting that well-being should be identified not only with obvious technical advantage (the superiority of metal tools) but also with an abundance of clothing, and with the full covering of the body.

It would be hard to understand why a few fairly powerless Tahitians, or even one personally forceful Englishman, should have succeeded in imposing a Tahitian style of dress on the Samoans, whose political autonomy was in no sense compromised or threatened at this very early moment in contact history, and who clearly took pride in their own modes of comportment. Although Williams noted that some Samoan women sought to convert the Tahitian teachers' wives to the Samoan way rather than expressing any interest in changing themselves, however, some others opted for cloth. Williams noted not only that "Some few Samoans who have embraced Christianity have taken to wear cloth entirely" but also that "On Sabbath days...the Teachers have succeeded in inducing the whole congregation men & women to attend properly clothed & decently covered."[19] "Cloth" means bark cloth and not mats, and "decent covering" means that the women, or perhaps both the men and the women, were covering their breasts. Williams does not specifically mention *tiputa*, but these are presumably the upper-body garments he has in mind. There is one early Samoan poncho in the Australian Museum, which was, supposedly, collected by him. Even if this identification is spurious, Samoan *tiputa* were certainly being made by 1839, when the American explorer Charles Wilkes noted that Samoans were wearing *siapo* "wrappers" "and the *tiputa*, a kind of poncho, of the same material, after the fashion of the Tahitians."[20]

There are references in the missionary literature on Polynesia to converts wearing tapa ribbons to distinguish themselves from their pagan neighbors, but the point I want to make about these objects is that they were much more than mere markers of identities. To be sure, tapa clothes did indicate that a person was a Christian rather than a pagan Samoan, but I believe that the interpretative strategy of regarding things essentially as expressions of cultural, subcultural, religious, or political identities depends on too static and literal an approach to their meanings. We also need to go beyond another fairly obvious statement about the Samoan *tiputa*, which defines them as "local appropriations" of a more pervasive form. Again, it is certainly true that these are Samoan variations on a regional type, but it would be misleading if we suggested that "localization" was a Samoan project that motivated their production; it may instead be an aspect of their practice that has other motivations. Anthropological rhetoric at present tends to treat the global as something insidious that locals have an interest in assimilating or incorporating, but the critical metanarrative of plural appropriations is ours rather than theirs; their investments may be in strategies that neither collude with nor resist global relations.

In this case, I suggest that local Polynesian strategies used these material forms as a kind of technology, toward a new way of being in the world. Williams understood this; he was less interested in a badge or flag that declared a person's Christianity than in a technique of dress that altered the being of the convert, that manifested an inner redemption or at least the scope for one. If it is unlikely that the Tahitian teachers shared this theology, they had, in all likelihood, adopted the notion of personal modesty, and saw the wearing of new garments as a means to that end. The Samoans too, would surely not have adopted these clothes had they not themselves regarded them as a technique of conversion; but what conversion meant to them in 1832 is by no means easy to measure or define. We can be sure that their ideas of self-transformation differed from those of Williams and the Tahitian Christians, and the most suggestive evidence lies perhaps in Fauea's observations on the strength and superiority of Christian people, with their ships and their full dress; this indicates broadly that the fully-dressed body was an empowered body. We may infer, also, that the power of that body was conferred by tapa wrapping, by some kind of transmission of the sanctity that otherwise inhered in the use of tapa in more special ritual contexts. At any rate, if Samoans were transforming themselves, to some extent at the instigation of foreigners, they were also effecting a shift that was internal to Samoan culture and material culture. How far they were binding the values that cloth possessed in collective ritual uses in new forms that embraced the particular person is something about which I can only speculate.

If *tiputa* started out, in Samoa, by bearing a Samoan strategy of empowerment, these artifacts also entailed certain Christian values of individual self-presentation. The idea that a set of garments constituted one's "Sunday best" implied both a new temporal order and a new spatial orientation, which transformed the church from a space of worship into a theater in which people might display themselves in a novel way (see p. 16, fig. 6). While it is impossible to know what was actually going on in the heads of the Samoans who began wearing cloth, to some degree these transformations were implicated in their practices, in what they did and in the objects they deployed, rather than in what they thought or said. We may be missing the point if we seek discursive expressions of embodied habits and orientations.

Conclusion

I have previously argued that novel things can be assimilated to existing categories.[21] I aimed to demonstrate that indigenous peoples possessed the power to redefine introduced objects, but perhaps perforce implied that their strategies were conservative, in the sense that they attempted to preserve a prior order rather than create a new and unique one. Here I seek to move beyond the constraints of an either/or approach. The value of *tiputa*, I suggest, inhered in their doubleness; they were things that mobilized certain precedents, certain prior values that cloth possessed, on the one hand, but possessed novelty and distinctiveness on the other.

Tiputa were more than just Christian clothes; they were more than clothes that covered the body and effected a new modesty. They were also wrappings that were understood by Samoans, initially at least, to empower their bearers. *Tiputa* were also Sunday best; they gave a new Christian calendar visibility and practical meaning; they were not part of a repressive missionary law as much as a productive effort, to teach people that their sense of self-worth and pride might be invested in their self-presentation in church on Sundays. These artifacts were not just expressions of a new context but technologies that created that context anew.

This way of seeing things also helps us move beyond the longstanding dilemma of historical anthropology in Oceania, which has lurched between emphasis on continuity and discontinuity, between affirmation of the enduring resilience of local cultures and critique of the effects of colonial history. Artifacts such as *tiputa* are neither inventions of tradition nor wholly unprecedented forms. They are simultaneously implicated in the material history of Polynesian societies and departures from that history. Their fertile relation to both prior and other forms of cloth is perhaps like the productivity of a metaphor. Metaphors must have affinities with the terms to which they are applied, but one chooses a metaphor, not for those affinities, but for its particular differences, because one wants to turn or twist meanings in a new direction. Those who have studied the cultural history of the Pacific may have neglected the interests in turning and twisting. More often than we have acknowledged, the indigenous peoples of the region have been concerned not to "contextualize" things, but to use things to change contexts.

Notes

1. See, however, Alfred Gell, *Art and Agency: An Anthropological Theory* (Oxford: Clarendon, 1998), for an innovative discussion of the mediation of social agency by objects.

2. See Simon Kooijman, *Tapa in Polynesia* (Honolulu: Bishop Museum Press, 1972), for a fine survey of Polynesian tapa traditions, albeit one that perforce leaves many questions unresolved. Other surveys include Roger Neich and Mick Pendergrast, *Pacific Tapa* (Auckland: David Batemen, 1997) (also published as *Traditional Tapa Textiles of the Pacific* [London: Thames & Hudson, 1997]); and Nicholas Thomas,

Oceanic Art (New York: Thames & Hudson, 1995), chap. 6. There is no comparable review of Melanesian or island Southeast Asian bark cloth.

3. Teuira Henry, *Ancient Tahiti* (1928; reprint, New York: Kraus, 1971), 382.

4. Compare Alfred Gell, *Wrapping in Images: Tattooing in Polynesia* (Oxford: Clarendon, 1993).

5. Margaret Jolly, "'To Save the Girls for Brighter and Better Lives': Presbyterian Missions and Women in the South of Vanuatu, 1848–1870," *Journal of Pacific History* 26 (1991): 27–48; Margaret Jolly and Martha Macintyre, eds., *Family and Gender in the Pacific: Domestic Contradictions and the Colonial Impact* (Cambridge: Cambridge Univ. Press, 1989); Nicholas Thomas, "Colonial Conversions: Difference, Hierarchy, and History in Early Twentieth-Century Evangelical Propaganda," *Comparative Studies in Society and History* 34 (1992): 366–89; and Richard Eves, "Colonialism, Corporeality, and Character: Methodist Missions and the Refashioning of Bodies in the Pacific," *History and Anthropology* 10 (1996): 85–138.

6. For the fullest review, see Niel Gunson, *Messengers of Grace: Evangelical Missionaries in the South Seas, 1797–1860* (Melbourne: Oxford Univ. Press, 1978).

7. Five bark cloth *tiputa* and one woven fiber garment of similar form are among the Polynesian artifacts collected on the Cook voyages; see Anne D'Alleva, "Shaping the Body Politic: Gender, Status, and Power in the Art of Eighteenth-Century Tahiti and the Society Islands" (Ph.D. diss., Columbia University, 1997), 2:490–92.

8. James Cook, July 1769, in J. C. Beaglehole, ed., *The Journals of Captain James Cook on His Voyages of Discovery*, vol. 1, *The Voyage of the Endeavour, 1768–1771* (Cambridge: Cambridge Univ. Press, 1955), 126.

9. A chief of Borabora, Society Islands, is shown wearing a *tiputa* decorated with ferns and leaves in Louis Isadore Duperrey, *Voyage autour du monde*, vol. 1, *Histoire du voyage: Atlas* (Paris: A. Bertrand, 1826), pl. 15.

10. Kooijman, *Tapa in Polynesia* (note 2), 67.

11. London Missionary Society, *A Missionary Voyage to the Southern Pacific Ocean* (London: T. Gillet for T. Chapman, 1799), 371; and Anne D'Alleva, "Continuity and Change in Decorated Barkcloth from Bligh's Second Breadfruit Voyage, 1791–1793," *Pacific Arts: The Journal of the Pacific Arts Association* 13–14 (1995): 29–42.

12. Peter H. Buck, *Arts and Crafts of the Cook Islands* (1944; reprint, New York: Kraus, 1971), 431–34.

13. Richard M. Moyle, ed., *The Samoan Journals of John Williams, 1830 and 1832* (Canberra: Australian National University, 1984), 117.

14. Moyle, *Samoan Journals* (note 13), 232.

15. Moyle, *Samoan Journals* (note 13), 10–11.

16. Moyle, *Samoan Journals* (note 13), 237.

17. Moyle, *Samoan Journals* (note 13), 68.

18. John Williams, *A Narrative of Missionary Enterprises in the South Sea Islands* (London: John Snow, 1838), 572–74; Caroline Ralston, "Early Nineteenth-Century Polynesian Millennial Cults and the Case of Hawaii," *Journal of the Polynesian Society* 94 (1985): 307–31, esp. 310–11, suggests that both these quotations refer to the same speech, in the course of an argument against the view that Polynesian millennial movements were motivated primarily by an extraordinary desire for European property. The

Polynesian interest in guns, cloth, iron, ships, and so on is, however, extraordinarily widely attested to and does not mark a Polynesian thirst for "Western goods" as such but rather an interest in the indigenous forms of prestige and power that possession and deployment of those goods at once enabled and marked. See Nicholas Thomas, *Entangled Objects: Exchange, Material Culture, and Colonialism in the Pacific* (Cambridge: Harvard Univ. Press, 1991), chap. 3; and for further comment on the Williams passage, see Vanessa Smith, *Literary Culture and the Pacific: Nineteenth-Century Textual Encounters* (Cambridge: Cambridge Univ. Press, 1998), 5–6.

19. Moyle, *Samoan Journals* (note 13), 231.

20. Charles Wilkes, *Narrative of the United States Exploring Expedition* (Philadelphia: Lea & Blanchard, 1845), 2:141.

21. Thomas, *Entangled Objects* (note 18).

Forms of Andean Colonial Towns, Free Will, and Marriage

Tom Cummins

And thus our Catholic Kings have taken great care in mandating through many royal decrees, which they have dispatched since the beginning of the Conquest until now that with great care, that they (the Spaniards) bring them (the Indians) to live in towns socially founded.

—Alonso de la Peña Montenegro[1]

The archaeology of Spanish colonial America is largely unwritten.[2] Yet, it is hard to imagine a much greater and more rapid transformation of material culture than that which occurred in America in the sixteenth century, especially in Mexico and Peru. Pre-Columbian villages and cities either were laid to waste or were rebuilt to conform to Spanish expectations. In addition, native communities were formed newly and in new places. Spanish colonization of the Americas is, however, more often imagined as the history of the forceful conquest and then the subsequent exploitation and evangelization of the native population.[3] Spanish colonization of the Americas was many more things than just that. And if one were to imagine an intellectually critical colonial archaeology, it quite likely would be a project that focused on the physical manifestations of the central concern of both the state and the church: the systematic establishment of Christian order in the New World.

The creation of this order meant a process of formulating coherent political and theological policies within Spain, then transmitting and implementing the policies within colonial communities. As an art historian, I want to track this transmission as a set of forms establishing throughout the New World a universalizing order. The process of transmission and its transmutation begins with the written pages of theologians and politicians in Spain that are rephrased in doctrinal documents specifically written for indigenous communities. It is in these "local" documents that exist visual renderings by colonial officials of what that order should look like. Finally, these abstractions become the places where the texts and images were built and performed.[4] This process is not as direct and unmediated as sketched here, but its outline is clearly discernible in existing documents.

In particular, I want to trace the unexpected intersection between the planning and building of new native towns, the formation of native grammars, and the universalization of the norms of consanguinity through the sacrament of marriage. It is to consider how imperial imagination might become colonial habitus in terms of space, actions, and subjectivity.[5] In short, it is to imagine the intersecting spheres of colonial culture and the spaces where that occurs, and how a critical form of colonial archaeology could inform the imagining of people interacting in a colonial world.

Reducciones

> Among other things that his Majesty is obliged, and the Encomenderos in his name, is the teaching to the Indians human civility so that they may be instructed with much greater facility in our Holy Catholic Faith, which is the principal aim (of conquest), and thus it is just and blessed the order for them to be gathered in to towns.
>
> —Juan de Matienzo[6]

Bestowing Christian order on the New World was a royal obligation.[7] Its fulfillment was first a philosophical and then a pragmatic problem. It meant, philosophically, the formation of a civilized community of men, the *consortium hominium*. This was to be achieved, as Anthony Pagden has described, by creating a *civilis societas* of which the *civitas* (the city) was the most natural and perfect community; where the practice of virtue and pursuit of happiness were possible and man could achieve his purpose, his *telos*.[8] The city, however, was "not a human invention … but a device implanted by Nature in man for his own safety and survival," and God was the author of natural law. That is, natural law was the knowable reflection of the celestial order. This is precisely how one of Spain's most important sixteenth-century theologians Francisco de Vitoria, quoted above and to whom I shall refer later, framed the essentially Aristotelian argument in Christian terms in his *On Civil Law* written in 1528.[9] More important, in terms of natural law in the New World, Vitoria demonstrated clearly that Indians had the capacity for civility within Aristotelian categories. The Indian, as a being capable of reason, was also universally recognized in a Papal Bull, the *Sublimus Deus*, issued by Pope Paul III in 1537, conceding that Indians could receive the sacrament of baptism. Although Indians were already being baptized as part of the evangelizing efforts of the mendicant orders, the Papal Bull declared once and for all that all the inhabitants of the New World could become Christians, and therefore the polis into which they were to be formed would be transformed eventually into a spiritual community with a quasi-mystical presence.[10] That is, the *consortium hominium* would become the *congregatio fidelium,* the brotherhood of all men in Christ with the possibility of eternal salvation.

The pragmatics of these metaphysics were first put into play in the New World through the issuance of a number of Royal Ordinances that officially initiated the extraordinary building campaigns of new towns throughout the viceroyalties. One of the earliest *cédulas* (written authorization or royal decree), issued by Charles V in 1551, establishes the indissoluble link between the building of towns and the teaching of Catholic doctrine:

It has always been the aim to impose with great care and particular attention the best means possible so that the Indians may be instructed in the Holy Catholic Faith and Evangelical law, and for this to be done with the greatest ability our Council of the Indies was called together various times [as well as] other Priests and the Prelates of New Spain to meet by order of the Emperor Charles V [and] who with the desire to succeed in the service of God and ours, resolved that the Indians be gathered [*reducidos*] into towns, [and] not live dispersed and isolated among the mountains and hills depriving themselves completely of temporal and spiritual benefit.[11]

I first want to pay close attention to the Spanish term used to designate the process and to name the form of resettlement. They both come from the word *reducir,* a verb the significance of which expands to define the organization of speech, space, and culture. Most immediately, Indians were to be *reducido,* or gathered, into *reducciones,* or towns. That is, *reducir* was a policy that was physically manifested in the *reducciones.* It was through this process that Indians would first become the *consortium hominium* that eventually, with religious instruction, would become the *congregatio fidelium.*

It is in the Andes, however, that *reducir* came to be associated with the most radical reorganization of native social space, much more so than in Mexico, where there already existed a more substantial urban tradition. The implication of the *reducción* in the Andes was the massive relocation of dispersed peoples living in isolated settlements into a concentrated urban setting. Although the ostensible reason was to congregate them so that doctrine could be efficiently taught, the *reducción* was strongly associated with political and economic goals. By physically bringing Andeans into a much more confined space, Spaniards had much easier access to their labor and goods. This certainly was one of the aims of the Viceroy, Francisco de Toledo, who in the 1570s attempted to forcibly relocate almost the entire population of the Andeans into these *reducciones.*[12] His intentions were multifold, but paramount was the organization and mobilization through the *reducciones* of Indian labor for the great silver mine of Potosí.[13]

Reducir, however, was conceptually greater than the physical concentration of previously dispersed individuals into a physically more restricted space. *Reducir* implies a sense of ordering according to a universal, preexisting structure. In terms of the resettlement of Andeans, *reducir* was about the organization of social space and a *reducción* was but one manifestation of *reducir.* In 1611, for example, Covarrubias, who wrote the first Spanish dictionary, defined *reducido* as "convencido y vuelto a mejor orden" [convinced and brought to a better order]; "convencer a uno" means "reducirle a que mude parecer." It also connoted "ser llegado a razón" [to be brought to reason].[14]

Reducido was the process of bringing into being a more perfect state. Christianity was at the metaphysical center of this colonial ordering process. This is clearly expressed in a Jesuit annual letter from Bogotá that speaks about conversion as an act of "reduc[ing] them [the natives] to the true knowledge of the holy God" (*ridurle alla uera cognitione di dio beneditto*).[15]

In other words, what is meant here is that Indians were taught Christian doctrine, and *reducciones,* also called *doctrinas,* constituted the physical space where this "reducing" took place.

Language, the form through which the Christian doctrine was transmitted, was also susceptible to such ordering. Antonio de Nebrija, who created the first Spanish grammar in 1492, explained as such:

> And as my thought and desire has always been to ennoble the things of our nation and to offer the people of my language works through which they can better spend the idle time than they do now spending it reading novels and histories filled with a thousand errors and lies, I decided before anything else [*reduzir en artificio*] to make a grammar of this our Spanish language so that from now and forevermore [whatever] would be written in it can remain in a tone and be esteemed throughout eternity. As we see what has transpired to those texts written in Greek and Latin [languages] which because they have been ordered by grammars have remained uniform despite the passing of many centuries.[16]

Nebrija uses the word *reducir* as the verb to indicate conceptually what is involved in the creation of a grammar. More important, *reducir* has a very precise meaning for Nebrija that becomes clear in his Spanish-Latin dictionary of 1495. For the Latin equivalent of *reducir,* he lists the word *redigo,* meaning, among other things, to bring to a specific state or condition.[17] That is, as a vernacular language that has been *reducido* to a grammar, the disparate parts of Spanish are submitted in Nebrija's *Arte* of 1492 to a higher order, an order found in Latin.

The date of publication of Nebrija's grammar was coincidental with the discovery of the New World, but its impact was not.[18] His Spanish and, more important, Latin grammars initially served as the models for the generation of grammars of indigenous languages in Mexico and Peru.[19] Both grammar and literacy were measuring sticks through which the Spaniards constructed a universal hierarchy in which Latin and Latin-derived alphabetically written languages occupied the highest rungs.[20] Most important, the ordering of native languages was also understood within the concept of *reducir.* So, for example, Fray Domingo de Santo Tomás wrote in his opening to the reader in his grammar, or *Arte,* of Quechua: "Christian reader please know how great have been my efforts and labors in wishing to create a grammar for Quechua within [a set of] rules and precepts."[21] Santo Tomás promises to bring Quechua under the dominion of order in the same sense as Nebrija. Santo Tomás, however, spatializes the process of *reducir* by rephrasing it, using the word *encerrar,* meaning to confine, contain, or embrace. Moreover, Quechua was to be placed "below" or "under" (*debajo*) the rules of a greater order, Latin. He employs a figural language creating a mental image of hierarchy that is spatially organized. The rules and precepts of Latin grammar were the confining structure to which *la lengua general* (a universal language) was to be *reducida.* This spatialization of language, implying the transformation from barbarity to civility, chaos to order, parallels the actual confinement of individuals within the *traza*, or the grid plan, of the *reducción*.

The ordering, *reduction,* of spoken Quechua to the laws of grammar made it graphically representational and, therefore, knowable at an intellectual level. This ordering permitted the language of the Inka to be elevated to the colonial status of a universal language, or *la lengua general.* As the general language to be known, taught, and used throughout the Andes, it became the filter through which Spanish passed into regional languages.[22] The possibility that Quechua could be so ordered was due to the fact that that order was already latent, a part of the divine plan, as Santo Tomás writes in 1560 at the beginning of his *Arte:* "This language is so agreeable with Latin and Castilian in its structure that it looks almost like a premonition that the Spaniards will possess it."[23] This latent harmony and order revealed God's plan in all things as brought forth by Spanish conquest, a kind of linguistic "manifest destiny."[24] That is, just as Peru with its rich gold and silver mines might be imagined to have beckoned like a bride to be taken by its suitor, the Spanish captain,[25] so too Peru's language, Quechua, might be imagined to have waited in readiness to surrender itself to its suitor, Latin. Andean language and precious metals were destined to be possessed by the Spaniards for the greater glory of God's order. This logic was clearly articulated in all three of its parts — riches, taking possession, and bringing to order (*reducir*) — almost at the beginning of Spanish conquest. In the Papal Bull of Alexander VI dated 4 May 1493, *Inter caetera divinae,* the Pope lauds Ferdinand and Isabella, who, on learning that the recently discovered islands had gold, spices, and other precious things, took it on themselves to spread the Catholic faith. Following "the example of your renowned royal progenitors, you proposed with divine blessing to take control of these mainlands and aforesaid islands, their natives and inhabitants, and to bring them to [*reducere*] to the Catholic faith."[26] The Latin root *reduco,* which implies physical movement toward something as well as to bring to a certain state or condition, of the Spanish verb *reducir* is used to suggest the transformation from an incomplete state of being to a completed one. In the case of language, Quechua revealed itself, as expressed by the Dominican Santo Tomás (see above). Such an understanding of *reducir* and *reducción* was not an innocent revelation. It restored a lost unity brought about by the building of the Tower of Babel and the dispersal of nations and tongues. The biblical multiplicity of languages and nations, of which Quechua and the Andes were a result, was, according to Santo Tomás's fellow Dominican Bartolomé de Las Casas, the cause of idolatry.[27] The capacity to bring languages hitherto unknown to each other into harmony restored a once lost unity. That Christianity could therefore be preached as result of this reunification would mean a final end to idolatry.[28]

Just as language was *reducida* into a logic of grammatical parts based upon a universal system, so too the physical layout, the *traza* of the *reducción,* was logically conceived as a set of interrelated parts that, when brought together, were a perfect order through which *policía* (civilized behavior) could

Fig. 1. Foundation plan of the Spanish villa of San Juan de La Frontera, 1562
Seville, Archivo General de Indias

Fig. 2. Ideal plan for an Andean *reducción*
From Juan de Matienzo, "Gobierno del Perú," 1567, MS 74, fol. 38r
New York, New York Public Library, Obadiah Rich Collection

be conducted in speech and action.[29] Furthermore, just as spoken language could be organized on the written page through this order, so too Andean social space could be ordered by the *reducción,* and be easily and repeatedly rendered in an abstract, graphic form. Space and sound were rendered through the same graphic system and the same conceptual logic. The order of space of the built environment was the grid and its multicomponent, yet universally organized, elements. Easily drawn on paper, the grid plans were replicated throughout the Andes. Moreover, the grid plan created homologous spatial arrangements for the citizens of the two republics so that one can find little difference between the plan of a Spanish town and that of an Andean town (figs. 1, 2).[30] The harmony between Spanish and Indian town plans was, however, understood to exist within a hierarchy. That is, just as Quechua was *reducida* according to the rules of Latin, so too Indian towns were understood to be *reducido* according to the Spanish town plan.[31]

More than merely an architectural plan,[32] the grid, when employed for the settlement of Andeans, was the *reducción,* a model for creating Christian order in a world in which antisocial and wild chaos lurked in the countryside.[33] The order of the urban grid was a visual manifestation of the divine order of Augustine's City of God, just as grammar was, and it was to be contrasted against the chaos of the *civitas diaboli,* the cities of the heathens. For Saint Augustine, as quoted by Las Casas, "the city is a multitude of men gathered in some bond of association or a multitude of men of one mind."[34] Augustine's concept of the City of God, however, became closely associated in the Americas with the physical building of new towns and cities. That is, a morphological relation was imagined to exist between the material appearance of the terrestrial city and the celestial one.[35] This relationship was continuously presented to the indigenous populations through sermons, catechetical instruction, and paintings. Felipe Guaman Poma de Ayala, the seventeenth-century Andean author and artist, gives a clear example of how the celestial city came to be imagined for the Andean through the new urban spaces built by the Spaniards. His drawing of the City of God (Ciudad del Cielo) depicts the celestial city as seen from a bird's-eye point of view (fig. 3). A large plaza dominates the cityscape, defined by the profiles and facades of the facing buildings. In the center appears the "fountain of life," identified in both Spanish (*aqua de vida*) and Quechua (*causay uno*) texts. Guaman Poma repeats the same composition for his drawing of Lima and most other colonial Andean cities (there is a total of forty-one drawings). In his rendering of Lima the celestial "fountain of life" becomes the terrestrial fountain and well. More important, the plaza is now a social space rather than a place of celestial joy, a place where state discipline is displayed with a gallows showing the execution of a criminal or rebel (fig. 4). Still, the analogy between the two is clear, for the punishment executed in Lima's plaza restores the social, moral, and political order that has been transgressed in the terrestrial realm, an order that is understood to reign universally in the celestial sphere.[36]

Guaman Poma's drawings of Lima and the City of God are much more fully realized views of a city than the grid plan used in foundation documents and maps made for other official inquiries. The elevations and architectural detail are more like urban portraits than the workmanlike grid plan, giving a particular character to the representation of urban space.[37] Only once does the Andean artist use the abstract grid plan as an image to render a specific Andean city. For the northern town of Riobamba, he draws the regularized blocks of the city with elevations of the north and south building of each block. This city image is in many ways much closer to other city views, such as that found in the 1673 plan of Panama City. Conceptually, then, the two forms for rendering the city are interchangeable, both expressing a kind of Neoplatonic essence. In both pictorial forms the morphological relationship to the City of God is first based on the centralizing space of the colonial urban plan, large and small alike. The plaza was the center of the *reducción*'s grid just as it was imagined as the defining feature for Lima and the Celestial City in Guaman Poma's drawings. Around this space, the places of the secular and religious power of the colonial order were distributed. Here native Andeans were required to live and participate in practices that made tangible the authority to which they were subjected.[38] This order and the authority it manifested preexisted its execution. That is, before a specific space was ordered (*reducido*) through architecture, it was carefully rendered in the graphic space of a plan, thereby ordering all civic space according to a universal norm.

Juan de Matienzo, in his *Gobierno del Perú* of 1567, was one of the first officials in Peru to articulate an Andean colonial response to a royal ordinance in regard to the building of new towns for the indigenous population. Referring to a *real provisión* of 9 October 1549, he drew and described the ideal form for what should comprise the grid pattern towns for Andeans. There is the sense here not only of bringing order to the actions of Indians but also of creating discipline through the production of confining spaces. He writes first that the *reducciones* should have not only jails and stocks but also a corral in which to place livestock that damage crops. The reasons for bringing Andeans into the *reducciones* are familiar ones in Spanish colonial discourse. Matienzo writes: "First of all, no one is ignorant of the disadvantages to the Indians of [their] being dispersed and hidden in *huaycos* and gorges, both with regard to their civil polity and their conversion, because they cannot be indoctrinated and will never learn to be human beings unless they live together in towns and there is no need to give more reasons for this because it is well known."[39]

Here Matienzo articulates clearly the relationship between conversion, and civil polity as a project of spatial reorganization of the inhabitants of Peru. He proceeds to describe the form of the new pueblos and draws a plan that visualizes the description. He writes: "The pueblo should be laid out in this way: each block should have four building lots. The streets should be wide, and there should be a plaza in the middle; the proportions should be those that the *visitador* thinks appropriate, depending on the number of people and the lay of the land."[40] Matienzo draws a plan of his textual

Fig. 3. Felipe Guaman Poma de Ayala
Ciudad del Cielo (City of God)
From Felipe Guaman Poma de Ayala, *Nueva corónica y buen gobierno,* 1615, Gl. kgl. S. 2232 4°, fol. 938
Copenhagen, Kongelige Bibliotek

Fig. 4. Felipe Guaman Poma de Ayala
La Ciudad de Los Reis de Lima (City of the Royalty of Lima)
From Felipe Guaman Poma de Ayala, *Nueva corónica y buen gobierno,* 1615, Gl. kgl. S. 2232 4°, fol. 1031
Copenhagen, Kongelige Bibliotek

description and suggests that one like it could be left in the hands of Indians to complete the construction of a *reducción* once it is laid out on the ground. It is a plan that is flexible but universal. He follows this by naming the principal structures, beginning with the church that should occupy an entire block. The house opposite the church should be for Spanish travelers. On another block there should be a house for the *corregidor* (a Spanish administrator or authority), behind which was to be built the jail as well as the house for the *tocuirco,* the judge and tribute collector in each *reparitmiento.*[41] The *curaca* (chief) was to be given two *solares* (lots) in order for them to demonstrate his traditional authority within the new colonial town.

At a universal level, Matienzo's plan for the *reducciones* in Peru follows closely the proscriptions found in the royal *cédula* of 1549. Promulgated in Valladolid, the *cédula* was sent to all the Spanish territories in the Americas. It advised that natives be gathered into new towns that were to be modeled after those already built in Mexico and, more specifically, in the province of Tlaxcala.[42] Certain features of Matienzo's plan are clearly taken from the Tlaxcalan model as described in the royal *cédula,* such as the jail and the structure that would house Spanish guests. It appears that these structures were never built in Andean *reducciones.* Deviation from the ideal plan was not important, however. The intention of the *cédula* was not necessarily to re-create the precise layout of the *reducción* built in Tlaxcala, although Matienzo certainly tried to do so. Rather, Tlaxcala became the royal paradigm for the *reducción* to be built throughout the Americas, because Tlaxcala represented the first and most successful transformation of indigenous communities into a Christian community.[43] The Tlaxcalans had been an early and critical ally for Cortés as he moved against the Aztec center of Tenochtitlán. Tlaxcalans became especially privileged by the crown, and in concert with their privileged place in the Viceroyalty, they quickly created a new city that corresponded to the Spanish administrative and architectural ideal. Matienzo seems to have embraced the royal edict with enthusiasm, perhaps because the reference to a specific Mexican model and the Tlaxcalans were significant as the Tlaxcalans demonstrated the capacity of Indians to organize themselves politically, spatially, even historically in a universal sense.[44] For example, the town council (*cabildo*) of Tlaxcala, which is composed of nobility, took an active role in seeing that the city was maintained on both a physical and a spiritual level. The *cabildo* even commissioned a history of its own participation in the Spanish conquest of Mexico to be sent to Philip II in 1552, as well as to have it painted in town hall of Tlaxcala.[45] A later copy, produced around 1580 by Diego Muñoz Camargo, not only proudly depicts the center of Tlaxcala with its municipal buildings but also unites the conquest of Peru and Mexico in a drawing in which Pizarro and Cortés present these territories as personified by key native participants to the king of Spain (figs. 5, 6).

Matienzo's plan, while conceptualized through what already had taken place in Mexico, nonetheless contains the essential elements of the Andean *reducciones.* Like the imagined space of history as personified by Pizarro and

Cortés in Muñoz Camargo's manuscript, this plan imagined a shared, universal urban space of the two viceroyalties. Moreover, by the end of the sixteenth century, following the extraordinary efforts of Viceroy Francisco de Toledo, Andeans came to live in towns that were very similar to what Matienzo had imagined and what had been built in Mexico.[46] The process of resettlement was an extremely labor intensive effort on the part of bureaucratic officials and Andeans alike. *Curacas* were responsible not only for leading their people into the new towns but also for overseeing the labor and material for the construction of the *reducción*. To ensure execution, *visitas,* or inspections, by Spanish officials of a territory were continuously conducted with the idea of first taking a census of everyone in a territory, and then, at times forcibly, the relocation of the scattered settlements into just a few rebuilt or newly built towns (*reducciones*).[47]

Some of these Andean *reducciones* today lie in ruins, long since emptied by abandonment and catastrophic mortality rates (fig. 7). Seen from an aerial view, the remains leave only the outline of the grid plan, as if the foundations had just been laid out as Matienzo suggests and is now ready to be completed by its future inhabitants, plan in hand. The ghostly outline of these towns as it appears today is a trace marking both its beginning and its end. Other sixteenth-century *reducciones* however, continued to thrive until today, and they still bear the structuring layout of the grid. Festival processions, most often beginning and ending at the facade of the church, take prescribed routes that angle through Andean towns near Cuzco, such as Pisac, Pacaritambo, and Ollantaytambo, as well as those far beyond. What is significant, perhaps, is that the regularized geometric grid that came to mark and transform the landscape could be visually appreciable to almost all Andeans. Moving from one valley to another, one most often approached these new towns by descending roads and paths such that one looked down on them spread out against the valley. The visual order of the town from that distance took on the same shape and scale as a sketched plan on paper when laid out on the floor or table for inspection or contemplation.[48] In much of the Andes, where places like Andahuaylillas and Sutatausa (*reducciones* in Peru and Colombia to be discussed below) were pressed up against the surrounding rising hills, the order and design as it was conceived on paper appeared in all its abstract geometrical parts as an actual town at one's feet, which as one walked toward and into the town became a different experience of space and form (fig. 8). The experience of the bird's-eye view in the Andes is not merely an imagined place of the viewer, something conjured up by the tricks of the artist's trade. It is a very common vantage point in the Andes from which a town was most often experienced before even entering into it. Moreover, the transformation of landscape and its appreciable appearance was not an unaccustomed experience for Andeans. The Inka and their predecessors had engineered a terrace and road system that reconfigured the rugged slopes and narrow valleys of the Andes into productive spaces that at the same time displayed remarkable geometrized beauty composed of

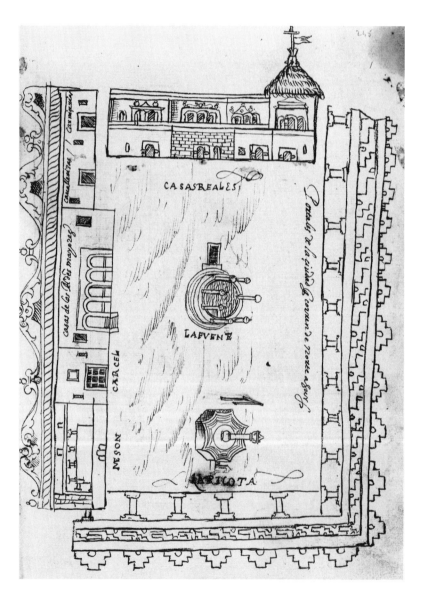

Fig. 5. Plaza Mayor of Tlaxcala, with elevations of the surrounding municipal buildings and church
From Diego Muñoz Camargo, *Descripción de la ciudad y provincia de Tlaxcala*, ca. 1583, MS Hunter 242 (u.3.15), fol. 245r
Glasgow, Glasgow University Library

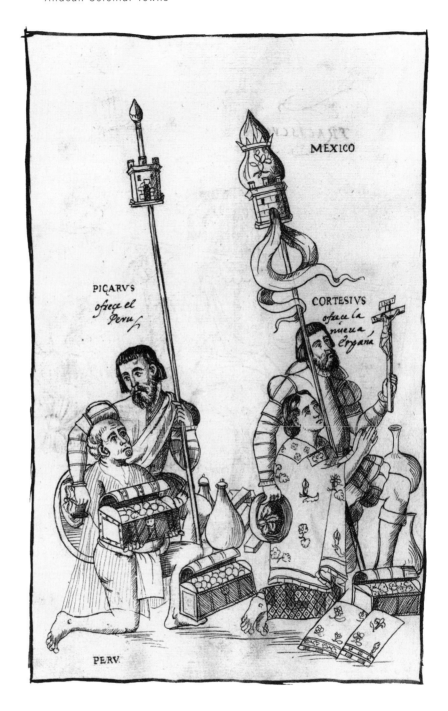

Fig. 6. Cortés and Pizarro present the personifications and riches of New Spain and Peru to Charles V
From Diego Muñoz Camargo, *Descripción de la ciudad y provincia de Tlaxcala*, ca. 1583, MS Hunter 242 (u.3.15), fol. 248v
Glasgow, Glasgow University Library

Fig. 7. Abandoned *reducción,* Colca Valley, early 1900s

Fig. 8. View of Pisac, Yucay Valley, from the road
connecting to Cuzco, 1995

Fig. 9. Inka terraces, Yucay Valley, near Cuzco, 1981

Fig. 10. Stepped design carved into rock with reflecting
pool, Quispihuara, above Cuzco, 1981

ascending terraces (fig. 9). More important, perhaps, in terms of an Inka aesthetic, the Inka used geometric abstraction as a sculptural style to mark sacred places throughout the landscape of Tawantinsuyu (the Inka Empire). For example, a boulder naturally set within a river could be carved with a negative step-fret design that could interact with water and its reflection when the river was dammed up so that it reconfigured the natural landscape into geometric abstraction (fig. 10). Such abstraction also carried over to two-dimensional figures, most especially in textile, the Inka's most important medium. Not only were designs abstract but there was no surface and ground distinction. Any comparable sense of abstract geometry in the Spanish arts, especially painting, did not give over to such "pure" expression; rather, it was manifested through perspective so as to deceive and convince the viewer. Only in the sphere of architecture in the form of the *reducción*, both as plan and reality, did anything come as close to what Andeans had already realized in their own aesthetic order.

The *reducción* was both a place and a form that could be beheld from afar, either across the valley or looking down into it. The experience of the *reducción* as an instrument of "civilizing" order was, therefore, appreciable by Andeans as an image of that order in the topography of their everyday lives. As a colonial town it represented itself to the Andeans not just as a map or plan placed in their hands but as a pattern to be inhabited, first by force and then by habit.

Central to the town's grid were two physical spaces of interrelated practices that, even if seen from the hills above, were understood as the center of religious experience. The first was that of the church, from which emanated the sound of the church bell calling inhabitants to hear mass, pray the rosary, and attend catechism classes; the territory within which such a sound carried was constituted as a legal community, mapped onto provincial space. The second space was the plaza that the church opened onto, and into which came processions of devotional images and their followers. The populace congregated several times a week in the atrium of the church as the doctrinal priest directed sermons at them, instructing them in the mysteries of Christianity. The facade of the church reached into the space further by the words of the priests who stood in the balcony before those called to the plaza. A catechism of 1576 written by the archbishop Luis Zapata de Cárdenas of Bogotá to which I will return outlines the socioreligious space between plaza and facade, community and priest: "And at the door [of] the town church, a large portal will be constructed, if possible, where there will be a pulpit for preaching to the infidels who have not yet entered into the ranks of the catechumens, because it is desirable that they understand that they are still not worthy of treating nor entering in that holy temple."[49] Zapata's building instructions for the portal are understood to be at once physical and metaphysical in its separation of the baptized from the nonbaptized. Zapata draws on the architectural metaphor for the Christian community as the City of God, as Las Casas wrote citing Gregory.[50] This doctrinal relationship was made explicitly clear to southern Andeans through the bilingual sermons of the Third Council of Lima published in 1585 and then republished as part of the sermons of Fernando de Avendaño in 1649. It cannot be known for sure where the sermons were preached to the natives, who could have been standing either before the portal in the plaza or inside the church. In the first sermon regarding the sacraments, however, this physical entrance space was evoked by likening baptism, as the entrance into salvation, to the church door, through which the faithful entered the church.[51]

The church's facade, therefore, not only dominated the plaza's space but also staged the physical and metaphysical interaction between the community and the priest. How this staging was created can be seen in an early-seventeenth-century church in the Muisca community of Sutatausa, located along the camino real and to the north of Bogotá, which was built following Zapata de Cárdenas's instructions. A door on the second story leads to where a balcony would have looked out onto the plaza and from which the priest would have preached to the community (fig. 11). A similar church was built in the *reducción* of Andahuaylillas, just south of Cuzco (fig. 12). This was the parish of Juan Pérez Bocanegra, a priest whose bilingual Quechua and Spanish book entitled *Ritual formulario* was published in Lima in 1631 as an important instructional text. I shall discuss Bocanegra's comments on the sacrament of marriage as well as those of Zapata de Cárdenas, found in his *Catecismo* of 1576, in relation to how marriage laws were first diagrammed in the manuscripts so as to then be enacted in the spaces of churches such as Sutatausa and Andahuaylillas. It is important here only to note that each church had a balcony from which the priest could address the native audience. The balcony, the place of utterance above the portal, marked the distinction between an interior space filled with doctrinal mural paintings, accessible only to those who had been baptized, and the plaza, where all members of the community participated in public gatherings.

These were the primary spaces of spiritual authority; however, the intrusion into the life of Andeans was not limited to the *reducción*'s space of Christian doctrine. The *traza*, the space of order of the *reducción*, also impinged directly on the social relations of the family that, as we shall see, was intimately connected to the spiritual reordering of the Andean subject.[52] Each domestic structure was now understood to belong to the nuclear family, whereas before the Andean architectural unit was the *cancha*, or compound of interconnected buildings that opened onto each other, allowing access to members of the extended family (fig. 13). This was the essential structure for the *ayllu*, or lineage group.[53] Colonial houses in a *reducción* were to be occupied solely by the nuclear family, and there was to be only one door leading into and out of the house, opening only onto the public space of the street that organized the grid. Several early-seventeenth-century schematic plans from the province of Santander and farther north suggest that this door of the house was the salient element that indicated separateness.[54] Each block of houses is drawn as a single rectangular shape. Only the doors, surmounted by

Fig. 11. Facade of the early-seventeenth-century church of Sutatausa (a Muisca *reducción,* north of Bogotá), 1996

Fig. 12. Facade with balcony of the early-seventeenth-century church of Andahuaylillas (a *reducción* south of Cuzco, parish of Juan Pérez Bocanegra), 1995

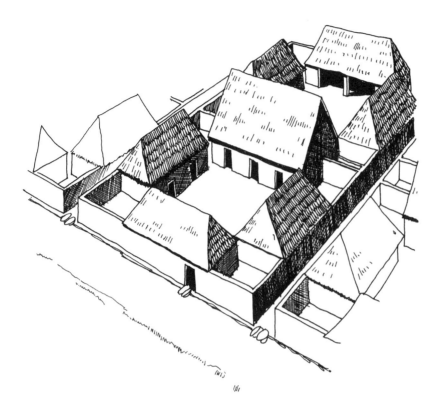

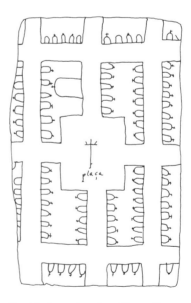

Fig. 13. Drawing of an Inka *cancha*, ca. 1530
After Graziano Gasparini and Luise Margolies, *Inca Architecture*, trans. Patricia J. Lyon (Bloomington: Indiana Univ. Press, 1980), fig. 179

Fig. 14. Copy of a plan of Lagunillas, ca. 1600
From "Visitas de Cundinamarca," vol. 5, fol. 885 Bogotá, Archivo General de la Nación

a cross, drawn in elevation and opening onto the facing street indicate the individual houses (fig. 14).

The reorganized space of the *reducción,* therefore, did not only mean that the Andean community as a whole now lived in closer proximity than ever before. The *reducción* implied a new domestic interior space in which the number of family members living together was now greatly restricted and those who continued to live together were more spatially segregated according to gender and degrees of consanguinity. The reasons were made explicit in the instructions of 1573 given by the Viceroy Francisco de Toledo to the *visitadores* who were to lay out the new towns of the *reducción:* "You shall lay out the Indian houses with the doors opening onto the public street, so that no house opens into the house of an other Indian, but that each has a separate house." The aim of stressing the single entrance was to inhibit sexual relations between close relatives that hitherto had been facilitated by the contiguous and connecting spaces of the *cancha,* which grouped extended families within a common enclosed courtyard that then had a doorway that opened to the public world.[55] The single and public entrance of the new colonial house could be policed by public vigilance in order to create Spanish norms of the family and to instill "decency." Not only were the new colonial dwellings to be organized according to the concept of a nuclear family; the interior spaces of these new domestic structures also were intended to structure the decorum of the nuclear family itself. Ideally the new houses were to be subdivided into private sleeping rooms occupied according to generation. The intent was to create a moral, architectural space, one that instilled a greater sense of shame in regard to sexuality, as Matienzo's describes: "And because the father, mother, sons and daughters live all together in one hut and sleep together, a separate room should be made in each house or hut for the daughters to sleep in; so that they do not learn like wild animals, observing their parents behaving immodestly; since I think this has been the reason that so many of them have grown so lewd and lascivious, and this would certainly help a great deal in keeping them from losing their sense of shame."[56]

The *reducciones* were, therefore, much more than the reordering of space for administrative purposes. The *reducción* was simultaneously a reordered space organized at its most basic modular unit for the performance of new rules of social relations, reformulating Andean consanguinity and marriage according to European norms. In other words, the *reducción* was first of all to be created in the *domicilium.*[57] The interior "private" spaces, now demarcated by walls of separation, marked degrees of kinship and the regulation of sexual customs that were subject to disciplinary punishment in the form of whipping in the town's plaza.[58] The "private," interior spaces were in this sense only an extension of the "public" space of the *reducción* and therefore were equally critical to the civil formation (*polícia*) of the *reducción's* inhabitants.[59]

An archaeology of *reducciones* might suggest the degree of success to which the interiors were divided into discrete spaces, and how those interiors were altered in order to accommodate local institutions and customs. Certainly, the intended order of *policía* was reworked to meet Andean concerns so that compliance took different forms. This is clear from the results of recent ethnohistorical and anthropological studies of specific *reducciones* that have demonstrated an active Andean engagement in the social and political articulation of the new colonial communities. For example, Gary Urton's work on the pueblo of Pacariqtambo, established as a *reducción* southwest of Cuzco, reveals how the leaders of the new town successfully worked to position the *reducción* within Inka mythic topography, thereby gaining a degree of prestige and power within the new colonial world.[60] Moreover, the streets of the *reducción* were assigned to members of the same *ayllu*, and the building and maintenance of the plaza's wall served in the reproduction of Andean social institutions.[61] The social and mytho-historical refashioning of the space of the *reducciones* is therefore critical to the understanding of how and why the *reducción* succeeded in the Andes. It also meant that at least some Andeans, especially the elite, took on for themselves the criteria of *policía*.[62] Of course, the aims of Spanish colonial indoctrination also were thwarted by native traditions, beliefs and their practice, and refashioned colonial cultural forms, such refashioning today is understood too often simply as forms of resistance.[63] There was resistance to the *reducción* as is clearly indicated by the repeated comments by viceroys throughout the seventeenth century. Most often Andean cultural resistance is analyzed, however, as residual rituals hidden and performed in the *reducciones* and outside of them in spite of all attempts of Catholic indoctrination. Certainly there is good reason for that. Colonial documents from the sixteenth and seventeenth centuries abound with descriptions of Andean rituals and their suppression. We therefore tend to think less about European rituals, especially religious ones, and what they did in the colonial formation of knowledge and the success of *reducciones* as places where many Andeans did reside.[64] At one critically important level in the formation of colonial culture, the institutionalized Christian performance codified previously diverse local practices into a single ritual system, thereby universally activating the spaces of the *reducción* by common cult. Ritual in relation to dogma was one form of internalization of the logic that created the new spaces of the *reducción*, especially the division of private space.

To Perform Marriage

If the intention for creating the *reducciones* was, in part, to create both exterior and interior spaces that marked the borders of a new domestic order, then one might expect that these moral distinctions had a recursive presence in Andean colonial urban spaces and their performance. That is, if *policía* aimed at creating normative conditions for a Christian understanding of moral behavior, especially in regard to incest, then it could not be left just to the policing walls of the interior spaces of the new Andean towns. Christian norms could not be established simply through prohibitions, marked spatially by the separation of walls and doors. *Policía* was, first of all, something public and affirmative, internalized as something natural, as something embodied, most often through ritual, as it was enacted in the regularized spaces of the *reducción*. That is, for the new colonial spaces of *reducción* to be Christian, *policía* required habits and customs that were embraced and performed by the inhabitants.

The institutionalization of Christian *policía* in the Americas therefore transformed the individual as a corporate member through ritual action, both in terms of civic celebrations and religious cult. The two spheres of ritual constantly overlapped in the same spaces of the *reducción* such that ritual could serve not only as practice but also as an explanatory model through which the experience of a political ritual involving an abstract concept might be used by analogy to explain to Andeans the mysteries of Christianity.[65] European Christian rituals could also be deployed through various nonperformative forms of representation as a means of communicating European knowledge and beliefs. Catholic ritual was, therefore, not just something to be performed temporally and spatially. Christian ritual was also a metapractice that not only enacted Christian cult but also produced an abstract state of knowledge that could be evoked outside of its phenomenological context to refer to the conduct and practice of *policía* in general. As such, it permitted, within the Spanish colonial enterprise, to interrelate state and religion as mutual spheres of authority in relation to forms of representation and their referent. In this sense, I disagree with Catherine Bell's recent definition of "ritualization" as a "matter of variously culturally specific strategies for setting some activities off from others, for creating and privileging a qualitative distinction between the 'sacred' and the 'profane,' and for ascribing such distinctions to realities thought to transcend the powers of human actors."[66] Ritual as a regularized spatiotemporal performance may be qualitatively different from quotidian activities; however, the elements of space and time are not contained by ritual's performance of the sacred. Ritual extends beyond its performance so as to link seemingly disparate elements of social phenomena within a defined public space. This is especially true within a Western colonial condition, where the prior spheres of profane and sacred become reorganized according to colonial norms. The social institution of marriage, as something common to both Andean and Spaniard, is critical in this intersection, as marriage for the Spaniard is performed within the context of Christian ritual rather than as a social contract within Andean norms. It is the Catholic Church that now defines the boundaries for proper or moral conditions of marriage, that is, laws of consanguinity and the formation of the nuclear family. It is, of course, the priest who should perform the ritual that brings forth the social institution of marriage as being something that is sanctified. The form of the *reducciones*, their doorways and separating walls, are to be understood within this reorientation of marriage and the proper kinship relations as being something sacred and critical to *policía*.

The performance of marriage as a Christian ritual produces a particular form of knowledge about Native social relations in the spaces of *reducciones* and participates in the same organizing principles as the *reducción*. By their mutual production and interaction, colonial space and ritual transformed those relations and the way we still conceive of them. That is, what rituals did in the spaces created for them then informs what we think we understand now about Andean kinship as it was organized. I, therefore, am concerned not only with the performative aspect of marriage as it takes place in the church, and in the numerous Andean paintings that commemorate the ritual either as something specific or universal. I am equally interested in marriage as a concept that by its ritual performance standardizes and thereby disciplines and orders diverse pre-Hispanic social practices to bring them within the domain of universal religion. More important in terms of art history, I am interested in the colonial representational practices through which Catholic marriage could come to standardize social relations throughout the Americas based on a unified concept of kinship.[67] More important, this graphic organization of kin relations parallels and intersects with the graphic rendering of the new Andean towns. That is, just as the universal plan of the *reducción,* such as that drawn by Matienzo, precedes the building of any particular town, so too a plan or diagram of the necessary conditions of marriage precedes any particular marriage.

Two doctrinal documents from the Andes are the focus here and, in particular, their images of consanguinity as they relate to marriage by Andeans now living in colonial towns. The first document is the *Catecismo en que se contienen las reglas y documentos para que los curas de yndios les administren los santos sacramentos,* written in Bogotá, Colombia, in 1576 by Luis Zapata de Cárdenas, the second bishop of Nueva Granada. The second document, *Ritual formulario e institucion de curas, para administrar a los naturales de este Reynos, los santos sacramentos,* was written in about 1620 by Juan Pérez Bocanegra, curate of Andahuaylillas and later canon in Cuzco's Cathedral, and was published in Lima in 1631. As the titles of both documents imply, they are instructional texts addressed to fellow priests and treat at length the mysteries of the Catholic Church and their external signs and sacramental rituals, as they pertain to the indoctrination of the native population. What is of interest is that in each document the written word is supplemented only once by the visual image in order to aid the priest further. More important, the recourse to the visual occurs at the same point in both manuscripts, and in relation to the conditions of kinship that must be recognized before marriage can take place.

This study is not the first to look at the institutionalization of marriage in the colonial period. Recent and important work, such as that of Patricia Seed, has focused on the fundamental links between the social and the religious through marriage. In general, however, the analytic emphasis of these studies follows in the wake of Michel Foucault's *History of Sexuality,* and does not locate the performance within colonial space. Rather, the Catholic ritual of confession in relation to sexuality has been the main analytic focus of colonial marriage by a number of scholars.[68] Many of these scholars point out that

pre-Hispanic marriage and marriage rituals are not necessarily a sacred contract, but are very much more a social one in which economic, political, and
social bonds are forged. Furthermore, while these bonds are also crucial for
European marriage, marriage in the Catholic Church became reemphasized as
a sacred act following the Council of Trent. It was one of the seven sacraments instituted by Christ and given external signs through specialized rituals
in which the body must be present and marked. After the Council of Trent
decree of 11 November 1563, however, the definitive ritual of Catholic marriage was established, and among other things it required witnesses to the cer-
emony and its celebration by a priest. Witnessing of a marriage in the Andes,
as we shall see, came to have an additional performative aspect in terms of the
community and its relationships according to consanguinity.[69]

Marriage, however, is categorically different from any other sacrament
available to the native in colonial Catholicism. Five of the sacraments, Baptism, Confirmation, Penance, Eucharist, and Extreme Unction are necessary
for salvation and are, therefore, obligatory. The other two sacraments, Priesthood and Marriage, are voluntary, however, and are entered into through
free will. Marriage as an expression of free will by Andeans is especially
important. Cardinal Zapata takes pains to explain why in his *catecismo* of
1576. He advises his fellow priests that the Indians should be encouraged to
marry for two interrelated reasons. They should enter into marriage because,
first, "as Indians they are incapable [*incapaces*] of professing the priesthood,
so that marriage is the only sacrament that they can freely profess... and
second if they do not marry they will either live in a state of concubinage
or they will cease to reproduce and the territory will become empty and
unproductive."[70] In this sense marriage stands at the opposite pole of confession in terms of the concept of free will in Christian doctrine. That is, for
their salvation, all natives must not only confess their sins but also acknowledge that the commission of each sin was an act committed by their own
individual free will;[71] however, the same free will can be enacted as a profession of faith by the entrance into the sacrament of marriage through the
grace of God.

Yet to enter freely into the sacrament of marriage is to accept first the conditions of freedom as laid out according to Catholic doctrine. Most important, any native who fully entered into the church by receiving the first four
sacraments and who then chose to marry undertook this sacrament within the
restrictions of consanguinity as now defined by the church. In other words,
one ideally could not marry within the fourth grade of linear and transversal
descent. Temporary dispensation for Indians to marry within the third grade
of consanguinity had been given by Pope Paul III in his Bull of 1537, *Altitudo
divini concilii*. This dispensation was permitted until such time that the
papacy should declare otherwise, which in fact subsequent popes never did.
Specific dispensation to marry even within the first grade was also granted in
the case of high Inka nobility.[72] Nonetheless, the Indians were taught the precepts of orthodox consanguinity as established in 1215 by the Fourth Lateran

Council, which changed the restriction of consanguinity from the seventh grade to the fourth grade.

The restriction was restated by the Spanish Dominican, Domingo de Soto (1494–1560), in his *Comentaria in IV Sententiarum* (Salamanca, 1557), IV, Dist. 40, art 5 prope 59. De Soto was one of Vitoria's star pupils and he summarized most of Vitoria's teachings in his *De iustia et jure*.[73] As one of Spain's most important jurists of both canon and civil law in the sixteenth century, he was sent by Charles V and Philip II to the Council of Trent in 1545. He also became confessor to Charles V, the emperor, in 1548.[74] He also was deeply involved with the philosophical and legal debates in Salamanca over the nature of the Indian and the Spanish conquest; therefore, his works were widely known in the Americas.

Nearly twenty years later, Zapata turns to the work of de Soto as his source for imposing on the converted natives of Nueva Granada, present-day Colombia. The native faithful were prohibited in general from marrying until the fourth level, be it in direct ascending or descending line, from the grandfather to the great-great grandson.[75] The transversal line of descent is equally prohibited, which he also describes in detail.[76] What is significant is that at this point in the manuscript Zapata makes recourse to an image of explanation by writing "as the figure that immediately follows makes very clear and obvious" (fig. 15). What Zapata provides for his fellow priests is a diagram that visualizes temporally and spatially the set of relations that a priest must understand and explain to the Indians as those kin relations that must be recognized in order to be able to marry. A modern reinterpretation of the drawing makes clearer for us what Zapata's diagram was intended to "make very clear and obvious" for sixteenth-century Spanish priests (fig. 16). The lines and terms refer to the degrees of consanguinity as a universal concept for the sacrament of marriage. That is, the image graphically provides for the priest a spatiotemporal form of the universal socio-kinship relations that determine the possibility of a marriage and its ritual enactment. Already in Mexico two books concerning the sacrament of marriage had been printed that provided similar diagrams. The first, *Speculum coniugiorum,* was written by Alonso de Vera Cruz and published by Juan Pablos on 26 December 1556 in Mexico City. A woodcut appears on page 307 illustrating the degrees of consanguinity to be recognized for marriage. The stem descends from Plato and, therefore, takes on a set of metaphorical relations (fig. 17). A second diagram appears in Bartolomé de Ledesma's *De septem novae legis sacramentis summarium* published in Mexico by Antonio de Espinosa just ten years later (fig. 18). In this woodcut, Adam and Eve form the trunk from which the five grades of consanguinity descend. As the biblical primordial pair, their image and their offspring were evoked throughout the colonial period in the teaching of sacrament of marriage.[77] Whether Zapata actually saw either of these two Mexican books or took his inspiration directly from a Spanish source is unclear. What is important, however, is that like the royal *cédulas* and plans that circulated throughout the Americas to give a common form to *reducciones*, there was a

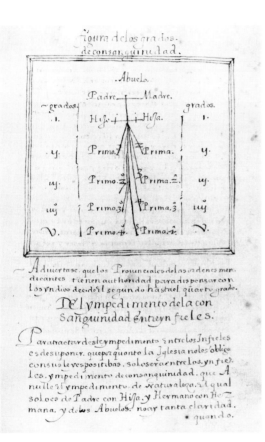

Fig. 15. *Figura de los grados de consanguinidad*
From Luis Zapata de Cárdenas, *Catecismo para la edificación y conversión de los naturales*, 1576, fol. 51

Fig. 16. Redrawing of *Figura de los grados de consanguinidad* (see fig. 15)

223

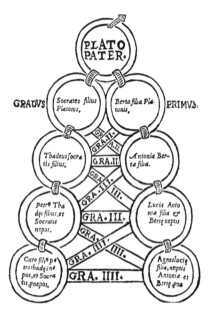

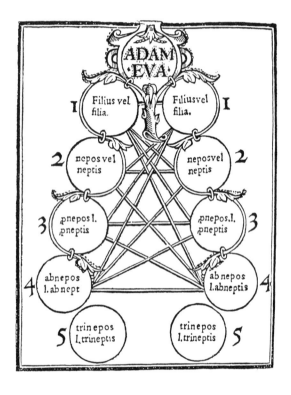

Fig. 17. Diagram of the grades of consanguinity
From Alonso de Vera Cruz, *Speculum coniugiorum* (Mexico: in aedibus Ioannis Pauli Brissensis, 1556), 307

Fig. 18. Diagram of the grades of consanguinity
From Bartolomé de Ledesma, *De septem novae legis sacramentis summarium* (Mexico: excudebat Antonius de Espinosa, 1566), fol. 352v

pictorialization of consanguinity that gave it a universal form as it was presented for indoctrination.[78]

Some fifty years later in his *Ritual formulario* of about 1620, Pérez Bocanegra turned from Zapata's universal form to one that was specific, both nominally and graphically.[79] He provided an elaborated illustration of the terms of consanguinity, offering it to his fellow priests "so that the degrees of consanguinity can be understood and seen more distinctly I have put this diagram [*ramo*] of the ascending and descending levels among males and females" (fig. 19).[80]

Here oral Quechua kinship terms are combined with Christian baptismal names within a diagram of European degrees of descent that are pictorialized by bust portraits of Inka royalty, signaled by the males who wear a royal fringe over their foreheads. Even the diagrammatic armature of the kin relations is more pictorial, having an architectonic appearance with a tympanum-like summit supported by the columnar arrangement of the two lines of descent. This diagrammatic structure already projects a sense of divine order to which marriage and rules of consanguinity intimately belong as a holy sacrament. In fact de Soto, the author who Zapata cites in 1576 as his authority for these rules, had himself conceived of *lex divina* as the creative *ratio* of God himself, and imagined it as set of norms or *regulae* used by God at the Creation just as an architect might use a set of drawings.[81] Pérez Bocanegra's woodcut seems to give de Soto's metaphysical analogy a visual concreteness for Peruvian priests in which the universal laws as reinforced by the Council of Trent are envisioned in the images of Andean subjects. The woodcut's architectonic armature lends a concreteness to the Andean relationships. And like Quechua, which Santo Tomás had found so agreeable with Latin and Castilian in its structure that it looked almost like a premonition that the Spanish would possess it, Andean kinship terms seemed to have existed so as to be ready for the Christian sacrament.

I therefore have no interest here whether the woodcut in some way or another captures the reality of Andean concepts of kinship, although that is the way it is usually cited. Rather, it is important to stress that both illustrations are meant to be didactic for European priests working in Andean native communities. The diagrams are not about knowing Andean customs of kinship but about making visible European knowledge that ultimately comes from divine law, such that it may come to include Andean kinship terms within a rational stemma of Christian order.

Johannes Fabian, in discussing Walter Ong's 1958 study of Ramus, the sixteenth-century theologian, notes that diagrams were unquestionably not only sixteenth century but also modern forms of the visual-spatial conventions whose function it was to give "method" to the dissemination of knowledge in our society. In particular, Fabian analyzes kinship charts as they are drawn by modern anthropologists. He writes that "if one reflects...on the nature of kinship charts (of the genealogical grid type), one finds that, ultimately, they are limited only by the size of paper on which they are drawn or

Fig. 19. Diagram of the grades of consanguinity
From Juan Pérez Bocanegra, *Ritual formulario . . .* (Lima:
por Geronymo de Contreras, 1631)

printed.... One is tempted to consider the possibility that anthropological kinship theories...are actually determined by the presentability of diagrams that fit onto a conventional printed page."[82]

This may be true for modern knowledge about kinship and its visual representation, but that is not at issue in these two early modern images of Andean kinship. At one level of representation, they are like modern kinship charts in that they are a visual method for the dissemination of knowledge within the society that produces them about another society. But in both sixteenth- and seventeenth-century images, the process of knowledge is reversed and the structure of kinship moves from the European to native. Both authors ask the priest to look at the diagrams so as to recognize Catholic kinship structure as it pertains to Christian marriage. One may ask why an image is needed here and nowhere else in the two manuscripts. Is it that the temporal and spatial conditions of any kinship formation somehow elude the capacity of written text to be easily rendered comprehensible for the reader and that the diagram does it better? In truth, I find it easier to understand the diagram than the written description, and visual clarification certainly is the intent of what Zapata and Pérez Bocanegra say that they are aiming for when they provide the images for their fellow priests. Surely, however, the rules of consanguinity were learned by the priests before ever entering a *reducción*. It is also quite possible that priests themselves redrew the diagrams for their own didactic use, instructing Andeans in Christian norms of consanguinity.[83]

It is, however, the performance of the marriage ritual itself through which one can come to understand how this visual intercommunication between Catholic priests became an internalized experience for Andeans and, therefore, a natural state of human relations within a divine order. Whether or not Andeans saw some form of these images is not critical in terms of their relation to the space of the *reducción*. What the images represented as a universal set of norms came to be embodied by Andeans through the performance of the marriage ritual itself, which took place in the *reducción*, before the entire community. This does not mean that Andean marriage rites and celebrations were eliminated. Rather, they were attached to and performed around Catholic ritual practice.[84]

As an issue of the exercise of free will within colonial society, every individual who decided on the sacrament of marriage first had to perform a self-examination in preparation for the sacrament. Confession is the most evident of these ritual acts of introspection. While this is the most radical act of individuation, however, the ritual of Catholic marriage is the vector between the individual and community in which all natives are ideologically and psychologically the subject of the Catholic priest. In preparation for the culminating act in which the bonds of matrimony between the two individuals are pronounced, the entire community first acknowledges the Catholic laws of consanguinity to which they are all the subject, and then performs a communal act of surveillance on the couple to be married. That is, on three separate celebrations of the Mass held before the wedding itself and for which the entire community was congregated on each occasion, the priest asked in Quechua or Aymara whether there was anyone who knew if the pair should not be married on account of their kinship.[85] Most important, the forms of consanguinity that established these boundaries theoretically had already been internalized by every individual who had married within the Catholic Church. Couples were examined just before their marriage in either Quechua or Aymara about their relationship to their future spouse in regard to each level of possible consanguinity. For example, the first question in regard to the ascendant and descendant line for the male is "Is this woman with whom you wish to marry your mother or your daughter?"[86] The first question in regard to the transversal line for the male is "Is this woman (with) whom you wish to marry your sister?" And so on.[87]

Pérez Bocanegra and Zapata intended the images of consanguinity to be an aid for their fellow priests in establishing correspondences between local kinship terms and universal terms of the sacrament. The images may have been spoken by priests during a marriage celebration in a *reducción*, but they also were embodied and enacted by almost every adult member of an Andean community. At every individual Christian marriage that followed the prescriptions and proscriptions of Pérez Bocanegra, the community stood with the local priest in the regularized space of the central plaza of the *reducción* and before the church.[88] The language of Quechua or Aymara through which the priest spoke to those gathered in this new space of order had been ordered or *reducido* just as the space in which it was spoken had been. Language, the symbolic system through which the Christian doctrine was taught, was susceptible to such ordering, and, therefore, language itself could be taught. Moreover space, especially domestic space of family relations, could be built in a way that demanded the primacy of the nuclear family. These relations themselves became performed communally in the only Catholic sacrament that evoked individual choice. Order could be recognized as something to be seen and experienced both in the layout of the *reducción* and in one's relation to family. Both conditions were susceptible to being laid out on a page to be seen and then to be lived. At one level of experience, colonial space, language, and human relations could all be quantified in terms of their parts and assembled into an order that represented God's design of civilization, a design that could be rendered visible through the plan or diagram.

Conclusion

One might say, then, that the ritual of Christian marriage colonized Andean kinship within an architectural space that reified these forms. The ritual and its rules universalized the Christian structure of kinship as being privileged, recognized by Andeans as structuring the boundaries of marriage. Books of baptism that registered the Christian names of Andeans opened the door of the church and the City of God; however, marriage as a Christian sacrament registered willing acceptance into that community. In fact, Pérez Bocanegra's diagram united baptismal names and Quechua kinship terms as a single whole. Of course, the texts and images of Zapata and Pérez Bocanegra represent an ideal of what was supposed to be understood and performed. Many of the *reducciones* had fewer than five hundred people in them, and many Andeans did not marry according to Catholic ritual.

Nonetheless, what is critical about the *reducciones* and the marriage ceremonies that, in the very least, were imagined to take place in them is that they formalized relationships according to a set of interrelated ideals. The sense of decorum could be seen to exist, at least for Spanish visitors, to the *reducciones*. The straight, intersecting streets that emanated from the plaza and the single entrance doors that opened on to these streets anticipated, by matching visually, the plans that had been drawn somewhere else and at some other time, such as those by Matienzo and others. *Reducciones* formed a stage for a normalcy that could be gauged against an ideal. So, too, the nuclear family that lived within the houses could be imagined to be acting within a set of expectations as illustrated in the diagrams drawn by Zapata and Pérez Bocanegra. As much as conquest and physical force, the establishment of the rules of order first manifested in the lines of diagrams and plans worked to shift universally the social and cultural norms of the Andes so that a colonial order could at least be recognized for what it might and should be, but which was not yet fully achieved.

Notes

1. Alonso de la Peña Montenegro, *Itinerario para parochos de Indios, en que se tratan las materias más particulares, tocantes à ellos, para su buena administración,* new ed. (1668; Antwerp: Hermanos de Tournes, 1754): "Y assi nuestors Catolicos Reyes han tenido gran cuydado en mandar por cedulas muchas, que han despachado desde las primeras Conquistas hasta aora, que con gran cuydado los reduzcan a vivir en Pueblos fundados socialmente."

2. Colonial archaeology in Latin America as an independent intellectual enterprise is almost nonexistent. Rather, the considerable internal and external financial resources and intellectual effort directed toward Latin American archaeology is focused on the pre-Columbian past of modern nation states. The reasons are multifold but certainly include economics (that is, tourism) and politics. Most often, archaeologists' work at colonial sites relates to restoration projects, such as those after the earthquake of 1950 in Cuzco or the national and European (Belgium and Spain) efforts in San Francisco and Santo Domingo, Quito, for the quincentenary. Thus while there are clearly defined research agendas for pre-Columbian archaeology as well as for colonial Latin American history, no such coordinated plan could be articulated for the archaeology of colonial Latin America. Notable exceptions include the work of Kathleen A. Deagan, *Spanish St. Augustine: The Archaeology of a Colonial Creole Community* (New York: Academic, 1983); and Charles R. Ewen, *From Spaniard to Creole: The Archaeology of Cultural Formation at Puerto Real, Haiti* (Tuscaloosa: Univ. of Alabama Press, 1991), both of which attempt to locate social and gender relations within the colonial archaeological record.

3. This image was created by Spaniards such as Bartolomé de las Casas, *Brevísima relación de la destrucción de las Indias* (1552; reprint, Madrid: Tecnos, 1992), in order to counter abuses in the Americas. It was then reframed by Protestant Europe to defame the Spaniards; see Lewis Hanke, *The Spanish Struggle for Justice in the Conquest of America* (Boston: Little, Brown, 1949), 88; and William S. Maltby, *The Black Legend in England: The Development of Anti-Spanish Sentiment, 1558–1660* (Durham: Duke Univ. Press, 1971).

4. As Roberto González Echevarría, *Myth and Archive: A Theory of Latin American Narrative* (Cambridge: Cambridge Univ. Press, 1990), 46, writes, "America existed as a legal document before it was physically discovered." The documents, he notes, were made and performed throughout the viceroyalties; see Ewen, *Spaniard to Creole* (note 2).

5. *Habitus* in the colonial world of Latin America has a particular analytic power, as it is sometimes possible to articulate the move to establish the rules before they become unconscious and embodied in everyday practice; see Pierre Bourdieu, *Outline of a Theory of Practice,* trans. Richard Nice (Cambridge: Cambridge Univ. Press, 1977).

6. Juan de Matienzo, *Gobierno del Perú (1567)*, ed. Guillermo Lohmann Villena (Paris: Institut Français d'Études Andines, 1967), 22: "Entre las otras cosas que su magestad tiene obligacion, y los encomenderos en su nombre, una es el enseñar a los Indios la policia humana para que pueden con mas facilidad ser enseñados en nuestra santa fee Catholica que es el principal intento, y asi muy justa y santa la provision para que se reduzcan a pueblos."

7. This was recognized almost immediately after Columbus's discovery of the New World by Pope Alexander VI in the draft of his *Inter Caetera Divinae* of 4 May 1493.

8. Anthony Pagden, *The Fall of Natural Man: The American Indian and the Origins of Comparative Ethnology* (Cambridge: Cambridge Univ. Press, 1982), 66–68; and Anthony Pagden, *European Encounters with the New World: From Renaissance to Romanticism* (New Haven: Yale Univ. Press, 1993), 2. See also Colin M. MacLachlan, *Spain's Empire in the New World: The Role of Ideas in Institutional and Social Change* (Berkeley: Univ. of California Press, 1988), 1–19; and Valerie Fraser, *The Architecture of Conquest: Building in the Viceroyalty of Peru, 1535–1635* (Cambridge: Cambridge Univ. Press, 1990).

9. Francisco de Vitoria, *Political Writings*, ed. Anthony Pagden and Jeremy Lawrance (Cambridge: Cambridge Univ. Press, 1991), xiv–xv, 9–10.

10. This logic is sustained in the articulation of Andean evangelization until at least the end of the seventeenth century, as expressed by Alonso de la Peña Montenegro in his *Itinerario para parochos de Indios* (see the modern critical edition: *Itinerario para párrocos de indios,* ed. Carlos Baciero et al., 2 vols. [Madrid: Consejo Superior de Investigaciones Científicas, 1995–96]).

11. *Recopilación de leyes de los reynos de las Indias*, vol. 2 (1681; reprint, Madrid: Ediciones Cultura Hispánica, 1973), 198 (bk. 6, titulo 3, ley 1):

Con Mucho cuidado, y particular atencion se ha procurado siempre interponer los medios mas convenientes, para que los Indios sean instruidos en la Santa Fé

Catolica, y Ley Evangelica, y olvidando los errores de sus antiguos ritos, y ceremonias vivan en concierto, y policia, y para que esto se executasse con mejor acierto se juntaron diversas vezes los de nuestro Consejo de Indias, y otras personas Religiosas, y congregaron los Prelados de Nueva España el año de mil quinientos y quarenta y seis, por mandado de el señor Emperador Carlos V. de gloriosa memoria, los quales con deseo de acertar en servicio de Dios, y nuestro, resolvieron, que los Indios fussen reducidos á Pueblos, y no viviessen divididos y seperados por las Sierras y Montes, privandose de todo beneficio espiritual, y temporal.

This understanding of town planning is reiterated in the *Laws of the Indies,* issued by Philip II on 13 July 1573: "They [the newly discovered areas] should be populated by Indians and natives to whom we can preach the gospels since this is the principal objective for which we mandate these discoveries and settlements be made"; cited and translated in Dora P. Crouch, Daniel J. Garr, and Axel I. Mundigo, *Spanish City Planning in North America* (Cambridge: MIT Press, 1982), 8.

12. This process had begun in the 1550s on the north coast of Peru; see Susan E. Ramírez, *The World Upside Down: Cross-Cultural Contact and Conflict in Sixteenth-Century Peru* (Stanford: Stanford Univ. Press, 1996), 67.

13. See Alejandro Málaga Medina, "Las reducciónes toledanas en el Perú," in Ramón Gutiérrez, ed., *Pueblos de Indios: Otro urbanismo en la región andina* (Quito: Ediciones Abya-Yala, 1993), 263–316; and Manuel M. Marzal, *La transformación religiosa peruana* (Lima: Pontificia Universidad Católica del Perú, 1983), 92–96.

14. Sebastián de Covarrubias Orozco, *Tesoro de la lengua castellana o española*, ed. Felipe C. R. Maldonado, rev. ed. Manuel Camarero, 2d ed. (Madrid: Editorial Castalia, 1995), 350.

15. This document (AGCG/R 1616: 116v) and its relation to *reducción* is discussed in Tom Cummins and Joanne Rappaport, "The Reconfiguration of Civic and Sacred Space: Architecture, Image, and Writing in the Colonial Northern Andes," *Latin American Literary Review* 26, no. 52 (1998): 174–201.

16. Antonio de Nebrija, *Gramática de la lengua castellana: Salamanca, 1492* (London: Oxford Univ. Press, 1926), 6–7:

I por que mi pensamiento y gana siempre fue engrandecer las cosas de nuestra nacion, y dar a los ombres de mi lengua obras en que mejor pueden emplear su ocio, que agora lo gastan leiendo novelas o istorias embueltas en mil mentiras y errores, acordé ante todas las otras cosas reduzir en artificio este nuestro lenguaje castellano, para que lo que agora y de aqui adelante en el se escriviere pueda quedar en un tenor, y estenderse en toda la duracion de los tiempos que estan por venir. Como vemos que se a hecho en la lengua griega y latina, las cuales por aver estado debajo de arte, aun que sobre ellos an passado muchos siglos, toda via quedan en una uniformidad.

17. Antonio de Nebrija, *Vocabulario español-latino* (Madrid: Real Academia Española, 1951); and Antonio de Nebrija, *Vocabulario de romance en latín* (Sevilla: Editorial Castalia, 1981).

18. For Nebrija's impact on the creation of grammars for the languages of New Spain, see the various essays in Ignacio Guzmán Betancourt and Eréndira Nansen Díaz,

Memoria del coloquio la obra de Antonio de Nebrija y su recepción en la Nueva España: Quince estudios nebrisenses, 1492–1992 (Mexico City: Instituto Nacional de Antropología e Historia, 1997); Walter D. Mignolo, "Literacy and Colonization: The New World Experience," in René Jara and Nicholas Spadaccini, eds., *1492–1992: Re/discovering Colonial Writing* (Minneapolis: Prisma Institute, 1989); and Walter D. Mignolo, *The Darker Side of the Renaissance: Literacy, Territoriality, and Colonization* (Ann Arbor: Univ. of Michigan Press, 1995).

19. Walter D. Mignolo, "Nebrija in the New World: The Question of the Letter, the Discontinuity of the Classical Tradition, and the Colonization of the Native Languages," *L'homme: Revue française d'anthropologie* 122–24 (1992): 187–209.

20. See Mignolo, "Literacy and Colonialization" (note 18); and Pagden, *Fall of Natural Man* (note 8).

21. Domingo de Santo Tomás, *Grammática o arte de la lengua general de los Indios de los reynos del Perú* (Cuzco: Centro de Estudios Regionales Andinos "Bartolomé de las Casas," 1995), 13: "Bien entiendo, christiano lector, quán sobre mis fuerzas es el negocio y obra que al presente tomo sobre ellos, en querer redduzir la lengua general de los reynos del Perú arte, queriendola encerrar debaxo de preceptos y cánones."

22. Bruce Mannheim, *The Language of the Inka since the European Invasion* (Austin: Univ. of Texas Press, 1991), 80–82.

23. See Santo Tomás, *Grammática* (note 21), 9: "Y, brevemente, en muchas cosas y maneras de hablar tan conforme a la latina y española; y en el arte y artificio della, que no paresce sino que fue un pronóstico que españoles la avían de posseer."

24. See Santo Tomás, *Grammática* (note 21), 5: "El armonía y orden, S.M., que Dios nuestro señor puso en las cosas dende las crió ocupando cada una en su officio de tal manera que unas a otras se ayudassen y todas sirviessen a la máchina del universo."

25. The analogy is found in the 1571 text *Parecer de Yucay;* see Isacio Pérez Fernández, *El anónimo de Yucay frente a Bartolomé de las Casas: Estudio y edición crítica del* Parecer de Yucay, *anónimo (Valle de Yucay, 16 de marzo de 1571)* (Cuzco: Centro de Estudios Regionales Andinos "Bartolomé de las Casas," 1995), 157–60. This analogy is repeated by José de Acosta in 1590; see José de Acosta, *Historia natural y moral de las Indias,* ed. Edmundo O'Gorman, 2d ed. (Mexico City: Fondo de Cultura Económica, 1962), 4.7, 143, as cited by Sabine MacCormack, *Religion in the Andes: Vision and Imagination in Early Colonial Peru* (Princeton: Princeton Univ. Press, 1991), 264.

26. Both the Latin text of *Inter Caetera Divinae* and its translation are to be found in William Eugene Shiels, *King and Church: The Rise and Fall of the Patronato Real* (Chicago: Loyola Univ. Press, 1961), 78–81, 283–87:

In quibus quidem insulis et terris jam repertis aurum, aromata et aliae quampluri-maeres prestiosae diversi generis et diversae qualitatis reperuntur. Unde omnibus diligenter et praesertim fidei catholicae exaltatione et dilatatione (prout decet cathilicos Reges et principes) consideratis, more progenitorum vestorum clarae memoriae regum, terras firmas et insulas praedictus illarumque incolas et habitores vobis divina favente clementia subjicere et ad fidem catholicam *reducere* proposuistis.

In 1668 Alonso de la Peña Montenegro, *Itinerario para parochos de Indios* (note 1), deploys the Spanish term *reducir* to the same effect in a chapter title: "Avifos muy provechofos à los Ministros Evangelicos, que se ocupen en reducir Infieles de Jefu-Chrifto."

27. Bartolomé de las Casas, *Apologética historia sumaria,* ed. Edmundo O'Gorman, 3d ed. (Mexico City: Instituto de Investigaciones Históricos, Universidad Nacional Autónoma de México, 1967), 383, as cited in MacCormack, *Religion in the Andes* (note 25), 221.

28. For an insightful analysis of Las Casas's discussion of idolatry and language, see MacCormack, *Religion in the Andes* (note 25), 220–21.

29. My thoughts and words here in terms of action and speech as constituent and contiguous elements of *reducción* are indebted to my discussions with and reading of the works of William F. Hanks; see his "Authenticity and Ambivalence in the Text: A Colonial Maya Case," *American Ethnologist* 13 (1986): 721–44; and *Language and Communicative Practices* (Boulder: Westview, 1996), 248–304. I thank him for his generosity and wisdom in working through these issues with me. For a discussion of *polícia* and its relation to architecture, *reducciónes*, and the colonization of Peru, see Fraser, *Architecture of Conquest* (note 8), 40–47.

30. Ideally, the two communities (Spanish and native) were socially and politically separated from one another. This was spatially organized by building Indian and Spanish towns. For a detailed description of the *república de los Indios* and the importance of *reducciónes*, see Juan de Solórzano y Pereira, "Política indiana sacada en lengua castellana de los dos tomos del derecho i governo municipal de las Indias," in idem, *Política indiana* (Madrid: Ediciones Atlas, 1972), bk. 2.

31. Whereas new towns were built for natives throughout the Americas in the sixteenth century, the terms by which they were categorized vary from region to region. In Mexico, for example, they are usually called *doctrinas* or *congraciones*. Only in the Andes is the term *reducción* used consistently to classify these new native towns. I suspect that this may be due to the different urban histories of the two areas; for example, in the Andes, new spaces had to be created to form *doctrinas*, whereas in Mexico, many indigenous towns were spatially reorganized so as to become *doctrinas*.

32. Art-historical and architectural-historical study of colonial town planning in the Americas has focused on the origins of the plan; see, for example, George Kubler, "Open Grid Town Plans in Europe and America, 1500–1520," in *Verhandlungen des XXXVIII: Internationalen Amerikanistenkongresses, Stuttgart-München, 12. bis 18. August 1968* (Munich: K. Renner, 1969–72), 4:105–22.

33. Angel Rama, *The Lettered City,* ed. and trans. John Charles Chasteen (Durham: Duke Univ. Press, 1996); and Bartolomé de las Casas, *In Defense of the Indians,* ed. and trans. Stafford Poole (DeKalb: Northern Illinois Univ. Press, 1992), 79–85.

34. Las Casas, *In Defense* (note 33), 80.

35. See Teresa Gisbert, *El paraíso de los pájaros parlantes: La imagen del otro en la cultura andina* (La Paz, Bolivia: Plural Editores, 1999), 191–93.

36. Henri Lefebvre, *The Production of Space,* trans. Donald Nicholson-Smith (Oxford: Basil Blackwell, 1991), 271, extends this relationship to the Renaissance town

in general, which perceived itself as "a harmonious whole, as an organic mediation between earth and heaven."

37. Raquel Chang-Rodríguez, "Las ciudades de primer nueva coronica y los mapas de las *Relaciones geográficas de las Indias:* Un posible vínculo," *Revista de crítica literaria latinoamericana* 20, no. 41 (1995): 95–119, suggests that Guaman Poma's images of Andean colonial cities derive from the maps made in response (*Relaciones geográficas)* to the official questionnaire sent out from Madrid by the court of Philip II so as to know the empire; see Barbara Mundy, *The Mapping of New Spain: Indigenous Cartography and the Maps of the* Relaciones Geográficas (Chicago: Univ. of Chicago Press, 1996), for an excellent analysis of the questionnaire and *Relaciones geográficas* made in Mexico. Although Felipe Guaman Poma de Ayala's inspiration derives from Martín de Murúa's manuscript *Historia del Perú* (1590), for which he did a number of drawings, the original sources may have come from the *Relaciones geográficas.* This is clearly the case for Guaman Poma's *Mappa mundi,* which is very similar to the map pointed out in MacCormack, *Religion in the Andes* (note 25).

38. For an excellent analysis of the relationship between power and the grid form of the *reducción,* see Alan Durston, "Un régimen urbanístico en la América hispana colonial: El trazado en damero durante los siglos XVI y XVII," *Historia* 28 (1994): 59–115; see also Fraser, *Architecture of Conquest* (note 8), 40–50. One of the state's most potent images of authority and discipline was placed in the center plaza, the *picota* (pillory); see Gonzáles Echevarría, *Myth and Archive* (note 4), 49; Constancio Bernaldo de Quirós y Pérez, *La picota en América*: *Contribución al estudio del derecho penal indiano* (Havana: J. Montero, 1948); and Constancio Bernaldo de Quirós y Pérez, *Nuevas noticias de picotas américanas* (Havana: J. Montero, 1952).

39. Matienzo, *Gobierno del Perú* (note 6), 22 (fol. 37v).

40. Matienzo, *Gobierno del Perú* (note 6).

41. This building and its function may be based on a similar structure built in the plaza of Tlaxcala, the *alhóndiga,* which was the depot for the collection of tribute grain; see Charles Gibson, *Tlaxcala in the Sixteenth Century,* 2d ed. (Stanford: Stanford Univ. Press, 1967), 126–27.

42. Matienzo, *Gobierno del Perú* (note 6), 23 (fol. 37r). A version of the *cédula* was sent to all the *audiencias* addressed locally but with universal aims. For the text sent to Bogotá, see *Audiencia de Santafé,* lrg. 553, leb. 1, fol. 99r; as cited in Juan Friede, ed., *Documentos inéditos para la historia de Colombia,* vol. 10, *1549–1550* (Bogotá: Academia de Historia, 1960), 154–55:

> ahora están cada casa por sí, y aún cada barrio, no pueden ser doctrinados como convendría, ni promulgarles las leyes que se hacen en su beneficio, ni gozar de los Sacramentos de la Eucaristía y otras cosas, de que se aprovecharían y valdarían estando en pueblos juntos y no derramados, y que todos los pueblos que estuviesen hechos… como se hace y acostumbra a hacer en la provincia de Tlaxcala y en otras partes, y que también tuviesen cárcel en cada pueblo para los malhechores y un corral de coso para meter los ganados.

43. Matienzo's reference to Tlaxcala is important because the Tlaxcalan people, as allies of the Spaniards in their conquest of Mexico, received certain rights and privi-

leges. Tlaxcala was also thought to be the first place where baptism took place in Mexico, with Hernán Cortés acting in 1519 as the godfather to the Tlaxcalan leaders; see Gibson, *Tlaxcala* (note 41), 30. The baptism became an iconographic theme by 1581 (Diego Muñoz Camargo, "Descripción de la ciudad y província de Tlaxcala..." [1585], fol. 254), and was reproduced several times in seventeenth-century Tlaxcalan paintings.

44. Interestingly, the acts of the *cabildo* (town council) of Tlaxcala, the principal city of the province of the same name, record in 1560 a resistance to Spanish attempts to congregate peasants into new towns, recommending instead that experienced noblemen be settled first in these locations, after which commoners would be brought in. See James Lockhart, Frances Berdan, and Arthur J. O. Anderson, *The Tlaxcalan Actas: A Compendium of the Records of the Cabildo of Tlaxcala, 1545–1627* (Salt Lake City: Univ. of Utah Press, 1986), 59–60, 104–5.

45. Lockhart, Berdan, and Anderson, *Tlaxcalan Actas* (note 44), 51.

46. Toledo was far from being completely successful in establishing *reducciónes* throughout Peru. In 1617 Viceroy Esquilache wrote to Philip III, saying that the policy of *reducciónes* was "conocida de todos, intentada de muchos y de ninguno conseguida" (known to all, tried by many, and achieved by none); cited in Marzal, *La transformación* (note 13), 89. The viceroy's comments demonstrate the ongoing problems of establishing and maintaining *reducciónes* in the viceroyalty of Peru, in part due to the work service in the mines, especially Potosí. Despite the ongoing complaints that Andeans had not been fully settled in towns, *reducciónes* did, in fact, become the major form of settlement for Andeans by the beginning of the seventeenth century.

47. For a detailed historical description and analysis of the process and its impact on a particular area, see Thomas A. Abercrombie, *Pathways of Memory and Power: Ethnography and History among an Andean People* (Madison: Univ. of Wisconsin Press, 1998), 237–61. For the census-taking as a transformative process in and of itself, see Armando Guevara-Gil and Frank Salomon, "A Personal Visit: Colonial Political Ritual and the Making of Indians in the Andes," *Colonial Latin American Review* 3 (1994): 3–36.

48. There is early evidence of maps drawn on the ground by the Inka. This was done in the valley of Yucay, near the Inka capitol of Cuzco, under the direction of Spanish administration so as to indicate salient landmarks of a valley. An Inka lord had the map made from a vantage point overlooking the valley, so that it could be used for mutual visual inspection and agreement between Inka and Spaniard; see Alonso de Alvarado, "Documentos de Yucay en le siglo XVI," *Revista del Archivo histórico del Cuzco* 13 (1970–71): 1–148, esp. 1–51.

49. Luis Zapata de Cárdenas, *Catecismo para la edificación y conversión de los naturales,* in Juan Guillermo Durán, *Monumenta catechetica hispanoamericana: Siglos XVI–XVIII* (Buenos Aires: Facultad de Teología de la Pontificia Universidad Católica Argentina "Santa María de los Buenos Aires," 1990), 2:161–289, esp. 258: "Y a la puerta [iglesia del pueblo] se hará, si fuere posible, un portal [portalón mm] donde estará un púlpito para predicar a los infieles, que aún no han entrado en el número de los catecúmenos, porque se desea que les den a entender que aún no son dignos de tratar ni entrar en aquelo santo templo."

50. Las Casas, *In Defense* (note 33), 80–81: "You shall not share any of it [the

sacrifice of the lamb] with unbelievers because they are outside the door of the Church since they lack baptism, which is the door of the Church as Gregory goes on to explain."

51. Fernando de Avendaño, *Sermones de los misterios de nuestra santa fé catolica, en lengua castellana y la general del Inca: Impugnanse los errores particulares que los Indios han tenido* (Lima: Jorge López de Herrera, 1648), pt. 2, fol. 1r:

> El primero (Sacramento) es el santo Bautismo, sin el qual ningun otro Sacramento vale nada, ni es nada; por esso el que no está bautizado, no piense que es casado con matrimonio de la Iglesia, ni piense que confessando sus pecados le valdrá la confesion. Asi como todos los que entran en esta iglesia entran por la puerta: asi tambien los que entran por en el numero de los fieles, y hijos de Dios, entran por el Bautismo, y no ay otra puerta para entrar en el cielo. . . . *Ñaupaquenmi Bautismo sutiyoc. Cai sacramentocunamamtapas ñaupaclla chasquissun. Cai Sacramnttocta mana ñaupac chasquispaca, pana huaquiñin Sacramentocuna (2r) chasquichhuā(n) chaipas, mana yupaitā(n) chasquichhuā(n) manarac baptizacuspatac, casaracucca manam casssaracuscan yupaichu, manarac baptizasca caspa confessacuspas confessacuscan manam yupaichu. Imanam cai iglesia yaicuspa, puncunactarac yaicumunchic, hinatacmi sancta Iglesia Christianocunap huñuccuiñunmana. Diospa churin caipac, yaicuita munaccunaca, bautizacusparac yaicunea. Bautismotacmi hanacpachap puncunca.*

See also folio 57r of the Sermanario in Concilio de Lima, "Tercero catecismo," in Juan Guillermo Durán, *Monumenta catechetica hispanoamericana: Siglos XVI–XVIII* (Buenos Aires: Facultad de Teología de la Pontificia Universidad Católica Argentina "Santa María de los Buenos Aires," 1984), 2:599–740.

52. The plaza itself became a space of first assembly and distribution of individuals to perform *mita* (obligatory labor service) either for the mines, such as Potosí, or for local Spaniards.

53. Diego González Holguín, *Vocabulario de la lengua general de todo el Perú, llamada lengua qquichua o del Inca,* 3d ed. (Lima: Universidad Nacional Mayor de San Marcos, 1989), 39.

54. For a discussion of early *reducciónes* in Colombia, see Alberto Corradine Angulo, "Urbanismo español en Colombia: Los pueblos de Indios," and Jaime Salcedo, "Los pueblos de Indios en el Nuevo Reino de Granada y Popayan," in Ramón Gutiérrez, ed., *Pueblos de Indios: Otro urbanismo en la región andina* (Quito: Ediciones Abya-Yala, 1993), 157–78, 179–203.

55. Franklin Pease G. Y., *Breve historia contemporánea del Perú* (Mexico City: Fondo de Cultura Económica, 1995), 45; see also Abercrombie, *Pathways of Memory* (note 47), 248, who cites and translates the passage from Toledo's instructions as published in *Francisco de Toledo: Disposiciones gubernativas para el virreinato del Perú,* vol. 1, *1569–1574* (Seville: Escuela de Estudios Hispano-Americanos, 1986), 34–35.

56. Matienzo, *Gobierno del Perú* (note 6), 24; Toledo, immediately after stipulating that doors open on to the public street, also insists for the same reasons on the separation of interior domestic spaces: "You shall procure that the houses of Indians are laid out such that the room of the wife and daughters and maids, is separated from that

of the male children and other male Indians of the house"; see *Francisco de Toledo* (note 55), 35, as cited in Abercrombie, *Pathways of Memory* (note 47), 248.

57. The house is the critical architectural unit for the *reducción* in terms of *policía*, at least according to Bourdieu, *Outline* (note 5), 89: "[I]t is in the dialectical relationship between the body and a space structured according to the mythic-ritual oppositions that one finds the form par excellence of the structural apprenticeship which leads to the em-bodying of the structures of the world, that is, the appropriating by the world of a body thus enabled to appropriate the world. . . . [I]nhabited space — and above all the house — is the principal locus for the objectification of generative schemes."

58. Ordenanzas 16 and 17 from "Ordenanzas generales para la vida comun en los pueblos de Indios," promulgated by Viceroy Toledo in Arequipa, 6 November 1575, in *Francisco de Toledo* (note 55), 226–27.

59. The relationships among domestic space, sexual relations, *reducciónes*, and creation of a social being is explicitly made by José de Acosta, *De Procuranda Indorum Salute* (Madrid: Consejo Superior de Investigaciones Científicas, 1984–87), 536–43, in a chapter entitled "Quibus Modis Salus Indorum per Saeculares Ministros Procurari Possit." This passage from Acosta, first published in 1588, is mentioned by Peña Montenegro in 1668, who notes that Acosta "dize (que se reduzcan a Pueblos copioso y concentrados) porque retirarse a vivir en los desiertos, no solo es faltar a la enseñança de la doctrina e instrucción en la Ley Evangelica, sino tambien a la conversación politica."

60. Gary Urton, *The History of a Myth: Pacariqtambo and the Origin of the Inkas* (Austin: Univ. of Texas Press, 1990).

61. Abercrombie, *Pathways of Memory* (note 47), 251–58; Gary Urton, "*Chuta*: El espacio del práctica social en Pacariqtambo, Perú," *Revista Andina* 2 (1984): 7–56; and Gary Urton, "La arquitectura pública como textual social: La historia de un muro de adobe en Pacariqtambo (1915–1985)," *Revista Andina* 6 (1988): 225–63.

62. For example the *kuraka* (chief), Juan Ayaviri de Sacaca, presents himself in "Memorial de Charcas [1584–98]," fol. 12 (cited in Silvia Arze and Ximena Medinaceli, *Imágenes y presagios: El escudo de los Ayaviri, Mallkus de Charcas* [La Paz, Bolivia: Hisbol, 1991], 15), in the following terms:

Yten. As being in said town in your royal service, I dress myself very elegantly in costly Spanish clothes in order to be respected and feared.

Yten. I am a man of twenty-six years, of good appearance, good stature, and polished good manners such that I am no different in my bearing, dress, and speech than courteous and courtly Spaniards.

63. The most articulate analyses of the remaking of symbolic cultural forms such as ritual into a means of resisting and inverting authority have been made by Mikhal Bakhtin, *Rabelais and His World*, trans. Hélène Iswolsky (Bloomington: Indiana Univ. Press, 1984); and James C. Scott, *Weapons of the Weak: Everyday Forms of Peasant Resistance* (New Haven: Yale Univ. Press, 1985).

64. There are many notable exceptions to this sweeping statement, such as Hanks, "Authenticity" (note 29); Marzal, *La transformación* (note 13); Linda Curcio-Nagy, "Giants and Gypsies: Corpus Christi in Colonial Mexico City," in William H. Beezley,

Cherly English Martin, and William F. French, eds., *Rituals of Rule, Rituals of Resistance: Public Celebrations and Popular Culture in Mexico* (Wilmington: SR Books, 1994), 1–16; Abercrombie, *Pathways of Memory* (note 47); and Carolyn Dean, *Inka Bodies and the Body of Christ: Corpus Christi in Colonial Cuzco, Peru* (Durham: Duke Univ. Press, 1999).

65. See, for example, Joanne Rappaport and Tom Cummins, "Between Images and Writing: The Ritual of the King's Quillca," *Colonial Latin American Review* 7 (1998): 3–32.

66. Catherine Bell, *Ritual Theory, Ritual Practice* (Oxford: Oxford Univ. Press, 1992), 74.

67. An underlying argument not developed here is that the first mapping of kin-ship relations of non-Western cultures so as to codify them is not to be located in the nineteenth-century modalities of Darwinian civil lawyers, such as Lewis H. Morgan, as recently discussed in Adam Kuper, *The Invention of Primitive Society: Transformations of an Illusion* (London: Routledge, 1988), but in Christian doctrine as applied to sub-ject peoples in the sixteenth and early seventeenth centuries in relation to the institution of marriage as a sacred ritual. As will be suggested, however, this mapping takes an inverse form to the one with which we are familiar in modern anthropology.

68. See, for example, J. Jorge Klor de Alva, "Sahagún and the Birth of Modern Ethnography: Representing, Confessing, and Inscribing the Native Other," in J. Jorge Klor de Alva, H. B. Nicholson, and Eloise Quiñones Keber, eds., *The Work of Bernadino de Sahagún: Pioneer Ethnographer of Sixteenth-Century Aztec Mexico* (Albany: Institute for Mesoamerican Studies, University at Albany, 1988), 31–52; Serge Gruzinski, "Individualization and Acculturation" and Asunción Lavrin, "Introduction: The Scenario, the Actors, and the Issues," in Asunción Lavrin, ed., *Sexuality and Marriage in Colonial Latin America* (Lincoln: Univ. of Nebraska Press, 1989), 1–43, 96–117; and Irene Silverblatt, *Moon, Sun, and Witches: Gender Ideologies and Class in Inca and Colonial Peru* (Princeton: Princeton Univ. Press, 1987).

69. For a discussion of the Tametsi decree and its impact on marriage in colonial Latin America, see Lavrin, "Introduction" (note 68), 6–7.

70. Zapata, *Catecismo para la edificación* (note 49), 284: "El sacerdote debe tra-bajar de les conservar este derecho, en especial siendo estos Indios ahora incapaces de profesar algún otro estado de los que la Iglesia tiene, sino el del matrimonio, y por los graves daños que de no casarse se siguen, como es estar siempre amancebados [con-cubaniage], o no multiplicarse y quedar las tierras desiertas."

71. See Gruzinski, "Individualization," (note 68), 97–99.

72. For a discussion of the early history of consanguinity in the New World and various dispensations, see Daisy Rípodas Ardanaz, *El matrimonio en Indias: Realidad social y regulación jurídica* (Buenos Aires: Fundación para la Educación, la Ciencia y la Cultura, 1977), 169–93.

73. Vitoria, *Political Writings* (note 9), 366, editor's note.

74. Domingo Ramos-Lissón, *La ley según Domingo de Soto* (Pamplona: Ediciones Universidad de Navarra, 1976), 22–23.

75. Ramos-Lissón, *La ley según* (note 74), 22–23: "Los fieles están impedidos por este impedimiento hasta el cuarto grado, ora sea en recta línea, ascendiendo o

descendiendo desde el abuelo hasta taratnieto, y algunos dicen que en recta línea todos son prohibidos; pero opinón es que el abuelo que distase de su descendendiente en quinto grado, que no se prohíbe."

76. Ramos-Lissón, *La ley según* (note 74), 22–23:

Y en línea transversal igual como dos hermanos que son en primero grado y dos primos hermanos en segundo, y dos primos segundos en tercero, etc., y en desigual como el tío con la sobrina, o al cuarto con la sobrina, al contraio, y al que primo de mi padre conmigo; el que es primo segundo del padre de la moza con quien se ha de casar, que éstos están en el grado más distante, como si uno es mi primo hermano y tiemne una nieta, la tal y yo estaemos en cuarto grado, y su bisnieta de mi prima hermano estará conmigo en el quinto grado, en el cual y al los deudos fieles, no son prohibidos casarse, como muy clara y patentemente lo da a entender la figura que se sigue presente.

77. For example, the Quiteña artist Miguel de Santiago depicts Adam and Eve being married by a priest to represent the sacrament of marriage in his didactic series of paintings entitled *Doctrina cristiana* (circa 1660).

78. Both the *Speculum* and *De Septem* circulated in the viceroyalty of Peru, forming a part of Francisco de Avila's library; see Teodoro Hampe Martínez, *Cultura barroca y extirpación de idolatrías: La biblioteca de Francisco de Avila, 1648* (Cuzco: Centro de Estudios Regionales Andinos "Bartolomé de las Casas," 1996), 130, 148. Zapata, however, may have taken it from a *Catecismo* of 1574 composed by Matyr Coma and printed in Spain for use by priests in Spain; see R. Tom Zuidema, "The Spanish Contributions to the Study of Amerindian Kinship Systems," in Serge Gruzinski and Nathan Wachtel, eds., *Le Nouveau Monde, mondes nouveau* (Paris: Editions Recherche sur les Civilisations, 1996), 643–64.

79. Juan Pérez Bocanegra, *Ritual formulario, e institucion de curas . . . con aduertencias muy necessarias* (Lima: por Geronymo de Contreras, 1631).

80. Pérez Bocanegra, *Ritual formulario* (note 79), 602: "Y para que los grados de consanguinidad se conozcan y vean mas distinctamente, pongo este ramo y figura entre ascendeintes y descendientes varones y mugeres."

81. Domingo de Soto, *Fratris Dominici Soto Segobiensis . . . libri decem* De iustitia et iure (Antwerp: Philippvm Nvtivm, 1567), 7v–8r, as cited in Pagden, *Fall of Natural Man* (note 8), 67.

82. Johannes Fabian, *Time and the Other: How Anthropology Makes Its Object* (New York: Columbia Univ. Press, 1983).

83. Diego Valadés, *Rhetorica Christiana* (Perugia: Petrumiacobum Petrutium, 1579), depicts a Franciscan monk who is examining couples in regard to the degrees of consanguinity using a tree and branches to visualize them.

84. For contemporary descriptions of Andean marriages, see Juan M. Ossio Acuña, *Parentesco, reciprocidad, y jerarquía en los Andes: Una aproximación a la organización social de la comunidad de Andamarca* (Lima: Pontificia Universidad Católica del Perú, 1992), 215–49.

85. Pérez Bocanegra, *Ritual formulario* (note 79), 601–2:

Notum fit ect. Sea notorio a todos los presentes que N. varon, y nuestra muger de tal familia y Parroquia con el ayuda de Dios, pretenden contraer entre si matrimonio; por lo qual amonestamos a todos a cada qual que si alguno supiere que entre ellos ay algun impedimento de consanguinidad, ú de afinidad, ú de cognacion espirtual, ú otro qual quiera que impida entre los el matrimonio; luego nos lo avise y esto lo amonestamos, primera vez, (si fuere la primera) o segunda vez (si fuere la segunda) o tercera vez (si fuere la terecera denunciacion).

(Be it known to all those present that our man and our woman of such and such a family and parish with the help of God seek to marry, because of which we admonish each and everyone of us if anyone knows that amongst them there is some impediment of consanguinity, or affinity, or spiritual cognation or other that wishes to impede among them marriage; then advise us of it and this we admonish, first time (if it were the first) or the second (if it were the second) or the third time (if it were the third declaration).)

86. Pérez Bocanegra, *Ritual formulario* (note 79), 603:

De Impedimento consanguinitatis, in linea ascendenti, & descendenti.

1 Grado. Esta india con quien te quieres casar, es tu madre, ó tu hija?

2 Grado. Es tu abuela, ó tu nieta?

3 Grado. Es madre de tu abuelo, ù de tu abuela?

4 Grado. Es nieta de tu nieto, ù de tu nieta? O es abuela de tu abuelo, ù de tu abuela?

(Concerning impediments of consanguinity, ascending and descending lines.

1 Grade. Is this *india* with whom you wish to marry your mother or your daughter?

2 Grade. Is she your grandmother or your granddaughter?

3 Grade. Is she mother of either your grandfather or your grandmother?

4 Grade. Is she granddaughter of either your grandson or your granddaughter? Or is she the grandmother of either your grandfather or grandmother?)

87. Pérez Bocanegra, *Ritual formulario* (note 79), 604:

De Impedimento consanguinitatis, in linea transversal, equaliter distantium?

1 Grado. Esta india con quien te quieres casar es tu hermana?

2 Grado. Es hija de tu tio, ù de tia?

3 Grado. Es hija del hijo de tu hermano, ù de tu hermana?

4 Grado. Es hija del nieto de tu hermano, ò hermana, ù de tu abuela ù bisabuela?

(Concerning impediments of consanguinity, in transverse lines, of equal distance.

1 Grade. Is this *india* with whom you wish to marry your sister?

2 Grade. Is she the daughter of either your uncle or your aunt?

3 Grade. Is she the daughter of the son of either your brother or your sister?

4 Grade. Is she the daughter of the grandson of either your brother or your sister, or is she the daughter of your grandmother or your great grandmother?)

88. Valadés, *Rhetorica* (note 83), notes that couples were examined using an illustration of descending and ascending lines of relations and in the presence of native witnesses.

Material Culture and the Roots of Colonial Society at the South African Cape of Good Hope

Stacey Jordan and Carmel Schrire

An old but familiar question often asked of archaeologists is how might we infer identity from residues. In prehistoric archaeology the answer is often derived from the residues themselves that are reified to denote identity, as in the case of the Mound Builders or the Lapita people, or quantified, as in the case of the Late Magdalenians. Where the historical archaeology of colonialism is concerned, this question assumes greater complexity because the contact that is the hallmark of colonial times was played out in a series of moves. People formed separate enclaves, only to breach them through immigration, emigration, trade, marriage, interbreeding, and warfare, until a creolized community was realized. The essays in this volume focus on various points in the archaeological imprint of this process, comparing situations like Punic and Greek enclaves in Europe with seemingly unbreached European fortresses in West Africa. In South Africa, with its infamous preoccupation with identity that is known as "apartheid," colonial contact engendered institutional racism, and archaeology has a powerful ability to explore the antecedents of this policy through the material signature of colonization in this creole society.

As Mary Douglas and Baron Isherwood wrote of material goods, "Even the choice of kitchen utensils is anchored to deep preconceptions about man and nature."[1] This analysis of the European-style coarse earthenware found in Dutch colonial contexts at the Cape of Good Hope seeks to interpret the forms, makers, and usages of earthenware as a material signature of colonialism—a signature that was neither European nor indigenous, but rather that of a creolized society, which emanated from Africa, Asia, and Europe, and dealt with the interests of officials, farmers, citizens, slaves, and indigenous folk. Going beyond a mere cataloging of artifacts and personages, we might examine the role of material culture in negotiating community, identity, and status at the Cape settlement of the Dutch East India Company (Dutch Verenigde Oostindische Compagnie, or VOC), and reveal the relationships between people by unraveling the social realities and social fantasies of the Cape community.

At issue here is how utilitarian artifacts operate beyond their mundane function. Artifacts are not merely products but also instruments used by actors in the social system.[2] By focusing on the individual experiences in which everyday artifacts play a part, historical archaeology reveals how commonality and community are constructed. This is particularly relevant in what Mary Louise Pratt has termed contact zones, those "social spaces where cultures meet, clash, and grapple with each other, often in contexts of highly asymmetrical relations of power."[3] In these contexts material culture can play a large role in the attempt to define both oneself and others. While Pratt focuses on the pedagogical arts that mediate communities in contact, negotiating and reinforcing authority and authenticity, her ideas become even more useful when broadened to include the material arts of contact zones, the various processes by which material culture helps mediate and construct social realities. The ideologies embedded in these processes—the images of social reality that players seek to impose on others—may be inferred from analyses of artifacts like the VOC coarse earthenware, the "symbolic surrogates" of individual interrelations.[4]

Artifacts, however, may not necessarily be read as a text that encodes a singular meaning. They represent instead a certain incongruity, simultaneously reflecting varying intentions, actions, and social signals: "When the material world and the actions of those who create it, come into contact with it, and use it for whatever ends, are all seen as statements in a discourse, it is the ambiguity arising out of the multiple meanings material objects carry—the polysemic status of artifacts—that provides the entry for explanation."[5] In recognizing this polysemic aspect of material culture, artifacts can be seen as representations of the emergent nature of social groups, statuses, and identities; the ways they have been historically produced; and the ways they have been contested.[6] Seeing artifacts as elements in this contestation rather than as markers of unity or cohesion makes it possible for us to examine the complex workings of identity and community construction on the everyday level.[7]

The style, circumstances of production, and contexts of use of locally produced coarse earthenware present just such a "disunity" through which to glimpse the social dynamics at the colonial Cape of Good Hope. Style is viewed here not as a marker of identity but rather as our access to dialogues of difference and processes of differentiation. To examine style is to consider the entire process of the pot—its transformation from clay raw material, its formation by the potter, its selection by consumers, and its use.[8] Seen as "the visible outcome of a particular manner of acting, specific to time and place, based on a conceptual outlook, a system of values and standards of appropriateness," style becomes a means to understanding the social practices and meanings in which all these particular activities are embedded and enacted.[9]

Background

The Cape settlement was founded at the site of present-day Cape Town by the VOC in 1652 as a refreshment station for those delivering shipments between Holland and the East Indies (fig. 1). It constituted the "frontier fortress of India" on the periphery of their Batavian-Javan sphere.[10] At the Cape, the VOC encountered the indigenous Khoikhoi, with whom they traded in cattle

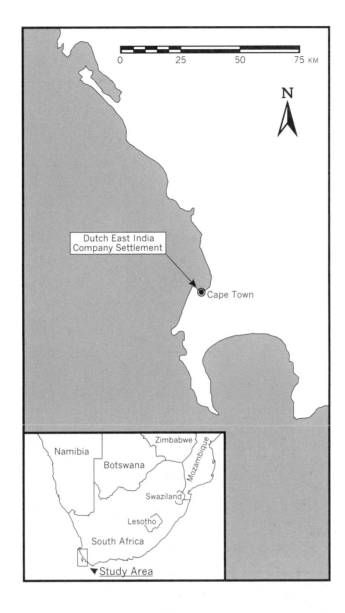

Fig. 1. Earliest VOC settlement, Cape of Good Hope

Fig. 2. Peter Kolb (German, 1675–1725)
Trade relations between the VOC and the indigenous people at the Cape of Good Hope
From Peter Kolb, *The Present State of the Cape of Good Hope...*, trans. Guido Medley
(London: printed for W. Innys, 1731), vol. 1, frontispiece

Fig. 3. Cape course earthenware porringer, or handled bowl
(CA9OMT vessel 86), excavated from the castle moat

and sheep to supply the passing ships (fig. 2). It soon became clear that this exchange was insufficient to support the Indies trade, and within five years, former soldiers of the VOC became farmers on the grazing lands of the indigenous people. By 1684, the Cape was self-supporting but increasing VOC control stifled production and development so that the station became a drain on company resources.[11] As the VOC plummeted into debt, its stations became ripe for plucking, and in 1795, the Cape fell to British forces, who held it as the Cape Colony — with a brief interregnum by the Napoleonic Batavian Republic (1803–6) — for the next 150 years.

The initial VOC colony of 132 European employees was emplaced in a land of hunters, gatherers, and herders, collectively called "Khoisan" (see fig. 2). The colony grew to encompass numerous European settlers, indigenous Africans, Indonesian slaves joined by smaller numbers of enslaved from other parts of Asia and Africa, Chinese convicts, and other political prisoners drawn from the Dutch seafaring empire. By 1806, Europeans made up at least half of the 55,000 inhabitants of the new Cape Colony, and the prediction of the first commander, that the settlers would "in due course break altogether with Holland and one day make this place their Fatherland" had long come to pass.[12] The settlement was neither African nor European; the Cape was a cosmopolitan society with a syncretic *indische*, or Eurasian culture, its genetic interactions encoded in most people, its lingua franca — low Portuguese —

spoken throughout the settlement, its Cape Dutch architecture built by Indonesian craftsmen for colonial masters, and its creole cuisine blending master, servant, and slave foodways.[13]

The archaeological signature of the Cape is drawn from a multiplicity of sites excavated over the past thirty years, including VOC sites and shipwrecks, British frontier and town dwellings in the eastern Cape.[14] Ceramic collections from sites occupied in those times reflect the Cape's position as a crucial node in its trade network, with a preponderance of Asian porcelain, a lesser amount of coarse earthenware, and minor quantities of Asian and European stoneware and refined earthenware.[15] Whereas foreign wares reflect trade, demand and supply, status, and utility, locally made ceramics have the potential to reveal much more. Only coarse earthenware was made locally and, by distinguishing it from similar European wares, one can reveal how effectively mundane material objects like utility pottery function in the creation and negotiation of the social world at the Cape (fig. 3). The coarse earthenware is analyzed with regard to production history, source, typology, distribution, and potters.

Production History

Coarse earthenware was first produced at the Cape in 1665, thirteen years after the founding of the station. Coarse wares were uncommon on outbound ships, and Cape officers generally used pewter (called "tin") vessels.[16] The local, hand-formed, indigenous vessels, with their round or pointed bases, seldom feature in significant quantities in colonial contexts and might not have been available as trade goods or suitable for European hearths. Lacking ceramic vessels, the garrison ate from a common trencher or from the cooking pots themselves, using spoons, shells, and hands.[17] Commandant Wagenaer was disgusted at this spectacle and requested earthenware potters to join the company in 1663. The first potter arrived by 1665, when the earliest vessels were produced. Glazed with a locally made lead glaze and fired in a kiln located near the VOC Castle of Good Hope (the company's headquarters), these goods were set out for VOC use and general sale.[18] The last recorded potter is listed in 1790, five years before the end of VOC rule. After this, the arrival of the British signaled an end to the local tradition, with the importation of industrially produced refined earthenwares that produced a new archaeological signature for the Cape.

Source

The provenance of the local European-style coarse earthenware was revealed using thin-section petrography, which characterizes the aplastic component of ceramic samples in order to infer the geological source of the raw materials employed.[19] The analysis was aimed not only at characterization but also at differentiating local from imported European wares. Archival records revealed no evidence for importation of clays or temper to the Cape, but insist that local wares emanated from a clay source near the Castle of Good Hope

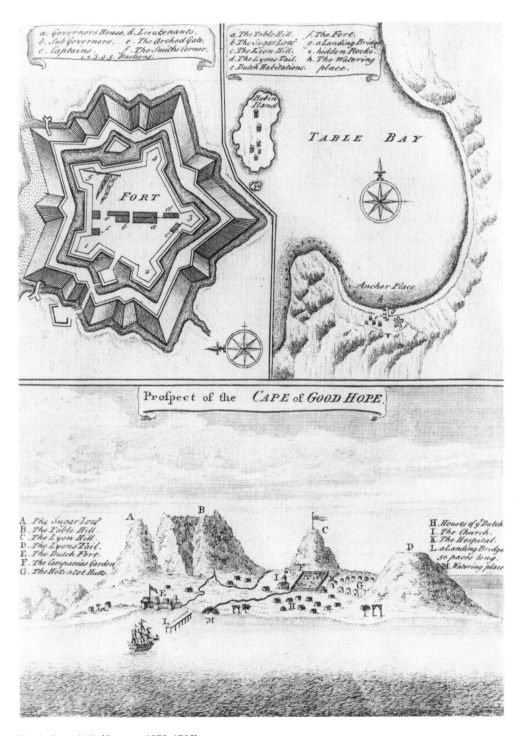

Fig. 4. Peter Kolb (German, 1675–1725)
Prospect of the Cape of Good Hope [VOC castle labeled "The Fort"]
After Peter Kolb, *The Present State of the Cape of Good Hope...*, trans. Guido
Medley (London: printed for W. Innys, 1731), vol. 2, 4, 12

in the Table Valley (fig. 4).[20] Whereas the European wares came predominantly from the variable alluvial material sources located along the Rhine-Meuse River system and therefore have no single petrographic profile, the distinctive geology of the Cape provides a highly characteristic petrographic signature for ceramic raw materials emanating from this area.

European-style coarse earthenware excavated from VOC sites was first divided into suspected European and suspected local wares on the basis of decoration, form, and fabric. Given the lack of white or buff firing earthenware clay raw material at the Cape, only red-bodied vessels without white clay slip decoration were considered as possible local products.[21] All suspected local samples shared a single petrographic profile emanating from a residual granitic source like that of the Cape. This was in marked contrast to the profiles of suspected imports, which not only lacked this signature but also emanated from heavily weathered raw material of nongranitic origin, consistent with the fluvial deposits of northwest Europe.

Typology

Excavated Cape coarse earthenware is dominated by kitchen forms. The open fire cooking forms found in seventeenth-century Europe are duplicated here in tripod cooking pots, skillets, saucepans, and dripping pans.[22] Building on Richard Schaefer's typology of Dutch ceramics, not only can we reveal the local forms produced at the Cape but we are also able to see the forms that are missing.[23] The local Cape vessels are directly related in form to wares from seventeenth- and eighteenth-century Netherlands and Germany, and fall into four categories of usage — namely, storage; food preparation; food and beverage service; and smoking, heating, and lighting (fig. 5). An extensive review of free burgher and free black probate inventories supports these categories and adds a few more vessels, including flowerpots, milk pans, and chamber pots.[24] The local products encode a general lack of decoration, resembling vessels from eighteenth-century potteries in the northeast United States; this simplification has been related to imperfect learning, limited raw materials, labor scarcity, and increasing consumer demand.[25]

Distribution

The distribution of these wares in three archaeological sites provides further insight into their role in the new colonial society. Three sites were examined in detail, occupied from the last quarter of the seventeenth century to the middle of the eighteenth century. Two sites, the Van der Stel Moat and F2, are located at the VOC castle in central Cape Town, and the third is the VOC provisioning post for its ships at Oudepost I, lying some 100 kilometers to the north of the castle (see fig. 1).

The moat collection was excavated from outside the castle's Van der Stel Gateway and consists of material that apparently emanated from the kitchens within and was dumped in the moat between 1703 and circa 1750 (fig. 6). Food preparation vessels dominate; specifically large, locally produced

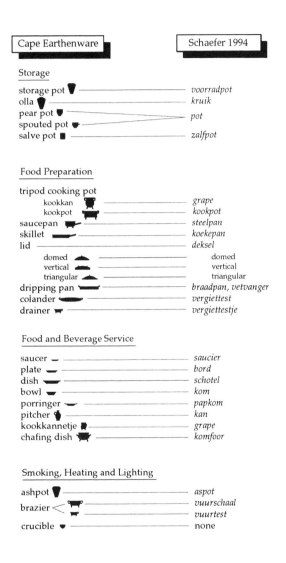

Fig. 5. Typology of Cape coarse earthenware in relation to the nomenclature of Richard Schaefer's typology of Dutch ceramics

Fig. 6. W. L. Walton (British, active 1834–55), after Thomas William Bowler (English, 1812–69)
The Entrance to the Castle [excavations were made to left of entrance]
From Thomas William Bowler and W. R. Thompson, *Pictorial Album of Cape Town, with Views of Simon's Town, Port Elizabeth, and Graham's Town* (Cape Town: J. C. Juta, 1866), pl. 6

Fig. 7. Excavation of the VOC lodge at Oudepost I, Cape of Good Hope, 1986

Fig. 8. Cape tripod cooking pot (CA90MT vessel 61), excavated from the Van der Stel Moat site at the VOC castle

tripod-cooking pots used over an open fire to stew large quantities of mutton and rice for the garrison. The F2 assemblage from the castle granary, dated from 1674 to the early eighteenth century, is refuse in primary context and is dominated by imported vessels. Unlike the moat collection, it contains equal amounts of food preparation and food and beverage service forms. The Oudepost collection, dated from 1669 to 1732, is dominated by food and beverage service vessels, which probably reflect the very small garrison of six to ten men stationed there. The tendency was for each man to fend for himself rather than sup from a communal trencher as was done at the castle. In addition, unlike those at the castle sites, the majority of vessels here were imported, probably obtained from passing ships whose passage was the very raison d'être of the outpost (fig. 7).

The incidence and nature of coarse earthenwares at these sites contrast with those found in other Dutch colonial sites. Enormous amounts of utilitarian pottery were produced in the United Provinces, and European red-bodied coarse earthenware alone constitutes 39 percent of the excavated assemblages from Fort Orange, a Dutch West India Company (DWIC) post in New Netherland.[26] This contrasts markedly with the meager amounts exported to the Cape. Unlike the Cape, New Netherland was the destination for DWIC ships, which were loaded at that location with the bounty of the fur trade and apparently there was no disadvantage in carrying mundane goods like earthenware to the budding middle-class households of the settlement. For the VOC, however, it was more cost-efficient to produce coarse earthenwares at the Cape station and save the space in outbound ships for the lucrative goods needed for trade with the East.

These sites show that wares made at the Cape reflect a shifting foodways system. European and New Netherlands subsistence relied heavily on dairy industries. The Cape, however, served as a refreshment station providing butchered meat to passing VOC ships, and hybrid Khoikhoi-European sheep were the basis of this system. European cattle were not imported in significant numbers until the late eighteenth century, postponing the development of a dairy industry. Here, the large tripod cooking pots are consistent with the Cape's role as a butchering station for VOC ships, suggesting the continuation in some form of the meat and vegetable stews prevalent in Europe (fig. 8). These cooking pots, however, were also used to steam and boil new staples like Asian-grown rice and to incorporate new spices in dishes prepared at the Cape. While the uses of the Cape earthenware were changing, their shapes echoed those of the European domestic tradition, perpetuating a memory of origins while functioning materially in a new, creolized economy, and a new *indische* cuisine.

The Potters

The VOC kept such detailed written records that its employees were dubbed "soldiers of the pen." A search of the muster and free burgher rolls, contracts, wills, death notices, criminal and civil case records, taxation records, and

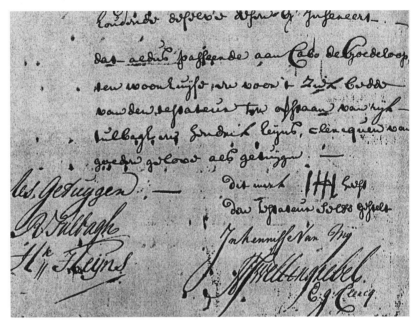

**Fig. 9. Final page of VOC potter Jan Holdhuijsen's will,
1721, with Holdhuijsen's scrawled initials at center right**
Cape Town, Cape Town Archives Repository

deeds, housed in the State Archives in Cape Town and the Rijksarchief in The
Hague, revealed at least nineteen men who served as potters at the Cape
between 1666 and 1790. The resultant profile shows that all were European,
with origins that reflected the wide recruitment to the company, coming
mainly from Germany and the Netherlands, but also from as far afield as
Lisbon, Portugal; and from the Hanseatic, now Polish, cities of Kolberg and
Stettin. They signed on for the customary five-year contract, and usually operated as potters for three to seven years, although some remained in the occupation for up to twenty-one years. They generally worked only half a year as
potters, being hired out as farm laborers, or *knegten,* for the rest of the year.
Unlike the VOC garrison and other artisans, potters lived in a house near the
kiln and worked under the supervision of a company lieutenant. Being company servants first and foremost, they had no guild like their European coun-
terparts and were poorly paid compared to other artisans.

The life histories of the potters vary; some rose to the level of slave-owning
freemen, others stayed poor and locked into servitude to the VOC or served as
farm laborers to a free burgher. One potter entered the court records as a
petty thief and departed them fourteen years later, signing his own will with a
simple scratch of initials (fig. 9). Another became a free burgher and married

well but was murdered by his own slave. A third married well but tended to prefer the company of people from his earlier, lower ranked life. In general, these poor and illiterate craftsmen followed a trajectory from VOC servitude to freedom in the lower echelons of Cape society, passing their time in the inns and smoky taverns that lined the busy shore. Their material signature, encoded in their pots, reflects their origins as well as the emergent creole culture in which they lived.

In summary, the coarse earthenware at the VOC Cape emanates from both Europe and the local Cape potting industry. Some vessels were imported from the homeland in the early years of the Dutch settlement, and local coarse earthenware production began in 1665. These vessels were made for private and company use, and their archaeological context reflects their functions, with large vessels associated with intensive cooking for the garrison in the VOC castle while smaller vessels were associated with individual use at a small VOC outpost. The form of the local products hints at a retention of European identity; however, these vessels mirror something else, namely, the needs of the newly emergent creole society at the Cape. Here, staple foods were a far cry from the dairy-, wheat-, and pork-based cuisine of Europe. Instead, we find a creole cuisine—based on mutton, rice, and spices—planted, harvested, imported, and cooked by an emergent creole society of settlers, servants, and slaves trawled in from northwest Europe, Africa, Asia, and Indonesia, in the great mercantile net of the VOC. It is the articulation of a European tradition into something new that is the hallmark of these modest wares; therefore, it is necessary to contextualize the social implications of these findings in a wider context.

Discussion

The VOC Cape was an entrepôt for the circulating goods of mercantile capitalism, with the settlement embedded in both a global market economy fueling European expansion as well as an internal economy maintaining the Cape Colony itself.[27] By the eighteenth century, a syncretic culture blending elements from all parts of the VOC mercantile empire had grown at the Cape. Emphasizing the cultural homogeneity of the colonial Cape, however, overlooks the struggles to negotiate and articulate status and identity in this new economic, demographic, and cultural environment. In traditional historiography, there is a trichotomy wherein "European," "Khoikhoi," and "slave" are the operative labels used to discuss the history of colonial interaction. Much of this work invents an egalitarianism for all Europeans that masks status ambiguities within the company community itself.[28] As noted by Peter Kolb, an observer in 1731, this community was divided into "Two Classes, call'd the *Qualified* and the *Unqualified*. The Qualified are all the Officers of the Administration; and the Clerks and Book-keepers under them. The Unqualified are the Soldiers, Artificers and Common Servants."[29]

Recognizing the complexities of the garrison's position within the European community of the Cape directs this analysis away from an essentializing colonizer-colonized dichotomy. The question becomes, where did the European VOC employees, including officers, artisans, and servants, who made and used the coarse earthenwares of our study, fit within the Cape settlement's mix of statuses and identities?

Being a statelike entity with its own administration and legal jurisdiction, the company needed to maintain authority, and as such it was faced with the need to control not only the indigenes in its new colonial fold but also its own social subordinates. The company's successes were being forged at the same time that distances were widening in Europe between the cultivated Dutch elite, who increasingly followed French styles, and the masses of common farmers, agriculturalists, and townspeople.[30] The proportion of Dutch nationals in the company's service was higher in commissioned ranks than among the enlisted men, and it was these members of the elite who first set sail with their notions of propriety and rank to make the goods of the world their own.[31] Given their excessive preoccupation with official rank and social status, we find that laws specifically made material culture a physical expression of these differences, creating status displays by circumscribing access to commodities so that material symbols served as ammunition both between factions of the Cape's elite and between the elite and the entire underclass of slaves, garrison members, and poor Europeans.[32]

While all other artisan crafts were the domain of slaves or free blacks, the VOC relied on European potters. The importation of European potters meant the importation of a vernacular style, the "bedrock design notions" inherited by artisans and perpetuated, deeply embedded, unquestioned, inculcated by instruction and insinuation.[33] Exactly why these potters were imported to the Cape is one of the "paradoxes, contradictions, and disjunctions [that] are the keys to getting inside."[34] Given that at the Cape, as elsewhere in the Dutch mercantile empire, membership in the European community was no longer delineated by simple material, linguistic, or racial markers, we suggest that the style of the locally produced coarse earthenware helped articulate the statuses and identities being negotiated.[35] The role of the Cape potters and their European-style products must be examined then in an increasingly creolized world where foodways, material culture, and demographics already reflected the contact of multiple cultures.

The unqualified VOC employees at the Cape were of European heritage, but were often treated no better than slaves. As early as 1686, the Cape's rulers established a curfew of 9:00 P.M. for all slaves and company servants, soldiers, and sailors.[36] By 1731, it was law that "no *Hottentot* or Common Sailor should smoak in the Streets" under penalty of lashing.[37] The garrison and slaves were sometimes provisioned with the same fish from Saldanha Bay, and at times, garrison and slaves even wore similar clothing.[38] Numerous interactions are recorded between these parties. In 1677 some soldiers wore VOC clothes issued by the company to its slaves and traded in turn by the slaves for tobacco and rice. Privately owned slaves operated as hawkers of foods and other products on the streets of Cape Town, allowing everyday social interaction between European consumers, slave consumers, and slave vendors. Social contact between slaves and the VOC garrison also took place in the taverns and inns of the Cape settlement.[39] According to Robert Shell, both slaves and men in the lowest ranks of the Cape's European community exhibited their unrest in "violence, murder, rape, gambling, homosexuality [and] bestiality."[40]

Although elite perceptions of company servants locate them in an uncomfortable social tension—company on the one hand, and servant on the other—the Cape garrison and slaves were exploited and managed in quite similar ways.[41] In 1717 the Cape governor rejected a proposal for permanent company artisans, remarking that "such persons who would come here in that capacity, would often be of bad character—men who had wasted their substance at home," and concluding that "we are amply provided with drunkards who keep our hands full."[42] By the end of the century, a treatise on the Cape made clear the general opinion of the company's underclass, asking and answering the issue: "What kind of people are these soldiers in the Company's service? Everybody knows that they are…the dregs of European society, that they are bad people, who have been forced to leave Europe and go to Asia, that they are mostly people who have been taken into military service by compulsion, by force and by ruse."[43] In other words, despite an "identity of interests" between lower-class Europeans and slaves, there was a certain liminality in the lowest echelon of the European community, as for example in the *knegten*, who were European servants loaned out as wage laborers by the VOC, as well as free poor whites, who often ended up sandwiched between the slave owners and the slaves, embodying the marginality of all poor VOC servants—European, yet still in bondage.[44] On the opposite pole, elite functionaries of the VOC shared not only a language of communication but also one of profit. The settlement's administrators and officers were men of privilege, initially of European birth although increasingly after 1730 the Cape-born sons of free burghers.[45] Each took what Benedict Anderson calls an administrative pilgrimage on his way up the company hierarchy; on this journey, an officer encountered "as eager fellow-pilgrims his functionary colleagues…. In experiencing them as travelling-companions, a consciousness of connectedness ('Why are *we…here…together?*') emerges, above all when all share a single language-of-state."[46]

Like women in nineteenth-century colonial contexts, the VOC European servants experienced the "cleavages of racial dominance and internal social distinctions very differently than men [in this case, elite men] because of their ambiguous positions, as both subordinates in colonial hierarchies and as active agents of imperial culture in their own right."[47] Inherent in colonial encounters is not only the creation of the "Other" but also the redefinition of the various "Selves" that the colonizing community comprises. Community itself becomes a *product* of contact. Simon Schama recognizes the Dutch sense of community as a result of the confluence of recent historical experience and geographic constraints.[48] The same can be said for the Dutch sense of colonial community, where the results of recent global movements brought different peoples together in new social contexts.

Under these circumstances, the locally produced coarse earthenware may be viewed as Commandant Wagenaer initially intended it to be, namely, as an instrument to help maintain a European identity within a world of obscured sexual, social, and status boundaries. The insistence on European potters and, by extension, European forms by Cape officials, was an attempt to construct for the garrison what Anderson calls an "imagined community" through a material identification with the European homeland. A "deep, horizontal comradeship" created loyalty to the greater body, which, although it might not have realized it at the time, was well on its way to creating a kind of corporate nationalism out of the dynamics of mercantile capitalism, in which items like the Cape's local coarse earthenware could become part of the material expression and phenomenological experience of just such an imagined community.[49]

The familiar material forms demanded by the company officers, however, did more than reinforce a community identity of "European." They also reflected the distinctions within this colonizing group. Archaeological and documentary evidence reveals how VOC servants and freemen dined from the local coarse earthenware as well as communal wooden trenchers, while Company officers dined from imported porcelains and matching pewter services at their tables.[50] The castle moat debris, emanating as it did from the garrison kitchen, shows coarse earthenware to have been instrumental in food production for at least this part of the company population. Despite the presence of this functional and locally available ceramic, however, the company continually requested metal vessels from Europe to provision the officers and the free burgher farmers.[51]

In comparison to the rather limited suite of vessel forms found in the excavated coarse earthenware at the Cape, imported metal vessels encompassed not only cooking pots, plates, and dishes but also fish kettles, porringers, and salt and mustard pots, indicating that it was not only the raw materials that distinguished elite and nonelite but also the range of forms they used.[52] Imported iron and copper cooking vessels are listed in inventories of the company's warehouses throughout the eighteenth century, and burgher Adam Tas notes the officers' exploitation of these indirectly in his comments of early that century, saying "if there be timber from home in the Castle, the gentlemen make off with the best; their iron they draw from the Castle store."[53] Locally produced earthenwares, then, appear to have been selected *against* by the VOC officers in favor of imported metal and porcelain vessels, rendering earthenware into a symbol of both "Europeanness" *and* low status.

Through these material items, the VOC elite acted to maintain both cultural differentiation and internal hierarchy at the polycultural Cape. The differential use of coarse earthenware helped create an "iconography of rule."[54] It reinforced a general identity within which the nonelite segment of the Cape's European population — the VOC servants — would continue to be socially and economically subordinate, by maintaining their tenuous position between company and subaltern.[55] European-style coarse earthenware integrated lower-class Europeans into the colonizing community but symbolically excluded them from the very power that European identity had the potential to confer. Keeping in mind the dialectic nature of material culture, however, it is important to view these artifacts not simply as a means by which the VOC elite sought to keep *themselves* in control but, equally as important, as the way they convinced themselves of their power to define and structure social reality. Likewise, the distinction between slave and free person at the Dutch colonial Cape was materially marked by the fact that slaves alone were not allowed to wear shoes at any time.[56] On a grander scale, symmetrical house facades, gridded street plans, and geometric fortification architecture were "public transcripts" of domination, part of elite attempts to spatially order and symbolically control the colonial world.[57] Such architectural ordering is also seen in other colonial contexts, like that of the Andean colonial settlements discussed by Cummins in the present volume.[58]

Such material signs, however, also incorporate elements of the "low/bottom/other" in their form, in that the elite required symbols of that which it was not in order to define that which it was.[59] Ornate symmetrical facades that elaborated common structures and underclass areas of town, provided a constant reminder of the elite quality of life.[60] Coarse earthenware was one such signifier of the common and mundane at the Cape. Precisely because it was not a commodity at the VOC entrepôt, this ceramic became part of the political discourse at the settlement.[61] It served as the element of the "low" in the total colonial ceramic suite whose absence from some contexts of use—by the elite, for example—helped define the "high." The meaning and symbolism of ceramics are shaped not only by the status of their user, the social context of their use, and access to them but also by the ability to choose *not* to use them.[62] Just as the increased variety of ceramic wares resulting from global trade allowed for new and more elaborate displays of status, so too did the limited range of ceramics available to certain portions of the Cape population mark their own circumscribed status.

Beyond attempts to define "Europeanness" and the status hierarchy, locally produced ceramics also served in negotiations of power and identity in the households of the broader population. There were very few European women at the Cape, numbering only a few hundred, in contrast to the many thousands of company employees and free settler men.[63] Many came from orphanages in the Netherlands, and usually found themselves marrying into the households of the more prosperous citizens.[64] French Huguenot refugee women and the wives of early settlers and officials composed the rest of the small European female population. The already unbalanced sex ratio widened further when the VOC ceased to underwrite the immigration of free settler families in 1717.[65]

The solution to this situation was for men of European origin to marry outside of their group. Robert Ross has suggested that it was the lower echelon of the European male community that bore the brunt of this imbalance, marrying disproportionately "into the mass of 'non-white' underlings, for no doubt it was these people who were the least able to find white wives."[66] While marriage was not permitted between slaves and free persons, the marriage of garrison members to free black women — some of whom they themselves emancipated — was not uncommon, nor was concubinage and cohabitation with women still enslaved.[67] In this way non-European women from all parts of the VOC's eastern trade network entered into colonial households, as domestic slaves and wives, and encountered the material tools of European domesticity. These circumstances gave Cape wives of European descent greater value in yet another way, carrying both "the identity of difference from the transgressive miscegenation" as well as the cultural heritage of European domesticity.[68] Thus households were changing, and mostly among those very European men the VOC officers sought to keep in their fold.

The gendered division of the Dutch spatial world, where men were positioned outside the household and women within, is reflected in the genre art of the time, which in turn echoes Jacob Cats's prescription of 1628 that "The husband must be on the street to practice his trade, The wife must stay at home to be in the kitchen."[69] A Dutch wife's duties centered on her role as the domestic administrator, supervising servants; shopping; planning, preparing, and cleaning up after the week's meals; and caring for the goods of the house among other chores.[70] But beyond ruling the domestic sphere, the housewife had an equally important role: the physical manifestation of moral order. "The laws that commanded the Dutch to conspicuous observation of their washing rituals were moral rather than material... to be clean was to be patriotic, vigilant in the defense of one's homeland, hometown and home against invading polluters and polluted invaders."[71] Central to this is the cleanliness not only of the state but also of the implied body. This polluted invader, this threatening "exotic," was embodied at the Cape by the slave woman, permeating the boundaries of the European community both culturally and physically. How, then, were slave women and their descendants to be incorporated into that symbolic core of morality, the Dutch household?

The property laws of the Cape, based on Roman-Dutch law, made women a valuable commodity. Elite, property-owning families were often connected through matrilineal links, and widows could sometimes control significant estates.[72] At the same time, however, a woman automatically became a legal minor when she married or remarried, while the groom was automatically granted majority and control of property, regardless of age.[73] Thus, although social networking and the domestically based black markets in goods may have given some Cape women a measure of freedom, the daily experience of women was still one of institutionalized disempowerment.[74]

Home and family was the foundation of the Dutch commonwealth.[75] At the same time that the European style of the local products was meant to re-enculturate VOC servants in this new polycultural context, it was also meant to acculturate female slaves and free black women — often the wives and daughters of Europeans — into the fantasy of the Dutch household, the moral backbone on which the United Provinces relied so heavily. Even abandoned

Khoikhoi babies, all female, were taken in by European families in their wide-ranging attempts to bring the "Other" into the European community via the home and family.[76] Other measures of social control included the VOC maintenance of census rolls of the *eenlopenden* — free, single European men — through which the company "closely monitored their lives until they were safely married. These lists, of persons assumed to be potentially unstable characters — 'singletons,' as they were dubbed — were kept as a security measure ... colonial authorities at the Cape viewed the family as the bedrock of the society and the economy."[77] Not only did European men need to enter the stabilizing force of the "Dutch" household, but more important, so did the slave women and their descendants who increasingly dominated the domestic units of the Cape settlement. As in Batavia, the child-rearing and domestic roles of wife were now being taken on by colonized Asian or Creole women.[78] In the domestic realm of these polycultural colonial contexts then existed the paradox of "the impossibility and necessity of creating the other as other — the different, the alien — and incorporating the other within a single social and cultural system of domination."[79]

At the Cape, the local European-style earthenware was used to mediate this contradiction. In both its form and use, the local coarse earthenware was a means of measuring the degree to which the ideal of the Dutch household as maintained by well-to-do male colonists was preserved. In *Patria*, the Fatherland, Dutch genre images of households and domestic utensils communicated "the tireless perseverance and strength needed to master fleshly self-indulgence."[80] At the distant Cape, the local earthenware itself served as such a visual icon. The European-style ware produced was symbolic not only of an imagined European community but also of women's position in the colonial hierarchy as defined by both gender and heritage. As in the New World colonies, the respective identities, roles, and positions of women and slaves were denoted by the objects they used; in this light, the coarse earthenware produced by the VOC becomes a representation of more than "European-ness."[81] In its domestic use by wives and slaves it also became a means through which common men passed on a degree of their former subordination, again constructing themselves as higher in status through their own non-use of these European domestic utensils (fig. 10; cf. excavated vessel in fig. 8).

As elsewhere in the colonial world, control over membership in the Cape's colonizing community required control over all aspects of sex, marriage, and domesticity among both Europeans and their colonial subordinates.[82] The European-style coarse earthenware produced by the VOC was an instrument in the elite's attempts to reconstitute community and moral boundaries in the face of breached bodily boundaries. To re-create the Other in one's own image — to bring the Other into one's own community of cultural and moral practice — was to conquer.

How, then, was the local coarse earthenware employed by these women in the household? European-style coarse earthenware was one of the elements used by slave women and free black wives in the course of daily food

Fig. 10. Lady Anne Barnard (English, 1750–1825)
Our Undercook, ca. 1800
From A. M. Lewin Robinson, ed., *The Letters of Lady Anne Barnard Written to Henry Dundas, from the Cape and Elsewhere, 1793–1803* (Cape Town: A. A. Balkema, 1973), 51

preparation. These ceramics differed from the foods and utensils used in the foodways of Indonesia, the homeland of many Cape slaves. The diets of Southeast Asians were dominated by starch from rice and tubers; animal protein from buffalo, pig, goat, chicken, duck, shellfish, cephalopods, and boiled fish; and fruits such as coconut, mango, and banana.[83] Raw seafood, vegetables, and fruits were often dressed with relishes like coconut milk, rasped and roasted coconut meat, pepper and salt, or limes mixed with the chili peppers introduced from America in the sixteenth century.[84] Nuts, tamarind sauce, tree sap vinegars, parsley, basil, mint, coriander, eggplant, onion, garlic, turnips, beans, peas, lentils, and melons were also part of the sixteenth-century diet.[85] *Atjar*, described as a "salad or minced onion," was a common part of the Indonesian meal.[86] Also prevalent were the satays, descendants of the Middle Eastern kebab, which accompanied Arab Muslim traders into the area.[87] In this dish the meat "is served at table cut in pieces which are spitted ladder-like on little wooden sticks. They serve the fish in *sagu* leaves like a pastry."[88]

Where utensils are concerned, bamboo, shells, and leaves were more often used than ceramic wares.[89] Ceramics were present, but unlike the wheel-thrown European earthenwares, early ceramics of southeast Asia were generally hand-coiled, unglazed earthenware finished with an anvil and a beater. These globular, wide-mouthed, pit-fired vessels were later accompanied by unglazed bottles and *kendi*, spouted bottles that copied forms produced in India.[90] The common earthenware pot was used to store liquids and pickled goods, with similar smaller containers for sauces, pastes, and preserves.[91] This traditional round-bottomed vessel form was sometimes used for rice preparation and service, although rice was also steamed or roasted in leaves over open fires.[92] Until recently, cooking in the Celebes took place on "simple hearths of hard earth where pots and pans were set on three stones over a fire of wood or coconut shells."[93] In Southeast Asia today, coarse earthenware pots "are the most regularly used and preferred cooking utensils in many homes, especially for rice, and for tamarind or lime based soups," as well as for "fermenting fish and storing grains, wine, or water."[94] Local earthenware production decreased with the increasing use of porcelain vessels in Southeast Asian households after the fourteenth century.[95] While elites on these islands used porcelain and copper vessels, leaves apparently served as dishes and cups for common people.[96]

These foods and utensils differed strongly from the basic ones used in northwest Europe, where the common diet relied heavily on cheese and butter, wheat bread for the wealthy and rye for the commoner, beans, vegetables, and fruits. Gruels of old bread soaked in milk sat on the poorest tables. Meats like beef, pork, mutton, and poultry, often salted or stewed, as well as fresh and cured fish, provided animal protein.[97] *De verstandige kok of sorghvuldige huyshouder* (The Wise Cook or the Painstaking Householder), a seventeenth-century middle-class Dutch cookbook, recommended a diet of fresh meat once a week, and cheese, bread, stews, salads, and fresh vegetables.[98] Vegetables readily available to northwest Europeans were onions, cabbages, parsnips, turnips, beets, carrots, salsify, peas, beans, cucumbers, endive, scallions, and leeks, prepared in the metal and ceramic tripod cooking pots, saucepans, and skillets discussed above.[99]

In transplanting people and foods to the Cape, ingredients of both Indonesia and Europe were used in new combinations and prepared in new ways. Rice, often steamed in leaves or fire-roasted, was now boiled in European-style coarse earthenware vessels. The ubiquitous coconut of the East dropped out of the everyday diet in the transition westward.[100] The *atjar* relishes of the Indonesian isles became a favorite condiment at any meal, enjoyed especially by Cape ladies. Abbé de la Caille, visiting the Cape between 1751 and 1753, observed: "The women are particularly fond of achards, that is to say vegetables or fruits salted and preserved in vinegar, with an abundance of spices."[101] Meats and fish at the Cape were preferred salted, smoked, or dried, then lightly grilled with pepper and bread soaked in hot water.[102] Satays and curries became part of the colonial cuisine. While pepper and curries were initially used to disguise unsavory meat, curried quail cooked in "the old Dutch way" was considered a great delicacy by the turn of the twentieth century.[103] The culinary prowess of slave women and their descendants was legendary, and continued especially in old Cape families of Dutch descent, who had Malay and Indian cooks.[104]

This creole foodways system, where domestic slaves and slave women who married European men passed their cultural influence into the household through the kitchen, is reflected in the inventories of seventeenth- and eighteenth-century Cape households, which included:

> water cans and buckets, a grater, a funnel, pestles with mortars, cleavers, a chopping knife with a board, an "overkeerbort," grids, tongs, a blowpipe, chimney chains, a trivet, coffee mills, a rice block and a chopping board. Cooking vessels were mostly in copper, such as the numerous specialized pans including tart pans, "poffer" pans, skimmer pans, a baking pan and long-handled pans, one of which was a frying pan. Other copper vessels were kettles/cauldrons or boilers, a colander, casseroles and a ewer with iron feet.[105]

The *rijstblok*, or rice block, is particularly revealing: it is a typically Asian utensil used for domestic rice processing, and its presence in the inventories reflects the basic changes occurring in Cape foodways, households, and material culture. One of the most fundamental contributions of Asia to the Cape diet was imported rice, which would become a staple at the settlement. In Antonia Malan's extensive analysis of probate inventories, a rice block was present in at least two-thirds of a transcribed sample dating between 1701 and 1821, suggesting that the *rijstblok* "was in fact a normal item of the Cape household."[106] It is a small item, but a powerful indicator that here, as elsewhere in the Dutch seaborne empire, specifically at its headquarters in Batavia, company men and free farmers who married into the Asian or Creole population, singularly failed to "induce their Asian and Eurasian womenfolk to forgo their Indo-Portuguese cultural mores and to adopt the Dutch way of life."[107]

If the material appearance of the Cape kitchen remained predominantly European, the foods prepared there were not. While traditional Dutch dishes cooked in the European-style earthenware were themselves connected to "a morally wholesome and thriving family life," they included new Eastern spices and flavors, which "with their heady fragrance and pagan origin were to be mistrusted as likely to beguile men away from home cooking and plain morality."[108] In this context both the use and symbolic meaning of the locally produced coarse earthenware were transfigured into conduits for the increasingly creolized foodways, and emblems of the creolized population growing at the Dutch colonial Cape of Good Hope. Despite the fact that the vessel forms were intended to be icons of Dutch domesticity and morality, they actually contributed to a specifically colonial Eurasian culture, participating in the creolization of both the foodways milieu and the Cape household itself.

A similar creolization of the colonial ceramic signature as a whole occurred in the sixteenth- and seventeenth-century Spanish settlement of Saint Augustine, Florida. Here, aboriginal utility ceramics are the predominant ware from Spanish colonial households, reflecting "the close cultural and physical admixture of the Spanish and Indian groups in the colony."[109] Like the Cape station, Saint Augustine was manned by a military garrison of single men, and European women appear to have constituted less than one-third of the total European population.[110] According to Kathleen Hoffman, "The shortage of Spanish women resulted in one of the most dramatic and fundamental transformations of Spanish culture into a Spanish colonial culture—a pattern of intermarriage, both formal and informal, between Spanish men and Native American women dating from the earliest years of creolization."[111]

In this context, the replacement of utilitarian Spanish lead-glazed vessels with Native American vessels may be a material marker of the increased presence of indigenous women in Spanish households, as both wives and servants. While display- and tablewares as well as social symbols like architecture remained predominantly European in form, the indigenous ceramics used by women in the households brought elements of native culture into the private spaces of the settlement. Kathleen Deagan notes the greater impact of indigenous culture among the lower levels of Saint Augustine society, where nonelite Spanish colonists with few resources may have more readily adopted elements of native material culture and lifeways—precisely the kind of change the Dutch East India Company intended to avoid with its European-style coarse earthenware.[112] At the Cape the situation is reversed, with imported Asian porcelains and creolized architecture as markers of social status and European-style utilitarian earthenwares as carefully placed reminders of cultural loyalties. While the face of the total ceramic assemblage at Saint Augustine differs from that of the Cape, however, it is clear that the changing household dynamics in both colonial situations is reflected not only in ethnic creolization but also in the creolization of the domestic ceramic signature.

Although the Cape ceramic signature as a whole was a product of creolization, there is no single creolized ware equivalent to the Colono ware found on colonial sites of the eastern United States and the Caribbean. This coarse, unglazed, distinctively non-European pottery, which was excavated from late seventeenth- and eighteenth-century contexts, was possibly produced predominantly by enslaved African Americans.[113] Despite the lack of creolized ware, locally produced VOC earthenware operated much like Colono ware, as a material manifestation of contact and changing social dynamics in the colonial situation, and as a reflection of the process of interaction here.[114] Just as Colono ware might not merely be a technical replication and cultural retention of African traits, the Cape coarse earthenware is a product of the new and complex social relations of the colonial context. With its influx of new staples like rice, new Eastern spices, and new servants in the form of Eastern slaves who were valued for their culinary skills, the Cape became the locus of a conceptual struggle against an ongoing cultural creolization, manifested even in the local foodways. The VOC officials were appropriating not only the landscape of Africa but also the new natural resources they encountered, attempting to redefine them through preparation in a European-style suite of material items. Despite the icons of European foodways, domesticity, and morality drawn from the Cape clay, however, the VOC settlement was undergoing subtle and irreversible change.

Conclusion

While common VOC servants were using the local European-style redwares to cook and eat, so too were the slave women — integrated as wives and domestic slaves into colonial households — using these vessels in their everyday activities. Both of these groups of VOC subordinates incorporated the European-style local products, with their iconographic recollections of "Dutchness," into their material and symbolic worlds.

"Identity" says Stuart Hall, "is formed at the unstable point where the 'unspeakable' stories of subjectivity meet the narratives of a history, of a culture."[115] This unstable point, the meeting of the colonial experience and the ideals of Dutch culture, created the contradictions that material culture was used to manage. While the historical and cultural references made by the European-style coarse earthenware were representations of the elite's sociocultural ideologies, material culture was not simply the static representation of a particular identity.[116] Rather, it was one of many tools by which identity at the Cape was shaped and enacted, with the garrison using a familiar material form from the European homeland, and slaves and free blacks using this icon of Dutch domesticity in their creolized foodways system.[117]

The locally produced coarse earthenware was a material tool in reconfiguring notions of community at the Cape. To recognize its "Europeanness" is not to characterize its presence in the archaeological record as a marker of European identity but rather to see it as part of the ongoing struggle to define and redefine self and community at the VOC settlement. The form of the local coarse earthenware, together with the uses to which the vessels were put, constitute the cognitive context in which artifacts functioned and provide the basic key to understanding the significance of coarse earthenware at the settlement.[118]

The Cape coarse earthenware provides a window into the global and local movements that contributed to the creation of a colonial material culture. A variety of economic, social, and geographic factors created the situation in which the local European-style earthenware was preferable to the European product. Understanding the history of pottery production and the forms created at the seventeenth- and eighteenth-century Dutch Cape provides a context in which to see how these European-style pots were both reflective of and instrumental in the creation and negotiation of social reality at this nexus of different worlds. These vessels reflect the fissures and social paradoxes, the simultaneity of community, inequity, identification, and liminality, which defined the Dutch colonial Cape of Good Hope.

Notes

1. Mary Douglas and Baron Isherwood, *The World of Goods* (New York: Basic, 1979), 73.

2. Mary C. Beaudry, Lauren J. Cook, and Stephen A. Mrozowski, "Artifacts and Active Voices: Material Culture as Social Discourse," in Randall H. McGuire and Robert Paynter, eds., *The Archaeology of Inequality* (Oxford: Basil Blackwell, 1991), 174.

3. Mary Louise Pratt, "Arts of the Contact Zone," in David Bartholomae and Anthony Petrosky, eds., *Ways of Reading: An Anthology for Writers*, 4th ed. (Boston: St. Martin's, 1996), 530.

4. Charles E. Orser Jr., *A Historical Archaeology of the Modern World* (New York: Plenum, 1996), 33.

5. Beaudry, Cook, and Mrozowski, "Artifacts" (note 2), 158.

6. Margaret W. Conkey, "Experimenting with Style in Archaeology: Some Historical and Theoretical Issues," in Margaret W. Conkey and Christine A. Hastorf, eds., *The Uses of Style in Archaeology* (Cambridge: Cambridge Univ. Press, 1990), 12.

7. See Suzanne Desan, "Crowds, Community, and Ritual in the Work of E. P. Thompson and Natalie Davis," in Lynn Hunt, ed., *The New Cultural History* (Berkeley: Univ. of California Press, 1989), 47–71.

8. Michael Shanks, "Style and the Design of a Perfume Jar from an Archaic Greek City State," in Robert W. Preucel and Ian Hodder, eds., *Contemporary Archaeology in Theory: A Reader* (Oxford: Basil Blackwell, 1996), 374.

9. Tracey Cullen, "Social Implications of Ceramic Style in the Neolithic Peleponnese," in W. D. Kingery and Esther Lense, eds., *Ancient Technology to Modern Science* (Columbus, Ohio: American Ceramic Society, 1985), 78.

10. George McCall Theal, *Chronicles of Cape Commanders* (Cape Town: W. A. Richards, 1882), 183; and Jean Gelman Taylor, *The Social World of Batavia: European and Eurasian in Dutch Asia* (Madison: Univ. of Wisconsin Press, 1983), 4–5.

11. Robert Ross, *Beyond the Pale: Essays on the History of Colonial South Africa* (Johannesburg: Witwatersrand Univ. Press, 1994), 25.

12. Gababeh Abrahams, *The Archaeological Potential of Central Cape Town* (Pasadena: Munger Africana Library, California Institute of Technology, 1985), 19; and Harm J. De Blij, *Africa South* (Evanston: Northwestern Univ. Press, 1962), 23–30.

13. Richard Elphick and Robert C.-H. Shell, "Intergroup Relations: Khoikhoi, Settlers, Slaves and Free Blacks," in Richard Elphick and Hermann Giliomee, eds., *The Shaping of South African Society, 1652–1820* (Cape Town: Longman, 1979), 157.

14. See, for example, Katherine Cruz-Uribe and Carmel Schrire, "Analysis of Faunal Remains from Oudepost I, an Early Outpost of the Dutch East India Company, Cape Province," *South African Archaeological Bulletin* 46 (1991): 92–106; Martin Hall, *A Study in the Archaeology of Early Colonial Settlement: Cape Town in the Seventeenth, Eighteenth, and Early Nineteenth Centuries*, report submitted to the Human Sciences Research Council (Cape Town: Archaeology Contracts Office, 1991); Martin Hall, *Archaeological Work at Sea Street, Cape Town*, report submitted to Old Mutual Properties (Cape Town: Archaeology Contracts Office, University of Cape Town, 1991); Martin Hall et al., "The Archaeology of Paradise," *Goodwin Series, South African Archaeological Society* 7 (1993): 40–58; Martin Hall and Ann Markell, eds., *Historical Archaeology in the Western Cape* (Cape Town: South African Archaeological Society, 1993); Martin Hall et al., "'A Stone Wall Out of Earth That Thundering Cannon Cannot Destroy'? Bastion and Moat at the Castle, Cape Town," *Social Dynamics* 16, no. 2 (1990): 22–37; Martin Hall et al., "The Barrack Street Well: Images of a Cape Town Household in the Nineteenth Century," *South African Archaeological Bulletin* 45 (1990): 73–92; Ann Markell, Martin Hall, and Carmel Schrire, "The Historical Archaeology of Vergelegen, an Early Farmstead at the Cape of Good Hope," *Historical Archaeology* 29, no. 1 (1995): 10–34; Carmel Schrire, *Digging through Darkness: Chronicles of an Archaeologist* (Charlottesville: Univ. Press of Virginia, 1995); Bruno E. J. S. Werz, "The Excavation of the *Oosterland* in Table Bay: The First Systematic Exercise in Maritime Archaeology in Southern Africa," *South African Journal of Science* 88 (1992): 85–89; Bruno E. J. S. Werz and Jane E. Klose, "Ceramic Analysis from the VOC Ship *Oosterland* 1697," *South African Journal of Science* 90 (1994): 522–26; and Margo Winer and James Deetz, "The Transformation of British Culture in the Eastern Cape, 1820–1860," *Kroeber Anthropological Society Papers* 73–74 (1992): 41–61.

15. Antonia Malan, "The Material World of Family and Household: The Van Sitterts in Eighteenth-Century Cape Town," in Lyn Wadley, ed., *Our Gendered Past: Archaeological Studies of Gender in Southern Africa* (Johannesburg: Witwatersrand Univ. Press, 1997), 293.

16. H. C. V. Leibbrandt, *Precis of the Archives of the Cape of Good Hope: Journal, 1699–1732* (Cape Town: W. A. Richards, 1896), 116–32; and H. C. V. Leibbrandt, *Precis of the Archives of the Cape of Good Hope: Letters Despatched from the Cape, 1652–1662* (Cape Town: W. A. Richards, 1900), 3:229.

17. Zacharias Wagner, *Dagregister en briewe van Zacharias Wagenaer, 1662–1666*, ed. Anna J. Böeseken (Pretoria: Staatsdrukker, 1973), 305.

18. Wagner, *Dagregister* (note 17), 222.

19. Stacey C. Jordan, Duncan Miller, and Carmel Schrire, "Petrographic Characterization of Locally Produced Pottery from the Dutch Colonial Cape of Good Hope, South Africa," *Journal of Archaeological Science* 26 (1999): 1327–37.

20. H. C. V. Leibbrandt, *Precis of the Archives of the Cape of Good Hope: Requesten (Memorials), 1715–1806*, vol. 3, *P–S* (Cape Town: South African Library, 1988), 992.

21. This information on local clays comes from Sharma Saitowitz, Department of Archaeology, University of Cape Town.

22. A. P. E. Ruempol and A. G. A. van Dongen, *Pre-Industrial Utensils, 1150–1800: Museum Boymans-Van Beuningen, Rotterdam, Department of Applied Arts and Design* (Rotterdam: Museum Boymans-Van Beuningen, 1991), 164.

23. Richard G. Schaefer, *A Typology of Seventeenth-Century Dutch Ceramics and Its Implications for American Historical Archaeology* (Ann Arbor: University Microfilms, 1994).

24. Antonia Malan, "Households of the Cape, 1750 to 1850: Inventories and the Archaeological Record" (Ph.D. diss., University of Cape Town, 1993).

25. See Sarah Peabody Turnbaugh, "Introduction," and F. J. E. Gorman, D. G. Jones, and J. Staneko, "Product Standardization and Increasing Consumption Demands by an Eighteenth-Century Industrial Labor Force," in Sarah Peabody Turnbaugh, ed., *Domestic Pottery of the Northeastern United States, 1625–1850* (Orlando, Fl.: Academic, 1985), 1–28, 119–32.

26. Paul Huey, *Aspects of Continuity and Change in Colonial Dutch Material Culture at Fort Orange, 1624–1664* (Ann Arbor: University Microfilms, 1988).

27. Robert Ross, "The Occupations of Slaves in Eighteenth-Century Cape Town," in Christopher Saunders and Howard Phillips, eds., *Studies in the History of Cape Town*, vol. 2 (Cape Town: History Department and Centre for African Studies, University of Cape Town, 1984), 1.

28. See Robert C.-H. Shell, *Children of Bondage: A Social History of the Slave Society at the Cape of Good Hope, 1652–1838* (Hanover: University Press of New England, 1994), xxix.

29. Peter Kolb, *The Present State of the Cape of Good Hope...*, trans. Guido Medley (1731; reprint, New York: Johnson Reprint, 1968), 1:354–55, italics in original.

30. Simon Schama, *The Embarrassment of Riches: An Interpretation of Dutch Culture in the Golden Age* (New York: Knopf, 1987), 597.

31. Charles R. Boxer, *The Dutch Seaborne Empire, 1600–1800* (London: Hutchinson, 1965), 81.

32. Boxer, *Dutch Seaborne Empire* (note 31), 210; Arjun Appadurai, *The Social Life of Things: Commodities in Cultural Perspective* (Cambridge: Cambridge Univ. Press, 1986), 25; and Martin Hall, "High and Low in the Townscapes of Dutch South America and South Africa: The Dialectics of Material Culture," *Social Dynamics* 17, no. 2 (1991): 41–42.

33. James R. Sackett, "Style and Ethnicity in Archaeology: The Case for Isochrestism," in Margaret W. Conkey and Christine A. Hastorf, eds., *The Uses of Style in Archaeology* (Cambridge: Cambridge Univ. Press, 1990), 39.

34. G. Sider, "When Parrots Learn to Talk, and Why They Can't: Domination,

Deception, and Self-Deception in Indian-White Relations," *Comparative Studies in Society and History* 29, no. 1 (1987): 4.

35. For a discussion of community membership and identity in other Dutch colonial contexts, see Anne Stoler, "Carnal Knowledge and Imperial Power: Gender, Race, and Morality in Colonial Asia," in Micaela di Leonardo, ed., *Gender at the Crossroads of Knowledge: Feminist Anthropology in the Postmodern Era* (Berkeley: Univ. of California Press, 1991), 51–101.

36. Wayne Dooling, "The Castle: Its Place in the History of Cape Town in the VOC Period," in Elizabeth van Heyningen, ed., *Studies in the History of Cape Town*, vol. 7 (Cape Town: Univ. of Cape Town Press, 1994), 19.

37. Kolb, *Present State* (note 29), 1:346.

38. H. C. V. Leibbrandt, *Precis of the Archives of the Cape of Good Hope: Journal, 1671–1674 and 1676* (Cape Town: W. A. Richards, 1902), 167, 244.

39. Dooling, "The Castle" (note 36), 18–19.

40. Shell, *Children* (note 28), 76. See also Robert Hughes, *The Fatal Shore* (New York: Knopf, 1987), 264–72, for a similar discussion of the early eighteenth-century penal colony in Australia.

41. Ross, *Beyond the Pale* (note 11), 85.

42. *The Reports of Chavonnes and His Council, and of Van Imhoff, on the Cape; with Incidental Correspondence* (Cape Town: Van Riebeeck Society, 1918), 75.

43. Petrus J. Idenburg, *The Cape of Good Hope at the Turn of the Eighteenth Century* (Leiden: Universitaire Pers, 1963), 32–33.

44. Dooling, "The Castle" (note 36), 21; and Shell, *Children* (note 28), 11, figs. 1–3.

45. Nigel Worden, Elizabeth van Heyningen, and Vivian Bickford-Smith, *Cape Town: The Making of a City: An Illustrated Social History* (Claremont, South Africa: D. Philip, 1998), 52.

46. Benedict Anderson, *Imagined Communities: Reflections on the Origin and Spread of Nationalism,* rev. ed. (London: Verso, 1991), 55–56.

47. Stoler, "Carnal Knowledge" (note 35), 51.

48. Schama, *Embarrassment* (note 30), xi.

49. Anderson, *Imagined Communities* (note 46), 7.

50. H. C. V. Leibbrandt, *Precis of the Archives of the Cape of Good Hope: Journal, 1662–1670* (Cape Town: W. A. Richards, 1901), 6; Leibbrandt, *Precis . . . Letters from the Cape, 1652–1662* (note 16), 3:116; and Rowland Raven-Hart, *Cape Good Hope, 1652–1702: The First Fifty Years of Dutch Colonisation as Seen by Callers* (Cape Town: A. A. Balkema, 1971), 116.

51. Leibbrandt, *Precis . . . Letters from the Cape, 1652–1662* (note 16), 2:300, 3:229.

52. Leibbrandt, *Precis . . . Journal, 1699–1732* (note 16), 152–53.

53. Leibbrandt, *Precis . . . Journal, 1671–1674 and 1676* (note 38), 256–67; and Leo Fouché and Anna J. Böeseken, eds., *The Diary of Adam Tas, 1705–1706,* trans. J. Smuts (Cape Town: Van Riebeeck Society, 1970), 173.

54. Stoler, "Carnal Knowledge" (note 35), 54.

55. Yvonne Brink, "Places of Discourse and Dialogue: A Study in the Material Culture of the Cape during the Rule of the Dutch East India Company 1652–1795"

(Ph.D. diss., Univ. of Cape Town, 1992).

56. Shell, *Children* (note 28), 225.

57. Hall, "High and Low" (note 32), 70.

58. Tom Cummins, in this volume.

59. Peter Stallybrass and Allon White, *The Politics and Poetics of Transgression* (New York: Cornell Univ. Press, 1986), 42.

60. Hall, "High and Low" (note 32), 52.

61. Appadurai, *Social Life* (note 32), 30.

62. Anne Yentsch, "The Symbolic Divisions of Pottery: Sex-Related Attributes of English and Anglo-American Household Pots," in Randall H. McGuire and Robert Paynter, eds., *The Archaeology of Inequality* (Oxford: Basil Blackwell, 1991), 193.

63. Shell, *Children* (note 28), 290.

64. Theal, *Chronicles* (note 10), 265.

65. Shell, *Children* (note 28), 290.

66. Ross, *Beyond the Pale* (note 11), 137.

67. W. Bird, *State of the Cape of Good Hope in 1822* (1823; reprint, Cape Town: Struik, 1966), 74–75; and Ross, *Beyond the Pale* (note 11), 5.

68. Martin Hall, "Patriarchal Façades: The Ambivalences of Gender in the Archaeology of Colonialism," in Lyn Wadley, ed., *Our Gendered Past: Archaeological Studies of Gender in Southern Africa* (Johannesburg: Witwatersrand Univ. Press, 1997), 227.

69. Yentsch, "Symbolic Division" (note 62), 204.

70. Schama, *Embarrassment* (note 30), 422.

71. Schama, *Embarrassment* (note 30), 378.

72. Antonia Malan, "Beneath the Surface — Behind the Doors: Historical Archaeology of Households in Mid-Eighteenth-Century Cape Town," *Social Dynamics* 14, no. 1 (1988): 276; and Shell, *Children* (note 28), 302–3.

73. Malan, "Beneath the Surface" (note 72), 276.

74. See Malan, "Beneath the Surface" (note 72), 295, for a discussion of the freedoms such activities allowed.

75. Schama, *Embarrassment* (note 30), 386.

76. Kolb, *Present State* (note 29), 1:145.

77. Shell, *Children* (note 28), 217.

78. Taylor, *Batavia* (note 10), 59.

79. Sider, "Parrots" (note 34), 7.

80. Schama, *Embarrassment* (note 30), 384.

81. Yentsch, "Symbolic Divisions" (note 62), 197.

82. Stoler, "Carnal Knowledge" (note 35), 53.

83. Angela Hobart, Urs Ramseyer, and Albert Leemann, *The Peoples of Bali* (Oxford: Basil Blackwell, 1996), 48; and Christian Pelras, *The Bugis* (Oxford: Basil Blackwell, 1996), 118, 226.

84. Alice Yen Ho, *At the South-East Asian Table* (Kuala Lumpur: Oxford Univ. Press, 1995), 20; and Pelras, *Bugis* (note 83), 228.

85. Hubert T. T. M. Jacobs, ed. and trans., *A Treatise on the Moluccas, c. 1544* (Rome: Jesuit Historical Institute, [1971]), 59.

86. Jacobs, *Treatise* (note 85), 145.

87. Ho, *Asian Table* (note 84), 14.

88. Jacobs, *Treatise* (note 85), 141.

89. Dawn F. Rooney, *Folk Pottery in South-East Asia* (Singapore: Oxford Univ. Press, 1987), 18.

90. Rooney, *Folk Pottery* (note 89), 6–10.

91. John Guy, *Ceramic Traditions of South-East Asia* (Singapore: Oxford Univ. Press, 1989), 9; and Rooney, *Folk Pottery* (note 89), 18.

92. Rooney, *Folk Pottery* (note 89), 20; and Ho, *Asian Table* (note 84), 46.

93. Pelras, *Bugis* (note 83), 227.

94. Ho, *Asian Table* (note 84), 67.

95. Barbara Harrisson, *Later Ceramics in South-East Asia, Sixteenth to Twentieth Centuries* (Kuala Lumpur: Oxford Univ. Press, 1995), 76.

96. Jacobs, *Treatise* (note 85), 43–45, 143.

97. Fernand Braudel, *The Structures of Everyday Life: The Limits of the Possible*, trans. Siân Reynolds (New York: Harper & Row, 1981), 197; and Schama, *Embarrassment* (note 30), 155–88.

98. P. Nijland, *De verstandige kok of zorghvuldige huyshouder* (Amsterdam, 1669), cited in Schama, *Embarrassment* (note 30), 158–59.

99. Schama, *Embarrassment* (note 30), 169.

100. S. Patterson, "Tasty Little Dishes of the Cape," in Jessica Kuper, ed., *The Anthropologists' Cookbook* (New York: Universe, 1977), 125.

101. Raven-Hart, *Cape Good Hope* (note 50), 29.

102. Abbé De la Caille (1751–53), cited in Raven-Hart, *Cape Good Hope* (note 50), 29.

103. Braudel, *Structures* (note 97), 221; and Hildagonda J. Duckitt, *Hilda's "Where Is It?" of Recipes* (London: Chapman & Hall, 1891), 199.

104. Duckitt, *Hilda's "Where Is It?"* (note 103), viii.

105. Gabeba Abrahams, "Foodways of the Mid-Eighteenth-Century Cape: Archaeological Ceramics from the Grand Parade in Central Cape Town" (Ph.D. diss., University of Cape Town, 1996), 218; see also Ross, *Beyond the Pale* (note 11), 7–8.

106. Malan, "Beneath the Surface" (note 72), 109.

107. Boxer, *Dutch Seaborne Empire* (note 31), 223.

108. Schama, *Embarrassment* (note 30), 159, 165.

109. Kathleen A. Deagan, "The Material Assemblage of Sixteenth-Century Spanish Florida," *Historical Archaeology* 12 (1978): 31.

110. Kathleen Hoffman, "Cultural Development in *La Florida*," *Historical Archaeology* 31 (1997): 27.

111. Hoffman, "Cultural Development" (note 110), 28.

112. See Kathleen A. Deagan, "Spanish-Indian Interaction in Sixteenth-Century Florida and Hispaniola," in William W. Fitzhugh, ed., *Cultures in Contact: The Impact of European Contacts on Native American Cultural Institutions, A.D. 1000–1800* (Washington, D.C.: Smithsonian Institution Press, 1985), 281–318.

113. See Leland Ferguson, *Uncommon Ground: Archaeology and Early African America, 1650–1800* (Washington, D.C.: Smithsonian Institution Press, 1992); and

Orser, *Historical Archaeology* (note 4), 117–23, for an extensive review of the literature on Colono ware. For a counter argument, see L. Daniel Mouer et al., "Colonoware Pottery, Chesapeake Pipes, and 'Uncritical Assumptions,'" in Theresa A. Singleton, ed., *I, Too, Am America* (Charlottesville: Univ. Press of Virginia, 1999), 83–115.

114. Orser, *Historical Archaeology* (note 4), 122.

115. Stuart Hall, "Minimal Selves," in Houston A. Baker Jr., Manthia Diawara, and Ruth H. Lindeborg, eds., *Black British Cultural Studies: A Reader* (Chicago: Univ. of Chicago Press, 1996).

116. Christopher R. DeCorse, "Culture Contact and Change in West Africa," in James G. Cusick, ed., *Studies in Culture Contact: Interaction, Culture Change, and Archaeology* (Carbondale: Center for Archaeological Investigations, Southern Illinois University, 1998), 358–77.

117. See Cullen, "Social Implications" (note 9), on the notion of ceramics as a tool in shaping identity during the Neolithic.

118. DeCorse, "Culture Contact" (note 116), 369.

Biographical Notes on the Contributors

Tom Cummins is associate professor of art history at the University of Chicago, where he also serves as director of the Center of Latin America Studies. He is coeditor of *Native Traditions in the Postconquest World* (1998) and *Native Artists and Patrons in Colonial Latin America* (1995), and author of *Huellas del Pasado* (1996) and *Toasts with the Inca* (2002).

Adolfo J. Domínguez is professor of ancient history at the Universidad Aútonoma de Madrid in Spain, where he specializes in the history of archaic Greece and the ancient history of Spain. His publications include *La colonización griega en Sicilia* (1989), *La polis y la expansión colonial griega* (1991), and *Los griegos en la Península Ibérica* (1996). He is a contributor to *Esparta y Atenas en el siglo V* (1999) and *Greek Pottery from the Iberian Peninsula: Archaic and Classical Periods* (2001).

Peter van Dommelen currently lectures in Glasgow University's department of archaeology. Between 1991 and 1999 he codirected the Riu Mannu regional survey project in Sardinia, which has been a joint project of Leiden and Glasgow Universities since 1997. He is also coeditor of *Archaeological Dialogues*. His interests include postcolonial approaches to ancient and (early) modern colonialism and settlement and survey archaeology in the late prehistoric and early historical western Mediterranean.

Stacey Jordan is a senior archaeologist with Mooney & Associates, a community planning and environmental consulting firm in San Diego, California. Her research has focused on Dutch colonial South Africa, ceramic production and use, and the construction of identity. She has published on a diversity of topics, including ceramic petrography, typologies, foodways, and the social history of South Africa's colonial European underclass.

Kenneth G. Kelly is assistant professor of anthropology at the University of South Carolina, where he teaches historical and African archaeology. His research focuses on developing a transatlantic perspective on the archaeology of the African Diaspora, and its impacts both in West Africa and the Caribbean. His work is published in a variety of edited volumes and journals, including *World Archaeology* and *Ethnohistory*.

Claire Lyons is collections curator at the Getty Research Institute, where she oversees acquisitions, exhibitions, and programs related to archaeology and ancient art. She is the author of *Morgantina: The Archaic Cemeteries* (1996) and coeditor of *Naked Truths: Women, Sexuality, and Gender in Classical Art and Archaeology* (2000). She has also written extensively on the history of archaeology, antiquities, collecting, and cultural property issues.

Irad Malkin is professor of ancient Greek history and director of the Center for Mediterranean Civilizations at Tel Aviv University, and coeditor and founder of the *Mediterranean Historical Review*. His areas of research include Greek religion, colonization, ethnicity, and Mediterranean History. His writings include *Religion and Colonization in Ancient Greece* (1987), *Myth and Territory in the Spartan Mediterranean* (1994), and *The Returns of Odysseus: Colonization and Ethnicity* (1998). He edited *Ancient Perceptions of Greek Ethnicity* (2001).

John Papadopoulos is a professor in the department of classics at the University of California, Los Angeles. Formerly the associate curator of antiquities at the J. Paul Getty Museum, he has published widely on the archaeology of the classical world, including *Torone I: The Excavations of 1975–1978* (2001), *Ceramicus Redivivus* (2002), and *The Early Iron Age Cemetery at Torone* (forthcoming)

Carmel Schrire is professor of anthropology at Rutgers, the State University of New Jersey. She has published widely on the archaeology, ethnohistory, and ethnography of hunters, herders, and colonists in Australia, the Arctic, and South Africa. She is author of the prize-winning *Digging through Darkness: Chronicles of an Archaeologist* (1996) and *Tigers in Africa: Stalking the Past at the Cape of Good Hope* (2001).

Gil Stein is professor in anthropology at Northwestern University. His areas of specialization include the evolution of complex societies, political economy of early states, urbanism, Near Eastern archaeology, and ancient colonies. Among his writings are *Rethinking World Systems: Diasporas, Colonies, and Interaction in Uruk Mesopotamia* (1999), and he coedited *Chiefdoms and Early States in the Near East: The Organizational Dynamics of Complexity* (1994).

Nicholas Thomas is professor of anthropology at Goldsmiths College, University of London. He has written widely on cross-cultural exchange, European colonial cultures, and contemporary art in Oceania. His most recent writings include *Possessions: Indigenous Art/Colonial Culture* (1999) and a scholarly edition of George Forster's *Voyage Round the World* with Oliver Berghof (2000).

Illustration Credits

Unless otherwise noted, illustrations are from the collections of the authors and are reproduced with their permission. The following sources have also granted permission to reproduce illustrations in this book:

3, fig. 1   Research Library, Getty Research Institute, Los Angeles, acc. no. 96.R.127

3, fig. 2   Research Library, Getty Research Institute, Los Angeles, ID no. 86-B4271

4   Research Library, Getty Research Institute, Los Angeles, acc. no. 94.R.8

6   Research Library, Getty Research Institute, Los Angeles, ID no. 88-B2657

10   ACHAC Collection, Research Library, Getty Research Institute, Los Angeles, acc. no. 970031

16   Research Library, Getty Research Insitute, Los Angeles, acc. no. 94.R.8

19   Werner Nekes Collection, Research Library, Getty Research Institute, Los Angeles, acc. no. 93.R.118 (box 2*)

38   Courtesy Dr. Guillermo Algaze, Department of Anthropology, University of California, San Diego

76–78   © Proyecto de Escultura Ibérica, Universidad Autónoma de Madrid. Photo: J. Blánquez

125   ACHAC Collection, Research Library, Getty Research Institute, Los Angeles, acc. no. 970031

132, 136   Drawings: Erick van Driel, Leiden

158   Courtesy John Griffiths Pedley. Photo: © 1990 Aaron M. Levin

163   Courtesy Archivo Fotografico dei Musei Capitolini, Rome, neg. no. ??????

164   Courtesy Soprintendenza per i Beni Archeologici delle province di Napoli e Caserta

167, fig. 4   Courtesy John Griffiths Pedley. Photo: © 1990 Aaron M. Levin

167, fig. 5   Drawings: Fritz Gehrke. Courtesy Soprintendenza per i Beni Archeologici delle province di Napoli e Caserta

168   Courtesy Ny Carlsberg Glyptotek, Copenhagen, inv. H.I.N. 379 (I.N. 2295)

189   Research Library, Getty Research Institute, Los Angeles, acc. no. 93.R.90 (no. 18)

192   Collection of the Museum of New Zealand Te Papa Tongarewa, neg. B.029030

204, fig. 1   Ministerio de Educación y Cultura Archivo General de Indias, MP. Buenos Aires 9

204, fig. 2   Obadiah Rich Collection; Manuscripts Division; The New York Public Library; Astor, Lenox and Tilden Foundations

207   Photos: From the facsimile edition, Felipe Guaman Poma de Ayala, *Nueva corónica y buen gobierno (codex péruvien illustré)* (Paris: Institut d'Ethnologie, 1936)

210, 211   Courtesy Department of Special Collections, Glasgow University Library

212, fig. 7   Photo: Aerial Explorations, Inc., New York. From Philip Ainsworth Means, *Fall of the Inca Empire and the Spanish Rule in Peru, 1530–1780* (New York: Charles Scribner's Sons, 1932)

216   Drawings: Matt Hunter

223, fig. 15   Obadiah Rich Collection; Manuscripts Division; The New York Public Library; Astor, Lenox and Tilden Foundations

223, fig. 16   Drawing: Matt Hunter

226   Courtesy John Carter Brown Library, Brown University

253   Courtesy Cape Town Archives Repository (CAR), CJ2651:126

261   Courtesy National Library of South Africa, Cape Town Division

Index

Page references to illustrations are in italic.

Abomey (Dahomean capital), *98*, 102
acculturation, 5–7; vs. Middle Ground, 153
administrative technology: Anatolian, 53, 56; Middle Ground and, 156; Uruk, *38*, *39*, 47, *48*, 53–55
Africa: European trading presence in, 13, 33–34, 35, 96–117; settler colonies in, 29. *See also specific regions*
African American pottery, 265
Afro-Brazilians, 14, 116; architecture of, 112–15, *113, 114*
Agadja, King of Dahomey, 102
agency: archaeological evidence for, 98; in colonial situations, 13, 123; individual, idea of, 7; objects/artifacts and, 8, 9, 17, 196, 241–42
Alberro, Solange, 152
Alexander VI, Pope, 203, 230n.7
Algaze, Guillermo, 40
Algeria, French colonialism in, 15, 122, 124–26, *125*, 144n.22
Allada (West Africa), 100, *101;* Dahomean conquest of, 102
ambiguity: colonial, 7, 15, 124–26, 128, 129; of objects in social life, 182
ambivalence, colonial, 15, 128, 129; in Sardinia, 133–37, 142
Anatolia: ceramic forms from, 43, *45*, 51; food preferences in, 49; seals from, 53, *56;* Uruk expansion into, 12, *26*, 27–28, 37–58. *See also* Hacınebi Tepe
Anderson, Benedict, 256, 257
Andes, Spanish colonization in, 18, 199–229; Christian ritual and, 218–19; and conversion to Christianity, 18, 199, 200–201, 203; and housing arrangements, 214–17, *216;* and language, 18, 202–3; and marriage, 219–28; and spatial arrangements, 203–5, *204*, 209–14, *212, 215*, 228, *229;* and town-building,

18, 200–201, 203–18, *204, 207. See also reducciones*
Angkor Wat (Cambodia), French colonial mission in, *3*
Annaba (Algeria), 15, 124–26
apartheid, 20, 241
archaeology: and colonial subject, creation of, 2–5; on intercultural interaction, 98–100; role of, 1; as text, 11
architecture: African, European influence on, 106–8, *107;* Afro-Brazilian, 112–15, *113, 114;* in Andean colonial towns, 213–17, *215, 216;* Dutch, on Cape of Good Hope, *250, 258;* and ethnic identity, identification of, 36; Iberian, Greek influence on, 83–85, *85;* as instrument of change, 8; Punic/Sardinian, 133, 134, *135, 140*, 140–41; in Uruk colonies, *38*, *39*, 43, *46*
Aristonothos krater, 161–62, *163*
Aristotle, 170
art, as instrument of change, 8
artifacts: bias in exhibition of, 5; and identity, 8–9, 12, 241, 257, 258, 260, 265–66; polysemic status of, 242; and texts, relationship between, 15. *See also* objects
Asia: European trade diasporas in, 33–34, 35. *See also* Southeast Asia
assimilation, 5–7; diaspora, 35
Auger, Raoul: *Jeu de l'Empire français, 10*
Augustine, Saint, 205
autonomy, diaspora, 33, 50, 73; of Uruk enclave in Anatolia, 52, 55, 57–58
Avendaño, Fernando de, 214

bark cloth, 17, 183–87, *185, 186*, 190; ritual significance of, 184, 193
Barnard, Lady Anne: *Our Undercook, 261*
Bartlett, Robert, 154, 155
Basset, Urbain: French colonial mission in Angkor Wat, Cambodia, *3*

Bay of Naples. *See* Campania
behavioral patterning, 47–49, 55
Bell, Catherine, 219
Bénabou, Marcel, 122
Benin. *See* Dahomey; Hueda
Bérard, Jean, 155
Bhabha, Homi, 9, 15, 128–29, 139, 142
Bickerman, Elias, 171
bitumen, 47, 51–52
Bougainville, Louis-Antoine de, 191
Bourdieu, Pierre, 18, 237n.57
Bowler, Thomas William: *The Entrance to the Castle*, 250
Britain: colony on Cape of Good Hope, 245; comparisons with Roman colonialism, 122; trade diaspora in India, 34
Broughton, T. R. S., 122
Buchner, Giorgio, 160
Burkert, Walter, 161, 162

Caille, abbé de la, 263
Cambodia, French colonial mission in, *3*
Campania, 151–72; as colonial frontier, 153, 172; ethnic groups in, 151, 159; Greek-Etruscan interaction in, 15–17, 153–54, 161–62, 169–70; Middle Ground in, 153–54, 158–59, 160, 172; pottery from, Greek epic motifs on, 161–65, *163, 164,* 166, *167*
cancha, 214, *216,* 217
Cape of Good Hope, *19,* 241–66, *243;* Dutch settlement at, 18–20, 241, 242–43, *247, 250;* earthenware from, *245,* 246–54, *251,* 257, 258, 260; food preferences on, 252, 254, 263–64; indigenous people of, 242–45, *244;* social classes on, 254–58; syncretic culture of, 20, 245–46, 254; women at, 258–60, *261, 263,* 265
Cárdenas. *See* Zapata de Cárdenas, Luis
Carthage: after First Punic War, 138. *See also* Punic settlements
Casas de Juan Núñez (Iberia), sculpture from, 74, *77,* 78
Cats, Jacob, 259
ceramics. *See* pottery
Charles V, Holy Roman Emperor, 200, 222
Chinese trade diaspora, 33, 34
Chippindale, Christopher, 11
Christianity, conversion to: clothing as vehicle for, *16,* 17–18, 191, 194, 195; and marriage, 219–28; in Polynesia, 187, 191, 193–94; ritual as vehicle for, 218–19; Spanish colonization of

Americas and, 18, 199, 200–201, 203, 205; urban structure as vehicle for, 213–14, 218
Christo (Christo Javacheff), 184
Cicero, 138, 139
cities. *See* towns
City of God, 205; Guaman Poma's drawing of, 205–6, *207*
class structure, colonial, 20; on Cape of Good Hope, 254–58. *See also* elites
cloth(ing): as conversion vehicle, *16,* 17–18, 191, 194, 195; and cultural transformation, 183; as empowerment, 194, 195, 196, 237n.62; in Polynesia, 183–87, *185, 186,* 190–91, *192;* ritual significance of, 184, 193
Cohen, Abner, 28, 30, 31, 73
colonial (term), 121, 141, 142
colonial culture, 141–42, 172
colonial frontier, 154; Campania as, 153
colonial identity: ambiguity in, 124–26; construction of, 129; and indigenous identity, blending of, 139–41; myth and, 15–17; religion and, 15, 17–18
colonialism: and archaeology, 2; vs. colonization, 67; comparative approach to, 9–11; and cultural hegemony, 67; and cultural transformation, 182; definitions of, 12, 28, 65, 88n.11; dualist representations of, challenging of, 123–26, 141; European model of, 27, 28–29; vs. imperialism, 65; indigenous agency in, 13; modern vs. ancient, 5, 65, 121–22, 128, 155; without colonies, 67, 72, 86. *See also* colonization; *specific colonial situations*
colonies: classical terminology for, 121–22; colonialism without, 67, 72, 86; vs. diasporas, 35; neutral definition of, 29–30; organizational variability in, 35; trade, 35–36 (*see also* trade diasporas); traditional view of, 29
colonization: vs. colonialism, 67; definitions of, 11–12; and mother-city identity, 156; narratives of, 15–17; nonterritorial, 153; as normative process, 17; overlapping means of, 154; phenomenon of, 1; resistance to (*see* resistance to colonialism); and resource exploitation, 14, 27, 65, 87n.1
colonized (colonial subject): agency by, 13; identity construction for, 2–5, 69, 71–72; stereotypes of, 128–29
Colono ware, 265

Connan, Jacques, 52
Contestan script. *See* Greco-Iberian alphabet
Cook, James, 190
copper pin, Uruk, *46*, *47*
corporate identity, of trade diasporas, 31, 32
Cortés, Hernán, 208, *211*, 235n.43
Covarrubias Orozco, Sebastián de, 201
creolization: of food, 263–64; of pottery, 264–65; in South Africa, 20, 254, 263–64; in West Africa, 106, 112–15
cultural hegemony, colonialism and, 67, 70
cultural identity, trade diasporas and, 31, 32
cultural poetics, 17
cultural transformation, objects and, 182–83
culture: active construction of, 123; colonial, 141–42, 172; mediating, 152
Cummins, Tom, 18
Curtin, Philip, 34, 73
Cyclops. *See* Polyphemos

D'Agostino, Bruno, 160, 169
Dahomey (West Africa), 13, 108–9; and European trade, 96–117; geographical location of, *98*; relations with Europeans, 109, 116; and slave trade, 102. *See also* Ouidah
Davis, Richard, 8
Deagan, Kathleen, 264
DeCorse, Christopher R., 105, 112, 116
de Hoz, J., 82
Demaratos, Bakchiad, 161
Dening, Greg, 155
de Soto, Domingo, 222, 225
diasporas, 31; vs. colonies, 35. *See also* trade diasporas
diet. *See* food preferences
difference: grounds for, 14; trade diasporas and emphasis on, 32
dominance: colonial model of, 29, 30, 35, 65–67, 182; colonial model of, testing of, 27–28, 57–58; diaspora, 33–34, 50, 73; postcolonial theory on, 127
Domínguez, Adolfo, 12
Douglas, Mary, 241
dress. *See* cloth(ing)
Dunbabin, T. J., 127
Dutch colonies: in Indonesia, 34; in West Africa, 106
Dutch East India Company, at Cape of Good Hope, 18–20, 241, 242–45, 247,

250; earthenware produced under, *245*, 246–54, *251*, 257; social classes under, 254–58; women of, 258–60, *261;* written records of, 252–53, *253*
Dutch West India Company, 252

earthenware, Dutch-style, *245*, 246–54, *251*, 257; analysis of, 20, 241, *242;* symbolism of, 257, 258, 260, 265–66; typology of, 248, *249*
Eleusis amphora, 177n.54
elites, local: cooperation in colonialism, 13; emulation by, vs. trade diaspora, 37; European presence in Africa and, 96, 102; Greek presence in Iberia and, 70, 72, 73, 75, 82, 85, 86, 92n.52; trade diasporas and, 32–33
Elmina (Ghana), 13, 97–98, 105; architecture of, European influences on, 106–8, 112; artifacts recovered from, 105, 106; cultural transformation at, 115; European establishment at, *104*, 105; Savi contrasted with, 108
emporion, 159; model of, 72
Emporion (Iberia), 68–70, 72, 84, 85, 86
Espinosa, Antonio de, 222
ethnicity: definition of, 90n.30; recognizing through material culture, 36; as social phenomenon, 17, 71–72; of trade diaspora, 32
Etruscans, 153; in Campania, 159, 160, 169; city development by, 179n.74; Greek mythology and, 156–57, 161–72; and Greeks, interactions of, 153–54, 161–62, 169–70, 181n.100; and *symposion*, 165–66
Euboian Greeks, 157, 161, 168–69
Europe: diet in, 262–63; glass trade beads from, 9; medieval colonization in, 154, 155, 157. *See also specific countries*
European colonialism model, 28–29; vs. ancient colonialism, 5, 65, 121–22, 128, 155; dominance assumptions of, 29, 30, 65–67; vs. prehistoric trade networks, 27, 28; testing of, 27–28, 57–58
European trade diasporas, 33–34, 35, 96–117
évolué, 126, 137

Fabian, Johannes, 225
family structure: on Cape of Good Hope, 258–60; colonization and ordering of, 219–28; and housing units, Andean, 214–17, *216*

Faraone, Christopher, 178n.63

Fauea (Samoan chief), 194, 195

Felix de Souza, Francisco, 112

Ferdinand, King of Castile, 203

Finley, M. I., 29

food preferences: Anatolian, 49; on Cape of Good Hope, 252, 254, 263–64; and ethnic identity, identification of, 36; European, 262–63; Southeast Asian, 262; Uruk, 47–49

Forster, George, 190

Foucault, Michel, 13, 127, 220

Freeman, Derek, 191

free will, marriage as exercise of, 221, 227

French colonialism, 10; in Algeria, 15, 122, 124–26, 125, 144n.22; in Cambodia, 3; comparisons with Roman colonialism, 122

Gauguin, Paul, 183

Ghana. See Elmina

glass trade beads, 9

Glewhe. See Ouidah

Gold Coast (Africa), 98, 100. See also Elmina

Gortynaia (Cortona), 170

Gras, Michel, 160

Greco-Iberian alphabet, 80–83, 81

Greek colonialism, 154; in Iberia, 12, 65, 67–87; in Mediterranean, 67, 68, 121; Middle Ground in, 155–56; vs. modern Western colonialism, 128; myth in, 69, 156–59

Greeks: in Campania, 159; colonial narratives of, 15–17, 154, 158; cultural superiority of, notion of, 67; and Etruscans, interactions of, 153–54, 161–62, 169–70, 181n.100

Greenblatt, Stephen, 17

Grimshaw, Beatrice: The New Woman in Niue, 188

Gruzinski, Serge, 12

Guaman Poma de Ayala, Felipe, drawings of, 205–6, 207

Habuba Kabira (Syria), 39, 52; artifacts from, 38, 43; bitumen from, 47, 52

Hacınebi Tepe (Turkey), 26, 27, 39; administrative technology at, 47, 48; architecture at, 43, 46; behavioral patterning at, 47–49, 55; bitumen at, 47, 51–52; ceramics at, 42, 43, 44, 45; conclusions about, 55–58; location of, 40, 41; Mesopotamian-Anatolian inter-

action at, 50–55; occupation phases at, 40–43, 41; stone tools at, 52–53

Hall, Stuart, 265

hegemony: cultural, colonialism and, 67, 70; Foucault's notion of, 13

Hellanikos, 171

Hesiod, 166, 169

history: decolonization of, 9; as textuality, 11, 17

Hoffman, Kathleen, 264

homeland: Middle Ground in relation to, 156; trade diasporas and, 34

Homeric epics: as colonial narratives, 15–17, 154; iconography of, 161–62, 163, 166, 167, 168, 177n.54; spread of, 161–72, 181n.100

host communities: and colonies, relations between, 29, 30; and trade diasporas, 31, 32–34, 35, 39–40, 49–55

housing: in Andean towns, colonial, 214–17, 216, 236n.56; Fon vs. Afro-Brazilian, 112–15, 113; Punic, from Sardinia, 140, 140

Hueda (West Africa), 13, 98, 101; coronation of king of, 103; Dahomean conquest of, 102, 108; and European trade, 95n.87, 96–117; relations with Europeans, 105–6, 108, 109, 116; slave trade and, 100. See also Savi

Hughan, Allan: Case canaque — Uarail, 4; Sortie de la messe à Vau, 16

hybridization, colonial, 7, 15, 142

Iberia: architecture in, Greek influence on, 83–85, 85; in Greek colonialist discourse, 68–69; Greek settlements in, 12, 65, 67, 72–73; origins of name, 68; Phoenicians in, 65, 68, 72, 74, 91n.37; resistance to colonialism in, 79–80, 83, 86–87; stone sculpture in, Greek influence on, 71, 73, 74–80, 76, 77, 78, 84; writing system in, Greek influence on, 71, 73, 80–83, 81

Iberian script, 80, 83

identity: archaeology and creation of, 2–5; artifacts/objects and, 8–9, 12, 241, 257, 258, 260, 265–66; colonial (see colonial identity); corporate, of trade diasporas, 31, 32; ethnic, construction for colonized people, 69, 71–72; indigenous, ambiguity of, 15, 124–26; internal vs. external, 72

ideology, trade diasporas and, 31–32

Iliad, Nestor's cup in, 165

imperialism: vs. colonialism, 65; vs. imperium, 122

imports, assumptions about, 123–24

India: British archaeologists in, 2; British trade diaspora in, 34; Jains in, 33

Indian(s): Papal Bull on, 200; term, in Spanish colonialist discourse, 69. *See also* Inka

indigenous identity, ambiguity of, 15, 124–26

indigenous peoples: agency in colonialism, 13; evolving attitudes toward, 5–7. *See also* colonized; elites, local

Indonesia: diet in, 262; Dutch trade diaspora in, 34

Inka: *cancha* of, 214, 216, 217; geometric abstraction used by, *212*, 213; maps drawn by, 235n.48; terrace and road system of, 209–13, *212*

Ionian alphabet, 80

Isabella, Queen of Castile, 203

Ischia. *See* Pithekoussai

Isherwood, Baron, 241

Italy: Greek settlements in, 121, 122–23, 151; imported Greek vessels in, 123–24. *See also* Campania; Sardinia

Jenkins, Richard, 72

Jewish trade diasporas, 33, 34

Jordan, Stacey, 18–20

Kelly, Kenneth, 13–14

Khoikhoi, 20, 242–45, *244*

King, A. D., 65–66

kinship: Andean concepts of, 18, 225; anthropological theories of, 225–27; in Christian doctrine, 222–25, *223*, *224*, *226*, 238n.67. *See also* family structure

Klor de Alva, J. Jorge, 69

Kolb, Peter, 254

Kooijman, Simon, 190

Kymē (Cumae), 151, 159, 160

labeling, in colonialist agenda, 68–69

La Fonteta, Phoenician city at, 72

Lakonian vase, 177n.54

language(s): Iberian, 82; Middle Ground and, 156; ordering of, colonization and, 18, 202–3, 225, 228

La Pícola (Santa Pola, Alicante), 73, 84–85, *85*, 86

Las Casas, Bartolomé de, 203, 205

Latin America: colonial archeology in, 199, 229n.2. *See also* Andes; Mexico

Ledesma, Bartolomé de: diagram of consanguinity, 222, *224*

Leiden-Glasgow Riu Mannu project, 130, 138

Libya, Greeks in, 154

Lightfoot, Kent, 1

Lilliu, Giovanni, 137

Lima (Peru), Guaman Poma's drawing of, 205–6, *207*

literature: vs. archaeology, 11; as instrument of change, 8. *See also* texts

London Missionary Society (LMS), 187, 193

Los Villares (Iberia), sculpture from, 74, *76*, *77*, 78

Lycophron, 170, 171

Magna Graecia, 121, 151, 154. *See also* Greek colonialism

Malan, Antonia, 263

Malietoa (Samoan chief), 193

Malkin, Irad, 15, 69

Marfudi (Barumini), *nuraghe* at, *140*, 140–41

marginality, diaspora, 32–33, 73

marriage, Spanish colonization and, 219–28; consanguinity rules regarding, 222–25, *223*, *224*, *226*; ritual of, 227–28

Marsiliana d'Albegna tablets, 161

Matienzo, Juan de, 200, 206–8, 209, 217

mediating culture, 152

Mediterranean: colonialism in, 2, 121, 122; early scholarship on, 5; Greek settlements in, 67, 68, 121; Phoenician settlements in, 121, 146n.49. *See also specific regions*

Mesopotamia: fourth-millennium, 26. *See also* Uruk trade diasporas

Mexico, Spanish colonization in, 152–53, 201, 208; and baptism, 235n.43; and town-building, 208, *210*, 233n.31

Middle Ground, 7, 15, 151–59; in Campania, 153–54, 158–59, 160, 172; coast in, 155; cultural, 171; Greek colonial, 155–56; Greek-Etruscan, 153–54, 162; internal operation of, 156; origins of theory, 152

migration, vs. colonization, 30

missionaries: absence of ancient equivalents to, 128; in Polynesia, 187, 193

moral community, trade diaspora as, 31

Mother Hubbard-style clothing, *16*, *17*, 183

Muñoz Camargo, Diego, 208

myth: in formation of colonial identities, 15–17, 172; Greek, spread of, 69, 156–57, 161–72

naming, in colonialist agenda, 68–69, 72
natural resources, Iberian, Greek exploitation of, 14, 27, 65, 87n.1
Neapolis (Sardinia), 130, *131*, 133, 134–37, 142
Nebrija, Antonio de, 202
Nestor's cup, 162–65, *164*, 178n.59, 178n.63
nomina, 156
North Africa, French colonization of, 15, 122, 124–26, *125*
North America, colonization of, 151, 152; Spanish, 152–53, 201, 208, 264
Nostoi, 165, 166–68
nuraghi, 133, *140*, 140–41

objects: as active agents, 8, 9, 17, 196, 241–42; ambiguity in social life, 182; biographical accounts of, 8; colonial, interpretations of, 129; and cultural transformation, 182–83; entangled, 97, 108; imported, assumptions about, 123–24; and individuals, interaction of, 20; reevaluation of role of, 8. *See also* artifacts
Oceania. *See* Polynesia
Odysseus: Etruscan adoption of, 165, 166, 168–69, 170–71, 172; iconography of, 161–62, *163, 168*; as transcultural icon, 15, 152, 153; travels of, as colonial narrative, 15–17, 154, 158, 166
oikist cults, 170
Olmos, R., 70
Ong, Walter, 225
Osborne, Robin, 14, 68, 89n.17
Otaheite. *See* Tahiti
Othoca (Sardinia), 130, *131*, 134
Ouidah (Dahomean town), 13, 97, *98*, 102; Afro-Brazilians at, 112, 116; architecture at, 112–15, *113, 114*; European forts at, 109, *110*; spatial organization at, 109, *111*

Pablos, Juan, 222
Pacific. *See* Polynesia
Pagden, Anthony, 200
Paul III, Pope, 200, 221
Peña Montenegro, Alonso de la, 199, 230n.10, 233n.26, 237n.59
Pérez Bocanegra, Juan, 214, 220; diagram

of consanguinity, 225, *226, 228*; *Ritual formulario*, 239n.85
Peru. *See* Andes
Philip II, King of Spain, 208, 222; *Laws of the Indies*, 231n.11
Phoenicians: in Campania, 159, 178n.59; in Iberia, 65, 68, 72, 74, 91n.37; in Mediterranean, 121, 146n.49; in Sardinia, 138
photography, ethnographic, *3, 4, 5*
pied noirs, 126, 144
Pisac (Peru), 209, *212*
Pithekoussai (Ischia), 123, 151, 159, 160; amphora from, 166, *167*; Nestor's cup from, 162–65, *164*, 178n.59
Pizarro, Francisco, *211*
poetics, cultural, 17
polícia (civil formation), 217, 233n.29; Christian rituals and, 218–19
Polybius, 138
Polynesia: bark cloth in, 183–87, *185, 186*; conversion to Christianity in, 187, 191, 193–94; indigenous dress in, 190–91, *192*
Polyphemos, blinding of, 15–17, 161, 162, *163*, 177n.54
ponchos, Polynesian, 190–91, *192*, 194–95; duality of, 196
Pontecagnano (Picentia), 160, 169
Porcuna ensemble, 75, *78*
Portuguese colonialism: in Southeast Asia, 34; in West Africa, 116
postcolonial theory, 126–27, 141, 142
Potosí silver mines, 18, 201, 235n.46
pottery: African American, 265; Anatolian, 43, *45*, 51; creolization of, 264–65; Dutch-style (*see* earthenware, Dutch-style); Euboian, 169; Greek epic motifs on, 161–65, *163, 164, 166, 167*; Iberian, Greek influence on, 69, 70, *71*, 72, 80, *81*; Punic, from Sardinia, *132, 134, 136*; Southeast Asian, 262; Uruk, *38, 39, 42, 43, 44*, 51
power: cloth(ing) and, 194, 195, 196, 237n.62; postcolonial theory on, 127; relationships of, variation in, 30, 35
Pratt, Mary Louise, 242
Pulaaku, 33
Punic settlements on Sardinia, 14–15, 130–37, *131*; architecture of, 134, *135*; pottery from, *132, 134, 136*
Punic War, First, 138

Quechua language, 18, 202–3, 225, 228

racism: in nineteenth-century colonial representations, 127–28; institutionalization of, colonial contact and, 241

Ramus, 225

reducciones, 18, 200–201, 203–18; aesthetic experience of, 209–13; church in, 213–14, *215*; housing units in, 214–17, *216*, 237n.57; plaza in, 213, 236n.52; resistance to, 218; spatial arrangements in, 203–5, *204, 207, 209, 212*, 229; success of, 217–18, 235n.46; use of term, 233n.31

religion: and colonial identity, 15, 17–18; polytheistic, accommodating nature of, 159; and trade diasporas, 32. *See also* Christianity

resistance to colonialism, 7, 123; African, 106; Iberian, 79–80, 83, 86–87; Latin American, 218, 235n.44

resource exploitation, colonization and, 14, 27, 65, 87n.1

Ridgway, David, 160, 181n.100

Riedel, F.: *Vue du Promontoire du Bonne Espérance*, 19

ritual(s): Christian, and civil order in colonial Andes, 218, 219–20; cloth(ing) and, 184, 193; and colonial identities, formation of, 15, 18; as instrument of change, 8; marriage, 227–28

Roman civilization: adoption of Greek myths by, 172; encounters with barbarian tribes, 5, 6; as model, 5

Roman colonialism: French and British comparisons with, 122; in Iberia, 65; in Sardinia, 14–15, 138–40

Ross, Robert, 258

Rouillard, P., 79

Said, Edward, 9, 14, 65, 68, 69, 126, 127

Saint Augustine (Florida), Spanish settlement at, 264

Samoa, 17; cloth(ing) in, 184, 191, *192*, 194–95; conversion to Christianity in, 191, 193–94; customs in, 191–92

Santley, Robert, 36

Santo Tomás, Fray Domingo de, 202, 203, 225

Sardinia, 14–15; interior of, colonial culture in, 137; northern half of, 139; Punic colonial settlements on, 130–37, *131*; Roman rule in, 138–40

Savi (Hueda capital), 13, 97, *98*; architecture at, *107*, 108; artifacts recovered from, 105–6, 108; Dahomean conquest of, 102, 108; Elmina contrasted with, 108; European establishment at, *104, 105*; Ouidah contrasted with, 109

Scaurus, M. Aemilius, 138

Schaefer, Richard: typology of Dutch ceramics, 248, *249*

Schama, Simon, 256

Schrire, Carmel, 18–20

Schwartz, Mark, 52

sculpture: Iberian, Greek influence on, 71, 73, 74–80, *76, 77, 78*, 84; Inka, *212*, 213; Punic, 134, *136*

seals: Anatolian, 53, *56*; Uruk, 38, 47, *48*, 53, *54*

Seed, Patricia, 220

Self vs. Other, 7, 151; Cape of Good Hope and, 256–57, 260; Greek colonialism and, 71; in identity definition, 72; rejection of model, 15

settler colonies, 29

sexual relations, housing units and regulation of, 217

Shell, Robert, 256

Sicily: Greek presence in, 121, 154; imported Greek vessels in, 123

sickles, Uruk, *46*, 47, 52

skyphoi, black-glazed, 169

Slave Coast (Africa), *98*, 100

slaves, on Cape of Good Hope, 255–56, 258; female, 259, 263, 265

slave trade: and European trade posts, 13; impact on African societies, 14, 99, 100

Smith, Anthony, 172

South Africa, 20, 241; creolization in, 20, 254, 263–65. *See also* Cape of Good Hope

Southeast Asia: Chinese trade diaspora in, 33, 34; diets in, 262; French colonialism in, *3*; Portuguese colonialism in, 34

Spain: Jews in, 34. *See also* Iberia

Spanish colonization: in Andes (*see* Andes); in Mexico, 152–53, 201, 208; in Saint Augustine, Florida, 264

spatial arrangements, colonization and: in Andean towns, 203–5, *204*, 209–14, *212, 215*, 228, 229; in West Africa, *104, 105*, 109, *111*

sphinxes, Iberian, 74

Spitz, G.: Family group, *189*

Spivak, Gayatri, 9

Stein, Gil, 12, 67, 73

stereotypes, in colonial encounters, 128–29, 139

stone sculpture, Iberian, Greek influence on, 71, 73, 74–80, *76*, *77*, *78*, 84
stone tools, Uruk, *46*, 47, *52–53*
Strabo, 68, 87, 89n.13, 169
Strøm, Ingrid, 160
suffetes, 138, 146n.59
Sürenhagen, Dietrich, 52
symposion, 152, 161, 165–66, *167*
Syria, Uruk colonies in, *26*, 27, 37, 39. *See also* Habuba Kabira

Tahiti, 17; bark cloth production/use in, 184, *185*, *186*, 190; conversion to Christianity in, 187; indigenous dress in, 190; reputation of, 191
tapa. *See* bark cloth
Tarquinia, Tomba dell'Orco II, *168*
Tarquinius Priscus, Lucius, 161
Tas, Adam, 257
textiles: Inka, designs on, 213; in Uruk trade diasporas, 53. *See also* cloth(ing)
texts: artifacts and, relationship between, 15; history as, 11, 17; in study of colonization, 11. *See also* literature
Tharros (Sardinia), 130, *131*, 133; architecture of, 134, *135*; artifacts from, 134, *136*
Theopompos, 170
Thomas, Nicholas, 11, 17, 80
Thucydides, 171
Timaios, 171
Tinepé (West Africa), *98*, 99
tiputa, 190–91, *192*, 194–95; dualism of, 196
Tlaxcala (Mexico), 208, *210*, 234n.43
Toledo, Francisco de, 201, 209, 217, 235n.44, 236n.56
tophet sanctuaries, 134, 138, 146n.49
towns: Andean, Spanish colonization and, 18, 200–201, 203–18, *204*, *207*; Etruscan, 179n.74
trade: and European colonialism in Africa, 95n.87, 96–117; and Greek colonialism in Iberia, 70, 72, 82, 86
trade diasporas: definition of, 30; distinctive identity of, 31, 32; evolution of, 34–35; Greek, in Iberia, 73, 85; and homeland, 34; and host communities, 31, 32–34, 35, 39–40, 49–55; identification in archaeological record, 36–37; Mesopotamian, 12, *26*, 27–28, 37–58; model of, *28*, 30, 73; theoretical framework of, 55–57; unifying ideology and, 31–32

Trajan's Column (Rome), 6
Turkey. *See* Anatolia; Hacınebi Tepe

Urton, Gary, 218
Uruk trade diasporas, 12, *26*, 27–28, 37–58; administrative technology of, *38*, *39*, 47, *48*, 53–55; architecture of, *38*, *39*, 43, *46*; bitumen used by, 47, 51–52; ceramics of, *38*, *39*, *42*, 43, *44*, 51; and host communities, 39–40, 49–55; stone tool production and use by, *52–53*
Utruse. *See* Odysseus

van Dommelen, Peter, 14–15, 65
Vera Cruz, Alonso de: diagram of consanguinity, 222, *224*
Vitoria, Francisco de, 200, 222
VOC (Verenigde Oostindische Compagnie). *See* Dutch East India Company
votive statuettes, Punic, 134, *136*

Wagenaer (Commandant on Cape of Good Hope), 246, *257*
wall cones, Uruk, 43, *46*
Wallerstein, Immanuel, 49
Walton, W. L.: *Lowering the Great Winged Bull, 3*
Webster, Jane, 88n.11
West, Martin, 179n.73
West Africa, 96–117; architecture of, 106–8, *107*, 112–15, *113*, *114*; coast of, *98*, 100, *101*; European forts at, *104*, 105, 109, *110*, *111*; spatial arrangements in, *104*, 105, 109, *111*
White, Richard, 15, 152
Wilkes, Charles, 194
Williams, John, 191
women: at Cape of Good Hope, 258–60, *261*, 263, 265; at Saint Augustine colony, 264
writing system: Greek, spread of, 157, 161, 169; Iberian, Greek influence on, 71, 73, 80–83, *81*

xenoi, in Greek mythology, 157, 159

Young, Robert, 11
Yovogan, 109, 112

Zapata de Cárdenas, Luis, 213, 214, 220, 221, 239n.78; diagram of consanguinity, 222, *223*, 228

Issues & Debates
A Series of the Getty Research Institute Publications Program

In Print
Art in History/History in Art: Studies in Seventeenth-Century Dutch Culture
Edited by David Freedberg and Jan de Vries
ISBN 0-89236-201-4 (hardcover), ISBN 0-89236-200-6 (paper)

American Icons: Transatlantic Perspectives on Eighteenth- and Nineteenth-Century American Art
Edited by Thomas W. Gaehtgens and Heinz Ickstadt
ISBN 0-89236-246-4 (hardcover), ISBN 0-89236-247-2 (paper)

Otto Wagner: Reflections on the Raiment of Modernity
Edited by Harry Francis Mallgrave
ISBN 0-89236-258-8 (hardcover), ISBN 0-89236-257-X (paper)

Censorship and Silencing: Practices of Cultural Regulation
Edited by Robert C. Post
ISBN 0-89236-484-X (paper)

Dosso's Fate: Painting and Court Culture in Renaissance Italy
Edited by Luisa Ciammitti, Steven F. Ostrow, and Salvatore Settis
ISBN 0-89236-505-6 (paper)

Nietzsche and "An Architecture of Our Minds"
Edited by Alexandre Kostka and Irving Wohlfarth
ISBN 0-89236-485-8 (paper)

Disturbing Remains: Memory, History, and Crisis in the Twentieth Century
Edited by Michael S. Roth and Charles G. Salas
ISBN 0-89236-538-2 (paper)

Looking for Los Angeles: Architecture, Film, Photography, and the Urban Landscape
Edited by Charles G. Salas and Michael S. Roth
ISBN 0-89236-616-8 (paper)

In Preparation
Claiming the Stones/Naming the Bones: Cultural Property and the Negotiation of National and Ethnic Identity
Edited by Elazar Barkan and Ronald Bush
ISBN 0–89236–673–7

Representing the Passions: Histories, Bodies, Visions
Edited by Richard Meyer
ISBN 0–89236–676–1

Designed by Bruce Mau Design Inc.,
Bruce Mau with Chris Rowat and Daiva Villa
Coordinated by Suzanne Watson
Type composed by Archetype in Sabon and News Gothic
Printed by Southern California Graphics on Cougar Opaque
Bound by Roswell Bookbinding

Issues & Debates
Series designed by Bruce Mau Design Inc., Toronto, Canada

Short  Collection

UNIVERSITY
CANCELLED
GLASGOW
LIBRARY